'This highly informative and penetrating study lifts the veil on some of the most significant developments of the modern era. It is one of the few books that are really "must reading" for those who hope to understand how the world is evolving.' Noam Chomsky

'What's wrong with having the global media controlled by a handful of corporations, which happen to be amongst the largest corporations on earth? In Edward Herman's and Robert McChesney's closely reasoned, lucidly argued analysis, the result of this concentration of power is that we get a range of views not much wider than that permitted in the old Soviet press, though of course cunningly tarted out with trivia and trash. There's no hope for democracy, they conclude, unless the media can be pried free from the sticky fingers of the billionaire class.' Barbara Ehrenreich

'The book is a revelation and a trenchant reminder of the centrality of the media in the social and democratic fabric. It is also a marvelous example of the essential bond between top class scholarship and passionate social commitment.' Peter Golding

'The global media lords march to the beat of commercialism, autocracy and low grade sensuality. Read all about it in The Global Media by Herman and McChesney and get motivated to do something for democratic communications.' Ralph Nader

THE GLOBAL MEDIA

THE NEW MISSIONARIES OF CORPORATE CAPITALISM

EDWARD S. HERMAN
AND
ROBERT W. MCCHESNEY

=) emma - birthday
=7 Betsy

CASSELL
LONDON AND WASHINGTON

Cassell
Wellington House
125 Strand
London WC2R 0BB

PO Box 605
Herndon, VA 20172

First published 1997
Paperback reprinted 1997

British Library Cataloguing-in-Publication Data
A catalogue record for this book is available from the British Library.

ISBN 0-304-33433-2 (hardback)
    0-304-33434-0 (paperback)

Library of Congress Cataloging-in-Publication Data
Herman, Edward S.
    The global media: the new missionaries of corporate
    capitalism
    Includes bibliographical references and index.
    ISBN 0-304-33433-2. --- ISBN 0-304-33434-0 (pbk.)
    1. Communication, International. 2. Mass media — Economic aspects.
    3. Mass media — Political aspects. I. McChesney, Robert Waterman,
    1952-   . II. Title
    P96. I5H46 1997   97-1950
    302.2—dc21   CIP

Typeset by Patrick Armstrong, Book Production Services, London
Printed and bound in Great Britain by Creative Print and Design (Wales), Ebbw Vale

CONTENTS

The communication media are monopolized by the few that can reach everyone. Never have so many been held incommunicado by so few. More and more have the right to hear and see, but fewer and fewer have the privilege of informing, giving their opinion and creating. The dictatorship of the single word and the single image, much more devastating than that of the single party, is imposing a life whose exemplary citizen is a docile consumer and passive spectator built on the assembly line following the North American model of commercial television.

EDUARDO GALEANO

LIST OF ACRONYMS

ABC	American Broadcasting Company
ACT	Action for Children's Television
AFP	Agence France-Presse
AMARC	World Association of Community Radio Broadcasters
AOL	America Online
AP	Associated Press
BBC	British Broadcasting Corporation
BSkyB	British Sky Broadcasting
CBC	Canadian Broadcasting Corporation *and* Caribbean Broadcasting Company
CBS	Columbia Broadcasting System
CCTV	Chinese Central Television
CIA	Central Intelligence Agency
CLT	Compagnie Luxembourgeoise de Télédiffusion
CNN	Cable News Network
CPBF	Campaign for Press and Broadcasting Freedom
ESPN	Entertainment and Sports Network
FAIR	Fairness & Accuracy in Reporting
FCC	Federal Communications Commission
FDI	foreign direct investment
GAMA	Global Alternative Media Association
GATS	General Agreement on Trade in Services
GATT	General Agreement on Tariffs and Trade
GDP	gross domestic product
GII	Global Information Infrastructure
IFC	International Finance Corporation
IFIs	international financial institutions
IMF	International Monetary Fund
ITU	International Telecommunication Union
JSkyB	Japanese Sky Broadcasting
M&A	mergers and acquisitions
MTV	Music Television
NAFTA	North American Free Trade Agreement
NAM	Movement of Non-Aligned Nations
NATO	North Atlantic Treaty Organization

NBC	National Broadcasting Corporation
NET	National Educational Television
NWICO	New World Information and Communication Order
NZOA	New Zealand on the Air
PBS	Public Broadcasting System
SALs	structural adjustment loans
SAPs	structural adjustment programs
TCI	Tele-Communications, Inc.
TNC	transnational corporation
UNCTAD	United Nations Conference on Trade and Development
UNESCO	United Nations Educational, Scientific, and Cultural Organization
UPI	United Press International
WTO	World Trade Organization
WWW	World Wide Web

ACKNOWLEDGMENTS

The authors' names are given in alphabetical order on the title page. Edward S. Herman is primarily responsible for Chapters 5 and 6, and Robert W. McChesney for Chapters 2, 3 and 4. They share responsibility equally for the Introduction and Chapters 1 and 7.

The authors would like to express their thanks to the following individuals for help in the preparation of this book: Mark D. Alleyne, Joe Atkinson, Nicholas Baran, Dustin Beilke, Daniel Biltereyst, Pauline Chakravartty, Vivek Chibber, Andrew Clement, Alan Cocker, Susan Davis, Doug Dowd, John Downing, Patricia Edgar, Dianne Feeley, Andrew Feldman, John Bellamy Foster, George Gerbner, DeeDee Halleck, Rod Hill, Jesse Hirsh, Geoffrey Leeland, John Lent, Arthur Lipow, Patricia Lombroso, Elizabeth Mahan, Rick Maxwell, Vicky Mayer, Michael McCauley, Mark Crispin Miller, Edward L. Palmer, Manjunath Pendakur, Jon Pollack, Marc Raboy, Dan Schiller, Herb Schiller, Inger L. Stole, Keyan Tomaselli, James Winter, and Ruth Zanker. The authors are, of course, responsible for any errors or flaws that remain.

INTRODUCTION

Since the early 1980s there has been a dramatic restructuring of national media industries, along with the emergence of a genuinely global commercial media market. The newly developing global media system is dominated by three or four dozen large transnational corporations (TNCs), with fewer than ten mostly U.S.-based media conglomerates towering over the global market. In addition to the centralization of media power, the major feature of the global media order is its thoroughgoing commercialism, and an associated marked decline in the relative importance of public broadcasting and the applicability of public service standards. Such a concentration of media power in organizations dependent on advertiser support and responsible primarily to shareholders is a clear and present danger to citizens' participation in public affairs, understanding of public issues, and thus to the effective working of democracy.

In this book we trace the emergence of the global media system and chronicle the political, economic and technological factors that have led to its ascension. We examine how the operation of the global media is affecting media structure and performance, and their political and cultural impact in a number of countries around the world. We also review some of the local and national responses to the spread of a global media system. Our purpose is to contribute to an understanding of the economic and political dynamics of growth and the effects of the globalization of the media, while pointing up alternative and arguably more democratic media structures and policies. Chapter 1 provides a historical overview of the rise of the global market system and the development of a global media from telegraphy, film, and shortwave radio to the current era of consolidation and growth. In Chapters 2 and 3 we analyze the specific dynamics of the global media market and we profile the strategies and holdings of the very largest media TNCs. In Chapter 4 we show how the global media are incorporating the Internet and digital communication systems into their orbit. Chapters 5 and 6 present the heart of our analysis of the implications of the globalization and commercialization process, looking first at the United States and then at several other nations around the world. In Chapter 7 we discuss the various arguments contending that the evolving global commercial media system is benign or of limited power, so that it is unnecessary to be concerned about its activities and effects. We also chronicle the array of ongoing activities and struggles to establish a more public service-oriented media around the world.

Media operations abroad are not new; book, film and music production have been dominated by TNCs for decades. The striking new arena for global commercial development is television (TV), and in the pages that follow we devote special attention to global commercial broadcasting. In most nations there remain vibrant national media – usually newspapers and magazines – and these along with assorted other local and national cultural institutions need to be examined to provide an accurate picture of any particular national media culture. Yet in our view TV is the defining medium of the age, and it provides the basis for an integrated global commercial media market. Indeed, the recent surge of growth in global media, as well as their scope, degree of interpenetration and integration of national economies, and uncertain consequences for the welfare of ordinary people, suggest that something very special is on the horizon. Rather than being the 'end of history,' a new phase of history is opening up in the 1990s.

ROLE OF THE MEDIA: CONCEPT AND IMPORTANCE OF THE PUBLIC SPHERE

In contemporary societies people communicate in many ways: by direct personal encounters at home and in public places; by phone, fax, and mail; by attending schools, churches, concerts, theatrical productions, and public gatherings and lectures; and by listening to, reading, and watching the media. As the media are not the exclusive means of communication, when they are technically deficient or grossly propagandistic other forms may fill the gap, however imperfectly.[1] The media are especially important in large and technologically advanced countries where most of the citizenry never meet 99 percent of their fellow citizens and the media serve as a kind of proxy.

As a major collective source of information and images, the media perform many functions and serve numerous personal needs. At the personal level they provide a link to the larger society and at least indirect connections to other human beings, and in varying degrees a sense of connectedness and solidarity. (The media can, however, strengthen people's sense of isolation and make them more fearful of the world outside.[2]) They provide emotional outlets, evoking anger and feelings of sympathy, stress, and release. The media provide amusement, entertainment and distraction. And they provide information (or myths and disinformation) about the past and present that helps to create a common culture and system of values, traditions and ways of looking at the world. The media also sometimes service minorities and subcultures within larger communities, providing them with local news and entertainment and allowing them to see themselves and the world through their own lenses.

At the political level, the media play a central role in the working of democracies. Historically, a critical feature of movements toward democracy has been the creation of a 'public sphere,' meaning all the places and forums where issues of importance to a political community are discussed and debated, and where information is presented that is essential to citizen participation in community life.[3] The concept is important because a democratic society depends on an informed populace making political choices. In large and complex societies public participation in political processes is already limited largely to occasional expressions of opinion and protests and the periodic selection of representatives. For this weak participation to be minimally effective the public has to know what is going on and the options that they should weigh, debate, and act upon.

In the view of Jürgen Habermas and others, the public sphere works most effectively for democracy when it is institutionally independent of the state and society's dominant economic forces. Although such autonomy is difficult to develop and maintain, the point of democratic communication policy-making is to strive toward this goal, although within this institutional schemata there are many different shapes a public sphere may assume. To some, the public sphere is exemplified by nonprofit, noncommercial public service broadcasters like the British Broadcasting Corporation (BBC), that tend to be relatively independent and therefore capable of some degree of 'objectivity.' A public sphere arguably can work as well or better when there is a wide range of media, each partially or wholly independent of the state and commercial control, that engage in public affairs and journalism in a partisan fashion. Indeed, this is the type of media culture associated historically with the most democratic political systems. The crucial factor in making this type of democratic public sphere viable is that there be no restriction on the range of political viewpoints and that resources be allocated in such a way that powerful economic and political actors cannot drown out the ideas of media representing the less powerful segments of society.

The media are not the only instruments of a public sphere. Libraries, schools, churches, trade unions, and other voluntary associations are examples of public sphere institutions where citizens can meet and discuss their problems and interests. The media, however, are the preeminent vehicles of communication through which the public participates in the political process, and the quality of their contribution to the public sphere is an important determinant of the quality of democracy. If their performance is poor, people will be ignorant, isolated, and depoliticized, demagoguery will thrive, and a small elite will easily capture and maintain control over decision-making on society's most important political matters. We give heavy weight to the media's ability to contribute to the public sphere in our assessment of media form and structure.

A broad dichotomy is commonly made in discussing broadcasting between 'public service' programs, which nourish the public sphere, and entertainment programs, which are designed to amuse, distract, and pull in large audiences.[4] The two are not wholly incompatible and separate – entertainment programs can raise serious public issues and encourage thought and controversy; and public sphere programs may be mere propaganda, or so boring and careful to avoid offense as to serve very little public purpose. Nevertheless, the dichotomy holds, and is important; as we shall see, commercialized media tend to favor 'light entertainment' over either serious entertainment or public sphere programs.

THREATS TO THE PUBLIC SPHERE

The integrity and quality of the public sphere may be threatened by government control, the bias and self-censorship of private systems of control, or by external intrusions into media systems that shape them in accord with ends sought by powerful foreign interests. There may also be combinations of these forms of threat, with governments and powerful private interests working in tandem, or foreign agencies collaborating with local governments and/or private media groups.

Government control and censorship

Government control and censorship are well understood to be threats to the public sphere, not only in authoritarian states but in those with parliamentary institutions. For example, in Great Britain, the government has regularly censored by withholding information and threatening prosecution under the Official Secrets Act.[5] It has legislated and bullied public and private media to contain investigative reporting, censored news on the struggle in Northern Ireland,[6] and engaged in highly deceptive and expensive propaganda campaigns to achieve its public relations objectives (often with mainstream media cooperation).[7]

The U.S. government has also frequently used 'national security' as a pretext for withholding important information on public matters like radiation experiments on civilians,[8] the threat of radiation wastes, and foreign policy actions.[9] Massive secret police and coordinated information policy campaigns have been deployed by the state to fight civil rights activists like Martin Luther King, Jr.,[10] and oppositional movements to foreign interventions and wars.[11] Inflation of the Soviet military threat by means of concocted evidence in the Cold War years was standard operating procedure.[12] U.S. government agencies like the CIA have also enrolled mainstream and foreign journalists to plant stories that were often untrue.[13]

In many countries, physical threats to journalists and extensive use of bribery have helped make the media servants of government propaganda. For example, in Guatemala, forty-eight journalists were murdered in the years 1978–85, and media dissent has been understandably modest;[14] and in Mexico, dozens of murders of journalists[15] have been supplemented by extensive bribery – the *embute* (cash payment) and *la mordida* (the bite) are together 'the favored method that government bureaucrats and others have used to sway journalists.'[16] In Mexico these methods have long been supplemented by government control over newsprint supplies, so that papers criticizing the government may find their rations cut. Globally, straightforward government censorship is widespread.

Government control over broadcasting through ownership, regulation, and partial funding of public broadcasting services poses serious problems of government intrusion and damage to the public sphere. In quite a few cases public broadcasters are under direct government control and serve as straightforward propaganda agencies of the controlling party. This is true in a number of countries where former colonial government broadcasting monopolies were taken over by independent regimes and used in virtually the same authoritarian manner as previously.[17] In other cases governments long wielded a heavy hand, dividing channel control among the leading political parties (Italy), or otherwise compromising the independence and integrity of the public sphere (France, Spain, Portugal, Greece, Thailand).

In a number of cases, however, in recognition of the threat of political control, public broadcasting has deliberately been given a certain amount of distance and autonomy, along with a mandate to serve the public sphere without partisan bias. This autonomy and independence has had inherent limits as the public service operation is a creature of legislation and politicians, and can go only so far astray. The BBC is the classic case, and in an oft-quoted statement its long-time chief Lord Reith noted in his diary that 'They know they can trust us not to be really impartial.'[18] He is referring to the Members of Parliament and dominant establishment. In the BBC case, however, despite conservative attacks and hostility, the BBC did in fact cultivate the public sphere to a remarkable degree, and established a record of public affairs (as well as cultural) performance that compares very favorably with rival commercial media.[19]

Public broadcasting in the United States as well, while under severe political constraint and frequent attack, has cultivated the public sphere more attentively than the private commercial media. In fact, the government-sponsored Corporation for Public Broadcasting was allowed to come into existence in 1967 in substantial measure because the private broadcasters were sloughing off public sphere programs as unprofitable and were pleased to allow the responsibility to be taken over at taxpayers' expense. Furthermore, not only has public broadcasting taken over much of the responsibility for preserving a public sphere in TV broadcasting, as we will show below, despite its links to the government it has been bolder than the commercial networks in offering dissenting positions.

Private systems of control: self-censorship

The preoccupation in the West has been with government rather than private censorship. The U.S. First Amendment protection of free speech is addressed solely to government threats to abridge that right. The neglect of private threats to free speech rests on two considerations: they work without overt controls by following simple and seemingly 'natural' economic processes that marginalize dissent; and as the private system threats are from the media and their allied interests, media self-interest dictates silence.

Private systems of media control pose a threat to the public sphere for several reasons: first, they rest on ownership control and therefore will tend to represent a narrow class interest; and because of increasing economies of scale and scope, and other benefits of large size, media ownership tends to become more concentrated over time, aligning the media more closely with larger corporate interests. Second, privately owned media depend on advertising revenue and must therefore compete for advertiser attention and serve advertiser interests to prosper. Owner and advertiser domination give the commercial media a dual bias threatening the public sphere: they tend to be politically conservative and hostile to criticism of a status quo in which they are major beneficiaries; and they are concerned to provide a congenial media environment for advertising goods. This results in a preference for entertainment over controversy, serious political debate, and discussions and documentaries that dig deeply, inform, and challenge conventional opinion – that is, the media/advertisers' complex prefers entertainment over cultivation of the public sphere.

It is true that private media must attract audiences in order to serve advertisers, but they are free to do this in ways that protect owner interests and meet advertisers' standards. The prime objective is delivering affluent audiences to advertisers; audience service is a means, not an end, and will be implemented within a framework of private cost and benefit calculations. If children's programs do not interest advertisers because of children's limited spending capacity – or because advertising on children's programs is politically constrained – children will be poorly served. If they become an attractive sales vehicle for toy manufacturers, toy selling and programming will be integrated, unless constrained by nonmarket forces. The point is that children's needs are not the first order of business, and Stephen Kline asks why their interests must be derivative – 'why parents were being backed into a position where they were forced to resist the pressures of television.'[20]

Commercial media will not run programs on media concentration and advertiser effects on the media, and only rarely will they permit attacks on corporate (and advertiser) abuses of power. Self-interest prevents this: for example, Procter & Gamble, the world's number one corporate advertiser, explicitly prohibits programming 'which could in any way further the concept of business as cold, ruthless, and lacking all sentiment or spiritual motivation.'[21] It has also been shown that advertising money silences the media on issues important to advertisers. There is solid evidence, for example, that the more advertising money taken from tobacco companies by media institutions the less their willingness to permit discussion of the health effects of smoking.[22]

In short, the very logic of private media market control and behavior is antithetical to the cultivation and nurture of the public sphere. The development of a commercial media therefore results in serious forms of what economists call 'market failure,' in which the market yields less than optimal results, as we will show in describing the U.S. commercial model in operation (Chapter 5). The market-dominated media not only seek large audiences through entertainment, at the expense of the public sphere; they even tend to water down entertainment to avoid a depth and seriousness that might interfere with the commercial message.[23] They also exclude materials that the audience might want to watch but which might stir up controversy objectionable to advertisers.[24]

In economists' lingo, the benefits of the public sphere, such as a more politically informed citizenry, are 'positive externalities.' But those benefits accrue to the community at large and do not add to commercial media income, and hence will be ignored under competitive market conditions.[25] On the other hand, the market finds that violence and sex draw larger audiences, so that commercial entertainment offerings tend to be infused with these. But the exploitation of violence and sex can be socially detrimental, making the audience more fearful, insecure, and prone to violence. Put otherwise, the market can make money by programming that yields *negative* externalities, just as it improves its bottom line by ignoring the positive externalities of the public sphere.

MEDIA GLOBALIZATION EFFECTS

The central features of the media globalization of the past decade or so have been larger cross-border flows of media outputs, the growth of media TNCs and the tendency toward centralization of media control, and the spread and intensification of commercialization. The short-term effects of this process at the local and national level have been complex, variable, and by no means entirely negative. Among the positive effects, we may note first the global media's competitive pressure on, and threat to, state-controlled broadcasting systems that are sometimes complacent, stodgy, and performing poorly, and energized into extending and deepening their services.

Another positive effect of media globalization and commercialization is the rapid dissemination of the popular culture developed in the dominant commercial centers to the far corners of the earth. Its universal acceptance indicates that a widely felt need and demand are being met, and its global reach makes for a greater connectedness and linkage among peoples and the emergence of some kind of global culture. There is also some flow *toward* the cultural centers, and horizontal flows within regions as well, that may open new vistas and enhance understanding of different cultures within dominant and subordinate states.

A related positive effect of media globalization is its carrying across borders some of the fundamental values of the West, such as individualism, skepticism of authority, and, to a degree, the rights of women and minorities. These are frequently partially hidden in lyrics as well as drama, but the messages can be read between the lines and can help serve humane causes and disturb authoritarian governments and repressive traditional rules.

These positive effects of a globalizing media suggest the possibility of continued change, and net positive benefits – with a slowly globalizing media widening audience options, new technologies and channels maintaining or increasing diversity and offsetting centralizing tendencies, local and national media preserving their local character as they pick and choose among global media offerings, and public broadcasting systems declining only slowly and maintaining in substantial degree their public service character and quality.

Our view, on the other hand, is less optimistic. We regard the primary effect of the globalization process – the crucial feature of globalization, and manifestation of the strength of the great powers and TNCs whose interests they serve – to be the implantation of the commercial model of communication, its extension to broadcasting and the 'new media,' and its gradual intensification under the force of competition and bottom-line pressures. The commercial model has its own internal logic and, being privately owned and relying on advertiser support, tends to erode the public sphere and to create a 'culture of entertainment' that is incompatible with a democratic order. Media outputs are commodified and are designed to serve market ends, not citizenship needs.

Furthermore, by their essential nature the commercial media will integrate well into the global market system and tend to serve its needs. This means greater openness to foreign commerce in media products, channels, and ownership. As the media are commercialized and centralized their self-protective power within each country increases from their growing command over information flows, political influence, and ability to set the media–political agenda (which comports well with that of advertisers and the corporate community at large).

Although the global media continue their growth and consolidation, and the tide of commercialization and centralization remains strong, this process has met local and national resistance, which has sometimes slowed it down and helped to preserve indigenous cultural-political media space. Within any specific nation, domestic media, traditions, language, and regulation still play key, often predominant, roles in determining the media culture. The development of a global commercial media system is not a linear process but, rather, a complex one characterized by fits and starts; and while the trendline seems clear its future remains uncertain. It is to the understanding of this historical process and its implications for democracy that we dedicate this book.

1
THE RISE OF THE GLOBAL MEDIA

ads + sales / creating an environment

The emergence of a truly global media system is a very recent development, reflecting to no small degree the globalization of the market economy. Although global media are only one part of the overall expansion and spread of an increasingly integrated global corporate system, they complement and support the needs of nonmedia enterprises. On one hand, the global media play a central economic role, providing part of the global infrastructure for nonmedia firms, and facilitating their business just as the growth of domestic commercial media supports corporate growth within countries. The global media provide the main vehicle for advertising corporate wares for sale, thereby facilitating corporate expansion into new nations, regions, and markets. On the other hand, the global media's news and entertainment provide an informational and ideological environment that helps sustain the political, economic, and moral basis for marketing goods and for having a profit-driven social order. In short, the global media are a necessary component of global capitalism and one of its defining features.

Although the establishment of an integrated global media market only began in earnest in the late 1980s and did not reach its full potential until the 1990s, the roots of a global media system can be traced back decades, even centuries. In this chapter we outline the evolution of the global media from their modern origins to the present day. In our view, media, global or otherwise, can only be understood in a political economic context, so we will emphasize the relationship of media to capitalism. We devote most of our attention to the second half of the twentieth century and, within that, to the rise of neoliberal 'free market' policies in the 1980s and 1990s. This will explain why the global media system is so thoroughly dominated by western, and especially U.S., media firms. Moreover, as we are primarily concerned with the media's ability to provide a public sphere for democracy, our analysis of capitalism includes a discussion of its relationship to political institutions. Only by understanding global corporate capitalism's social and political implications can we possibly make sense of the global media's important social and political role.

THE ORIGINS OF GLOBAL MEDIA

Global media came into existence long after the emergence of local and national media. In Western Europe, the first great mass medium, newspapers – that dominated through the nineteenth century – required several centuries of social, economic, and political change following the invention of the printing press to find a hospitable climate. The rise of the press and literacy, and the accompanying emergence of journalism, were integral parts of the democratic revolutions and the modern notion of informed self-government. The social and political power associated with control over the media has been recognized from the very dawn of publishing; in all societies the questions of who owns and controls the media, and for what purposes, have been political issues.

Although media were almost entirely local and national phenomena until the twentieth century, modern capitalism has always extended across national boundaries. The outward drive of the new commercial capitalism of the fifteenth through eighteenth centuries was unrelenting. The movement of peoples (which included the massive slave trade), goods, and precious metals across the borders in this era was great and had huge consequences. The entire world was brought into the market system, and in the process European traders, shipowners, investors, and pirates generated much of the surplus that laid the foundation for the industrial revolution of the nineteenth century. However, this surplus was obtained to a significant degree by the 'plundering of . . . defence-less natives' that brought 'bankruptcy upon the greater part of the people' under European control, as Adam Smith noted in 1776.[1] This exploitative treatment of the peoples of India, Africa, the Dutch East Indies, Peru, Mexico, and Hispaniola, among others, weakened and established dependency relations among the victims that made them the 'Third World' and the 'less-developed countries' of the twentieth century.[2]

Media systems have tended to reflect the patterns of the overall political economy. In most western nations, the press was at first explicitly political, regulated and/or censored by the government, and subsidized by the state and/or political parties. As capitalism developed and the profitability of commercial publishing became clear, newspapers tended to come under business control and operate in accord with commercial principles. In general, commercial media developed as small enterprises in competitive markets, evolving over time into large enterprises operating in monopolistic or oligopolistic markets. As capitalist enterprises, competitive pressures pushed these firms into new media and related industries, sometimes into unrelated industries, and, eventually, toward international expansion. In a world of enormous disparities in national political economic development, it would be these western governments and media corporations that would become the primary, even exclusive, architects of global media.

Global media developed haltingly in the nineteenth century. Newspapers and periodicals were written almost exclusively for domestic audiences, which combined with language problems to limit their potential for export. In fact, to this day newspapers remain the media industry that is least integrated into the global media system. When much of the planet was formally colonized by Europe and the United States in the late nineteenth century, the colonial powers generally permitted their home-based press interests a role in shaping the colonial media systems, which were understood to be of major importance in maintaining imperial rule. (This would also be the case later, with the development of colonial radio systems.) The growth and expansion of capitalism encouraged the growth of new transportation and communication technologies to expedite commercial interaction. The coming of the telegraph and underwater cables in the mid-nineteenth century marked the dawning of the telecommunication age: for the first time, information could reliably travel faster than people. Increasingly, as global trade grew in importance, there was great commercial value in the rapid communication of world news via the wires.

Hence the wire-based international news agencies were the first significant form of global media. The French Havas, German Wolff, and British Reuters were commercial news agencies established in the nineteenth century as domestic enterprises, but with particular interest in foreign news. They produced the news and then sold it to newspaper publishers. Reuters, Havas, and Wolff established the 'Ring Combination' in the 1850s, a cartel which divided the entire world market for news production and distribution among themselves. When the U.S. Associated Press (AP) – a cooperative service formed by U.S. newspaper publishers – came along later in the nineteenth century, it gradually worked its way into the cartel. So did the commercial United Press, established by rival U.S. newspaper interests which felt discriminated against by the AP.[3]

From the beginning, global news services have been oriented to the needs and interests of the wealthy nations which provide their revenues. These news agencies were, in effect, *the* global media until well into the twentieth century, and even after the dawn of broadcasting their importance for global journalism was unsurpassed. Indeed, it was their near monopoly control over international news that stimulated much of the resistance to the existing global media regime by Third World nations in the 1970s, as is discussed below. Yet these news agencies were not so much media as wholesalers of content to other commercial media in their home nations primarily, but also to the media in many nations which could not support their own global news services. Only with the emergence of genuinely global media, in the late twentieth century, has the influence of the news agencies waned.

The crucial change for global capitalism, which laid the groundwork for the rise of global media, was the emergence and ascension of the transnational corporation (TNC). A TNC is one that maintains facilities in more than one country and plans its operations and investments in a multi-country perspective. The modern TNC emerged out of the steady growth of corporate enterprise in the wake of the Industrial Revolution in the nineteenth century. Increasing numbers of U.S. firms began to think of foreign markets in the 1870s and 1880s as they became national companies, found themselves with manufacturing surpluses, and sought to exploit their technical prowess and product differentiation advantages or to attain further economies of scale. British and continental European foreign direct investment (FDI) abroad also reached substantial levels before 1914; that of Britain was heavily concentrated in the Empire and the United States, whereas FDI of the continental powers was most often in other parts of Europe.

Money and capital markets among the Atlantic powers were already well integrated by the 1890s, and financial industries were already spreading aggressively abroad. The first real general surge in U.S. FDI and TNC growth came during and after the huge wave of mergers at the turn of the century. The TNC became increasingly significant during the twentieth century, and contributed most importantly to 'globalization' when its reach became wide, extending to many countries, when its facilities were more integrated and not independent ('stand alone'), and when there developed many firms of this character, thus making for a more profound integration of economic activity across borders.

FILM AND RADIO BROADCASTING

Two new media technologies – motion pictures and radio broadcasting – contributed to the development of global media in the first half of the twentieth century. In the case of motion pictures, unlike the earlier history of newspapers and magazines, there was no long drawn-out period of small-scale industrial competition followed by concentration. Instead, in keeping with the then ascendant corporate (and TNC) form of industrial organization, the film industry developed quickly into an oligopoly dominated by a handful of very large studios. Moreover, the film industry was the first media industry to serve a truly global market.

The members of this new oligopoly were almost all American, based in Hollywood, and with close ties to major financial interests on Wall Street.[4] As early as 1914, 85 percent of the world film audience was watching American films.[5] In 1925 American-made films accounted for over 90 percent of film revenues in the United Kingdom, Canada, Australia, New Zealand, and Argentina and over 70 percent of film revenues in France, Brazil, and Scandinavia.[6] Although the percentages declined with the rise of 'talkies,' the dominance of Hollywood was never challenged. The only barrier to complete U.S. control came from explicit state intervention in nations such as Britain and France to protect the domestic industries from obliteration. Throughout the first half of the century, motion picture production was preponderantly a European and North American phenomenon.

Radio broadcasting emerged around 1920 with the establishment of stations on the medium wavelengths.[7] Broadcasting was international by nature, because the airwaves respect no political boundaries, but its international utilization as signal transmission over long distances was expensive. Furthermore, broadcasting could only be conducted on a limited number of frequencies and only by a small number of broadcasters at any given time to avoid damaging interference. This was a particular problem in Western Europe with its large population, numerous nations, and relatively small land mass. A series of conferences in the 1920s and 1930s allocated the medium-wave frequencies among the various nations, leaving most with only a handful of channels to exploit. The question, then, of how best to develop the limited number of radio channels became a political battle in nearly every independent country in the world. In most nations, there was a general consensus that broadcasting served too important a function – akin to, say, education – to be left to commercial exploitation, thus leading to various forms of state-directed broadcasting systems. The most famous and successful of these systems was the British Broadcasting Corporation (BBC), which banned advertising and was supported by an annual license fee paid by listeners. As a rule of thumb, the more democratic a given society, the more publicly accountable would be its broadcasting system. At the other extreme from the 'public service' systems of Britain, Canada and The Netherlands were the centralized, tightly controlled and highly propagandistic state-run systems of Third Reich Germany and the Soviet Union.

In the United States, on the other hand, corporate interests were quick to grasp the commercial potential of radio as an advertising-supported medium, and they used their immense political leverage to seize control of the industry before a public service system could be established. The two dominant national networks – the National

Broadcasting Company (NBC)[8] and the Columbia Broadcasting System (CBS) – had successfully fought off and eliminated the opposition to commercial broadcasting by 1934.[9] NBC and CBS immediately sought to expand their commercial broadcasting empires globally, but they met severe resistance from the public service systems in the desirable wealthy nations. By affiliating with Latin American broadcasters, however, NBC and CBS were able to establish rudimentary Spanish-language 'Pan-American' networks for commercial broadcasting by the late 1930s. Yet the real profits in radio were to be made in the advanced nations. For example, in 1945, fully two-thirds of radio receivers were in the United States and Great Britain, and most of the remainder were in Western Europe.[10] As the enormous profitability of commercial broadcasting became evident, corporate and advertising interests throughout the world clamored for the creation of commercial broadcasting to replace the existing public service systems. By the 1930s, business interests had established several commercial English-language stations in France and Luxemburg aimed directly at Britain. The tension between commercial and noncommercial broadcasting remained throughout Europe and wherever else public service systems existed for the balance of the century.

Broadcasting became truly global with the development of the short-wave band (3,000 to 30,000 kilohertz) in the late 1920s. Shortwave broadcasting was less reliable than medium-wave broadcasting and was poorly suited to local or even national coverage. Due to the nature of the radio spectrum in the shortwave band, however, it provided an inexpensive means to broadcast globally from within the borders of a single nation. The initial shortwave broadcasters tended to be the national majors, like the BBC, NBC, and CBS, who merely rebroadcast much of their domestic programming on the shortwave frequencies for international consumption. Shortwave reception became quite popular, and by the late 1930s almost all radio receivers included shortwave bands. NBC and CBS quickly conceived of shortwave as a means to broadcast in numerous languages, permitting them to bypass all of the local national broadcasters and to broadcast U.S. commercial advertising directly into the world's homes. The experiment was carried the furthest in Latin America. Nonetheless, this was an idea well ahead of its time and neither NBC nor CBS found sufficient interest among U.S. advertisers to make the project viable. Indeed, shortwave broadcasting has never proved to be serviceable for commercial purposes; the global vision of CBS and NBC would have to wait for better times and more reliable technologies.

If shortwave broadcasting was inhospitable to commerce, it was a tool of extraordinary power for international politics, and no period has had more intense international politics than the 1930s and 1940s. The Soviet Union began foreign-language shortwave broadcasts in the 1920s and fascist Italy followed suit soon after. The Nazis commenced foreign-language shortwave broadcasting upon taking power in Germany and the BBC added foreign-language broadcasting to its English language service in 1938. By 1939, twenty-six nations were broadcasting in shortwave in languages other than their native tongues, and many of those nations were doing so in several languages. At its peak, the BBC was broadcasting in forty-six languages. Shortwave broadcasting became a major component of ideological warfare across the political spectrum. When the United States entered the war in 1941 it effectively took control of shortwave broadcasting from NBC and CBS and established the Voice of America as a shortwave broadcasting service funded and directed by the federal government. By the end of World War II, fifty-five nations had formal foreign-language shortwave broadcasting services.[11]

The experience with film, radio broadcasting, and propaganda in general elevated the importance of communication in the minds of policy-makers during the interwar years. There was little debate regarding the geopolitical and economic importance of control of media and, even more important, telephony and telecommunication systems. If, prior to World War I, U.S. media firms had rarely ventured abroad, U.S. firms were soon establishing themselves as global enterprises with the active support and encouragement of the U.S. government. These ventures met with resistance in Europe, but were more successful in Latin America, where the U.S. government policy was one of applying 'the principle of the Monroe Doctrine into the field of Communications.'[12] Accordingly, the U.S. government established the Office of the Coordinator of Inter-American Affairs in the early 1940s under Nelson Rockefeller with the express mission of expanding U.S. commercial and political influence over Latin American media and culture. By 1943, U.S. planners understood that after the war the United States would have a dominance of the world not seen since the heyday of the British Empire, as even its victorious allies were being reduced to rubble in the war effort. A major priority was for the United States to usurp the European role in international communication and thereby consolidate U.S. hegemony.

THE POSTWAR ERA: U.S. HEGEMONY AND TNC DOMINANCE

The ending of World War II in 1945 marked the beginning of a new era of rapid growth. The United States emerged from the war stronger than ever, while its capitalist world rivals were either defeated and devastated (former enemies, Germany and Japan) or allies who had suffered severe wartime damage and losses (Great Britain, France). With its unique power, the United States was able to organize a new world order serviceable to its political and economic interests. Just as Great Britain, at the peak period of its competitive power and hegemonic status, wanted open markets, so did the United States after 1945. It therefore pressed steadily for an ending of wartime capital controls and in favor of convertibility of currencies, a gradual reduction of tariff barriers through international agreements and bilateral arrangements, and open-door policies everywhere. It used the leverage from its control over the International Monetary Fund (IMF) and International Bank for Reconstruction and Development (World Bank), its direct loans and gifts under the Marshall Plan and other programs, and the Cold War, Soviet Threat, and North Atlantic Treaty Organization (NATO) to force open doors that might otherwise have been closed to its businessmen and bankers. The United States dominated foreign lending and FDI for almost two decades after 1945, and its great TNCs in the auto, chemicals, pharmaceutical, computer, petroleum, electrical machinery, and financial industries made enormous global advances. In 1960, the U.S. share of world FDI was a staggering 49.2 percent of the total. Although the U.S. portion of the global economy would decline thereafter with the rise of Germany and Japan as major economic powers and rapid growth elsewhere, the United States remained far and away the largest international investor, as well as dominant military power, in the late 1990s.

In the postwar period the United States championed the notion of the 'free flow of information' as a universal principle. With its new-found power, the United States was able to get the 'free flow' principle enshrined as official policy in the newly formed United Nations Educational, Scientific, and Cultural Organization (UNESCO). Free flow was at once an eloquent democratic principle and an aggressive trade position on behalf of U.S. media interests. The core operational idea behind the principle was that transnational media firms and advertisers should be permitted to operate globally, with minimal governmental intervention. In the view of U.S. policy-makers, this was the only notion of a free press suitable for a democratic world order.

The U.S. attempt to establish a global media system in its own image was aided by its influence over the postwar reconstruction of German, Italian, and Japanese media systems. U.S. officials pushed them as much as possible on the path to U.S.-style commercial systems.[13] But the United States met with only partial success in this effort as strong public broadcasters emerged in all three of these occupied countries. Beyond the U.S. sphere of influence, the Soviet Union led a group of self-described communist nations, including China after 1949, which opted out of the global capitalist system and refused to play by the rules of the market. Western leaders were gravely concerned by the spread of anti-market politics, and very quickly the Soviet Union and 'communism' replaced fascism as the primary threat to the status quo. By 1950 the global shortwaves had returned to ideological (Cold War) combat, helped along by the fact that they had limited reach in the lucrative western markets and were unattractive commercially. In the United States, for example, shortwave was no longer included on standard radio receivers in the postwar era. The U.S. Voice of America was soon the largest broadcasting organization in the world, and it complemented the covertly funded Radio Liberty and Radio Free Europe as well as the BBC World Service in ideological battle with the massive Soviet shortwave operations. Otherwise, the communist role in global communication was minuscule relative to the size of the communist nations. Although the Soviet Tass news agency ranked in size with the 'Big Four,' it had little influence outside of the communist world. As state-subsidized enterprises, communist media did not have the same commercial imperative to expand as did their capitalist counterparts, nor is there any reason to think a more aggressive posture would have met with success in global media markets. Indeed, whereas the communist economic and social model may have had some appeal to many people in the world as an alternative to capitalism – especially in the underdeveloped areas – the communist media system generated little enthusiasm anywhere.

It was in the postwar years that the contours of the contemporary global media system became apparent. An important factor helping to shape this system was the combination of the global power of the United States and the imperial legacy of Britain, which effectively made English the global 'second' language, if not the language of choice. This was of considerable value in assisting U.S. media activities abroad. At the same time, the dominant U.S. TNCs began to invest heavily overseas, and U.S. advertising agencies followed in their wake. The commercial media also moved abroad and began to consolidate and establish empires across formerly distinct media industries, with leading media firms acquiring significant holdings in film, music, publishing, and broadcasting. These were, and are, all long-term processes that did not realize their potential until the last decades of the century. The full effect of these developments became clear when they were linked with the extraordinary technological advances in communications of the latter part of the twentieth century, advances that permitted a degree of media conglomeration and global integration unthinkable in 1945 or even 1970.

Prior to 1945, aside from shortwave broadcasting, the dominant activities in global media had been those of the 'Big Four' news agencies and the global film industry centered in Hollywood. In the postwar period the German Wolff news agency, failing to recover from its affiliation with the Third Reich, collapsed, and the French Havas was recreated as the Agence France-Presse (AFP). In keeping with the U.S. role in the world, both the AP and the UP (to become UPI in 1958) gained ground globally on Reuters and AFP; aside from the Soviet Tass, this western grip on global print news agency reporting was unchallenged. The new 'Big Four' expanded their services to include radio. Television presented a greater challenge, and for that medium a handful of specific 'newsfilm agencies' emerged to provide television companies and networks with international newsfilm and videotape footage. Reuters allied with the BBC and several other broadcasting companies to establish Visnews, while UPI linked up with British commercial media broadcasting interests to form UPITN. The other two significant international newsfilm agencies were connected to the U.S. television networks CBS and ABC. As with the news agencies, international newsfilm was conducted by a select group of western firms, based in Britain and the United States.

The global film industry, too, remained primarily in the hands of a few U.S. firms – Columbia, Twentieth Century-Fox, United Artists, MCA (Universal), Warner Brothers, Metro-Goldwyn-Mayer, and Paramount – in the postwar years. Large domestic film industries emerged elsewhere, for example, in India and Japan. But the global export industry was synonymous with Hollywood. Film exports grew so rapidly that by the mid-1960s some U.S. studios were generating more income from foreign sources than from the U.S. market, though that would not become the general rule until the 1990s. By the 1960s, one-half of the non-communist world's motion picture theaters were offering dominantly Hollywood fare.[14]

In many respects the film industry remained at the forefront of advances in the global media system. Hollywood studios, for example, began to purchase foreign movie theaters to guarantee control of markets.[15] With a significant proportion of revenues generated outside of the United States, the Hollywood firms began to extend production overseas. The postwar surge of U.S. media included Hollywood's effective takeover of the British film industry, the remaining competitor for global audiences. As one British producer told the trade publication *Variety* in the 1960s: 'We have a thriving film production industry in this country which is virtually owned, lock, stock and barrel, by Hollywood.'[16]

The same patterns of increasing cross-border ownership, trade and global concentration were also emerging in the postwar book publishing industry. U.S. book exports grew from $12 million in 1945 to $50 million by 1960 and $175 million by 1970. Book imports, on the other hand, were generally less than one-half the value of exports.[17] Exports were less significant for U.S. book publishers than they were for film producers; they accounted for less than 10 percent of earnings in the early 1970s. By then the United States was producing 80,000 books per year, the United Kingdom 40,000 books, and France 30,000 titles per year. At the other extreme Ghana's annual production was 136, Nigeria's 1,316, and Kenya's 224. Nations like Brazil and India had significant domestic industries, but little export trade. Moreover, exports alone were a deceptive indicator of globalization. Many major publishers established overseas subsidiaries. For example, the largest British commercial publisher, William Collins, earned 20 percent of its revenues from exports in 1975 but nearly 60 percent of its revenues came from overseas activities. This made the entry and survival of local book publishers in Third World countries far more difficult. Finally, with the increased revenues and profitability in book publishing, there was a rise in concentration and a linking of publishing to larger global media corporations.[18]

Concentration and cross-media corporate control was also the pattern in the burgeoning global market for recorded music. Three of the five dominant transnational recording firms in the postwar period were based in the United States and each of these were subsidiaries of larger media concerns: CBS, Warner Brothers, and RCA. The other two recording giants were the British EMI and the Dutch PolyGram. These firms accounted for over 50 percent of global sales by the 1970s. Their elaborate global distribution, production, and promotional networks made it difficult for new competitors to succeed. Independent 'labels,' as they emerged, usually had to make deals with one of the five major firms in order to be competitive.[19]

The most dramatic and important media technology to emerge in the postwar period was television. As with other media, television usage was initially heavily weighted toward the advanced capitalist nations. As late as 1961 there were more television sets in the United States than in the rest of the world combined.[20] In the most lucrative European markets and in many of the newly independent Third World nations, television was established as a nonprofit and sometimes noncommercial national service, thus limiting the possibilities for global media expansion. What could be exploited commercially, however, was the pressing need for television programming. In this regard, the U.S. program producers had years of experience and economies of scale to make them virtually unbeatable in the world market. U.S. television programming sales abroad increased from $15 million in 1958 to $130 million in 1973.[21] Many nations imported a majority of their television programs and the United States was the main beneficiary. It exported twice as many hours of programming as all other nations combined in the early 1970s.[22] Due to U.S. broadcasting regulations (subsequently eliminated), the U.S. networks NBC, CBS, and ABC were restricted in what they could produce for domestic broadcast. Thus the major U.S. program producers, and therefore the major global TV production studios, were the film studios of Hollywood.

Despite these regulatory constraints, NBC, CBS, and ABC were hardly inactive as global TV players. They sought to export in the two program areas that they were permitted to control, news and sports, although these were minor in comparison to entertainment programming. Along these permissible lines CBS and ABC established global newsfilm services. As the broadcasting services of all the other industrial powers were nonprofit, the U.S. networks faced little direct competition as they attempted to establish commercial networks abroad. Wherever possible, the U.S. networks invested in local broadcasting companies. ABC was by far the most aggressive of the U.S. networks, and by 1965 it had financial stakes in fifty-four stations in twenty-four countries in Latin America, Africa, and Asia.[23] ABC also established WorldVision, a global commercial broadcasting network. This initial wave of U.S. television network expansion was only marginally viable. Dealing with a series of national bureaucracies and regulations was expensive and time-consuming, and global advertisers were primarily interested in the affluent Western European markets, where broadcast advertising was restricted or heavily regulated.[24]

It was advertising that had fueled the U.S. television boom of the postwar period, and similarly the rise of international advertising after 1945 stimulated the growth in global media. Advertising is a defining feature of late capitalism, reflecting the rise of product differentiation and oligopolistic competition. Advertising and product variation became primary competitive weapons of corporations in place of cut-throat price competition to protect and expand market share. Although local advertising was often dominated by retailers of varying size, the more significant national advertising was conducted primarily by firms listed in the Fortune 500. If anything, the club of corporations interested in global advertising was even more select. This was truly an arena for corporate powerhouses.

The United States accounted for 75 percent of global advertising in the 1950s. Despite a high rate of growth in the 1960s, U.S. advertising was less than 60 percent of the global total of $33 billion in 1973, reflecting the even faster increase elsewhere.[25] Nonetheless, the emergence of global advertising was pioneered mainly by U.S. advertising agencies, some of which eventually redefined themselves as *global* agencies, paralleling their opening of numerous overseas offices. In the 1950s, U.S. advertising agencies opened twenty-six overseas offices. In the 1960s that figure increased sevenfold to 181 new foreign offices.[26] In the early 1970s, seven of the world's ten largest advertising agencies were U.S.-based, and two others were partially U.S.-based. These were also the very largest agencies in the United States, and their percentage of non-U.S. revenues ranged from 26 percent to 72 percent.[27] As one United Nations official noted in the 1970s, 'United States agencies dominate the field almost completely.'[28] Much of the burst in global activity by U.S. agencies was in response to the demands of their U.S. corporate clients, many of whom were aggressively increasing their international activities.

The U.S. advertising industry, working for its own and its large corporate clients' interests, contributed significantly to the struggle to commercialize global broadcasting. Its members used, and helped make prosperous and politically powerful, commercial media abroad, and they regularly threw their weight behind efforts to commercialize publicly owned media. The J. Walter Thompson agency – based in the United States – was notorious for its behind-the-scenes role in the decision to introduce advertising to British broadcasting in the 1950s.[29] As early as 1960, advertising industry observers predicted that all but the communist world would experience commercial broadcasting within a generation. Indeed, by 1970 only Belgium and the Scandinavian countries still forbade television advertising altogether.[30] Most of the Third World nations which had hoped to establish public service systems also found the appeal of turning to advertising support difficult to resist. In the late 1960s, even All India Radio, which in the BBC tradition had a thirty-year record of opposition to commercial broadcasting, began to accept paid advertising. The nonprofit broadcasting systems of Europe and Asia remained intact, and often quite influential, but their missions were beginning to change in response to commercial and political imperatives.

THE NWICO DEBATE

By the 1970s the trajectory and nature of the emerging global media system were increasingly apparent; it was a largely profit-driven system dominated by TNCs based in the advanced capitalist nations, primarily the United States. At the same time, the world had changed considerably in the preceding quarter-century. During this period almost all of the European colonies in Asia and Africa gained political independence. And while the 1960s had seen growth in media usage in what came to

be called the Third World, there was little reason to expect the dispar-
ity between the media haves and have-nots to diminish for generations,
if at all. The revolutionary development of geosynchronous communication satellites in the 1960s and 1970s fanned the flames of concern
about global media. Satellites did for television – indeed for all sorts of
communication – what shortwave had done for radio broadcasting; it
made possible instantaneous, inexpensive global interactive communication and broadcasting, and of a much higher quality than shortwave
could ever achieve. Satellites held out the promise of making it possible
for Third World nations to leapfrog out of their quagmire into a radically more advanced media system, but at the same time satellites posed
the threat of transnational commercial broadcasters eventually controlling global communication, bypassing any domestic authority with
broadcasts directly to Third World homes.

Historically, communication policy debates had been almost exclusively local or national in scope. In many Western European capitalist
nations – as in the Third World – commercial media interests were
powerful but not omnipotent. There were strong traditions of nonprofit
media and communication services. The commercial interests battled
with other segments of society over communication policy. In the United
States, however, corporate media and communication firms ruled with
little opposition and the only communication policy battles of consequence were among business rivals. International communication politics, on the other hand, historically refereed relations between nation
states, accepting the existing balance of power as given. It tended to
favor technocratic responses to the international regulation of communication, and eschew controversy. Now, for the first time, global politics
dealt with the social implications of the emerging global media system.
Moreover, the major global institutions that dealt with communication
issues – the United Nations, UNESCO, and the International
Telecommunication Union (ITU) – now had majorities comprised of
Third World nations and sympathetic communist governments. The
impetus for the global media debate came from the Movement of the
Non-Aligned Nations (NAM), which comprised over ninety member
nations by the 1970s.

The NAM criticized the global media system at several different
levels. Global communication was attacked for the 'flagrant quantitative
imbalance between North and South' and the corresponding 'inequality in information resources.'[31] A central criticism revolved around the
western monopoly of global news services, with their almost exclusive
service to the needs of the developed nations. There was almost no
journalism by people in the nonaligned nations for the developed
nations or for each other. Likewise, the domination of entertainment

programming across the Third World was criticized as a cultural imperialism that implanted alien western values on audiences. The role of transnational media in undermining national sovereignty was another major concern. At its strongest, the NAM critique of global media was linked to a critique of global capitalism and economic imperialism; the global media were seen as working primarily to serve TNCs and advertisers, thus reinforcing the inequalities of the global economy. As one NAM resolution noted, 'a new international order in the fields of information and mass communications is as vital as a new international economic order.'[32] The nonaligned position included a socialist critique of capitalist media and a nationalist critique of imperialist media.

Although there was rough consensus on the critique, given the diversity of the NAM membership – which ranged from democratic socialist governments to corrupt dictatorships to stridently pro-capitalist nations – moving beyond the critique to meaningful reform proposals was more problematic. Indeed, the 1970s and 1980s campaign for a New World Information and Communication Order (NWICO) was more a rhetorical challenge than an organized political threat to the global status quo. For many of the nations, the actual commitment to the NWICO was limited; most Third World nations could have done far more than they were doing to promote indigenous media and alternative news services. Much of the campaign was a 'begging' operation, asking western media firms to curtail profitable operations (while getting nothing in return) and western governments to donate capital for Third World communication investment, for no apparent reason except the spirit of Christian charity. As such, this campaign was doomed to failure from the outset. The same problems plagued the campaign on behalf of a new international economic order.

Representatives of the developed nations naturally disputed the NWICO critique, and they argued strenuously against any changes that would seriously disturb the global media system. To the NAM, the state was the only body that could effectively represent the will of the people against the interests of powerful global corporations and institutions. In U.S. thinking the state was the sole enemy of a free press, and therefore only a market-based, profit-driven system could legitimately claim democratic credentials. Instead of increased state involvement with media and communication, the developed nations suggested that groups like UNESCO, ITU, and the World Bank should work to improve the communication infrastructure of Third World nations. To proponents of the NWICO, this was simply a continuation of postwar policies that had barely made a dent in the global media crisis.

The primary arena for the NWICO debate was UNESCO, which in 1976 established what became known as the MacBride Commission to study global communication and suggest solutions. In 1978, UNESCO passed a Mass Media Declaration, which referred to the 'moral, social, and professional responsibilities of the mass media.' Then, in 1980, the MacBride Commission issued its report, vaguely endorsing the NWICO. Upon receiving the MacBride Commission report, UNESCO passed a resolution in support of the call for eliminating global media imbalances and having communication serve national developmental purposes. UNESCO's resolution, and the MacBride Commission report itself, reflected compromise with western concerns; it rejected state media monopolies and supported 'freedom of journalists' and 'freedom of the press.' It accepted UNESCO's traditional support for a 'free flow' of information, adding a call for 'wider and better balance' and a 'plurality of channels and information.'[33]

These fuzzy generalities and contradictory appeals had little intellectual force and hardly moved U.S., British, or other great power leaders. These, and the TNCs and western media, never had the slightest sympathy for the NWICO, the media regarding it as a direct attack on their *modus operandi*. To the western establishment, the NWICO was anathema because it gave governments, and not markets, ultimate authority over the nature of a society's media. The western media mounted an aggressive, no-holds-barred attack in the 1980s against both the NWICO and UNESCO itself, as the agency that sanctioned the NWICO. Proponents of the NWICO were characterized as tinhorn dictators who wanted to censor the press to keep the truth from their peoples and the world. (For some of the NWICO's supporters, such a charge had credence.[34])

The heavily biased news coverage, however, gave U.S. readers no context for evaluating the nearly hysterical charges against the NWICO proposal and UNESCO, the bulk of whose activities had nothing to do with the NWICO.[35] The campaign was effective. Both the United States and Great Britain withdrew from UNESCO in 1985, and the chastened new leadership of UNESCO quickly retreated from NWICO controversies and rhetoric, confining media concerns to building infrastructure and training journalists. The UNESCO retreat reflected the weakening power of the Third World, with many Third World nations too concerned with survival and too dependent on western governments and the IMF and World Bank to take positions hostile to the dominant global interests. By the end of the decade, as Herbert Schiller contends, UNESCO was 'cowed and enfeebled,' and had become 'fully compliant with Western media interests.'[36] The withdrawal from UNESCO also reflected a broader change in U.S. and western politics in the 1980s, a move toward aggressive global pro-market policies, personified by Thatcher and Reagan and often referred to as neoliberalism.

....

THE TRIUMPH OF THE GLOBAL MARKET

In the 1980s a wave of global 'liberalization' gathered momentum, in which state enterprises were privatized, private businesses were deregulated, and government welfare state initiatives were cut back. Tariffs and national barriers to foreign investment and trade also came under sharp attack as impediments to economic growth and efficiency. This new economic, political, and ideological environment of the 1980s and 1990s has greatly stimulated TNC cross-border expansion and has more closely integrated the world economy. To some extent this was merely an acceleration of trends already in progress, but the breadth and scope of the changes suggest that a new phase of economic history may have opened up. It is this new stage of global corporate capitalism that has come to provide the basis for the formation of a global media system.

In financial markets, the modern integration process goes back at least to the development of the Eurodollar market in the 1960s, which led to a rapid growth of cross-border banking and eventually the emergence of a Eurobond market and wide array of other international financial markets.[37] International bank loans as a percentage of world trade quadrupled between 1964 and 1972, and cross-border bank credit to non-banks increased more than thirtyfold between the early 1970s and 1990 (from $54 billion to $1,708 billion). Global firms are more numerous in the fields of insurance, security dealing, and payment services. Many followed their non-bank customers abroad, but they now serve a global clientele. Investment and commercial banks are jockeying for position on a global basis.[38]

FDI rose from $68 billion in 1960 to $2.1 trillion in 1993; and despite its already high level in the mid-1980s, it tripled between 1985 and 1993. Much of this FDI involved investment among the 'triad' (United States, Western Europe, and Japan), and a large fraction was accounted for by cross-border acquisitions. Foreign companies acquired 3,643 U.S. firms valued at $245 billion between 1986 and 1990, and there were massive cross-border acquisitions in Great Britain and Western Europe in the same years.[39]

The number of TNCs in the fourteen developed countries has tripled over the last 20 years, from 7,000 to 26,000, and the overall number of TNCs in 1993 was 37,000, with 206,000 overseas affiliates. TNC asset holdings of this group are highly concentrated, however, with the 100 largest – all based in the fourteen developed countries – holding assets of $3.2 trillion, and about one-third of the global stock of FDI. By 1991 the output of the foreign affiliates of TNCs totaled $4.8 trillion and exceeded world exports of goods and services; this output had doubled in ten years.

A noteworthy feature of the evolving TNC universe has been the shift from relatively isolated 'stand alone' subsidiaries, that buy and sell inputs and outputs as virtually independent companies, to those that are more integrated with other TNC operations, with greater intrasystem specialization by plant within and between countries. This has become more economically feasible as a result of improved transportation and communication technology that facilitates close planning and coordinated operations. This intrafirm 'complex integration' has been reflected in the rise of intra-firm trade – in the early 1970s such trade was estimated to be about 20 percent of overall world trade; by the early 1990s it was estimated to have risen to one-third, and even more for U.S. TNCs.[40] Intrafirm trade would be even larger if TNCs were not resorting increasingly to farming out work ('outsourcing') at numerous levels of the economic process.

Globalization is also manifested in intercorporate alliances and sharing arrangements, which have proliferated enormously in the past several decades as means of speeding up market entry, obtaining technological knowledge, sharing expenses and risks, and limiting competition. One study estimates that loose agreements between U.S. and foreign firms are four times as frequent as wholly owned affiliates of U.S. firms. These alliances are encountered in all industries, but are especially common in automobiles, biotechnology and new materials industries, and information technology.

In short, globalization has gone far and is proceeding apace: increasing numbers of firms – financial and nonfinancial – plan investment and operations on a regional or global basis and run operations that are integrated across borders; these are supplemented by a dense set of cross-border relationships via alliances and outsourcing arrangements. As the UN Conference on Trade and Development (UNCTAD) puts it, integrated international production

reaches deeper into the fabric of international relations. As a result, it places economic activities that were previously subject solely to national control also under the common governance of TNCs. As this form of governance becomes more widespread and encompasses a larger share of world output, the nature of the world economy changes: national economies – still subject to domestic governance structures – are no longer linked through markets alone, but rather are increasingly integrated at the level of production, with this production (and attendant transactions) under the governance of TNCs. In addition, the linkages established through the governance are further strengthened by the flow across borders of norms, values and routines (business culture) that are becoming of central importance to international competition in a more integrated world economy.[41]

*institutions : banks &
lenders*

TNC System

THE INSTITUTIONS OF GLOBAL CAPITALISM

The growth of the TNC system has not been the result of blind market forces; powerful TNCs and national governments, especially those of the United States and Great Britain, have pushed it unflinchingly. Global corporate capitalism has also been greatly facilitated by the creation and growth of international financial institutions (IFIs) and the writing and implementation of a number of international and regional trade agreements since World War II. The IMF and World Bank were established under the Bretton Woods Agreement of 1944 to contribute to the stabilization and growth of the international economic order. The IMF was originally designed as a short-term lending agency to help countries suffering from temporary balance of payments deficits, and in this and other ways to help establish and maintain currency convertibility and stable exchange rates. The World Bank was envisaged as an international lender that would help finance postwar reconstruction and thereafter to underwrite expensive development projects. The World Bank was eventually supplemented as a development lending agency with the International Finance Corporation (IFC) (a division of the World Bank, formed to lend to poor countries) and the Inter-American Development Bank, which focuses on Latin American lending.

From their inceptions the IMF and World Bank have helped to serve the needs of TNCs, which thrive best in a world of stable currencies and economic growth. From their beginning, the IMF and World Bank have also pressed for conservative monetary–fiscal policies and encouraged private enterprise and open economies. The World Bank's lending has been heavily oriented to large infrastructure projects that were typically supplied and managed by TNCs; these projects also helped other TNCs entering those countries, and their financing tied the recipient governments more closely to the global corporate system. The IFC is explicit that it 'finances private sector investment in developing countries in partnership with private investors' and advises those governments to help them 'stimulate the flow of both domestic and foreign private savings and investment.'[42] The Bank has also been famous for favoring large private agricultural and other loans for outward-oriented enterprises, often at the expense of smaller operations serving indigenous markets.[43]

In the early 1980s, the IMF and World Bank took on a new role; they used their leverage with numerous distressed Third World borrowers to force their acceptance of Structural Adjustment Programs (SAPs) and Structural Adjustment Loans (SALs), which imposed conditions that were even more closely geared to the preferences of the global corporate system. These SAPs and SALs forced the borrowing countries to agree to give first priority to external debt repayment, private as well as government and IFI; it compelled them to adapt austerity programs of tight money and budget cutbacks focusing heavily on social expenditures affecting the poor and ordinary citizens; it forced a stress on cultivating exports, that help generate foreign exchange to allow debt repayment and that more closely integrate the borrower's economy into the global system; and it pushed privatization, allegedly in the interest of efficiency, but serving both to help balance the budget and to provide openings for TNC investment in the troubled economy.[44] These loans and lending programs sharply constrained the choices of Third World countries and, in the late 1980s and 1990s, members of the former Soviet bloc as well. Both the broad channeling effect as well as the details of the conditions attached to loans were perfectly attuned to the demands of the TNCs; the IFIs were serving as their agents.

The evolution of the international regimes of trade regulation reflect the same pattern. The General Agreement on Tariffs and Trade (GATT) traces back to the early post-World War II years and the attempt on the part of the then overwhelmingly dominant United States to establish a more liberal trading regime, complementing the more stable currency system to be facilitated by the IMF. Early GATT deliberations did succeed in getting tariff levels down but, significantly, they largely exempted agriculture and textiles, both of enormous importance to poor countries but with powerful protectionist constituencies in the United States and Europe. In the extended negotiations leading to the new GATT agreement of 1993 and the setting up of the World Trade Organization (WTO), the weakened condition of the Third World and more powerful position of the TNCs was evident. Tariffs were to be gradually reduced across the board, but the novel developments were the new protection for 'international property rights' and for foreign investments in host countries. The North American Free Trade Agreement (NAFTA) of 1994 between the United States, Canada, and Mexico also provided for tariff reductions but, more importantly, succeeded in establishing detailed protections for intellectual property rights and FDI.

Intellectual property rights comprise patents and copyrights which legalize monopoly advantage to their owners, mainly large companies in the United States and Europe. These rights interfere with 'free trade,' and will transfer large sums from the poor to the rich countries. For example, many poor countries have not recognized pharmaceutical patents and have produced or allowed production of cheap generic drugs in their own countries; this will be ended under the new regime of enforced intellectual property rights, to the benefit of the giant pharmaceutical companies of the great powers and to the detriment of Third

World drug buyers. And, as we discuss in Chapters 2 and 4, intellectual property rights in the form of copyright protection are crucial to the growth and profitability of the global media TNCs.

The new protections of foreign investment against host country discrimination reduce the power of weak countries to guard themselves against economic and cultural penetration and domination by advanced countries, and virtually eliminate their ability to take an alternative path to development. It is a notable fact that no country, past or present, including Great Britain, the United States, Japan, Germany, South Korea, or Taiwan, has taken off into sustained economic growth and moved from economic backwardness to modernity without large-scale government protection and subsidization of infant industries and other modes of insulation from domination by powerful outsiders.[45] The governments and institutions bargaining on behalf of the TNCs today, and through GATT and NAFTA, have been able to remove these modes of protection from less-developed countries. This threatens them with the possibility of extensive takeovers from abroad, thoroughgoing integration into foreign economic systems as 'branch plant economies,' preservation in a state of dependence and underdevelopment and, most particularly, an inability to protect their majorities from the ravages of neoliberal top-down development priorities.

In Europe, the European Community (EC, subsequently European Union, EU) was organized years ago in an effort to reduce intra-European tensions and to increase Europe's economic strength by means of regional trade integration. The Maastricht Agreement of 1991 is a follow-on attempt at closer regional integration. The EU and Maastricht both established a central authority to manage the trade regime; and Maastricht imposes budgetary, inflation rate, and exchange rate conditions for entry into a monetary union to begin in 1999. European countries have been struggling to get their budget deficits down to levels required by the entry target date.

The political design of all these regional and global trade agreements has been to remove decision-making powers from local and national legislatures in favor of impersonal market forces and/or supranational bureaucracies remote from popular control. States have, in effect, sought to reduce their own sovereignty, to 'constitutionalize' the rights of TNCs, agreeing to 'lock in' so-called 'reforms' and conditions making for a favorable climate of investment, in order to free the TNCs from the threat of future democratic alterations of this environment.[46]

Put otherwise, these trade agreements are all systems for regional or global deregulation. NAFTA indirectly deregulates wages, working conditions, and environmental controls in the affected areas by allowing capital to move easily into the deregulated environment of Mexico.

Maastricht's debt, inflation and exchange rate limits on its members impose the stability conditions preferred by the Bundesbank and global financial interests. Maastricht's Social Chapter was badly damaged by the Thatcher government's non-acceptance, and has been under steady pressure and erosion ever since; it is in fact incompatible with the fundamental principles of European integration, which locks the countries into 'a negative, market-making, deregulatory mode, and in an institutional trajectory that almost certainly rules out distributive intervention.'[47] NAFTA requires that government agencies operate on a strictly commercial basis, and it explicitly removes the possibility that governments can take on any new functions. GATT rules hold forth the possibility that local regulations to protect basic food supplies, reduce smoking, provide cheap medicines, limit pesticide use, and maintain environmental standards, can be overturned as unfair trade practices.

These international agreements were all negotiated in secret talks among executive branch leaders of the relevant governments, in close consultation with business representatives. Legislatures have been onlookers, and the general citizenry of the affected countries have been mere targets of propaganda, although sometimes allowed to ratify complex and vague agreements under intense pressure and propaganda from above.[48] The new institutions have considerable freedom to make decisions that may effectively veto national and local legislation. Subject to executive department and powerful business interest lobbying, they are a vehicle for overriding the parochial interests of democratic majorities in favor of the TNC global interest.

THE NEW POLITICAL IMPERATIVES

In this perspective, notwithstanding any purely economic/productivity merits, the global market economy has a starkly anti-democratic edge, if by democratic we mean that all or most people have any choice or influence over the central political and economic decisions affecting them. The paradox of the current era is that formal democracy extends to more of the globe's inhabitants than ever before, yet there is a pervasive sense of political powerlessness across most of these democratic nations. The decline in the power and leverage enjoyed by labor and nation states to act against the interests of TNCs and the global market goes a long way toward explaining this paradox.

The power of the TNCs and global market forces has grown with the increased mobility of capital, more integrated production across borders, and the steady increase in size and importance of the global financial and capital markets. The power of international finance was displayed in 1992 when Great Britain, with the support of powerful European allies, was unable to protect the pound when market opinion held that it was overvalued and must fall. In the wake of that market victory, which cost the European central banks an estimated $6 billion, Daniel Roche of Morgan Stanley stated frankly and complacently that 'governments have lost the power to control capital, and they probably have lost it forever', and Salomon Brothers strategist David Shulman pointed out that the very success of western financial leaders in opening up the world's economies 'has limited their control over events. . . . The day-to-day flows can swamp their ability to control things.'

Some analysts have pointed to the fact that TNCs still do the bulk of their business in their home countries and depend on their national states for support, inferring from this that the TNCs and global finance are still controllable by the state. They also point to vigorous state actions carried out in the Persian Gulf in 1991 and in the passage of the GATT and NAFTA agreements, showing that states can and do act globally.[49] They miss two critical points: first, TNC power operates at many levels (including the systems of communication and politics), and the gap between theoretical and practical controllability has greatly enlarged; and second, the constraints are asymmetrical – the state is limited in serving a popular constituency, not the TNC community (who supported the Gulf War, GATT, and NAFTA). This asymmetry has a powerful channeling effect on policy choices: redistribution policies to rectify inequality and increase domestic demand will be treated harshly by the market, which will insist on policies that improve 'competitiveness.' Competitiveness in the world market depends on keeping costs down – including wages, benefits, and taxes on business and the wealthy – and avoiding inflation. Virtually all policy choices that directly serve ordinary citizens threaten 'competitiveness' or inflation. By 1996 *Forbes* magazine exulted in the fact that the world's governments, be they ostensibly left or right, could no longer 'interfere' with the prerogatives of business without suffering an economic punishment that would bring them down; governments have effectively lost their power to govern. Political debate and institutions therefore have largely become irrelevant.[50] That pervasive sense of powerlessness referred to above is a very rational response to the existing situation.

On the other hand, while 'populist' policies are effectively vetoed by the powerful TNC and financial market communities, the latter support and encourage government policies that serve their own interests. Indeed, the state has played an extremely important role in the rapid growth of the new global economic and TNC order. As noted, such global spread has always depended in important measure on a stable political environment and 'favorable climate of investment,' which

demands not only state cooperation and support, but also the states' voluntary abnegation of rights to act contrary to TNC interests. TNCs
want assurances not only that they will not face political risks of unexpected regulatory and tax changes (let alone expropriation), but also that
monetary, budget, and labor policies will comport with their interests
(even if they may be hurtful to large numbers within the host countries).
And, increasingly, they have had the power to see that their preferences
are realized.

The discretionary power of Second and Third World states is even
more circumscribed than that of the great powers. The former and
weaker groups depend heavily on foreign credits and loans from the
IMF and World Bank, and they are more vulnerable to changes in conditions of market access and foreign aid from the dominant states.
Falling out of favor by failing to pay foreign creditors, expropriating foreign assets, imposing tariff increases or quotas on foreign goods, etc.,
quickly results in funding cutoffs, reduced aid, and in some cases boy-
cotts and even military attacks (Cuba, and Nicaragua in the 1980s).
Those who conform to neoliberal rules, like Carlos Salinas in Mexico
(1988–93), Carlos Menem in Argentina (1989–), and Boris Yeltsin in
Russia (1991–) are given lavish financial and public relations support; in
a sense the ability of these rulers to survive and even prosper while failing to serve their majority constituencies is largely based on the support
of these external interests, which become a very strategic, even if external, constituency.

A crucial factor in the decline of democracy has been the weakening
of labor, invariably a cornerstone in political movements for social
democracy. This, too, is a direct result of globalization. TNC investment
abroad can often be explained in terms of competitive (and anti-
competitive) strategies and by a desire for proximity to markets and
resources, but labor costs have been a very large consideration –
arguably the most important consideration – in cross-border investment,
and clearly the most important in terms of social and economic impact.
The new technologies and favorable political environment of recent
years have given the TNCs the ability to rearrange the global division of
labor by means of their FDI allocations. Investment and operations can
be gradually shifted from areas where wages, benefits, and taxes are
high, and regulations of working and environmental conditions are
costly, to places where the climate of investment is more business-
friendly. This arbitrage process has been in effect for many years, but the
new technologies and political conditions make it more efficacious. The
new capital mobility has shifted the balance of class power strongly in
favor of capital and against labor, which is spatially immobile. In the
new division of labor, capital can now tap the global 'reserve army of

labor,' enormously increased beyond the already large pools of labor in the Third World by the entry of China and the former Soviet bloc into the global market. Much of this global army is competent, energetic, and skilled; and much of it is located in authoritarian states that restrict independent labor organization. TNCs can move between these states and bargain for host government aid in further improving the climate of investment.

These conditions have placed increasing pressure on wages and working conditions in the developed countries with unions and previously high wages and benefits. In their new and powerful bargaining position, TNCs can threaten to move to low-wage areas unless 'concessions' are made and unless their home governments reduce business taxes and burdensome regulations. And in fact TNCs continue to move resources abroad, often with the active assistance of their own governments.[51] These developments have resulted in an ongoing crisis in the developed countries, as 'downsizing' and 'outsourcing' continue, unemployment and underemployment grow, wages and benefits stagnate and fall, and governments have no solutions to the problems except 'deregulating labor markets' – which would lower wages further, and possibly create some additional low-wage employment. The burden of adjustment to TNC efforts to improve their profits by reorganizing the global division of labor is falling on labor, and in the new world order this is deemed regrettable but entirely appropriate.

Although nation states and trade unions have been weakened by the globalization of the corporate system, their ability to act against the interests of TNCs has not been eliminated, only diminished. It is unclear how much political leverage labor and other non-corporate forces can muster, and what new forms of resistance might be. This will be determined in the future. But states and trade unions remain the major arenas and vehicles of political struggle. Moreover, the logic of the global system suggests that democratic forces will also need to organize across national lines to be effective, though this is mostly uncharted political territory.

IDEOLOGY OF GLOBAL CORPORATE CAPITAL

The world is in a paradoxical condition: technologies exist and are on the horizon that will radically improve labor productivity and could lead to higher living standards as well as the ability to address environmental damage and social inequality. Yet in the reigning 'free market' context productivity advances slowly, environmental threats grow, and inequality increases. The problem facing the victims and critics of the global corporate order is not that alternative courses are *technically* impossible – they are in fact more possible than ever before – as much as they are seemingly unthinkable. The triumph of TNC power has for the time being removed any feasible alternative, and the system's capacity to keep in check even mild social democratic reforms suggests that the 'problem of transition' to social democracy itself has become a formidable challenge.

This power is not only economic and political, but extends to basic assumptions and modes of thought; that is, to ideology. To no small extent the stability of the system rests upon the widespread acceptance of a global corporate ideology. Ideology has played the role of rationalizing and sanctifying inegalitarian relations in most societies historically – in premodern times it generally took the form of religion – and it is certainly necessary in the present order with its extreme and growing disparities in wealth, income, and power. As is natural, this ideology is embraced enthusiastically by those at the top of the socioeconomic pyramid, as they are prime beneficiaries of the status quo. But a strong ideology extends to non-beneficiaries and genuine victims, many of whom accept it in the face of contradictory experience. Those who question its postulate of benevolence may still not escape its assumptions of naturalness and inevitability, which induce quiescence and passivity. This is what makes ideology such an important mechanism of social control – far better than the risky option of employment of force.

So what are the main components of the new global corporate ideology? Its core element and centerpiece is the idea that the market allocates resources efficiently and provides *the* means of organizing economic (and perhaps all human) life. There is a strong tendency in corporate ideology to identify 'freedom' with the mere absence of constraints on business (i.e., economic, or market, freedom), thus pushing political freedom into a subordinate category. In defense of this priority system it is argued that economic freedom is basic and deserves top billing because in the long run it will allow or even cause political freedom to emerge. This is unproven and somewhat cynical in that it helps rationalize support of regimes that serve business well, but crush political freedom as part of the process of creating a 'favorable climate of investment'[52] – as with Pinochet in Chile, Marcos in the Philippines, and Suharto in Indonesia.

A second and closely related element of global corporate ideology is that government intervention and regulation tend to impose unreasonable burdens on business that impede economic growth. In this view, governments enlarge in a process of self-aggrandizement and in response to pressures of special interests. They should ideally confine themselves to the maintenance of law and order and the protection of private property; the market will do the rest. Government is best which governs least, except where business needs its support in the interest of 'competitiveness.' In the ideology of the market there is a closely related tendency to ignore or downplay 'externalities,' the existence of 'public goods,' and other forms of 'market failure,' which have been discussed at length by economists over the years and which would seem more relevant in today's interdependent and ecologically threatened world of rapid growth, proliferating chemicals, radioactive materials, and biological innovations. Market failure, however, implies a greater role for government, which conflicts with the ideological core, so it is not only mainly disregarded, but academic ideologues have developed theoretical models to show that the market does not fail,[53] or that failures are so small that their costs are less than are likely to follow from their attempted correction by inefficient governments.[54]

A third element of global corporate ideology is the belief that the proper objective of the economy and economic policy should be 'sustainable economic growth.'[55] Sustainable means non-inflationary, as inflation allegedly always tends to accelerate and eventually must be halted by draconian means. It is in fact very debatable whether low and moderate levels of inflation do accelerate,[56] but whatever the truth of the matter this criterion is extremely important to the professional investment community (bankers, brokers, mutual fund managers), as is evident in press reports of their near-hysterical reactions to reports of unexpected employment gains or 'unfavorable' wage settlements (wages go up too much). Their great and overriding fear is of inflation, and they much prefer slow growth, substantial unemployment and zero inflation to more rapid growth at the cost of even mild inflation. What is more, the financial markets have the power to enforce their preferences by their reactions to economic events.

Given the necessary control over inflation, the aim of macro-policy and criterion of progress, in corporate ideology, is economic growth, measured by real (inflation-adjusted) increases in gross domestic product (GDP) or per capita income. What is excluded from this schema of objectives is progress in the distribution of income or improvement in the condition of the poor. Globalization and other recent trends in technology and economic and political power have greatly increased income inequality and in many countries reduced the real incomes of those at the bottom of the income ladder[57] – and the corporate attacks on the welfare state have tended to reinforce these regressive tendencies of today's free market. It is understandable, therefore, that corporate ideology should focus on total and per capita growth: these figures not only show the progress benefiting those who underwrite the dominant ideology; they conveniently exclude measurement of the condition of

privatization

the non-beneficiaries and victims of the contemporary growth process.

A final important element of corporate global ideology is the belief in the desirability of privatization. This derives in part from the core belief that the market can do it all, and the derivative belief that the government is self-aggrandizing and inefficient. Getting the government to sell off its assets to private entrepreneurs will, in this view, improve efficiency. There are other motives underlying the recent enthusiastic support of privatization, however: one is the desire to weaken government. A government that owns and manages assets is likely to be more powerful and better informed than one that is outside markets; and it therefore poses the threat that, being potentially subject to democratic political control, it might effectively serve non-corporate interests. Making it small and dependent reduces this threat. A further motive is making money – either by fees in selling government properties or profits from buying government properties at favorable (below true market) prices, a phenomenon that is characteristic of a sizable fraction of privatized assets (they tend to be sold off by governments elected with the support of many of those interested in buying such assets, so that non-competitive selling and privileged buying is commonplace).[58]

The widespread acceptance and internalization of global corporate ideology rests on the enormous economic and political power of its sponsors. Its ideological domination is not complete, however, and in every country there are resistant classes, groups, cultural bodies, and individuals who expound alternative analyses, visions, and programs. But these are poorly funded, not effectively linked together, frequently work at cross purposes, and have little leverage in mainstream institutions and the mass media. Lavishly funded pro-corporate thinktanks, academics and public relations agencies, on the other hand, are significant propagators of the corporate ideology.[59] Their influence is large and growing in the media system. Corporate interests also dominate electoral campaigns with their ability to fund candidates, thereby minimizing the possibility of dissident voices entering the political debate.[60]

But it is the commercial media that play the central role in this process. The development of a global commercial media system that tends to regard corporate domination as natural and benevolent was and is the logical outgrowth of the 'free market' communication policies that have come to dominate globally in the 1980s and 1990s. The global media are the missionaries of our age, promoting the virtues of commercialism and the market loudly and incessantly through their profit-driven and advertising-supported enterprises and programming. This missionary work is not the result of any sort of conspiracy; for the global media TNCs it developed organically from their institutional basis and commercial imperatives. Nor are the global media completely mono-

commercial media a central logical premedia? May

lithic, of course, and dissident ideas make their occasional appearance
in virtually all of them. But their overall trajectory of service to the
global corporate system at many levels is undeniable.

THE GLOBAL MEDIA SYSTEM IN THE 1980S

Every bit as striking as the global media's emergence as exponents of the
ideology of global corporate capitalism has been the overall increase in
importance of media and communication as an economic component of
the global economy. In 1980 communication, broadly construed,
accounted for $350 billion or 18 percent of world trade. By 1986, the
annual worldwide output of the communication and information industries was valued at $1,600 billion and it was growing rapidly.[61] Along
with financial markets, communication and information have become
the most dynamic features of the globalizing market economy, and the
development of global commercial media has been crucial to the development of the global marketplace.
   Neoliberal policies have been applied aggressively to global media
and telecommunication, and have stimulated their commercial development. The twin hallmarks of neoliberalism were (and are) deregulation
and privatization. In communication, this has meant the simple denial
of the formerly important issues of whether the media had social, moral,
and political obligations beyond the pursuit of profit. In the 1980s these
policies were applied increasingly to national broadcasting and telecommunication systems that were traditionally regulated and often publicly
owned and operated. As these public services were often large and politically influential, the pace of deregulation, attendant commercialization,
and privatization ebbed and flowed, and it varied from nation to nation.
Even in the United States, where corporate power in the media field has
been exceptional, the attempt to thoroughly deregulate U.S. domestic
broadcasting was partially derailed by public and congressional opposition. Nonetheless, the commercial media lobbies have few rivals for
political influence and the general trajectory of the deregulation and
privatization process was unmistakable across the planet.
   The other critical development in the 1980s was the advance of communication technologies, spurred on by global business's demand for the
most rapid and reliable global communication networks possible. In the
1980s videocassette recorders and the expansion of satellite and cable
communication made the global distribution of media far more feasible.
Satellite services such as the Cable News Network (CNN), Music
Television (MTV), and the Entertainment and Sports Network (ESPN)
were launched in the United States and eventually grew into global

enterprises. Combined with privatization and deregulation, these new technologies also provided the basis for an extraordinary increase in the number of television channels, which sought commercial advertising and programming.

Consequently, the 1980s was a period of unprecedented expansion for global media, making the preceding thirty-five years appear almost like mounds of dirt against the backdrop of a mountain range. Hollywood's European exports (including films, television programming, and videotapes) increased by 225 percent between 1984 and 1988, to some $561 million annually.[62] Hollywood's worldwide exports doubled in value between 1987 and 1991 from $1.1 billion to $2.2 billion. (At the same time, film and television imports to the U.S. totaled $81 *million* in 1991.) Exports of recorded music also doubled from 1987 to 1991, to a total of $419 million by 1991. Moreover, the global market was increasing in importance relative to the domestic industry. In the second half of the 1980s, foreign sales increased from 30 percent to 40 percent of U.S. film and television industry revenues.[63] Using a broader definition of media products, Anthony Smith calculates that Hollywood's exports to Europe nearly doubled in the 1980s to reach a total of more than $5 billion by 1989.[64]

The number of hours of television watched globally nearly tripled between 1979 and 1991.[65] In the new deregulatory environment, global advertisers were eager to serve this transnational client base and provide commercial support to the burgeoning global television industry. Advertising in Europe more than doubled between 1980 and 1987, and it continued at that pace well into the 1990s. As one European advertiser put it in the late 1980s, the European Union considers advertising to be a 'vital component in the creation of a Single European Market.'[66]

Deregulation and new technologies not only stimulated global media expansion, they also provided the basis for a striking new wave of corporate consolidation in the media industry. In the United States, for example, where most of the major media firms had their headquarters, in the early 1980s fewer than fifty firms dominated the vast majority of output in the film, television, magazine, newspaper, billboard, radio, cable, and book publishing industries. Almost all of these firms operated in several media sectors. By the end of the decade that total was cut in half, due to mergers and acquisitions.[67] The very same process transpired in Western Europe. Perhaps the most intense process of concentration took place in the global advertising industry. After a wave of mergers and buyouts, by 1990 the leading seven advertising agencies accounted for $73 billion in billings. Five of these agencies were either U.S., or U.S. and British, while the other two were Japanese and French.[68]

Most important, the late 1980s gave birth to the development of a truly global media market, where the dominant firms were increasingly transnational firms. As the 1980s drew to a close, the leading transnational media firms, having activities located across the world, included, among others, Bertelsmann, Capital Cities/ABC, CBS Inc., Matsushita (owner of then MCA), General Electric (owner of NBC), Rupert Murdoch's News Corporation, Disney, Time Warner, Turner Broadcasting, and the Sony Corporation (owner of CBS Records and Columbia Pictures). By the early 1990s some of these firms – like News Corporation – rejected national identities and regarded themselves as global concerns. Although dominated by firms based in the United States, a critical development in the 1980s was the diffusion of ownership of the transnational media firms among investors and firms in the advanced capitalist world. Hence the Japanese hardware manufacturers Sony and Matsushita became members of the club through their purchases of U.S.-based media firms. Indeed, by 1990 over 10 percent of the U.S. workforce that worked for foreign-based firms worked in the film and television industries, a 2,000 percent increase over the same figure for 1980.[69] As Tunstall and Palmer note, 'Hollywood seems to have become steadily more powerful in the world, while becoming less American-owned.'[70] Herbert Schiller concluded that it was no longer appropriate to speak of American cultural imperialism, as much as one should speak of transnational corporate cultural imperialism with a heavy American accent.[71]

Yet even the stunning growth of the late 1980s was just the tip of the iceberg. All the major postwar global media trends were gaining momentum. Deregulation and privatization still had considerable ground to cover, and there remained enormous untapped potential for commercial expansion. In 1990, for example, European television advertising spending per household was only one-quarter of the U.S. rate.[72] Large sections of Asia had barely been incorporated into the global commercial media market. New technologies were on the horizon that could further revolutionize global media. A true global media market with its own logic and dynamics was emerging. The decade ended with the nascent global media industry in a state of flux. When Time merged with Warner Communications in 1989, Time's president stated that by the year 2000, worldwide media would be dominated by '6, 7, 8 vertically integrated media and entertainment megacompanies.'[73] One industry observer captured the spirit of the moment: 'By all accounts the 1990s promise a rate and speed of change that will make previous decades uneventful by comparison.'[74]

2
THE GLOBAL MEDIA IN THE LATE 1990s

In the 1990s, while media systems are still primarily national and local, the media that operate across borders continue to strengthen and have a steadily greater impact on indigenous systems. The dominant players treat the media markets as a single global market with local subdivisions. The rapidity of their global expansion is explained in part by equally rapid reduction or elimination of many of the traditional institutional and legal barriers to cross-border transactions. They have also been facilitated by technological changes such as the growth of satellite broad-casting, videocassette recorders, fiber optic cable and phone systems. Also critically important has been the rapid growth of cross-border advertising, trade and investment, and thus the demand for media and other communication services. In this chapter we address the state of the global media system at the end of the century and the main character-istics and trajectory of the still rapidly changing global media market.

OVERVIEW OF MEDIA GLOBALIZATION

Media and entertainment outlays are growing at a faster rate than GDP almost everywhere in the world and significantly faster in the Far East and Central Europe.[1] A 1996 survey of teenagers in television-owning households in forty-one nations finds that they watch on average six hours of television per day, and nowhere in the survey is the figure under five hours.[2] This has been a boon for the U.S. entertainment industry, as it dominates the global market for the production of television pro-gramming as well as film. Employment in the entertainment industry in Los Angeles alone has more than doubled from 53,000 in 1988 to 112,000 in 1995.[3] In Germany, for example, the twenty-one most heav-ily viewed films and nine of the top ten video rentals for 1995 were pro-duced by U.S. film studios.[4] 'The overseas market is a lot like the domestic market was 15 years ago,' one media executive states. 'It's wide open.'[5] As the U.S. market is the most mature in media and entertain-ment consumption, it is the global market that is drawing industry attention. One media industry analyst concludes that 'the long-term growth opportunities overseas dwarf what we think is likely to occur in the United States.'[6]

This growth trend is not without its interruptions; for example, in 1996, after a decade of increased output, the film studios reduced production in the face of a saturated market and some short-term losses.[7] The global music industry too had a sharp fall in its rate of growth in 1996, after years of double digit rates. The dominance of the United States should also not be exaggerated. Some of the key firms producing media and entertainment fare in the United States itself have significant foreign ownership. Non-U.S. media conglomerates, including the Japanese Sony (#5), Canadian Seagram (#15), Dutch Philips (#18), and Australian News Corporation (#27) all rank on the top thirty list of the non-U.S. firms with the largest U.S. investments.[8] Many other non-U.S. firms are participating fully in the media and entertainment boom around the world, particularly though not exclusively through the control of TV stations, cable systems, and other distribution channels.

Moreover, a major lesson of the 1990s has been that although Hollywood fare in film, television, and music has considerable appeal worldwide, this appeal has it limits. In Western Europe, the top-rated TV programs are nearly always domestically produced, and there is widespread recognition that audiences often prefer home-grown programs, if these have the resources to compete with Hollywood productions.[9] There has also been an increase in the export of cultural products by nations other than the United States in the 1990s, not only from Europe but from the developing nations.[10] Yet this only qualifies the mainly U.S. domination of the global media market; it does not challenge it. A 1996 advertising industry survey of 20,000 consumers in nineteen nations revealed that 41.5 percent of the respondents considered U.S. cultural fare to be excellent or very good, more than twice the figure for any other nation.[11] The United States enjoyed a trade surplus with Europe in media fare of $6.3 billion in 1995, more than tripling the media trade surplus between the U.S. and Europe for 1988.[12] 'In Europe,' one leading Italian film producer acknowledged, with the slight exception of France, 'we've been 90% colonized [by Hollywood] in terms of quantity of product on the market.'[13]

The leading global media firms are producing fare in languages other than English. For example, MTV, the global music television service, has begun to differentiate its content around the world and incorporate local music.[14] After the initial campaign to establish a pan-Asian television service faltered for lack of cultural specificity, its format was changed to incorporate local programming and languages.[15] 'We soon learned that one just can't pour Western programs down people's throats,' an executive of News Corporation's Asian Star Television Ltd. acknowledged.[16] A Disney executive states that 'For all children, the Disney characters are local characters and this is very important. They always speak local languages . . . The Disney strategy is to "think global, act local".'[17] As U.S.-based media giants earn a larger share of revenues abroad, they increasingly target different regions and nations of the world, and they enter joint ventures with local producers. Partially as a result, much of the domestically produced media content around the world increasingly has the flavor of Hollywood.[18]

The three media industries that entered the 1990s with the most developed global markets – book publishing, recorded music, and film production – have continued their growth in sometimes booming global oligopolistic markets. Book publishing is less concentrated than film or music, primarily due to language differences, yet the ten largest firms accounted for 25 percent of 1995's global sales of $80 billion. The world's three largest book publishers are owned by Bertelsmann, Time Warner, and Viacom, respectively the world's third, first, and fourth largest media conglomerates. Most of the other global book publishing giants are also affiliated with global media powers like News Corporation, Hachette, and Pearson. The top three book publishers alone accounted for over $10 billion in 1995 sales. The 1990s have been a period of rapid corporate consolidation both globally and in national markets. In Spain, France, and Germany, for example, the three largest book publishers command over 50 percent of the market. Industry analysts expect further consolidation, with the largest global publishers accounting for an increasing share of the market.[19]

Recorded music is the most concentrated global media market. The leading five firms, in order of global market share, are PolyGram (19 percent), Time Warner (18 percent), Sony (17 percent), EMI (15 percent), and Bertelsmann (13 percent). The only other player of any note is Universal (formerly MCA) (9 percent).[20] All but EMI are part of larger global media conglomerates. Some estimates show these six firms' combined sales as accounting for over 90 percent of the global market, while others place it closer to 80 percent.[21] The market boomed in the early and mid-1990s with a 10 percent increase in sales in 1995 to raise global revenues to $40 billion. Recorded music has successfully shifted to digital format as compact discs now account for 70 percent of revenues.[22] Global sales grew by 38 percent from 1992 to 1995. With western markets relatively mature, sales in the developing world are growing more rapidly.[23] A music industry trade publication forecasts that China's market for recorded music will increase by 900 percent between 1994 and 2001, to over $2.1 billion. In anticipation of this shift in demand, the 'big five' music firms and Universal are increasing their number of recording artists in the developing world.[24]

Global film production in the 1990s is dominated by the studios owned by Disney, Time Warner, Viacom, Universal (owned by Seagram), Sony, PolyGram (owned by Philips), MGM, and News Corporation. All but MGM are parts of large global media conglomerates. There are large and sometimes subsidized national film industries, but with only a few exceptions the commercial export market is effectively the province of these eight firms, several of which are not owned by Americans but all of which are part of 'Hollywood.' After the burst of U.S. expansion in the early 1980s, the percentage of non-U.S. revenue for the film industry increased from 33 percent in 1984 to over 50 percent in 1993, where it has remained.[25] 'The international business is exploding,' a Hollywood distributor stated in 1995, predicting that by 2000 non-U.S. revenues will account for 60–70 percent of studio income.[26]

Several factors suggest that global growth rates for the film studios will remain high for the foreseeable future. First, there is the construction of thousands of U.S.-inspired (often U.S.-owned) multiscreen theater complexes across the planet. 'Most of the world is severely underscreened,' one multiplex builder observed, and multiscreen theaters 'provide an environment that attracts audiences like magnets.' Some of the construction is being carried out by companies like Viacom, Universal, and Time Warner, which also produce films. 'Building theaters is kind of like drilling oil wells, only you get more gushers,' a film industry analyst concludes.[27] In Asia, where much of the construction is taking place, Time Warner forecasts annual growth rates of over 20 percent for the coming decade.[28] Second, the widespread diffusion of videocassette players has spurred the home video market, which brought in $8.8 billion, or over half of the film studios' 1995 global income.[29] Some expect the launching of digital video disks in the late 1990s to have the same stimulative effect on film sales in the late 1990s that the launching of CDs had for music sales in the late 1980s and early 1990s.[30] Third, the rise of multichannel commercial television broadcasting has created enormous demand for Hollywood fare. Several multibillion dollar deals signed in 1996 provided nothing short 'of a windfall for major Hollywood studios.'[31] The future may even be brighter; Universal's president states that 'Television in Europe is poised for extraordinary growth.'[32] Indeed, by 1997 Hollywood was in the midst of its greatest expansion in the number of 'sound stages,' or production studios for film, television, and video production in its history.[33]

The vast surge in demand may well have laid the foundation for an increase in worldwide film production, At the same time, however, the global film market rewards the largest budgeted films disproportionately.

high budgets + profitability of films.
why?

A 1996 *Variety* survey of 164 Hollywood releases concluded that films
with budgets greater than $60 million tended to be far more profitable
than less expensive films.[34] In 1996 just 13 of the 417 films released by
Hollywood studios accounted for nearly 30 percent of total box office.[35]
While the main studios are increasing their output to meet demand,
they are concentrating upon the production of 'blockbusters.'[36] With
the financial stakes so high, the implications for filmmaking tend to be
'homogenization of content and less risk taking,' as one Hollywood producer acknowledges.[37]

genres + cultures

One entertainment genre that needs little differentiation for global
commercial success is violence, and Hollywood has established itself as
the preeminent producer of 'action' fare. 'Kicking butt,' one U.S. media
executive states, 'plays everywhere.' The major U.S. studios find violent
fare as close to risk-free as anything they produce, and they have little
trouble locating non-U.S. interests willing to cover a share of production
costs in return for distribution or broadcasting rights in their nation or
region. 'For the U.S. studio it's an excellent deal,' the same executive
concludes. 'Even if the show bombs, the production cost is not drastic.
If it hits, it's all upside.' And with non-U.S. sales playing a larger role in
studio planning, violent fare for film and television looks set to command a larger segment of Hollywood output.[38]

THE COMMERCIALIZATION OF GLOBAL TELEVISION

It is with this worldwide surge of commercial television that the decisive
changes in global media in the 1990s are most apparent. The emergence of satellites and cable distribution of programming have dramatically increased the number of channels available in most nations in the
1990s. In Europe, for example, cable and satellite television revenues
increased on average by 30 percent annually from 1990 to 1994, and are
expected to grow at 25 percent per annum for the balance of the
decade.[39] This is also the trend worldwide. 'The marketplace for
subscriber-supported TV is in a vigorous upturn,' a Merrill Lynch
industry analyst concludes.[40] Goldman Sachs forecasts that the percentage of global TV households with either cable or satellite will increase
between 1995 and 2000 from 26 percent to 38 percent.[41] Politically, the
strong trend toward deregulation, privatization, and commercialization
of media and communication has opened up global commercial broadcasting in a manner that represents a startling break with past practice.
Throughout the world the commercialization of national television systems has been regarded as 'an integral part' of economic liberalization
programs.[42]

The commercialization and deregulation of national television systems worldwide began in the 1970s and 1980s, but it reached full speed
in the 1990s. It has taken place at the expense of the previously dominant state-run systems. One must not exaggerate the decline of public
broadcasting systems, as many still earn large audiences in competitive
environments.[43] Yet even successful public systems like those in
Germany and Sweden saw their audiences cut by nearly half between
1990 and 1995.[44] In the near future most nations with viable public systems will have access to literally hundreds of other channels. In this context it seems inevitable that the public broadcasting service will reach an
ever-shrinking audience. If the political environment were different, and
there was organized public support for viable nonprofit and noncommercial broadcasting, these services might be able to weather the multichannel onslaught. But in the current climate, where markets are
presumed to 'give the people what they want,' and commercial media
firms have increasing political power, most public broadcasting systems
find themselves under siege.[45] If public broadcasters continue on the
current course of shrinking audiences it is just a matter of time before
their public subsidy will be terminated. If public broadcasters attempt to
mimic commercial broadcasters to increase their audience size, by that
route also they lose legitimate claim to a public subsidy.[46] And as public
broadcasters lose their public subsidy, it requires them to become commercial enterprises in order to succeed.[47] In the United States, for
example, the national Public Broadcasting System now previews its
primetime schedule for leading New York advertising agencies in a
manner similar to the commercial networks.[48]

The response of the BBC and the Australian Broadcasting
Corporation to this dilemma has been to go commercial globally in
order to subsidize their domestic public service activities.[49] The BBC's
new chairman was selected in 1996 'to spearhead the BBC's international commercial activities,' according to the government minister
responsible for the appointment.[50] According to *Variety*, the BBC 'has
placed an expansionist commercial strategy right at the heart of its survival plan.'[51] The BBC has established alliances with Pearson PLC, Cox
Communications, and other firms to produce and distribute global television services.[52] The BBC launched the BBC World Service Television
as a global commercial venture in 1991. The point is to capitalize upon
the BBC brand name, considered to be the second most famous in the
world after that of Coca-Cola. It has already been effectively banned in
China and Saudi Arabia, unlike the explicitly commercial television
news services, because BBC journalism offended the rulers of those
nations.[53] In 1996 the BBC established joint ventures valued at close to
$1 billion with TCI-controlled Flextech and the U.S. Discovery

Communications (in which TCI has a 49 percent interest) to create over one dozen commercial television channels for global television markets.[54] Whether the BBC will be able to maintain public service standards while becoming an aggressively commercial enterprise remains to be seen. It is clear that the BBC has decided that its survival depends more upon locating a niche in the global media market than in generating political support for public service broadcasting. At any rate, this is an option that only a few public broadcasters from the wealthy (and arguably English-speaking) nations can pursue. For the balance of global public service broadcasters, the future would seem to be one of increasing domestic commercialization, marginalization, or both.

In the late 1990s the trend toward a global commercial television industry and the consolidation of a global media market is taking a quantum leap with the advance of digital television. Satellites already provide digital television, cable companies are beginning to employ digital converters, and terrestrial broadcasting will eventually switch over, in the next 10 or 20 years as all TV sets become exclusively digital. Although it is unclear what the eventual mix will be between satellite, cable, and terrestrial digital broadcasters, it is clear that digital television is a radical departure from its analogue predecessor. The shift to digital television improves technical quality, lowers production costs, and instantly expands the number of channels by a factor of five or six (and by the year 2000 by a factor of ten). When transmitted by satellite directly to minuscule home dishes, digital broadcasting can provide several hundred channels in 1997, and may deliver several thousand channels within a decade.[55] By the year 2000 nearly twenty million U.S. households are projected to have satellite dishes for digital television, and it will be a $7 billion market.[56] By 2004 Nielsen Media Research projects that nearly thirty million U.S. households will have digital satellite services and another seventy million predominately digital cable.[57] Growth should be comparable in Britain, which is a few years ahead of most of the rest of Europe.[58]

The exact contours of a satellite digital television universe remain unclear, but a few points are evident. First, only a fraction of the channels will have the programming traditionally associated with television. 'Research shows most people only watch eight to ten channels,' one executive noted.[59] The precise number will be determined by what is commercially viable, not what is technologically possible. The experience with cable television suggests that a handful of genres will proliferate and the vast majority of the channels will be provided by the very largest media firms.[60] 'Mergers and consolidations,' *Variety* observes, 'have transformed the cable-network marketplace into a walled-off community controlled by a handful of media monoliths.'[61] So what will occupy all the channel capacity of these digital satellite systems, or even the 200 or so channels of digital cable television? Many of the channels will be devoted to 'near video on demand,' in which one film may be run over a number of channels with starting times separated by only 10 or 15 minutes. This pay-per-view principle is also being widely applied to live sporting events. Many channels will be devoted to home shopping and explicit product marketing. Satellites can also broadcast digital data – such as electronic newspapers, multimedia or World Wide Web Internet sites – to businesses or to home subscribers' computers or TV sets.[62]

Second, within each of these regions the nature of the technology and the market is such that usually only one or two firms control the market. The fixed costs of establishing a digital satellite (or cable) television system are very high; it can only become profitable through covering wide areas and having a large market. Likewise, with current and foreseeable technology there are only a few optimal orbital locations for digital satellite broadcasting for each continent or global region; in the case of the United States and Mexico, for example, four slots at most are available to provide a viable service.[63] Although most digital systems will offer a similar array of commercial cable channels, those firms that are first to develop a marketable service and that can also provide a range of sporting events and films that are unavailable on competitor services have a distinct advantage. This has been the traditional pattern with cable and analogue satellite broadcasting and it appears to hold true for digital broadcasting. Technically, there is no reason that the digital broadcasting service providers need to act as anything more than distributors of other firms' television channels. However, the greatest profit is obtained when the system providers use their position to broadcast their own channels and programming as well.

Accordingly, the major global media firms are in the midst of what has been characterized as a 'winner-take-all battle' of 'digital star wars.' Although the full development of digital satellite television may take a decade or more, the crucial question of which firms will control these markets will probably be quickly determined.[64] Major joint ventures, usually centered in firms like News Corporation or General Motors' DirecTV, are in locked battle across the planet. In many nations and regions, a single firm already has a monopoly position and will likely scare away challengers. In most other regions or nations there will only be two or three contenders. The most competitive market is the United States. DirecTV has the early lead, but it faces challenges from Primestar, owned by General Electric and the major U.S. cable companies, U.S.S.B., owned by Hubbard Broadcasting, Dow Jones and others, and Sky Television, a joint venture of News Corporation, MCI, and Echostar.[65] The logic of this market, however, suggests that digital satellite television systems will soon be regional oligopolies, if not duopolies or even monopolies.

The emergence of global satellite television has led to a rearrangement of the global news industry. The 'big four' western news agencies – AP, UPI, Reuters, and AFP – still dominate the global print market while Reuters TV (formerly Visnews) and Worldwide Television News remain the dominant global television news agencies, but satellite television has brought into existence regional and global news channels.  The most prominent is CNN International, owned by Time Warner, which reaches over 200 countries and the vast majority of the world population. Although subsidized news services like the BBC World Service and the Voice of America still provide global news in numerous languages via the noncommercial and unprofitable channels of shortwave, they are battling to maintain their subsidies in a post-Cold War era; for example, Radio Canada, which broadcast in eight languages to 126 nations over the shortwave, was closed down in March 1997.[66] The commercial satellite news channels are where the growth has been occurring and where much, much more is to be expected.[67] At present they tend to reach a small elite audience, but they are increasingly becoming major providers of global journalism.[68] The BBC through its commercial World Service Television, and the remaining European public broadcasters through Euronews, have attempted to provide alternatives to CNN, with limited success.[69] One executive warns that Euronews may never gain the capital it needs to survive 'unless it decides to "commercialise" itself fully.'[70]

As advertising-supported vehicles, global news channels like CNN, directed at business and the global upper-middle classes, have proved quite lucrative.[71] With the digital increase in the number of channels, CNN faces increased competition, including two more global news channels launched in 1996, one by News Corporation and the other by NBC and Microsoft. As was the case with CNN, both plan to move quickly from the U.S. market to global service by 1997 or 1998.[72] CNN already has a Spanish-language service for Latin America and all the news channels are contemplating plans to broadcast in dominant regional languages as well as English. Roger Ailes, chairman of News Corporation's Fox News Channel, is explicit in stating that it will be directed at the needs of advertisers and the affluent audiences to which advertisers are attracted.[73] These news channels also offer their owners important political leverage in shaping public opinion and dealing with governments.[74] As a TCI executive acknowledges, much of TCI's and News Corporation's interest in a global television news channel is that 'they both know that news means control and a tremendous amount of influence.'[75] In all likelihood only two or three services can survive the anticipated round of competition; a risk factor for potential entrants that evidently caused Disney to cancel its plans to launch a news channel in 1996.

THE GLOBAL TREND TO DEREGULATION

These rapid changes in the global media system have been based on a 'new information order' of market freedom, and they have strengthened market rule. In the United States, for example, the First Amendment to the constitution has been increasingly interpreted as a statute that protects commercial speech from government interference.[76] Even the limited regulatory standards and enforcement of antitrust statutes to prevent media concentration that existed in the past have lessened to the point of irrelevance.[77] The 1996 U.S. Telecommunications Act, as one observer noted, opened up a 'Pandora's box of consolidation in the media industry,' as deregulation was the order of the day.[78] Encouraged by powerful media lobbies, this commercial spirit permeates all national debates concerning media. It also is true for regional bodies like the European Union, the home of outstanding public broadcasting systems but now devoted to establishing a single European market for commercial media. As a rule of thumb, the only basis for substantive media policy debates at the national level is when there are conflicts between powerful media interests. So it is that domestic media interests have been able to get some statutory protection from global media encroachment in the form of quotas and the like. But these campaigns for domestic protection have met with considerable resistance; in every nation there are powerful forces pressing the case for full integration into the global media market.[79]

At the international level, the dominant institutions and trade agreements continue to work toward the elimination of all barriers to the market. When the United States and Mexico signed a pact in 1996 to open up their respective satellite TV markets to the other, Federal Communications Commission Chair Reed Hundt termed the deal 'consistent with the spirit of NAFTA,' the regional free trade deal.[80] As the media have become increasingly central to the world economy, media policy matters have become the province of organizations like the IMF and the WTO. The IMF is committed to encouraging the establishment of commercial media globally to better serve the needs of a market economy. The WTO's mission is to encourage a single global market for commercial media, and to oppose barriers to this, however noble the intent.[81] In what may be a precedent-setting case, in January 1997 the

WTO ruled that Canada could not impose special taxes or tariffs on U.S. magazine publishers to protect Canadian periodicals. This was interpreted as strengthening 'Washington's case against cultural protection trade policies used by many other countries.'[82] In view of the global nature of the communication industries and technologies, there is an increasing acceptance of reduced national government control over vital areas of communication.[83] As a further case in point, the Geneva-based court of the European Free Trade Association ruled that Norway could not prohibit advertising aimed at children, as is the Norwegian practice,[84] on satellite broadcasts beamed into that country. Similarly, in 1996 the European Court of Justice informed Sweden that it could not ban advertising to children if the broadcasts originated in another EU state.[85] Likewise, EU rules require that France permit TV broadcasts of sporting events with liquor and alcohol advertisements, which violates French practice.[86] For less-powerful nations the prospect of impeding the global commercial market is even less plausible.

If in the 1970s global debate on media centered around the New World Information Order, notions of inequality, and the role of media in a democracy, the most prominent issue of the 1990s may well have become international copyright protection. Media firms lose several billion dollars annually to 'pirated' products; i.e., their films, books, or CDs are reproduced without the originating company and artist receiving compensation. In 1995, for example, it is estimated that China produced $1.8 billion, Russia $726 million, and Italy $515 million-worth of U.S. films, books, and recorded music without compensating the originating firm or artist.[87] Over 30 percent of the recorded music sold in Italy in 1995 was reportedly produced without respect to copyright.[88] China is said to account for 40 percent of the world's 'pirate' music market; it is a significant export industry.[89] There is grave concern among media firms that the shift to video compact disks will create 'unprecedented piracy' of films and television programs, 'that will make today's piracy look like petty theft.'[90] Along with pharmaceuticals, media and computer software copyright are the primary topics for global intellectual property rights negotiations.

Western media firms have commissioned their governments to lead the campaign against copyright violation. After threatening trade sanctions, the U.S. government reached an agreement with China in June 1996 for the latter to crack down on the 'pirate' media market.[91] The deal also abolishes China's quota of permitting only ten U.S. films per year to be imported to China, although China reserves the right to block importation if it finds that films violate its censorship standards.[92] Copyright protection is in fact a very complex issue; *The Economist* notes that much of copyright law is 'arbitrary' and designed for powerful interests.[93] Copyright and patents protect monopoly positions, keep prices high, and transfer income from poor to rich countries. The U.S. government aggressively insists upon a protection of intellectual property that provides maximum income to its own industry, while displaying minimal interest in the concerns of anyone else. The WTO has internalized this perspective, acting at the global level to attempt to enforce copyright protection. It has set the year 2000 as a deadline for nations to enact and enforce intellectual property protection.[94] In sum, the nature of global media policy debates conforms closely to the needs and desires of the largest and most powerful commercial actors.

localize content

GLOBAL CORPORATE MEDIA CONSOLIDATION

U.S.-based firms – though not necessarily owned by Americans – continue to dominate the global media market, and by all accounts they will do so for a long time to come.[95] In global media markets, U.S. firms can capitalize upon their historic competitive advantage of having by far the largest and most lucrative indigenous market to use as a testing ground and to yield economies of scale. Insofar as Hollywood and Madison Avenue have determined the formats for global commercial entertainment, this also accentuates the U.S. advantage.[96] U.S.-based firms can also take advantage of the widespread and growing international use of the English language, especially among the middle and upper classes.[97] Most of the large U.S-based media firms are in the process of moving from a 'U.S.-centric production and an international distribution network' model to a more transnational production and distribution model.[98] The increasing need for the media giants to 'localize' their content is encouraging them to 'establish wider international bases.'[99] Another factor in globalizing production is to take advantage of lower costs outside of the United States.[100]

The 1990s has seen an unprecedented wave of mergers and acquisitions among global media giants. What is emerging is a tiered global media market. In the first tier are around ten colossal vertically integrated media conglomerates. Six firms that already fit that description are News Corporation, Time Warner, Disney, Bertelsmann, Viacom, and TCI. These firms are major producers of entertainment and media software and have global distribution networks. Although the firms in the first tier are quite large – with annual sales in the $10–25 billion range – they are a notch or two below the largest global corporate giants, although all of them rank among the 500 largest global firms in annual sales. Four other firms that round out this first group include PolyGram (owned by Philips), NBC (owned by General Electric),

Universal (owned by Seagram), and Sony. All four of these firms are conglomerates with non-media interests, and three of them (Sony, GE, and Philips) are huge electronics concerns that at least double the annual sales of any first-tier media firm. None of them is as fully integrated as the first six firms, but they have the resources to do so if they wish.

There is a second tier of approximately three dozen quite large media firms – with annual sales generally in the $2–10 billion range – that fill regional or niche markets within the global system.[101] Most of these firms rank among the 1,000 largest global firms in terms of market valuation. These second-tier firms tend to have working agreements and/or joint ventures with one or more of the giants in the first tier and with each other; none attempt to 'go it alone.' As the head of Norway's largest media company stated, 'We want to position ourselves so if Kirch or Murdoch want to sell in Scandinavia, they'll come to us first.'[102] Finally, there are thousands of relatively small national and local firms that provide services to the large firms or fill small niches, and their prosperity is dependent in part upon the choices of the large firms.

In this period of flux all media firms are responding to a general market situation that is *forcing* them to move toward being much larger, global, vertically integrated conglomerates. One media industry observer characterizes the late 1990s as 'an all-out rush to claim global turf,' and 'a slugfest the likes of which have never been seen.'[103] A Wall Street media analyst states that 'the name of the game is critical mass. You need buying power and distribution. The ante has been upped. It's a global arena.'[104] 'The minimum hurdle for the size that you have to be has gone up,' a media consulting firm executive comments. 'Look, a couple of years ago, a $2 billion to $3 billion company was a well-sized company. Now there is really a concern from the executives of a lot of these companies that they are going to get left behind.'[105] Indeed, even in the current period of high growth it is just as likely that the number of major film and music producers for the global market will decrease rather than increase.

It is when the effects of horizontal and vertical integration, conglomeration, and globalization are combined that a sense of the profit potential emerges. First, there are often distinct cost savings. The media consultant who advised Viacom when it purchased Paramount in 1994 estimated that merely combining the two firms would immediately generate $105 million in cost savings.[106] This comes from fuller utilization of existing personnel, facilities, and 'content' resources. When a giant wishes to launch a new enterprise, it can draw upon its existing staff and resources. NBC or News Corporation, for example, are capable of launching global television news channels because they will use their journalists from their present staffs and other news resources. The marginal cost is quite low.[107] A second source of profitability deriving from conglomeration and vertical integration is the exploitation of new opportunities for cross-selling, cross-promotion, and privileged access. These benefits were given great emphasis in corporate explanations of the benefits of the Disney–ABC and Time Warner–Turner mergers, where they were regularly referred to as 'synergies.' It should be noted, however, that these gains are based on monopoly power, and are not gains to society any more than a firm's greater ability to levy higher prices would be. They are private and 'pecuniary' gains, not social and 'real' gains. The other side of the coin of effective cross-selling (etc.) is the exclusion of others, a reduction of competition, and pressure on rivals to follow the same exclusionary path.

When Disney, for example, produces a film, it can also guarantee the film showings on pay cable television and commercial network television, and it can produce and sell soundtracks based on the film, it can create spin-off television series, it can produce related amusement park rides, CD-Roms, books, comics, and merchandise to be sold in Disney retail stores. Moreover, Disney can promote the film and related material incessantly across all its media properties. Even films which do poorly at the box office can become profitable in this climate. Disney's 1996 *Hunchback of Notre Dame* generated a disappointing $99 million at the U.S. and Canadian box offices. According to *Adweek* magazine, however, it is expected to generate $500 million in *profit* (not just revenues), after the other revenue streams are taken into account. And films that are hits can become spectacularly successful. Disney's 1994 *The Lion King* earned over $300 million at the U.S. box office, yet generated over $1 billion in profit for Disney.[108] In sum, the profit whole for the vertically integrated firm can be significantly greater than the profit potential of the individual parts in isolation. Firms without this cross-selling and cross-promotional potential are at a serious disadvantage in competing in the global marketplace. This is the context for the wave of huge media mergers in the 1990s.

As the Disney example suggested, the 'synergies' do not end with media. Time Warner, Universal, and Disney all have theme parks and, likewise, Time Warner, Disney, and Viacom all have chains of retail stores to capitalize upon their media 'brands.'[109] Universal captures the spirit of the times in developing a five-year marketing plan for the 1995 film character 'Babe' to turn it into a 'mass-market cash cow.'[110] There will be a *Babe* film sequel in 1998, an animated *Babe* television series, along with *Babe* toys and books.[111] Universal is also launching 'brand galleries,' retail outlets based on its most well-known Universal Studios films and characters at its Florida and California theme parks. It is also designing plans for two other chains of retail stores, one to stand alone and another to be a 'boutique' inside existing chain retailers such as Toys 'Я' Us.[112] Viacom is part of a joint venture to launch a chain of 'Bubba Gump' seafood restaurants to capitalize upon the popularity of its *Forrest Gump* motion picture.[113] Turner Broadcasting aggressively markets its 'brands' from its huge movie and cartoon library to advertisers for use in commercials.[114] Both TCI and Disney are moving into the production of educational material, regarded as a lucrative market as the privatization and commercialization of U.S. schools gathers momentum.[115] Moreover, in view of their experience with commercial programming, media firms may be positioned to profit from the drive to bring advertising-supported fare into schools. The largest U.S. commercial education firm, Channel One, only blossomed after being purchased by media firm K-III.[116] By 1997 Channel One was being 'broadcast' to some 40 percent of all U.S. middle schools and high schools. Reebok, for example, has brought Channel One advertising into the heart of its marketing, using its school advertisements to promote the programs it sponsors over commercial television networks.[117]

The size and market power of the media giants also make it possible to engineer exclusive strategic alliances for cross-promotion with other marketing and retailing powerhouses. In 1996 Disney signed a ten-year deal with McDonald's, giving the fast food chain exclusive global rights to promote Disney products in its restaurants. Disney can use McDonald's 18,700 outlets to promote its global sales, while McDonald's can use Disney to assist it in its unabashed campaign to 'dominate every market' in the world.[118] PepsiCo. signed a similar promotional deal for a 1996 re-release of the *Star Wars* film trilogy, in which all of PepsiCo.'s global properties – including Pepsi-Cola, Frito-Lay snacks, Pizza Hut, and Taco Bell – were committed to the promotion.[119] Universal has taken this process the furthest, by keeping it in-house. In 1997 it began heavily promoting its media fare on parent corporation Seagram's beverage products, including Tropicana orange juice.[120] These link-ups between global marketers and media firms are becoming standard operating procedure, and they do much to enhance the profitability and competitive position of the very largest global firms.

It is important to note that these giant mergers, while enlarging profit opportunities in some respects, can run into difficulties, sometimes quite immense ones at that. The prices paid for the properties may be excessive and/or the interest payments on the debt incurred may prevent necessary capital expenditures and make the firm vulnerable to recession or other unexpected difficulties. Major mergers or acquisitions are often accompanied by the sale of assets to retire debt and refocus the firm's activities in areas where the firm has a large stake. In the late 1990s this process is being encouraged by Wall Street. Many corporate media stock prices have floundered during a bull market, putting severe pressure on corporate media managers to generate earnings growth in the short term. One investment banker observed that the largest media conglomerates will likely 'trim down to focus on businesses that are strong cash flow and high-growth, and get out of the businesses that aren't.'[121] In some cases the anticipated 'synergies' do not materialize or may be more than offset by difficulties in meshing with previously independent operations. Several global electronics giants, including General Electric and Sony, purchased major media firms thinking they could expand their profit potential through the complementary nature of media 'hardware' and 'software.' This has not yet proved to be the case. Matsushita found this route notably unrewarding, unloading (then) MCA to Seagram in 1995 after painful losses.

Firms grow and compete in the global marketplace by internal processes, reinvesting earnings to create new facilities, as well as by mergers and acquisitions. In establishing new ventures, media firms frequently participate in joint ventures with one or more of their rivals on specific media projects. Joint ventures are attractive because they reduce the capital requirements and risk of the participants and permit them to spread their resources more widely. Joint ventures also provide a more flexible weapon than formal mergers or acquisitions, which often require years for negotiation and approval and then getting the new parts assimilated. The ten largest global media firms have, on average, joint ventures with five of the other nine giants. They each also average six joint ventures with second-tier media firms. The full range of these activities will become apparent in Chapter 3. Media giants also use joint ventures as a means of easing entry into new international markets, teaming up with 'local international partners who best understand their own turf.'[122] This is a major route through which the largest national and regional media firms around the world are brought into the global market system. Joint ventures are not without their problems, as media partners can develop differing visions for the joint enterprise; along these lines Universal and Viacom had a dispute over their USA cable television network, and U.S. West has been dissatisfied with its shared operations with Time Warner.[123]

Beyond joint ventures, there is also overlapping direct ownership of these firms. Seagram, for example, owner of Universal, also owns 15 percent of Time Warner and has other media equity holdings.[124] TCI is a major shareholder in Time Warner and has holdings in numerous other media firms.[125] The Capital Group Companies' mutual funds, valued at $250 billion, are among the very largest shareholders in TCI, News Corporation, Seagram, Time Warner, Viacom, Disney,

Westinghouse, and several other smaller media firms.[126] The head of Capital Group's media investments, Gordon Crawford, is a trusted adviser to the CEOs of nearly all of these firms. He plays an important role in engineering mergers and joint ventures across the media industry.[127] In particular, through Capital Group's holdings in Seagram and TCI as well as its direct holdings in Time Warner, Crawford is one of the most influential shareholders in Time Warner.[128] More generally, in view of their great merger activity and rapid expansion, the media giants find themselves increasingly reliant on the largest Wall Street commercial and investment banks for strategic counsel and capital. A handful of global institutions like Chase Manhattan, Morgan Stanley, and Salomon Brothers have been key advisers in the major mergers of the mid-1990s.[129]

Competition in media markets is quite different from the notion of competition that dominates popular usage of the term. When politicians, business executives, and academics invoke the term 'competition,' they almost invariably refer to the kind found in economics textbooks, based upon competitive markets where there are innumerable players, price competition, and easy entry. This notion of competition has never had much applicability in communication markets. As noted, the 'synergies' of recent mergers rest on and enhance monopoly power. Reigning oligopolistic markets are dominated by a handful of firms that compete – often quite ferociously within the oligopolistic framework – on a non-price basis and are protected by severe barriers to entry. No start-up studio, for example, has successfully joined the Hollywood oligopoly in 60 years.[130] Whether the new studio DreamWorks, formed by Stephen Spielberg, David Geffen, and Jeffrey Katzenbach, succeeds, this is obviously an exceptional case, drawing upon the unique wealth and connections of its founders. If successful, DreamWorks will probably become a second-tier player specializing in providing content to media giants through joint ventures and working agreements.

Rupert Murdoch of News Corporation poses the rational issue for an oligopolistic firm when pondering the shakeout in the global media market: 'We can join forces now, or we can kill each other and then join forces.'[131] In this spirit, in 1997 Murdoch contacted Viacom CEO Sumner Redstone, informing him it was time they stopped 'being perceived as adversaries,' and that they should 'see what we can do together.'[132] Time Warner CEO Gerald Levin claims that with rapidly expanding economic opportunities 'there is enough new business, both domestically and internationally, that there won't be a war of attrition.'[133] And if the giants are pursuing this new business in joint ventures with major rivals in many local and national markets, the likelihood of cut-throat competition recedes markedly. John Malone, the

CEO of TCI, whose entrepreneurial drive is often noted, states that
'Nobody can really afford to get mad with their competitors, because
they are partners in one area and competitors in another.'[134] The *Wall
Street Journal* observes that media 'competitors wind up switching
between the roles of adversaries, prized customers and key partners.'[135]
In this sense the global media and communication market exhibits tendencies not only of an oligopoly, but of a cartel or at least a 'gentleman's
club.' Paine Webber's media analyst terms it the global 'communications kereitsu,' in reference to the Japanese corporate system of inter-
locking ownership and management.[136]

THE CENTRAL ROLE OF ADVERTISING

With the increasing globalization of the world economy, advertising has
come to play a crucial role for the few hundred firms that dominate it.
In 1995 the forty largest advertising corporations, all of which were
based in Western Europe, Japan, or the United States, spent some $47
billion on advertising worldwide, $26 billion of which was outside the
United States, an increase of nearly 20 percent over their spending in
1994. The top eight firms accounted for nearly one-half of the top
forty's advertising.[137] As *The Economist* puts it, 'much of the spending in
different countries comes from the same companies.' Procter & Gamble,
for example, is among the top ten advertisers in all but two of the ten
largest national advertising markets, and number one in three.[138] 'We're
in an era of global marketing warfare,' an expert on global corporate
'positioning' comments. 'The number one tactical weapon of the age is
advertising.'[139] Moreover, global advertising benefits from a stagnant
global economy as well as a vibrant one. 'With massive overcapacity in
industries worldwide,' *Business Week* observes, 'selling products is harder,
and differentiating goods more critical.' The development of global
commercial broadcasting is an integral part of the creation of a global
market. The long experience of the United States highlights how well
suited commercial television is to advertising. To help make this commercial bounty global, in 1996 the leading world advertising and broadcasting associations devised a single global standard for the purchase
and production of television advertising.[140]

Global advertising is expected to increase at a rate greater than GDP
growth for the foreseeable future. U.S. per capita advertising spending
in 1995 was $365 while in the U.K. (second in Europe to Switzerland) it
was $258, in Italy $97, and in China and India it was $3 and $1 respectively.[141] The rest of the world is in the process of having its level of ad-

vertising elevated toward the U.S. position. In 1970 the United States accounted for 60 percent of global advertising, whereas in 1995 it accounted for 47 percent. McCann-Erickson forecasts that global advertising will increase from $335 billion in 1995 to $2 trillion in 2020, with a further substantial decline in the North American percentage of the global total.[142] Yet the U.S. advertising market is hardly stagnant; it is growing at a pace well in excess of GDP growth in the middle and late 1990s.[143] Asia, Latin America, and Eastern Europe are where the greatest per capita increases are taking place.[144] The Leo Burnett Agency estimates that China's portion of Asian advertising went from 1 percent in 1991 to 8 percent in 1995, and it is projected to double to 16 percent in 1997.[145] Most of the growth in advertising spending is going toward television, while newspaper and magazine advertising shrinks as a proportion of the whole.[146]

Since the dawn of modern advertising, it has been axiomatic that it must be conducted by agencies independent of both the advertising firm and the media to be effective in the long run. Of the leading global advertising agencies, therefore, only Havas has extensive media holdings, over which it exercises indirect control. The leading advertising organizations also tend to be smaller than leading media firms, whose annual sales are as much as ten times greater.[147] In the 1980s there was a major wave of mergers and acquisitions among advertising agencies, especially in the United States, and global ambitions underlay much of the activity.[148] In the 1990s the trend toward consolidation has continued, only now the global concerns are central to the process. After a series of buyouts and mergers a 'big three' of global advertising organizations, each with a number of agencies around the world, has emerged. The three – the British WPP Group, the U.S. Omnicom Group, and the U.S. Interpublic – had combined gross revenues of $8 billion, and placed over $50 billion of advertising in 1995. The big three are followed by the Japanese Dentsu, British Cordiant, and U.S. Young & Rubicam, each of which is about half the size of the first three. The industry is effectively centered in New York, with a few key agencies based in Tokyo, London, Chicago, and Paris.[149]

In almost all developing countries the leading domestic agencies have sold out to one of the huge global advertising networks for fear of getting cut out of the action. The 'big three' own several agencies and through them maintain offices in over a hundred countries.[150] The U.S. and European advertising agencies ranked below the first five or six firms are now in a hurry to build 'critical mass outside the U.S.,' or else see themselves as likely catches 'for any one of the giants as they race to grow ever-bigger.'[151] According to *The Economist*, the 'consensus' is that perhaps one more advertising conglomerate 'will clamber into the first division,' while 'the rest will be eaten.'[152] Havas, the world's seventh largest advertising agency with 1995 billings of $6.2 billion, radically overhauled its organization in 1996 to make itself competitive on a global basis. It purchased six Latin American agencies and is expanding operations in Asia and China.[153] The French Publicis likewise has budgeted $350 million for the purchase of Latin American and Asian advertising agencies in 1996 and 1997.[154]

As the *Wall Street Journal* notes, to a considerable extent this global consolidation 'is being driven by the demands of increasingly international clients.'[155] 'Multinationals launching global brands in a strange country,' an Indian executive of the WPP Group observes, 'seek a sense of familiarity and sometimes prefer to deal with one agency worldwide.'[156] The clear trend in the 1990s has been for global firms like Colgate-Palmolive, Bayer, Coca-Cola, Intel, and numerous others to consolidate their advertising accounts – that had been spread among as many as fifty different agencies – into a single global agency.[157] Another common option is for transnational firms to consolidate their accounts into a 'club' of three or four huge agencies, as even the largest advertising groups are relatively weak in some regions.[158] 'It's about harnessing the global power of the brand,' an Interpublic executive states. 'The common thread is that they [the clients] want control of what their brands stand for, and the ability to develop that on a global scale.'[159]

The largest half-dozen global advertising organizations are also providing a wider range of services for their multinational clients. On the one hand, they complement their advertising services with global direct marketing networks. Non-advertising marketing activities account for half of WPP's income and one-third of Omnicom's income.[160] On the other hand, the largest global advertising agencies now own nine of the twelve largest global public relations (PR) agencies, most of which have offices in scores of nations. Like advertising, PR is a highly concentrated global industry; the top three global firms have as much income as the firms ranked four through sixteen, and the top three firms have twice the income of the firms ranked seventeen through fifty. By dominating global public relations, the global advertising giants can offer their corporate clients expertise in political lobbying, public opinion management, and influencing journalism surreptitiously across the world.[161]

The voracious marketing appetites and changing needs of advertising corporations provide many new opportunities for global media firms. Advertising volume is increasing rapidly both in the United States and globally. U.S. TV networks now broadcast 6,000 commercials per week, up by 50 percent since 1983. Half-hour programs, for example, have had their editorial time cut by as much as 10 percent to make more room for advertising.[162] As *Business Week* observes, 'the buying public has been virtually buried alive in ads.' Desperate to be seen and heard, advertisers are turning to new approaches, including 'stamping their messages on everything that stands still.'[163] In 1996, News Corporation's U.S. Fox television network ran commercial banners along the bottom of the screen during primetime shows, breaking a longstanding taboo, but with mixed results.[164] In 1997, in another precedent-setting example, a Swedish telecommunication firm offered reduced rates on its telephone service if customers would agree to listen to advertisements during their telephone calls.[165]

To circumvent this commercial blizzard, and consumer skepticism of traditional advertising, marketers are working to infiltrate entertainment. On one hand, this means making commercials appear like entertainment. Thirty- and 60-minute infomercials, once the domain of dubious enterprises, are now being employed by firms like Microsoft, Ford, and Eastman Kodak, offering state-of-the-art production values.[166] Infomercials are going global, and they 'sizzle in Asia,' according to the *Wall Street Journal*. 'Generally, if it works in America it works in Asia,' a Singapore-based U.S. media executive states.[167] The booming U.S.-based Quantum International (1997 sales: $400 million) buys 3,200 half-hours of infomercials in twenty-one different languages in sixty-five nations every week. Almost all of the infomercials are dubbed versions of the U.S. originals, and they 'heavily push the hype of U.S. consumerism.'[168] Another surging development is the effort of television channels like ABC to broadcast entertainment programs featuring products that are sold over the air, with the programs also including explicit commercial breaks for additional paid advertising. MTV has had some success with this format with its program, *The Goods*, but it is still in the infant stage. By 1997 the U.S. Sci-Fi cable channel, owned jointly by Viacom and Universal, had taken this genre the furthest; its weekly 'Sci-Fi Trader' series, which hawks science fiction-related material between interviews with sci-fi authors, is listed as a bona fide program in *TV Guide*, and it raked in advertising dollars from firms like AT&T, Coca-Cola, Procter & Gamble and Philip Morris.[169] As *Adweek* puts it, 'the network that cracks-the-code of marrying entertainment with selling will be richly rewarded.'[170]

This 'marrying' has resulted in further specialization; for example, there are over two dozen consultancies in Los Angeles whose business is linking marketers with film and television producers, usually to get the marketer's product 'placed' and promoted in films and TV programs.[171] In view of the global audience for U.S. films and television shows, this is an important marketing opportunity for leading firms. 'The connections between Madison Avenue and Hollywood have grown so elaborate,' *Business Week* concludes, 'that nothing is off-limits when studios and advertisers sit down to hammer out the marketing campaign.' The 1996 hit film *Mission Impossible*, for example, featured an Apple PowerBook Computer as star Tom Cruise's onscreen sidekick. In return, Apple plugged the film in a $15 million advertising campaign.[172] Apple had a similar deal with the 1996 News Corporation blockbuster, *Independence Day*, in which Jeff Goldblum saves the world from an alien invasion using his Apple PowerBook.[173] As an indication of Hollywood's new age, in 1997 Reebok sued Sony's TriStar Pictures, claiming TriStar had reneged on its promise to feature a Reebok commercial prominently in the concluding 'happy ending' scene of the film *Jerry Maguire*. Reebok earned this honor, it claimed, because it had spent $1.5 million in advertising and promotional support for the film. To Reebok, product placement is becoming a central means of selling. 'A great deal about a brand's image gets defined by who's wearing it and using it,' a Reebok executive explained. 'That's part of the fabric of who we are.'[174]

The most important method of commercializing films is to specifically produce films that lend themselves to the complementary merchandising of products: the revenues generated here can be greater than those generated by box-office sales or video rentals, as the Disney examples mentioned above highlighted. Time Warner and Disney generate over U.S.$1 and U.S.$2 billion in income respectively from their consumer products divisions. Indeed, Disney now looks to have its 'live-action' films generate the same merchandising revenues that have been associated with its animated films. This is becoming an important criterion for determining which films get made and which do not.[175] The ultimate result of the 'marriage of Hollywood and Madison Avenue' came with the 1996 release of Time Warner's film *Space Jam*, based upon Nike shoe commercials with Bugs Bunny and Michael Jordan and directed by 'the country's hottest director of commercials.' As *Forbes* magazine puts it, 'the real point of the movie is to sell, sell, sell.' Time Warner 'is looking to hawk up to $1 billion in toys, clothing, books, and sports gear based on the movie characters.' A similar film based on Nike advertisements with basketball star Penny Hardaway is expected to be produced in 1997. Moreover, the style of feature films has increasingly adopted the techniques of television commercials. One 1996 Hollywood film directed by a veteran of advertising – *The Rock*, with Nicolas Cage and Sean Connery – was characterized as 'like a series of vivid, focused, 60-second commercials.'[176]

In short, traditional notions of separation of editorial and commercial interests are weakening. Advertisers have a large and increasing role in determining media content. NBC has agreed to let IBM have final say over content in its new cable program 'Scan,' in return for IBM agreeing to sponsor the program on NBC's networks in North America, Asia, Europe, and Latin America. A U.S. advertising executive predicts that 'This is just a forerunner of what we are going to see as we get to 500 channels. Every client will have their own programming tailored to their own needs, based on their ad campaign.'[177] NBC and Viacom finalized a three-year deal in 1996 with Procter & Gamble whereby P&G will provide up to 50 percent of the financing for television series in return for access to advertising time on the show in the U.S. and globally.[178] P&G made a similar deal with Viacom and Bertelsmann to produce movies for European television.[179]

In a striking manifestation of the new era of global media and global advertising practice, in late 1996 Disney's ESPN began offering global buys to advertisers utilizing all its channels and properties around the world, and giving these clients exclusive participation in ESPN programming. No Fear jeans, for example, is to be identified with pivotal plays in replays of games on ESPN networks.[180] Even more sweeping, NBC and Young & Rubicam began negotiations for an unprecedented partnership that would give all the agency's clients integrated marketing and promotional opportunities on all of NBC's global properties, while permitting the agency input on programming decisions. In this way the oligopolistic nature of each industry comes to reinforce the monopoly power of firms in other industries.[181]

It is when one combines the effects of media conglomeration, corporate concentration, and hyper-commercialism upon media content that the nature of the global media system's culture comes into focus. Book publishing, for example, which for decades tended to have a relatively wide ideological and cultural range of output, has been brought squarely into the cross-promotional plans of the media giants.[182] 'The drive for profit,' a veteran U.S. book editor observes, 'fits like an iron mask on our cultural output.'[183] Even the most prestigious commercial magazine publishers concede that the traditional autonomy of editorial content has been replaced by a regime where 'everyone keeps an eye on profits.' And few corporate media magazine owners are especially concerned with prestige.[184] Scott Rudin, termed Hollywood's 'most prolific producer,' states, 'making movies has become so debilitating, so devoid of any enthusiasm for the material, for the talent involved.'[185] Corporate concentration and commercial pressures have also led numerous journalists to leave the corporate press in protest at the compromise of traditional standards.[186] In one example of how journalism fits into the operations of media empires, NBC News made the 1996 Summer Olympics its most frequently covered story for the year, with nearly 20 percent more coverage than that of its second most-covered story. The coverage of the Olympics for the other U.S. networks failed to even make their 'top ten' list of most-covered news stories for the year. Perhaps it was a coincidence, but NBC had the U.S. television rights to the Olympics.[187] Whether the commercial global media system 'gives the people what they want' is a subject we take up in later chapters. What is crystal clear is that the global media system is giving the largest media firms, their shareholders, and advertisers what they want. 'We're here to serve advertisers,' Westinghouse CEO Michael Jordan says. 'That's our *raison d'être*.'[188]

UNEVEN DEVELOPMENT OF THE GLOBAL MEDIA MARKET

Even if the market is becoming the worldwide method for organizing communication, and nonmarket principles and values are playing a much smaller role in determining the nature of media systems, the globalization–commercialization process does not operate at the same pace and to the same extent around the world. Each nation's indigenous commercial and/or noncommercial media system responds somewhat differently to the encroachment of global market forces, leading to continued variation in local markets. Moreover, nation states remain the most important political forces in communication and much else; the pace and course of media market liberalization varies from nation to nation and region to region, though the general trend toward deregulation is clear. In short, each country will have to be understood on its own terms as well as in the context of the global media market for the foreseeable future.

The core tendencies of the global market itself will also tend to produce a highly uneven worldwide media system. Commercial media markets are attracted to people with the money to purchase their products (and the necessary media hardware to use them), and to people with enough money to purchase the products that program sponsors wish to advertise. If global advertisers are interested in a sector of the population or a region, global media firms will move quickly to accommodate them. A nation like India provides a case in point. Over half of its 900 million population is entirely irrelevant to the global media market and, at present rates of change, will continue to be irrelevant for generations. But the prospering middle classes are another matter. 'There are 250 million people in the middle-class in India alone,' Disney's Michael Eisner observes, 'which is an enormous opportunity.'[189] And it has only begun to be incorporated into the global media market in any appreciable way in the past decade. The same can be said of upper and middle classes across Asia, the Middle East, and Latin America.

In the context of the market logic guiding global media firms, we can make a few observations about the manner in which the global system will evolve in different regions of the world. Although its share of global media consumption is declining, North America remains the most important market. It is difficult to imagine a firm being a global player without a significant presence there. Western Europe is almost as important, not only because of its wealth but because it still has room to grow to reach U.S. per capita levels of advertising and media consumption. At the other end of the spectrum is sub-Saharan Africa, which, aside from the business and affluent classes in South Africa, seemingly has been written off by global media firms as too poor to develop. It does not even appear in most discussions of global media in the business press. Global media firms tend to break the world down to North America, Latin America, Europe, and Asia. When the *Financial Times* published a world map to highlight MTV's global expansion, it simply removed Africa and replaced it with the names of the thirty-eight European nations that carry MTV.[190] In severe economic crises, many African nations have privatized their broadcasting systems, but there is little capital to provide radio and television services.[191] Due in part to 'feeble resources,' the *Financial Times* concludes, 'most African television is so excruciating unwatchable.'[192] Even in relatively rich South Africa, half of the homes have no electricity.[193] Left to the global media market, sub-Saharan Africa's media and communication systems will remain undeveloped, and even wither.

Eastern Europe has been the site of a painful transition from a state-dominated economy and media to one with increasing private ownership. As state media subsidies have been eliminated, advertising and subscription income have yet to provide much of a basis for a commercially viable press. As the *New York Times* concluded, the 'Russian Press Is Free, Free to Go Broke.'[194] Those papers that survive have tended to fall into the hands of businessmen and bankers who want to control vehicles of propaganda, and two of the three national TV stations have been acquired by businessmen-banker allies of the Yeltsin government (the other national channel is fully state-owned). One scholar characterized Russian television as 'an instrument to be exploited by criminals and authoritarian politicians.'[195] TV programming is heavily western-ized in both direct (imported) content and format – it is also Latinized, with Mexican *telenovas* very popular. Despite strong nationalistic undercurrents, the elites in Russia (and elsewhere in Eastern Europe) are denationalized, and it is reported that 'advertising (not only on TV) quite often used English as a sign of cachet, rather than Russian,' and that imported Western objects frequently have foreign language texts 'as a kind of guarantee of "non-Russo-Soviet" authenticity.'[196] Combined with the economic weakness, instability and dependency of the Russian economy and state (also true in varying degrees of other Eastern

European countries), this denationalization makes foreign entry and the imposition and advance of the commercial model relatively easy and sure, with uncertain time lags. The main impediment to this foreign penetration is likely to be the continuing authoritarian tendencies of the leadership and, not unrelated, continued economic and political instability. These forces and trends do not bode well for the emergence of a meaningful public sphere over the next decade. The bias of the newly commercializing and state-dominated and state-influenced media during the 1996 presidential election in Russia was so blatant that one Moscow citizen noted plaintively that 'Once again we need shortwave foreign broadcasts to know what's going on.'[197]

The situation is much the same in the rest of Eastern Europe, where the traditional state-subsidized media are disintegrating. The leading film studio of former Czechoslovakia is now used primarily for filming advertisements.[198] In another sign of the collapse of the once-powerful Eastern European film industry, in 1994 Hollywood studios commanded 93 percent of Hungary's film market.[199] While the collapse of the public sector in Africa has failed to rouse much enthusiasm for investment by global media firms, Eastern Europe seemingly holds more commercial promise. The new market-driven economies in Eastern Europe appear to be generating an affluent middle class alongside vast sections of the population mired in brutal poverty, not unlike the cases of Brazil or India. Global media firms have great interest in the new Eastern European middle classes, especially in the wealthier Poland, Hungary, and Czech Republic. Accordingly, media firms have moved into the desirable markets; for example, over half of Czech newspapers are owned by German and Swiss firms.[200] Western firms like Time Warner, Canal Plus, Disney, and Bertelsmann increasingly dominate television in those three nations.[201] 'We believe these countries are integrating more with the European community,' a U.S. commercial broadcaster observes, and as these economies recover, advertising in these nations 'will explode.'[202]

'Foreign-owned papers and private television expand the news spectrum' in Eastern Europe, observes the *New York Times*, 'but most show little interest in serious political coverage.'[203] The incorporation of Eastern Europe into the global media market is important in the eyes of Western policy-makers, as it will help to integrate the region into the global economy, and to produce the type of media and political culture where the market domination of society goes unquestioned.[204] The *Financial Times* refers to this as the necessary 'process of de-politicising the economy.'[205]

Latin America is seen as a high-growth area. It has a history of commercial media that, when combined with the continent-wide adoption of neoliberal economic policies, provides major opportunities for global media firms.[206] The region has only two languages, and English is widely understood among the upper and middle classes, making it easier to provide pan-Latin American services. A significant percentage of the region's 430 million people live in abject poverty, but there is a viable middle class, especially in nations like Brazil, Argentina, Mexico, and Colombia. Moreover, these middle classes have shown a fondness for Hollywood programming and advertised international brands.[207] Television sets are in 85 percent of Latin America's 100 million households, and between 11 and 15 percent have pay cable or satellite television.[208] This explains why Latin America has become a prime battleground for digital satellite television. Miami has emerged as the media capital of Latin America; most Latin cable and satellite channels are headquartered there, as is the coordination of Latin American advertising.[209] Latin America is now considered a 'top prospect for future growth' in advertising and marketing. IBM's Latin American marketing director describes the results of its 1995 direct marketing campaigns in Brazil 'as literally like sweeping gold off the street.'[210]

If Miami is the media capital of Latin America, Hong Kong and Singapore share that honor in Asia. Most of the global media giants base their East Asian activities in one of those locales. Asia is unquestionably the most coveted emerging market area for the global media giants. As one report puts it, 'The Asian market for cable and satellite services is huge and relatively untapped, offering practically unrivalled growth opportunities.'[211] The raw population is larger than that of the rest of the world combined, and it has enjoyed the highest rates of economic growth in the world in the 1990s. It is projected to remain the fastest growing region of the world well into the twenty-first century.

Asia's traditional drawbacks for global media firms are that it is far more heterogeneous than, say, Latin America, and Asian nations have had rather strict regulations over media. These regulations are gradually being removed and by all calculations Asia is and will continue to be the fastest growing global commercial media market. Indonesia, the fourth most populous nation in the world, had an entirely 'pirate' video market in 1991. It has now been brought into the global market system.[212] Between 1995 and 2003 India is projected to have a 50 percent increase in television set ownership, China and Indonesia a 33 percent increase, and Thailand and Malaysia a 25 percent increase. By 2003, Asia will have nearly 500 million television households, three times as many as in Western Europe, and nearly 180 million cable and satellite television households.[213] Television advertising revenues are forecast to nearly triple to $20 billion between 1995 and 2003.[214] 'With huge, growing economies, there's a big upside in media and entertainment in Asia,' an

Australian industry analyst observes. 'We are scouring places looking for
opportunities,' a U.S. investment manager states.[215] Even Japan, the
most developed Asian economy, has considerable room for commercial
media growth in comparison to the United States or Western European
nations.

The largest jewel in the Asian media crown is China, with its population of 1.2 billion people. Although still a political dictatorship under
the Communist Party, China has taken a decided turn toward becoming
a market economy. Advertising has become an accepted part of Chinese
life, and personal consumption of branded products is markedly increasing in prominence. 'Shanghai,' *Advertising Age* notes, 'is quickly embra-
cing the shopping mall culture.'[216] China's slogan for the development
of broadcasting is 'Those who invest, should benefit,' and by 1992
Chinese media were set on a path of explicit commercialization.[217]
Television has exploded in the past decade. The number of channels
increased from thirty-two in 1978 to nearly 600 by 1992. In 1994 there
were 230 million TV sets and 800 million viewers in China.[218] Color
sets were in 86 percent of China's urban households in 1994, and the
number of cable TV customers is expected to increase to between 80
and 100 million by 2000, making it the largest cable market in the
world.[219] (The Chinese have encouraged cable over direct-to-home
satellite TV as it is easier to regulate content.) The adoption of a market
economy has widened class divisions, and in the process has created a
viable middle class 'at least 100 million strong.'[220] All evidence suggests
that the Chinese commercial television market 'already is taking off,'
and the future may hold unfathomable riches for global media firms.[221]
All the global media giants are working quietly to gain entrance into the
Chinese television market, often through delicate negotiations with the
Chinese government.[222] Patience is the order of the day. The state-run
Chinese Central Television with its five channels still dominates, though
it is becoming an increasingly commercial enterprise. 'Once the change
in leadership stabilizes,' the president of NBC Asia predicts, looking to
China's near future, 'and the Government liberalizes, there will be
tremendous new demand.'

CONCLUSION

After another wave of global media deals in the summer of 1996, a leading Wall Street media industry analyst observed, 'It's the ninth inning in
a game that began in 1987, and that's the restructuring of the media
industry on a global scale.'[223] By 1997, the largest media giants like
Disney and Time Warner were increasingly providing their films to their

own television networks and cable channels in a privileged manner. This was leaving networks like NBC and CBS that lacked large production studios 'shut out' of the system, and suggested that another wave of mergers may transpire before the dust would settle.[224] How close the global market is to stabilization remains to be seen, but the contours are clearly visible. The firms that sit atop the global media market have transformed themselves seemingly almost overnight. Viacom, for example, a relatively obscure player in the U.S. media industry as recently as the late 1980s, is now one of the firms in the top half of the global first tier, having increased its sales sixfold from 1993 to 1997. Indeed, four of the top six first-tier global media firms did not exist in their present form in the 1980s. The two largest global media firms, Time Warner and Disney, both roughly doubled their annual revenues from 1994 to 1996, partly through internal growth, but mainly via acquisitions. The global media market is being constructed by these and other large firms seeking commercial gain in a congenial political and economic environment. It is now time to examine the nature, operations, and ambitions of the dominant media firms and their global empires.

3
Main Players in the Global Media System

In this chapter we profile the ten firms in the dominant first tier of the global media oligopoly. In doing so we will discuss the type of programming that is proving most lucrative commercially. The five largest media firms in the world in terms of sales – Time Warner, Disney, Bertelsmann, Viacom, and News Corporation – are also the most fully integrated global media giants. News Corporation, Time Warner, Disney, and Viacom have huge film and television production facilities and are in intense competition for success in the booming global commercial television market. Lacking such studios, Bertelsmann and TCI compete in different markets and manners, though both are moving toward more direct competition – and collaboration – in the global television market. We then look at four other firms – PolyGram, Seagram, Sony, and General Electric – that rank lower in the first tier. Any of these firms could vault to the very top of the global media market if they established that as a goal and successfully engineered the mergers and acquisitions necessary to bring it about. We conclude the chapter by discussing some of the second-tier firms in the global media market. These are the three dozen or so sizable firms that fill regional or niche markets and that often depend upon working arrangements with one or more of the giants in the first tier for their profitability.[1]

DOMINANT FIRMS IN THE GLOBAL MEDIA MARKET

Although **News Corporation** ranks fifth with approximately $10 billion in 1996 sales, it provides the archetype for the twenty-first century global media firm in many respects and is the best case study for understanding global media firm behavior. The News Corporation is often identified with its head, Rupert Murdoch, whose family controls some 30 percent of its stock.[2] Murdoch's goal is for News Corporation 'to own every form of programming – news, sports, films and children's shows – and beam them via satellite or TV stations to homes in the United

States, Europe, Asia and South America.'[3] Viacom CEO Sumner Redstone says of Murdoch that 'he basically wants to conquer the world. And he seems to be doing it.'[4] Redstone, Disney CEO Michael Eisner, and Time Warner CEO Gerald Levin have each commented that Murdoch is the one media executive they most respect and fear, and the one whose moves they study.[5] TCI's John Malone states that global media vertical integration is 'all about trying to catch Rupert.'[6] Time Warner executive Ted Turner views Murdoch in a more sinister fashion, likening him to Adolf Hitler.[7]

After establishing News Corporation in his native Australia, Murdoch entered the British market in the 1960s and by the 1980s had become a dominant force in the U.S. market. News Corporation went heavily into debt to subsidize its purchase of Twentieth Century Fox and the formation of the Fox television network in the 1980s. By the mid-1990s News Corporation had eliminated much of that debt. It also received an infusion of capital in 1995 when the U.S. telecommunications firm MCI – subsequently purchased by British Telecommunications (BT) and rechristened Concert – agreed to invest $2 billion in exchange for a 13 percent stake in News Corporation.[8] Although News Corporation is diversifying into film and television, it stills earns over half of its income from its profitable bedrock newspaper and magazine businesses.[9]

News Corporation's more significant media holdings include the following:

- Some 132 newspapers (primarily in Australia, Britain, and the United States), making it one of the three largest newspaper groups in the world;
- Twentieth Century Fox, a major film, television, and video production center, which has a library of over 2,000 films to exploit.
- The U.S. Fox broadcasting network;
- Twenty-two U.S. television stations, the largest U.S. station group, covering over 40 percent of U.S. TV households;
- Twenty-five magazines, most notably *TV Guide*;
- Book-publishing interests, including HarperCollins;
- A 50 percent stake (with TCI's Liberty Media) in several U.S. and global cable networks, including fX, fXM, Fox Sports Net;
- Fox News Channel;
- Asian Star Television, satellite service and television channels;
- Controlling interest (40 percent) in British Sky Broadcasting (BSkyB) (1996 sales: $1.6 billion);
- BSkyB has a 40 percent stake in U.K.'s Granada Sky Television satellite channel group;

- A 49.9 percent stake in Germany's Vox channel;
- A 30 percent stake in Sky Latin America digital satellite service;
- A 40 percent stake in U.S. Sky Television, a digital satellite joint venture with Echostar and Concert;
- A 50 percent stake in Japan Sky Broadcasting digital satellite service;
- Australian Foxtel cable channel;
- A 49.9 percent stake in India's Zee TV;
- The Spanish-language El Canal Fox in Latin America;
- U.K. Sky Radio;
- A 15 percent stake in the Australian Seven networks;
- India Sky Broadcasting digital satellite service;
- A 50 percent stake in channel V, Asian music video channel;
- A 45 percent stake in Hong Kong-based Phoenix Satellite Television Company.

News Corporation has equity joint ventures, equity interests, or long-term exclusive strategic alliances with the following:

- *First-tier media firms:* Time Warner, Viacom, TCI, Universal, Poly-Gram, Sony, Bertelsmann;
- *Second-tier media firms:* EMI, Canal Plus, Softbank, Granada, Globo, Televisa, MGM, BBC, Carlton;
- *Telecommunication/information firms:* Concert (BT-MCI).

News Corporation operates in nine different media on six continents. Its 1995 revenues were distributed relatively evenly between filmed entertainment (26 percent), newspapers (24 percent), television (21 percent), magazines (14 percent), and book publishing (12 percent). News Corporation has been masterful in utilizing its various properties for cross-promotional purposes, and at using its media power to curry influence with public officials worldwide. 'Murdoch seems to have Washington in his back pocket,' observed one industry analyst after News Corporation received another favorable ruling.[10] The only media sector in which News Corporation lacks a major presence is music, but it has a half interest in the Channel V music television channel in Asia.[11] In 1996 News Corporation also launched TK News, a joint venture to establish a strong presence in the burgeoning East Asian music market.[12] News Corporation earned 70 percent of its 1995 income in the United States and 17 percent in Britain. Most of the balance came from Australia and Asia.[13]

News Corporation's plan for global expansion looks to the areas where growth is expected to be greatest for commercial media: continental Europe, Asia, and Latin America. Until around 2005, Murdoch expects the surest profits in the developed world, especially Europe and Japan.[14] News Corporation is putting most of its eggs in the basket of television, specifically digital satellite television. It plans to draw on its experience in establishing the most profitable satellite television system in the world, the booming British Sky Broadcasting (BSkyB).[15] News Corporation can also use its huge U.S. Fox television network to provide programming for its nascent satellite ventures.[16] News Corporation is spending billions of dollars to establish these systems around the world; although the risk is considerable, if only a few of them establish monopoly or duopoly positions the entire project should prove lucrative. News Corporation calculates that digital satellite broadcasting will be able to offer many more channels – between 1,000 and 5,000 – and services than traditional cable broadcasting, or even cable broadcasting with digital converters. Murdoch is unambiguous about his goal: 'We want our Sky satellite service to be a completely ubiquitous brand everywhere in the world, just as we want Fox to be.'[17]

BSkyB is launching a digital satellite system in 1997 in Britain, where it looks to have an effective monopoly on the digital satellite market.[18] To protect its flank, in 1997 BSkyB announced its participation in a U.K. digital terrestrial television joint venture with Carlton Communications and Granada.[19] In the more competitive North American market, News Corporation is launching a digital television system – Sky Television – with Echostar and Concert (BT-MCI). News Corporation and MCI purchased the final remaining frequencies for North American satellite broadcasting in an FCC auction in 1996 for $683 million. News Corporation plans to launch Japanese Sky Broadcasting (JSkyB) in a joint venture with Sony and the Japanese firm Softbank in 1998. The Japanese media market has been the least exploited by the global media giants among the developed countries. News Corporation already provides two Japanese-language digital cable channels, Star Plus and Star Movies.[20]

In the developing world, News Corporation has two digital satellite systems. One is Sky Latin American, a joint venture held equally (30 percent each) with the two leading Latin American media firms, Globo of Brazil and Televisa of Mexico. TCI has the remaining 10 percent.[21] The other is India Sky Broadcasting (ISkyB), which draws from News Corporation's experience with the analogue Asian Star Television, which it purchased in 1993.[22]

Star TV has switched from a pan-Asian English-language format to a strategy of providing Asian language programming in the main regional languages over several channels.[23] It now provides twenty-three entertainment, music and sports channels – only four of which are primarily in English – to cable systems and satellite television households in fifty-three nations. According to the Leo Burnett advertising agency, in 1996 the Star channels have at least four times the audience of any other cable or satellite channel in Asia.[24] In 1994, Star TV took a 49.9 percent stake in Zee Telefilms, the largest private Indian satellite broadcaster, with a network of entertainment channels in at least four Indian languages and an in-house production studio.[25] Since then Star has dominated the Indian cable and satellite television market.[26] Star TV provides a service to fifty-three Asian nations, reaching 31 percent of the TV households in India, 61 percent in Taiwan, 25 percent in Hong Kong, and 19 percent in Bangladesh. It dominates the Indonesian market. Nonetheless, Star TV is losing some $100 million dollars annually and industry analysts estimate that News Corporation will need to invest another billion dollars before it can turn a profit in Asia.[27] Undaunted, in 1996 TCI took a 7.5 percent stake in Star Television.

What would probably assure Star TV of untold riches would be to have its channels placed on China's booming cable television systems or, better yet, to broadcast Star TV channels directly to Chinese customers via satellite. Murdoch has worked assiduously to gain access to the Chinese market, but has found the Chinese government resistant to his overtures. Yet Star TV is not without a Chinese audience. Although the Chinese banned home satellite receiving dishes in 1993 to emphasize the development of cable, the People's Liberation Army nonetheless manufactures small dishes and a huge quasi-legal market for them exists. Since Star TV is carried on the same satellite as the Chinese state broadcasting system, CCTV, its signal is impossible to block. One study concludes that in 1995 Star Television was available in 30 million Chinese homes, or 13 percent of Chinese TV households.[28] Eager to improve his standing, Murdoch discontinued carrying the BBC World Television Service in 1994 as it was disliked by China's rulers.[29] Then, in 1996, to expedite its entry into China, News Corporation scrapped its main Chinese channel, replacing it with channels produced by the Phoenix Satellite Television Company, a joint venture based in Hong Kong in which News Corporation has a 45 percent stake. Chinese investors hold the balance. Phoenix now offers three entertainment and sports channels to China. In 1997, News Corporation established a Chinese Internet service in a joint venture with the *People's Daily*, the Communist Party newspaper. The *Financial Times* characterized the purpose of the joint venture as aiming 'at gaining favour for News Corp which has ambitions to spread its Star satellite TV service via China's fast-growing cable network'.[30] After seeing how News Corporation's persistence eventually paid off with British Sky Broadcasting, one competing media executive stated that 'other companies have nightmares that they will wake up one day and discover that Murdoch controls all the access to China.'[31]

News Corporation is almost as concerned with producing content as with owning distribution channels. Aside from tried-and-tested filmed entertainment and music videos, 'the sure-fire winners' in global television are news, animation, and sports. 'That's where the synergy [*sic*] and cash flow growth are,' says Times Warner president Richard Parsons.[32] News Corporation trails one or two of the other global media giants in each of these areas, and it is devoting considerable resources to improving its position in each of them. Global television news has been the domain of Time Warner's CNN, but News Corporation introduced the Fox News Channel in the United States in 1996 to better utilize its vast journalism resources. The Fox News Channel will be rolled out globally in 1997 and 1998. News Corporation is also considering the launch of a Spanish-language version in 1997 or 1998.[33]

Time Warner and Viacom have led in the global market for children's television with their respective Cartoon Network and Nickelodeon,[34] but News Corporation has children's channels operating in Latin America and Australia, and plans for new kids' channels in Asia and Europe in 1997.[35] The large firms all hope that children's television will prove as lucrative globally as it has in the United States; U.S. advertising spending on kids' TV programming increased by 70 percent from 1991 to 1996.[36] News Corporation's U.S. children's programming on the Fox Network has been a huge commercial success, and in 1996 a distinct Fox Kids Channel was launched for cable and satellite distribution. In the realm of animated feature-length films, Disney has enjoyed a virtual monopoly on output. With no royalties to pay stars, large cross-selling and cross-promotional possibilities, and the ability to easily dub into any foreign language, animated films are ideal products for the global media market. News Corporation (and Time Warner) have constructed new state-of-the-art digital animation studios so that they will be able to compete with Disney in this market.[37] The new firm Dream-Works is the only other company with the talent and facilities to compete at this level.[38]

Nonetheless, News Corporation has devoted its greatest energy to dominating global TV sport; here the goal is not merely to have one of the leading channels or services, but to overwhelm the other media giants. A 1996 survey of teenagers in forty-one nations found that professional basketball was perhaps the most popular TV programming, followed by soccer.[39] Murdoch regards sport as the single most important means to help gain competitive advantage in developing News Corporation's global digital television system.[40] He calls it News Corporation's 'battering ram' for entry into new markets.[41] 'Sport will be the universal glue for global content, even more than movies,' the CEO or TCI International states.[42] Why is sport uniquely valuable to media firms? It is inexpensive and easy to produce and it is best viewed live. Sport is therefore ideal for pay-per-view and it 'is one of the few genres of programmes that television audiences have shown they will pay to watch.'[43] Moreover, sport is ideal for advertising, as it attracts those 'with the fattest wallets: men in the prime of life.'[44] In 1995 sport generated 10 percent of all U.S. television advertising revenues.[45]

Led by the United States, where the commercial television–sport nexus crystallized in the 1960s and 1970s, professional sport leagues are evolving into sophisticated marketing organizations capable of capitalizing upon their stars and 'brands' in grand symbiosis with advertisers and commercial media.[46] Sport is a seemingly perfect product for integration into the global media market. Beyond advertising, worldwide firms spent $13.5 billion in 1996 merely to be sponsors of sports events.[47] The North American National Basketball Association's (NBA's) games are broadcast to 175 countries. 'There is a strong connection between playing a game, being a fan, watching it, interacting with it at the retail level,' the NBA's marketing head states. 'This is why Coca-Cola and McDonald's became our first two global partners' (in 1994). Advertisers 'can count on a sports league' to provide 'an integrated approach to marketing they can take advantage of.'[48] Reebok is an official sponsor of the new women's American Basketball League, using its position to outfit players and promote its wares.[49] 'No one can deny the far-reaching influence of today's corporate power brokers on the evolution of professional sports as an extremely valuable business and entertainment property,' the president of *Sporting News* concludes.[50] The icing on the cake is that sport does not antagonize political authorities like other forms of programming. It provides drama and excitement while remaining politically uncontroversial and trivial. If anything, its competitive/aggressive characteristics make it well suited for use in campaigns to stir up patriotic fervor.

News Corporation learned the importance of sport for commercial television when the purchase of rights to broadcast Premier League soccer and NFL football were decisive factors in making BSkyB and the Fox network profitable in the 1990s. News Corporation discovered it could use the NFL with considerable success in cross-promotional campaigns with its other media properties. Since then, News Corporation's 'assault' on sports broadcasting has been characterized by *Sporting News* as 'the corporate equivalent of a no-huddle, two-minute drill.' It calls Murdoch 'the most powerful man in sports.'[51] News Corporation established Fox Sport Net in 1996, a series of regional U.S. cable channels featuring live sport coverage. Also in 1996, News Corporation and TCI established a joint venture as equal partners to create a global sports television network. They will provide the channel to cable television systems around the world and use it to attract audiences to their various satellite and cable television systems.[52] By 1997 Fox Sports Americas was already providing a 24-hour sports channel to Spanish-speaking Latin America, and a Portuguese-language Fox sports channel was introduced in Brazil in a joint venture with Globo.[53] News Corporation and TCI will be going head-to-head with Disney's ESPN, the present global sports television leader. When ESPN launched ESPN2 in the early 1990s it established itself as the 'fastest growing [U.S.] network in the '90s.' As an ESPN executive states, 'I don't think anyone can guess how big this genre might get.'[54]

Perhaps the central battle for media giants is to purchase television rights to the most popular sports events. News Corporation is in intense competition with most of the other media giants for the rights to telecast European professional soccer, the World Cup, the summer Olympics, and the leading North American professional team sports. In addition to NFL football, Fox has rights to NHL hockey and U.S. Major League baseball. News Corporation has most of the television rights to rugby matches in the world.[55] Because the supply of existing sports events is less than the global demand, rights fees are soaring. For example, Kirch agreed to pay six times more for the non-U.S. television rights to the 2002 and 2006 World Cups – $2.2 billion – than were paid for the three World Cups in the 1990s.[56] As a result of this influx of 'corporate cash,' a Dutch sports editor told *Business Week* in 1996 that European 'soccer has changed more in the last year than in the previous hundred.'[57] Kirch and Bertelsmann, for example, are urging that soccer shift to three periods, rather than two halves, to increase their opportunities for placing advertising.[58] In addition, advertisers and media are pressuring amateur sports to enlarge commercial exploitation; ESPN and General Motors have urged U.S. universities 'to create a more efficient and reliable structure to market their cash-cow football properties.'[59] Beyond working over the existing supply of sport, media firms are actively creating new sports leagues and events to provide the basis for commercial television broadcasts. News Corporation is the leader among the media giants in this regard. It has a 49 percent stake in the NFL's World League, an attempt to launch U.S. style football in Europe.[60] In 1996 News Corporation created a rival Australian rugby 'Super League' to provide programming for its television stations, and Murdoch is said to have considered establishing a rival professional golf tour.[61] In sum, spectator sport is in the process of being transformed radically by the global media system with which it is intertwined.

Time Warner is the largest media corporation in the world, with 1997 sales approaching $25 billion. It was formed in 1989 through the

merger of Time Incorporated and Warner Communications Incorporated. In 1992 Time Warner split off its entertainment group, and sold
25 percent of it to U.S. West, and 5.6 percent of it to each of the Japanese conglomerates Itochu (1996 sales: $151 billion) and Toshiba (1996
sales: $47 billion). It regained its position as the world's largest media
firm from Disney with the 1996 acquisition of Turner Broadcasting.
Time Warner is moving toward being a fully global company, with over
200 subsidiaries worldwide. In 1996 approximately two-thirds of Time
Warner's income came from the United States, but that figure is
expected to drop to three-fifths by 2000 and eventually to less than one-
half.[62] Time Warner expects globalization to provide growth tonic; it
projects that its annual sales growth rate of 14 percent in the middle
1990s will climb to over 20 percent by the end of the decade.[63] Music
accounts for just over 20 percent of Time Warner's business, as does the
news division of magazine and book publishing and cable television
news. Times Warner's U.S. cable systems account for over 10 percent of
income. The remainder is accounted for largely by Time Warner's
extensive entertainment film, video, and television holdings.[64] Time
Warner is a major force in virtually every medium and on every continent. Its holdings include the following:

- Twenty-four magazines, including *Time*, *People*, and *Sports Illustrated*;
- The second largest book-publishing business in the world, including
  Time Life Books (42 percent of sales outside of the United States) and
  the Book of the Month Club;
- Warner Music Group, one of the largest global music businesses with
  nearly 60 percent of revenues from outside the United States;
- Warner Brothers film studio, also a major producer of television programs;
- Majority interest in WB, a U.S. television network launched in 1995
  to provide a distribution platform for Time Warner films and pro-
  grams. It is carried on the Tribune Company's sixteen U.S. television
  stations that reach 25 percent of U.S. TV households;
- Global leading motion picture theater company, with over 1,000
  screens outside of the United States;
- Fifty percent of DC Comics, publisher of *Superman*, *Batman*, and sixty
  other titles;
- HBO, the largest pay cable channel in the world;
- Cinemax pay cable channel;
- Six Flags theme park chain;
- Warner Brothers Movie World theme park in Germany;
- Retail stores, including over 150 Warner Bros. stores and Turner
  Retail Group;

- The second largest cable system in the United States, controlling twenty-two of the largest 100 markets;
- A library of over 6,000 films, 25,000 television programs, books, music, and thousands of cartoons ripe for commercial exploitation;
- Several U.S. and global cable television channels including CNN, Headline News, CNNfn, the Airport Channel, TBS, TNT, Turner Classic Movies, The Cartoon Network, as well as the new CNN–SI all-sports news channel (meant to capitalize upon the cross-production and cross-promotion potential of CNN and *Sports Illustrated*);
- A 50 percent stake (with Viacom) in Comedy Central channel;
- A 33 percent interest in the cable Sega channel;
- A 33 percent stake in Court TV channel (with NBC);
- A 25 percent interest in Atari, 14 percent interest in Hasbro;
- Significant interests in non-U.S. broadcasting joint ventures including Germany's N-TV, New Zealand's Sky Network Television, European music channel VIVA, and Asian music channel Classic V;
- Ownership of the Atlanta Hawks and Atlanta Braves professional sports teams.

Time Warner has equity joint ventures, equity interests, or long-term exclusive strategic alliances with the following:

- *First-tier media firms:* Viacom, TCI, Sony, News Corporation, Bertelsmann, NBC;
- *Second-tier media firms:* Kirch, EMI, Kinnevik, Tribune Company, Cox, Hachette, United News & Media, PBL, Comcast;
- *Telecommunication/information firms:* US West, Bell South, Ameritech, AT&T, Oracle.

As with News Corporation, Time Warner has zeroed in on global television as the most lucrative area for growth. Unlike News Corporation, however, Time Warner has devoted itself to producing programming and channels rather than developing entire satellite systems. Time Warner has but two main non-U.S. distribution system ventures. In conjunction with shareholders Itochu and Toshiba, Time Warner is launching Titus Communications, a cable television company in Japan. In that battle they will be competing directly with a TCI joint venture and indirectly with News Corporation's JSkyB.[65] Time Warner is also one of the largest movie theater owners in the world with approximately 1,000 screens outside of the United States, and further expansion projected.[66] The Time Warner strategy is to merge the former Turner global channels – CNN and TNT/Cartoon Channel –

with their HBO International and recently launched Warner channels to make a four-pronged assault on the global market. These channels are expected to find homes on cable systems and the impending digital satellite systems.[67]

HBO International has already established itself as the leading subscription TV channel in the world; it has a family of pay channels and is available in over thirty-five countries. HBO Asia is booming; its subscriber base increased from under 250,000 in 1994 to 1.2 million in 1996. It is available in twelve Asian countries and will be launched in at least six more, including India, by the end of the decade. HBO Asia is a Time Warner joint venture with stakes also held by Viacom, Sony, and Seagram.[68] The firms owning HBO Asia have contracts granting it exclusive continental rights to their films for pay television purposes.[69] HBO Asia was initially viewed as a vehicle for the distribution of films; its success has made it revise its plans that now include launching 'a raft of new channels' across Asia in the late 1990s.[70] HBO in Latin America has several profitable channels (some in Spanish and Portuguese), including a movie channel, a music channel, and a 'family' channel. HBO's Latin American activities are already profitable. HBO President Jeffrey Bewkes states that global expansion is HBO's 'manifest destiny.'[71]

CNN International, a subsidiary of CNN, is also established as the premier global television news channel, beamed via ten satellites to over 200 nations and 90 million subscribers by 1994, a 27 percent increase over 1993. It provided 20 percent of CNN's total income in 1995 and the amount is climbing rapidly. CNN has become especially profitable, with operating margins of more than 35 percent.[72] CNN International built a new studio in Hong Kong, to better cultivate the booming East Asian market. In 1995 CNN enjoyed a major breakthrough in India when it became the first private broadcaster to be given access to the highly desirable satellite controlled by Doordarshan, the state-owned television network.[73] The long-term goal for CNN International is to operate (or participate in joint ventures to establish) CNN channels in French, Japanese, Hindi, Arabic, and perhaps one or two other regional languages.[74] CNN launched a Spanish-language service for Latin America in 1997, based in Atlanta.[75] CNN International will also draw on the Time Warner journalism resources as it faces new challenges from news channels launched by News Corporation and NBC-Microsoft.

Before their 1996 merger, Turner and Time Warner were both global television powers with the TNT/Cartoon Network and Warner Channels, drawing upon their respective large libraries of cartoons and motion pictures. The TNT/Cartoon Network – reaching 30 million homes in Europe and Latin America compared to 22 million in the

United States – has proved to be a global goldmine.[76] It is Latin America's most watched cable television channel. The Latin American Warner Channel shows classic Bugs Bunny cartoons 75 percent of the time, and it garnered 1.5 million subscribers in its first eight months on the air in 1995.[77] Now these channels will be redeployed to better utilize each other's resources, with plans being drawn up to develop several more global cable channels to take advantage of the world's largest film, television, and cartoon libraries.[78] In addition to Latin America, Warner Channels have been launched in Europe and Australia.[79] In 1996, Time Warner signed a long-term multi-billion dollar strategic alliance with Kirch to provide a German Warner Channel to its DF1 satellite joint venture with News Corporation. The deal also includes the sale of Time Warner film rights to Kirch and permits Time Warner to take a 5 to 10 percent equity position in DF1.[80]

With 1997 sales of nearly $24 billion, **Disney** is the closest challenger to Time Warner for the status of being the world's largest media firm. In the early 1990s Disney successfully shifted its emphasis from its theme parks and resorts to its film and television divisions. In 1995, Disney made the move from being a dominant global content producer to being a fully integrated media giant with the purchase of Capital Cities/ABC for $19 billion, one of the biggest acquisitions in business history. Disney now generates 31 percent of its income from broadcasting, 23 percent from theme parks, and the balance from 'creative content,' meaning films, publishing, and merchandising.[81] The ABC deal provided Disney, already regarded as the industry leader at using cross-selling and cross-promotion to maximize revenues, with a U.S. broadcasting network and widespread global media holdings to incorporate into its activities.[82] According to *Advertising Age*, consequently Disney 'is uniquely positioned to fulfill virtually any marketing option, on any scale, almost anywhere in the world.'[83] It has already included the new Capital Cities/ABC brands into its exclusive global marketing deals with McDonald's and Mattel toymakers.[84] Although Disney has traditionally preferred to operate on its own, CEO Michael Eisner has announced Disney's plans to expand aggressively overseas through joint ventures with local firms or other global players, or through further acquisitions.[85] Disney's stated goal is to expand its non-U.S. share of revenues from 23 percent in 1995 to 50 percent by 2000.[86]

Disney's holdings include the following:

- Several major film, video, and television production studios including Disney and Buena Vista;
- Theme parks and resorts, including Disneyland, DisneyWorld, and stakes in major theme parks in France and Japan;

- Consumer products, including more than 550 Disney retail stores worldwide and products that capitalize upon the Disney 'brands';
- Three music labels including Hollywood Records and Walt Disney Records;
- Book publishing, including Hyperion Books and Chilton Publications;
- The U.S. ABC television and radio networks;
- Ten U.S. television stations and twenty-one U.S. radio stations;
- A 14 percent stake in Young Broadcasting, which owns eight U.S. television stations;
- U.S. and global cable television channels Disney Channel, ESPN, and ESPN2;
- Holdings in Lifetime (50 percent), Arts & Entertainment (37 percent), and History Channel cable TV channels;
- Newspaper and magazine publishing, including seven U.S. daily newspapers and three specialty magazine publishing companies;[87]
- A 20 to 33 percent ownership in five European commercial television companies: the continent-wide Eurosport network, the Spanish Tesauro SA, the German terrestrial channel RTL2, the German cable channel TM3, and Scandinavian Broadcasting System SA, which capitalizes upon the commercial broadcasting boom across Northern and Central Europe, launching new channels in Austria, Hungary, and Finland in 1997;
- A 50 percent stake in Super RTL, a German children's station which it shares with Bertelsmann;
- Controlling interests in the NHL Anaheim Mighty Ducks and the Major League Baseball Anaheim Angels;
- A 20 percent stake in TVA, a Brazilian pay-TV company.

Disney has equity joint ventures, equity interests, or long-term exclusive strategic alliances with the following:

- *First-tier media firms:* Bertelsmann, NBC, TCI;
- *Second-tier media firms:* Kirch, Hearst, CLT, DreamWorks, Canal Plus, TFI, Cox, Comcast;
- *Telecommunication/information firms:* Ameritech, SBC, GTE, Bell South, America Online, U.S. West.

Historically, Disney has been strong in entertainment and animation, two areas that do well in the global market. To protect itself from encroachment upon its global domination of the lucrative animated film market, in 1997 Disney signed a 10-year exclusive joint venture to produce at least five films with Pixar, the computer animation specialists responsible for the 1995 hit *Toy Story*. Disney also took a 5 percent stake in Pixar.[88] The deal with Pixar reveals how even the most dynamic smaller media firms need to align themselves with a media giant to prosper in the global market. The deal also gives Disney more material as it seeks to expand in the booming global children's television market.

In 1996 Disney reorganized, putting all its global television activities into a single division, Disney/ABC International Television. Its first order of business is to expand the children- and family-oriented Disney Channel into a global force, capitalizing upon the enormous Disney resources. Disney is also developing an advertising-supported children's channel to complement the subscription Disney Channel.[89] For the most part, Disney's success has been restricted to English-language channels in North America, Britain, and Australia.[90] Disney's absence has permitted the children's channels of News Corporation, Time Warner, and, especially, Viacom to dominate the lucrative global market. Disney launched a Chinese-language Disney Channel based in Taiwan in 1995, and is developing programs 'compatible with China's ancient civilisation and tradition' to curry favor with China's leaders. Disney claims its Chinese children's radio programming already reaches 400 million Chinese since its July 1996 inception.[91] Disney plans to launch Disney Channels in France, Italy, Germany, and the Middle East.[92] The Disney Channel will also become connected to ABC's Panda Club children's service which is telecast in China and India. 'The Disney Channel should be the killer children's service throughout the world,' Disney's executive in charge of international television states.[93] The second order of business for Disney's global television division is to establish joint ventures 'in film channels around the world in order to gain the maximum advantage from the films it produces,' and owns.[94]

With the purchase of ABC's ESPN, the television sports network, Disney has possession of the unquestioned global leader. ESPN has three U.S. cable channels, a radio network with 420 affiliates, and the ESPN SportsZone website, among the most heavily used locales on the Internet.[95] One Disney executive notes that with ESPN and the family-oriented Disney Channel, Disney has 'two horses to ride in foreign markets, not just one.'[96] ESPN International dominates televised sport, broadcasting on a 24-hour basis in twenty-one languages to over 165 countries. It reaches the one desirable audience that had eluded Disney in the past: young, single, middle-class men. 'Our plan is to think globally, but to customize locally,' states the senior VP of ESPN International. In Latin America the emphasis is upon soccer, in Asia it is table tennis, and in India ESPN provided over 1,000 hours of cricket in 1995. ESPN has quietly enjoyed unusual success in China.[97] Chinese state broadcaster CCTV purchases ESPN content to fill nearly half of the programming on its all-sports pay channel, CCTV-5.[98] In addition to localizing content,

Disney will respond to global challenges from News Corporation and Time Warner by launching multiple channels of ESPN.[99]

Disney plans to exploit the 'synergies' of ESPN much as it has exploited its cartoon characters. 'We know that when we lay Mickey Mouse or Goofy on top of products, we get pretty creative stuff,' Eisner states. 'ESPN has the potential to be that kind of brand.'[100] Disney plans call for a chain of ESPN theme sports bars, ESPN product merchandising, and possibly a chain of ESPN entertainment centers based on the Club ESPN at Walt Disney World. ESPN has released five music CDs, two of which have sold over 500,000 copies.[101] 'If it's sports,' one trade publication concludes, 'ESPN's brand is all over it.'[102] In late 1996, Disney began negotiations with Hearst and Petersen Publishing to produce *ESPN Sports Weekly* magazine in 1997, to be a 'branded competitor to *Sports Illustrated*.'[103]

ESPN has even launched its own annual sports event, the X Games, to be aired globally over all ESPN networks. The X Games were created to attract the audience of young males whom advertisers find so elusive on television. As *Adweek* notes, unless marketers rallied to do sponsorships and buy commercial advertising time, the X Games would not exist.[104] 'Extreme sports,' one sports marketing executive states, 'have huge appeal around the world.'[105] They feature trendy sports like bunjee jumping and skateboarding. As one marketing executive states, 'the X Games are a perfect extension of the Mountain Dew brand personality.' Taco Bell's marketing head praises the X Games for delivering a 'pure audience.' The event has been a hit with advertisers and Winter X Games will be launched in 1997. By producing the event itself, ESPN can bring advertisers in as long-term partners, combining events with marketing campaigns. It can create a valuable 'brand' that is the property of ESPN, and for which it will never have to compete to win broadcast rights.[106] ESPN executives concede that the X games may 'seem bogus' but note that they attract 'blue-chip advertisers'.[107] So as not to be left out in the cold, News Corporation televised globally the inaugural World Championship Extreme Games from South Africa in 1996, and have purchased the rights to do the same with the winter version in 1997.[108]

None of the remaining three firms in the first tier of media giants has quite the range and scale of News Corporation, Time Warner, or Disney. **Viacom** is smaller, with a 1997 income exceeding $13 billion, and only 20 percent of that comes from outside of the United States.[109] CEO Sumner Redstone, who controls 39 percent of Viacom's stock, orchestrated the deals that led to the acquisitions of Paramount and Blockbuster in 1994, thereby promoting the firm from $2 billion in 1993 sales to the front ranks. Viacom generates 33 percent of its income from its film studios, 33 percent from its music, video rentals, and theme parks, 18 percent from broadcasting, and 14 percent from publishing.[110] Redstone's strategy is for Viacom to become the world's 'premier software driven growth company.'[111]

means

Viacom's holdings include the following:

- Thirteen U.S. television stations;
- U.S. and global cable television networks, including MTV, M2, Nickelodeon, Showtime, TVLand, Paramount Networks, and VH1;
- A 50 percent interest in Comedy Central channel (with Time Warner);
- Film, video, and television production, including Paramount Pictures;
- Blockbuster Video and Music stores, the world's largest video rental stores;
- Five theme parks;
- Book publishing, including Simon & Schuster, Scribners, and Macmillan;
- A 50 percent interest in USA cable network, providing the largest U.S. cable channel audience, and USA Network Latin America;
- A 50 percent interest in the U.S. UPN television network with Chris-Craft Industries;
- A 75 percent interest in the TV production company Spelling Entertainment.

Viacom has equity joint ventures, equity interests, or long-term exclusive strategic alliances with the following:

- *First-tier media firms:* Time Warner, News Corporation, Universal, PolyGram, Sony;
- *Second-tier media firms:* Kirch, Chris-Craft, Pearson;
- *Telecommunication/information firms:* Nynex, Sprint.

Viacom's growth strategy is twofold. First, it is implementing an aggressive policy of using company-wide cross-promotions to improve sales. It proved invaluable that MTV constantly plugged the film *Clueless* in 1995, and the same strategy will be applied to the Paramount television program based on the movie. Simon & Schuster is establishing a Nickelodeon book imprint and a 'Beavis and Butthead' book series based on the MTV characters.[112] Viacom also has plans to establish a comic-book imprint based upon Paramount characters, it is considering creating a record label to exploit its MTV brand name, and it has plans to open a chain of retail stores to capitalize upon its 'brands' à la Disney and Time Warner.[113] In 1997 Paramount will begin producing three Nickelodeon and three MTV movies annually. 'We're just now beginning to realize the benefits of the Paramount and Blockbuster mergers,' Redstone stated in 1996.[114]

Second, Viacom has targeted global growth, with a stated goal of earning 40 percent of its revenues outside of the United States by 2000.[115] As one Wall Street analyst puts it, Redstone wants Viacom 'playing in the same international league' with News Corporation and Time Warner.[116] Redstone and an entourage of Viacom executives spent the first six months of 1996 traveling across Europe, Asia, and Latin America making deals. Their most striking accomplishment was to reach a five-year, $1.5 billion deal to provide Kirch with programming for its European television networks, including the Kirch digital television service DF1.[117] Viacom also made similar deals with Scandinavia's Kinnevik and with the French digital television service TPS, partially owned by Bertelsmann.[118] Viacom now has a strong European distribution platform for its output. Since 1992 Viacom has invested between $750 million and $1 billion in international expansion.[119] 'We're not taking our foot off the accelerator,' one Viacom executive states.[120] Blockbuster alone plans to spend over $600 million to expand the number of non-U.S. video stores from 1,000 to 4,000 by 2000, with the goal of effectively dominating the global video rental retail market, and then expanding into other retail areas. With the U.S. market saturated, Viacom hopes 'to make the American couch potato a worldwide phenomenon.'[121] In a joint venture with Universal, Viacom is one of the largest film theater owners in Western Europe, and plans to expand elsewhere.[122] Viacom's only foray into global television systems is with a small Kuwaiti digital satellite joint venture called Gulf DTH.[123]

Yet global television is where Viacom is devoting the most resources, and Viacom is pressing to see that its main channels are adopted by cable and satellite systems around the world. Viacom is establishing a series of new Paramount Channels to provide films and programming from the Paramount library. Viacom's strategy is to employ joint ventures with local partners and other media giants to develop more new channels; it has a joint venture with PolyGram in Asia and one with News Corporation in the United Kingdom.[124] Viacom is also rolling out its premium channel Showtime and the USA Network to global markets; both are widespread in Latin America. USA Network Latin America already has 4.5 million Latin American subscribers.[125] Viacom's two main weapons are Nickelodeon and MTV. Nickelodeon has been a global powerhouse, expanding to every continent but Antarctica in 1996 and 1997 and offering programming in several languages. It is already a world leader in children's television, reaching 90 million TV households in seventy countries other than the United States – where it can be seen in 68 million households and completely dominates children's television.[126]

MTV is the preeminent global music television channel, available in 250 million homes worldwide and in scores of nations. In 1996 Viacom announced further plans to 'significantly expand' its global operations.[127] MTV also features 'extreme' sports, in competition with News Corporation and Disney's ESPN. Moreover, MTV airs several animated series on all of its global channels as well as via independent broadcasters. The biggest global success of MTV's animation division has been 'Beavis and Butthead.' *Variety* proclaims the 'heavy-metal morons' to be 'international superstars.'[128] MTV has used new digital technologies to make it possible to customize programming inexpensively for different regions and nations around the world. It can also offer this selectivity to advertisers.[129] In Asia it already has three distinct MTV channels, including one in Mandarin. MTV has become a major force in the $40 billion per year global music trade with its near monopolistic power.[130] It faces competition in Europe from Viva, launched by a joint partnership of the five largest music companies, and competition in Asia from Channel V, produced by News Corporation in alliance with the major music companies.[131] As CNN and ESPN have responded to competition, MTV intends to withstand the challenge by adding more music channels and by further localizing content.[132]

Bertelsmann is the one European firm in the first tier of media giants. It is the third largest media group in the world with sales of approximately $15 billion in 1996. The Bertelsmann empire was built on global networks of book and music clubs. Music and television provide 31 percent of its income, book publishing 33 percent, magazines and newspapers 20 percent, and a global printing business accounts for the remainder. In 1994 its income was distributed among Germany (36 percent), the rest of Europe (32 percent), United States (24 percent), and the rest of the world (8 percent).[133] Its holdings include the following:

- Major recording studios Arista and RCA;
- German television channels RTL, RTL2, SuperRTL, Vox;
- A stake in German Channel Club RTL;
- Stakes in Dutch television channels RTL4 and RTL5;
- Stakes in French television channels M6 and TMC;
- A stake in British Channel 5;
- Eighteen European radio stations;
- A 37.5 percent stake in Premiere, Germany's leading pay-TV channel;
- Book publishing, with around forty publishing houses, concentrating

on German-, French-, and English-language (Bantam and Double-day Dell) titles;
- Leading book and record clubs in the world;
- Newspaper and magazine publishing, including over 100 magazines including several U.S.-based magazines.

Bertelsmann has equity joint ventures, equity interests, or long-term exclusive strategic alliances with the following:

- *First-tier media firms:* Time Warner, Disney, Universal, PolyGram, News Corporation, Sony;
- *Second-tier media firms:* Kirch, Canal Plus, United News & Media, Havas, CLT, EMI, Pearson, BBC;
- *Telecommunication/information firms:* America Online.

Bertelsmann's stated goal is to evolve 'from a media enterprise with international activities into a truly global communications group.' By 1995 the Asian market accounted for almost 10 percent of Bertelsmann's income.[134] In 1996, it established a joint venture with the Japanese Mitsui (1995 sales: $181 billion), the world's second largest firm in terms of revenues, to create a 'distribution arm' in Asia.[135] Bertelsmann's strengths in global expansion are its global distribution network for music, its global book and music clubs, and its facility with languages other than English. It is working to strengthen its music holdings to become the world leader, through a possible buyout of or merger with EMI and through establishing joint ventures with local music companies in emerging markets.[136] Bertelsmann is considered to be the best contender of all the media giants to exploit the Eastern European markets, and it has already established book and music clubs in Hungary, Poland, and the Czech Republic.[137]

Bertelsmann has two severe competitive disadvantages in the global media sweepstakes. It has no significant film or television production studios or film library, and it has minimal involvement in global television, where much of the growth is taking place. Bertelsmann began to address this problem in 1996 by merging its television interests (Ufa) into a joint venture with Compagnie Luxembourgeoise de Télédiffusion (CLT), the Luxemburg-based European commercial broadcasting power. According to a Bertelsmann executive, the CLT deal was 'a strategic step to become a major media player, especially in light of the recent European and American mergers.'[138] CLT is a major player in commercial broadcasting in Germany where it effectively controls 25 percent of the market, as well as across the continent, in Britain, and in Eastern Europe.[139] The Ufa–CLT joint venture is the largest European commercial television broadcaster, with 1996 sales of $3.5 billion.[140] As a result of the merger, Bertelsmann–CLT has greater leverage when negotiating deals with content producers. Bertelsmann's stated long-term goal is to form an international television network.[141] These ambitions were set back, if not ended, when Bertelsmann's efforts to launch a joint venture for German digital satellite television collapsed in 1996 and the market was seized by Kirch. Had the German venture worked for Bertelsmann, it probably would have provided the basis for digital television ventures elsewhere in Europe and the world.[142]

TCI is smaller than the other firms in the first tier, with a 1996 income of approximately $7 billion, but its unique position in the media industry has made it a central player in the global media system.[143] TCI's foundation is its dominant position as the leading U.S. cable television system provider. CEO John Malone, who has effective controlling interest over TCI, has been able to use the steady cash influx from the lucrative semi-monopolistic cable business to build an empire. To assist global and non-cable expansion, Malone has split TCI's diverse activities into four divisions: TCI proper, which handles the U.S. cable system; Liberty Media, which handles TCI's investments in media content; TCI International, which coordinates TCI's global cable interests; and TCI Satellite Entertainment, which handles TCI's satellite television activities. All but TCI proper have global interests. Malone understands the importance of the U.S. cable base to bankroll TCI's expansion; in 1995 and 1996 he bought several smaller cable systems to consolidate TCI's hold on the U.S. cable market.[144] TCI faces a direct and potentially very damaging challenge to its U.S. market share from digital satellite broadcasting. It is responding by converting its cable systems to digital format so as to increase channel capacity to 200.[145] TCI is also using its satellite spin-off to position itself in the rival satellite business and retain some of the 15 to 20 million Americans expected to switch from cable broadcasting to satellite broadcasting by 2000.[146] In addition to owning two satellites valued at $600 million, TCI holds a 21 percent stake in Primestar, a U.S. satellite television joint venture with the other leading U.S. cable companies, and General Electric which already had 1.2 million subscribers in 1996.[147] TCI is pondering the launch of a distinct U.S. digital satellite service in 1997, and there is a possibility that it will incorporate its Primestar activities into this new service.[148]

TCI has used its control of cable systems to acquire equity stakes in many of the cable channels that need to be carried over TCI to be viable. TCI has significant interests in Discovery Communications, QVC, Fox Sports Net, Court TV, E! Entertainment, Home Shopping Network, and Black Entertainment TV, among others.[149] In 1996, TCI negotiated the right to purchase a 20 percent stake in News Corporation's new Fox News Channel in return for access to TCI systems.[150] Through Liberty Media, TCI has interests in ninety-one U.S. program services. As former Liberty Media president Peter Barton puts it, 'I'm in the center of the traffic lane for a lot of deals, a lot of ideas . . . and a lot of money.' Barton terms Liberty Media the 'Berkshire Hathaway of the media business,' in reference to the Warren Buffett holding company that profits from stock-ownership in other firms.[151] Nor does TCI restrict its investments to cable channels and content producers. It has a 10 percent stake in Time Warner as well as a 20 percent stake in Silver King Communications, where former Fox network builder Barry Diller is putting together another U.S. television network.[152] Many of the firms TCI has stakes in, like Time Warner and Discovery Communications, are active globally.[153] For example, Discovery, in which TCI has a 49 percent stake, already has seven channels in Asia and the Pacific with 7 million subscribers.[154] All told, TCI's joint ventures and media equity holdings are too numerous to mention.

TCI has applied its expansionist strategy to the global as well as domestic media market. On one hand, TCI develops its core cable business and has become the global leader in cable systems, with strong units in Britain, Japan, and Chile. The TCI path to global expansion in cable is to act directly through TCI International or, where necessary, to employ joint ventures with local partners who can better deal with local politicians, businesses, and cultures. Merrill Lynch estimates that TCI International's cable base outside of the United States will increase from 3 million subscribers in 1995 to 10 million in 1999. TCI will have twice as many more subscribers through its global joint ventures. In Japan, for example, a TCI executive predicts its equally split Jupiter Communications joint venture with Sumitomo Corporation will be as large as the U.S. TCI 'within a decade.'[155]

On the other hand, TCI uses its cable resources to invest across all global media and to engage in numerous non-cable joint ventures. 'When you are the largest cable operator in the world,' a TCI executive states, 'people find a way to do business with you.'[156] It already has thirty media deals outside of the United States, including a venture with Sega Enterprises to launch computer game channels, a joint venture with News Corporation for a global sports channel, and a 10 percent stake in Sky Latin America. TCI and Dow Jones have a joint venture, Asia Business News, that provides 24-hour business news television channels, including one in Japanese.[157] TCI also has majority interests in the cable and programming companies Flextech in the United Kingdom, and Cablevision in Argentina. It has a joint venture with Canal Plus to produce French-language television programming.[158] Japanese-based Jupiter Programming, another joint venture with Sumitomo, will provide children's, sports, news, shopping, and entertainment programming for six to eight broadcast channels by 1997.[159] More important, Jupiter Programming, in conjunction with five leading Japanese commercial television broadcasters, is launching Jet TV, a TV channel broadcasting according to viewers' choices of Japanese, Thai, Chinese, or English to ten Asia-Pacific nations in 1997.[160] Although Jet TV is in direct competition with Star TV, in 1996 TCI took a 7.5 percent stake in Murdoch's Asian TV venture.[161] As John Malone puts it, 'everything comes our way.'[162]

TCI is the wild card of the first-tier global media firms. It has significant holdings in countless media companies and formal joint ventures or important large-scale relationships with just about everyone, so its fate has a direct effect upon all the other giant media firms. By the late 1990s, TCI's core U.S. cable television business has become stagnant. The cable business also faces direct challenges from satellite television and indirect challenges from telephone companies as it attempts to move into the Internet. For TCI to compete requires huge investments in digital technology but TCI is also encumbered with a staggering debt load that limits its ability to raise capital. Because of this, TCI will probably be involved in major dealmaking as it shuffles its assets to become more competitive. Malone states that TCI will continue its international expansion with no let-up, and that the restructuring will concentrate on U.S. holdings. At any rate, when and if TCI's late 1990s impasse is resolved, it may well lead to a reshuffling of the global media deck.[163]

ROUNDING OUT THE FIRST TIER

Four firms join the above six media giants in the first tier of a global media oligopoly: Universal (Seagram), Sony, PolyGram (Philips), and NBC (General Electric). Unlike the six giants, each of these four firms' media properties are only part of broader industrial conglomerates, and only in the case of Universal are the media holdings close to 50 percent of the parent corporation's activities. In addition, each of these four firms is less vertically integrated than any of the aforementioned six. In the coming years, as the market crystallizes, it seems likely that each of these firms will be active dealmakers.

Effectively controlled by the Bronfman family, the global beverage firm Seagram purchased **Universal** (then MCA) from Matsushita for $5.7 billion in 1995. Matsushita was unable to make a success of MCA and had refused to go along with MCA executives who had wanted to acquire CBS in the early 1990s.[164] Universal is expected to account for approximately half of Seagram's $14 billion in sales in 1997. Over half of Universal's income is generated by the Universal Studios' production of films and television programs. Universal is also a major music producer and book publisher and operates several theme parks.[165] Universal's assets yield high returns and Paine Webber characterizes Universal as a 'sleeping giant.'[166] Seagram CEO Edgar Bronfman's plan is to follow the lead of the other media giants and 'exploit MCA's brand names throughout the world.'[167] Under Frank Biondi, Universal opened twenty-seven new overseas offices in 1996 and announced plans for 'aggressive international expansion.'[168] An example of this is the planned opening of a Universal theme park in Japan in 2001, as well as proposed theme park openings for East Asia and Europe, where a Universal executive states: 'there is a tremendous opportunity and appetite for Universal's branded entertainment.'[169] Universal announced plans to invest $200 million in theaters, retail stores, and amusement parks in China by 2000, hoping to position itself to exploit the 'huge potential' in the Chinese entertainment market as it increasingly opens up to foreign firms.[170] Universal also has plans to establish trendy 'smart shopping malls' in major cities around the world, and its movie theater joint venture plans to expand from 400 non-North American theaters to 2,200 theaters in 10 years' time.[171]

As many of the broadcast networks and cable channels vertically integrate with production companies, Universal has fewer options for sales and is less secure in its future.[172] It has a 50 percent interest in the cable USA Network and the Sci-Fi Network with Viacom, but the two firms are locked in battle over control of the networks.[173] In 1996, Universal negotiated a strategic alliance with NBC and signed two contracts each worth $1.5 billion, one with the German television network RTL, owned in part by Bertelsmann, and the other with Kirch.[174] The RTL arrangement provides for the two firms to co-produce up to twenty-five television series in the next decade.[175] Universal also has a 50 percent stake (in a venture with Ufa–CLT) in RTL7, a company to provide Polish cable and satellite television channels.[176] The Kirch contract calls for Universal to establish two German channels – its first non-U.S. channels – for the Kirch DF1 digital satellite venture. Universal CEO Frank Biondi called these 'bedrock' deals that will provide the basis for further global expansion.[177] In the meantime, Universal's global leading television production studio saw a 25 percent increase in non-U.S. sales in 1996, and it expects to generate 60 percent of its revenues in non-U.S. sales in the late 1990s.[178]

PolyGram is about the same size as Universal, with estimated sales of $6 billion in 1997. The enormous Dutch electronics firm Philips (FY 1996 sales: $38 billion) owns 75 percent of PolyGram's stock. PolyGram, like Universal, is a production firm concentrating on music and films. PolyGram used its massive music industry profits to enter the film industry with a Hollywood studio in the early 1990s. In 1997 it established a television production unit, also based in Hollywood. This unit will distribute PolyGram films for television and produce original TV programming.[179] Fifty percent of PolyGram's sales are in Europe, 25 percent in the United States, and much of the balance is in Asia. Its music division dominates, accounting for 75 percent of sales.[180] As it is virtually debt-free, PolyGram is well positioned to build up its film and television production; it acknowledges that it can no longer be profitable, with half the output of the other major studios.[181] PolyGram has actively pursued acquiring film studios, and was interested in MCA before Matsushita clinched its secret sale to Seagram.[182]

Sony is similar to PolyGram, in that its media holdings are concentrated in music (the former CBS records) and film and television production (the former Columbia Pictures), each of which it purchased in 1989. Music accounts for about 60 percent of Sony's media income and film and television production account for the rest. Sony is a dominant entertainment producer, and its sales are expected to surpass $9 billion in 1997.[183] As Sony's media activities seem divorced from its other extensive activities – Sony expects $50 billion in sales in 1997 – there is ongoing speculation that it will sell its valuable production studios to vertically integrated chains that can better exploit them.[184] Sony was foiled in its initial attempts to find synergies between hardware and software, but it anticipates that digital communication will provide the basis for new synergies.[185] Sony hopes to capitalize upon its vast copyrighted library of films, music, and TV programs to leap to the front of the digital video disc market, where it is poised to be one of the two global leaders with Matsushita.[186] Sony also enjoys a 25 percent share of the multi-billion dollar video games industry; with the shift to digital formats these games can now be converted into channels in digital television systems.[187]

During the past year, Sony has attempted to make up for its lack of a U.S. television network and cable channels. On the one hand, it signed a deal with CBS to create a company to produce programming for the U.S. broadcast network.[188] On the other hand, Sony is aggressively investing in international cable and satellite television channels. It now has global joint ventures with thirteen different companies and sixteen television channels, including two in Germany, five in Latin America, two in East Asia, and perhaps the top-ranked Hindi language cable channel in India.[189] Sony will spend an additional $500 million in the late 1990s making new investments in global satellite and cable channels.[190] In March 1997 it announced that it was taking a one-third stake in Japan Sky Broadcasting, joining News Corporation and Softbank. Sony is also intent on making deals with broadcasters, like the ten-year, $950 million agreement it reached in 1996 to provide the Kirch Group's European networks with films and television shows.[191]

General Electric is one of the leading electronics and manufacturing firms in the world with nearly $80 billion in sales in 1996. Non-U.S. revenues have increased from 20 percent of GE's total in 1985 to 38 percent in 1995, and they are expected to reach 50 percent by 2000. **NBC's** $5 billion in 1996 sales and nearly $1 billion in profit are a small proportion of GE's total, but after years of rapid growth NBC is now considered to be the core of GE's strategy for long-term global growth.[192] NBC owns U.S. television and radio networks and eleven television stations. It has been aggressive in expanding into cable, where it now owns several cable channels outright, as well as shares in some twenty other channels including the Arts & Entertainment networks, and is a partner in Primestar, the cable companies' U.S. satellite television venture.[193] Only News Corporation has equaled NBC's aggressive purchasing of broadcast sports rights; it has secured the U.S. rights to six of the next seven Olympic Games, the NBA, and it has kept the rights to broadcast professional football.[194] Their strategy of 'corner[ing] all the crown jewels in sports' has led NBC's climb to record profits by 1995.[195] General Electric's most dramatic gesture that it regards NBC as a key part of its growth plans is NBC's 1996 alliance and joint investment with Microsoft to produce cable news channel MSNBC, along with a complementary online service, MSNBC Interactive. From this initial $500 million investment, NBC and Microsoft plan to expand MSNBC quickly into a global news channel, followed perhaps by global entertainment and sports channels. NBC and Microsoft are also developing a series of TV channels in Europe aimed at computer users.[196]

MSNBC is part of NBC's three-pronged attack on global markets, along with its business channel CNBC and its NBC entertainment channel. Both CNBC and NBC Europe are widespread in Europe; in fact, NBC Europe has been a remarkable success and is seen in 69 million European households.[197] A 1996 agreement with Canal Plus will make NBC's cable channels the first U.S. networks to be carried over French digital television.[198] NBC has launched business and entertainment channels for Asia, and will do the same for Latin America in 1996 and 1997. In 1997, in a joint venture with the National Geographic Society, NBC introduced the National Geographic Channel, with plans for it initially to target markets in Latin America, Europe, and Asia.[199] NBC hopes to use its long experience of working with large advertisers and agencies in the United States as a competitive advantage in drawing them toward its global networks.[200]

SECOND-TIER FIRMS IN THE GLOBAL MEDIA MARKET

The second tier of firms in the global media market are those that fill regional or niche markets. These firms are all quite large, and most have annual sales in the late 1990s of several billion dollars. Many are built on newspaper empires, cable broadcasting systems, or broadcast chains that have evolved into national or regional media conglomerates. As national and regional conglomerates, they enjoy some of the cross-selling and cross-promotional benefits and economies of scale that the first-tier firms enjoy globally. In Asia and Latin America, some of the second-tier firms work closely as the local conduits for the first-tier media firms. They can take advantage of their facility with local languages, their prominent roles in national and regional economies, and the considerable influence they wield over domestic political authorities. In the United States and Western Europe, some of these second-tier firms fill niche markets, for example producing business news or offering satellite TV services. As the global market consolidates, so do the various national markets, with fewer and fewer owners of domestic media services. 'The whole global media industry is converging,' a U.K. media analyst notes.[201] The second-tier firms are actively strengthening their holds on their domestic and regional media markets. Some of these second-tier firms – like Kirch, Advance Publications, United Media, Thomson, Globo, Televisa, Westinghouse, Canal Plus, Hachette, or Havas – may attempt to become full-blown first-tier global media giants; to do so would require the firms to engage in aggressive mergers and acquisitions involving, at the least, like-sized firms. It will be just as likely for second-tier terms to be the objects of attempted buyouts, as suitors will believe they can enhance such a firm's profit potential by drawing its assets into a fully integrated global empire.

Nearly half of the second-tier firms are from North America. Canada has three second-tier firms in Thomson Corporation (1995 sales: $7.3 billion), which is moving from newspapers to electronic publishing; the newspaper group Hollinger, which controls fifty-eight of Canada's 108 daily newspapers;[202] and the cable television market leader Rogers Communications (1996 sales: $2 billion). Thomson and Hollinger both have global interests.

Two new U.S. firms striving for global niche markets are Dream- Works and DirecTV. DreamWorks intends to be a production studio for film, television programming, and music. With a $2 billion capitalization including $500 million from Microsoft co-founder Paul Allen, DreamWorks is the first firm to attempt to launch a competitive major studio in Hollywood in fifty years. Its success is predicated on the talents, capital, and contacts of its founders, David Geffen, Stephen Spielberg, and former Disney executive Jeffrey Katzenberg. DreamWorks has a 400-strong animation staff and is taking aim at Disney's monopoly over animated feature films. 'I mean, they are about the destruction of Disney,' Rupert Murdoch states.[203] DreamWorks also plans to become the industry leader in applying digital and computer technologies to entertainment fare.[204] DreamWorks plans to assure outlets for its work by signing agreements with television networks.[205]

DirecTV is owned by Hughes Electronics, a subsidiary of General Motors, and AT&T. Hughes (1995 sales: $15 billion) is a defense and electronics firm that is drawing upon its expertise in military satellite technology to tap into the digital satellite boom. When GM sold most of Hughes's military operations to Raytheon in 1997, it maintained its ownership of DirecTV.[206] AT&T provides its global marketing network to sell DirecTV in conjunction with its own services.[207] This is proving to be a formidable combination. It has the leading digital satellite service in the United States, and has clear global ambitions. In late 1996, DirecTV overhauled its management to position itself to compete in the rapidly consolidating global digital satellite television market.[208] It also purchased PanAmSat, which gave it fourteen satellites providing content to 100 nations.[209] DirecTV introduced Galaxy Latin America in a joint venture with Venezuela's Cisneros Group and commercial broadcasting companies from Mexico and Brazil.[210] It also owns a 42.5 percent stake in DirecTV Japan, a joint venture with Matsushita and other Japanese companies.[211] In both instances DirecTV's primary competition comes from News Corporation. DirecTV has additional tentative plans to launch satellite services in joint ventures in Spain, India, and China.[212]

The largest U.S. second-tier firm is Westinghouse, which purchased CBS for $5.4 billion in 1995 and Infinity Broadcasting for $3.7 billion in 1996. Added to its existing network of radio and television stations, these acquisitions created a powerful U.S. broadcasting group with a major television network, two radio networks, and TV stations that cover one-third of the U.S. population in the largest markets. Westinghouse is one of the two largest U.S. radio broadcasters, with eighty-three stations concentrated in seventeen of the largest markets, and collecting at least 17 percent of the revenues in each of the ten largest U.S. radio markets. In New York, Chicago, Philadelphia, and Boston, Westinghouse has approximately 40 percent of the radio revenues.[213] Broadcasting will account for over half of Westinghouse's 1996 sales of $10 billion.[214]

Westinghouse announced plans in November 1996 to split its media properties from its stagnant industrial operations, so that the unleashed broadcasting company – with the name CBS Corp. – could develop 'into a major media company.'[215] As terrestrial broadcasting is currently a profitable industry, but in slow decline, Westinghouse is expected to diversify in the near future, and to think globally. It already produces more of its own content than any other television network and is a major syndicator of radio fare. It plans to use its broadcast properties to spawn a production arm, both on its own and in a joint venture with Sony.[216] To begin to capitalize on 'synergies' in a manner similar to the first-tier media firms, Westinghouse has plans to create music and book publishing subsidiaries that will initially concentrate on spin-offs from CBS-owned radio and television programs.[217] In 1996, Westinghouse purchased TeleNoticias, a Spanish-language news channel broadcast to twenty-two Latin American nations, renamed it CBS/TeleNoticias, and announced plans to spin-off a distinct Spanish-language news channel aimed at the U.S. Latino population.[218] CBS/TeleNoticias established a Portuguese-language network specifically for Brazil in 1997.[219] CBS also launched its first U.S. cable channel, 'Eye on the People,' in 1996. 'This is the start of a very aggressive plan we have,' the Westinghouse executive in charge of CBS/TeleNoticias said.[220] In 1997 Westinghouse paid $1.55 billion in stock to acquire two major North American cable channels, the Nashville Network and Country Music Television, from Gaylord Broadcasting. The channels are expected to mesh well with Westinghouse's eight large market U.S. country music radio stations.[221] As the *Financial Times* put it, Westinghouse is just 'one final leap' from 'where it wants to be – in the land of the media giants.'[222]

The remaining U.S. second-tier media firms include:

* Dow Jones (1996 sales: $2.5 billion);
* Gannett (1996 sales: $4.0 billion);
* Knight-Ridder (1996 sales: $2.9 billion);
* The New York Times (1996 sales: $2.5 billion);
* Times-Mirror (1996 sales: $3.5 billion);
* Washington Post Co. (1996 sales: $1.8 billion);
* Tribune Co. (1996 sales: $2.2 billion);
* Reader's Digest (1996 sales: $3 billion);
* Hearst (1995 sales: $2 billion);
* McGraw-Hill (1995 sales: $3 billion);
* Advance Publications (1995 sales: $4.9 billion);
* Comcast (1996 sales: $3.4 billion);
* Cablevision Systems (1996 sales: $1.1 billion);
* Cox Enterprises (1996 sales: $3.8 billion).

Although Europe has spawned only a couple of first-tier global media firms, it provides the home base for even more second-tier global media firms than North America. The growth of European commercial and pay television has vaulted several firms into prominence. The French Canal Plus (1996 sales: $3 billion) is the leading pay television firm in Europe following its 1996 merger with Nethold. It provides analogue or digital television in most European nations, and is especially prominent in Scandinavia, Central Europe, France, Spain, and Belgium.[223] Canal Plus is also a partner with Bertelsmann and Kirch in the leading German pay television channel, Premiere, with 1.2 million subscribers. Yet Canal Plus is more than a television carrier; it also owns a 5,000-title film library, perhaps the largest in Europe, and it produces television programs in a joint venture with TCI.[224] In the turbulent world of European digital television, it is probable that Canal Plus will be involved in future mergers, acquisitions, and/or joint ventures. It terminated a 1994 joint venture with Bertelsmann to develop European pay television when Bertelsmann merged its television holdings with those of CLT in 1996.[225]

No European firm has capitalized upon commercial and pay television more than the Kirch Group (1996 sales: $4 billion). A German media conglomerate, Kirch has a 35 percent stake in the Axel Springer newspaper group and widespread German commercial broadcasting holdings.[226] Kirch also has a 7 percent investment in Italy's Mediaset and a 25 percent stake in Spain's Tele5 television.[227] Although Kirch 'has been the major-domo of European television for some time,' as one industry analyst puts it, it is Kirch's development of digital television that stands to spur the firm's growth. Kirch launched DF1 as Germany's first digital satellite service in 1996. Kirch solidified its hold on the digital satellite market by signing billion-dollar exclusive long-term pay TV deals with all of the major Hollywood studios, and by purchasing non-U.S. broadcast rights to the 2002 and 2006 World Cups. Bertelsmann, Kirch's only potential rival for control of Europe's most lucrative digital satellite television market, has thrown in the towel.[228] Kirch has a 57.5 percent stake in Telepiu, the concern that launched Italy's first and only digital satellite service in 1996.[229] In 1996, Kirch went beyond television systems to purchase a 7.5 percent stake in the U.S. New Regency film studio, which is distributed by Time Warner.[230] If digital satellite television proves lucrative, Kirch will unquestionably become 'one of the most powerful media groups in Europe,' if not the world.[231]

Four especially large European media firms are the French Havas and Lagardere Group (Hachette), the Italian Mediaset, and the Anglo-Dutch Reed Elsevier. Each of these firms is a powerhouse in its regional or specific media market, and one or more of them may join the set of vertically integrated global media firms. Havas (1996 sales: $8.8 billion) is primarily an advertising agency, but it has extensive holdings in European commercial broadcasting through its 34 percent stake in Canal

Plus and a 10 percent stake in CLT. Havas is also the world's fifth largest publishing group.[232] As a Morgan Stanley media analyst puts it, Havas's challenge remains to find ways to 'build on the synergies' between its disparate activities.[233] Hachette (1994 sales: $5.3 billion) is a French and European magazine and book publishing giant, with smaller interests in broadcasting. It derives 17 percent of its income from (mostly magazine) sales in the United States.[234] Mediaset (1996 sales: $2 billion) is the media conglomerate which split off in 1996 from Silvio Berlusconi's Fininvest, the third largest private company in Italy. Still controlled by Berlusconi, Mediaset may well be the most dominant national media company in the world, with three national broadcasting channels, magazines, radio stations, and newspapers. Mediaset's future is uncertain, however, because of corruption charges surrounding Berlusconi and his political activities. (See our discussion of Italy in Chapter 6.[235]) Its current strategy is to use its strength in Italy to move into Italian mobile telephony and telecommunications in an alliance with British Telecommunications, rather than expand regionally or globally.[236] That Mediaset would make a superb addition to a global media giant is clear; Rupert Murdoch negotiated long and hard to purchase it in 1995 but to no avail. Reed Elsevier (1995 sales: $5.5 billion) is a leader in scientific, business, technical, and reference publishing. It has $5 billion for new acquisitions and has committed itself to dominating the electronic publishing and information markets.[237]

The remaining European second-tier media firms include the following:

- The German Axel Springer (1993 sales: $3 billion);
- The German Verlagsgruppe Bauer (1993 sales: $1.7 billion);
- The Italian RCS Editori Spa (1993 sales: $1.6 billion);
- The French CEP Communication;
- The Dutch Wolters Kluwer (1994 sales: $1.7 billion);
- The Dutch VNU (1994 sales: $1.4 billion;
- The Swedish Kinnevik (1996 sales: $1.8 billion);
- Spanish media conglomerate Prisa Group, which has expanded into Latin America;
- Spanish commercial broadcaster Antena 3, which has also expanded into Latin America;
- The British Carlton Communications (1996 sales: $2.5 billion);
- The British Granada Group (1996 sales: $3.6 billion);
- The British Pearson PLC (1996 sales: $2.9 billion);
- The BBC (1995 U.K. revenues: $3.5 billion);
- The British Reuters (1995 sales: $4.1 billion);
- The British United News & Media (1996 sales: $2.9 billion);

- The British EMI (1996 sales: $5.4 billion);
- The European CLT, which has merged its activities with Bertels-mann's Ufa television division (1996 sales: $3 billion);
- The French Television Francais 1 (TF1) (1996 sales: $1.8 billion).

The balance of the world also provides some second-tier media firms. At present these firms are all smaller than their Western European and North American counterparts, but in view of the prospective growth in parts of the developing world, some of these firms should grow quite rapidly. In Eastern Europe, however, they tend to be foreign-owned. As one observer puts it, Eastern Europe's 'Catch-22' is 'How to create cap-italists without capital.'[238] The global media giants like Time Warner, Bertelsmann, Canal Plus, and Disney (through its interest in SBS) are filling the void as they battle for control of commercial broadcasting, especially in the more lucrative Central European markets.[239] Their strongest competition comes from the U.S. Metromedia (1995 sales: $1.7 billion) and Central European Media Enterprises (CME), which have both targeted Eastern Europe for the development of commercial broadcasting.[240] CME was formed by U.S. cosmetics heir Ronald Lauder, who hoped to capitalize upon his contacts after serving as a diplomat in the region. The CME strategy is to get the licenses for at least one of the limited number of terrestrial broadcast channels in each country and then to deliver large audiences to advertisers. CME's think-ing is that satellite or cable television will do limited business in Eastern Europe for the foreseeable future.[241] CME's first channel, 'Nova' in the Czech Republic, has been wildly successful, gaining over 70 percent of the Czech market in its first year and generating $40 million in profit.[242] CME now owns eleven Eastern European television stations and has a stock market value of $800 million, six times its annual revenues.[243] Its empire extends from the Czech Republic to Romania, Slovenia, Ukraine, Poland, Germany, and Slovakia and it is planning to move into Bulgaria and Hungary.[244]

Latin America, on the other hand, has at least four second-tier firms in the global market: the Argentine Clarin, the Venezuelan Cisneros Group, the Brazilian Globo, and the Mexican Televisa. Each of these four firms is the dominant media conglomerate in its national market and each, to varying degrees, is expanding regionally and globally. Clarin (1996 sales: $1.2 billion) has holdings in television, cable, and print media. It has teamed with Globo to develop Brazilian cable tele-vision systems and it is considering working with TCI to develop Chilean cable systems. Clarin was a partner in the launch of the cable news network TeleNoticias.[245] The Cisneros Group (1995 sales: $3.2 bil-lion) is an industrial conglomerate which has moved aggressively into media. It is the primary partner of DirecTV in Galaxy Latin America and it has media and telecommunication joint ventures with Motorola, Sprint, Microsoft, AT&T, BellSouth, Televisa, and Hearst. Cisneros owns television stations in Venezuela, Trinidad, and Chile and is a partner in a Spanish digital television joint venture. 'We want to be a very large force in Latin America,' the Cisneros CEO states, 'and throughout the hemisphere.'[246] Globo (1996 sales: $2.2 billion) dominates Brazilian television with a 60 percent audience share. Globo's network is the fourth largest in the world after the three major U.S. webs, generating $1.5 billion in 1996. Globo is prominent in other Brazilian media as well (see also Chapter 6). It exports television programming to nearly sixty nations, with Portugal being the primary customer outside of Latin America, but the total value of its exports was only $30 million in 1996.[247] Globo remains primarily a Brazilian firm, though it is becoming more regionally minded. It has allied with AT&T and Brazil's largest private bank to bid for the coming privatization of Brazil's telephone system.[248] Globo's most ambitious project may be its 30 percent stake in the Sky Latin America digital satellite service, alongside News Corporation, TCI, and Televisa.[249] Brazil had the world's fastest growing pay television market between 1994 and 1996, and there is room for much more growth. Globo has already established several channels for the 'Sky Brasil' service of Sky Latin America.[250]

Televisa (1996 sales: $1.2 billion) has been the most aggressive Latin American media firm both regionally and internationally. *Business Week* observes that Televisa 'wants to crash the global major leagues.'[251] Although Televisa dominates Mexican media with interests in broadcasting, cable, and publishing, it is facing increased competition and smaller margins. Its response is 'to go global like never before.'[252] It has purchased television stations in Peru and Chile, and has acquired the world's largest publisher of Spanish-language magazines. Televisa has a stake in the U.S. Hispanic cable channel Univision.[253] Televisa's television melodramas – telenovelas – are exported to over 100 countries, and are especially popular when dubbed in China, India, and Turkey. They accounted for 85 percent of Televisa's $71-million-worth of 1995 program exports.[254] Yet Televisa is not satisfied with being the preeminent Spanish-language media company in the world; it is now producing low-budget English-language melodramas for U.S. audiences and broadcasting them to the southwestern United States from a series of stations along Mexico's northern border. Televisa's Tijuana station is a Fox affiliate (News Corporation). If Televisa's foray into English programming succeeds, it intends to expand its activities to Europe and Asia.[255] Like Globo, Televisa has a 30 percent stake in Sky Latin America. 'This is the most important project we have,' Televisa's chief financial officer states.[256] Televisa is also contemplating an investment in Spanish digital satellite television.[257]

Asia, the Middle East, and the Pacific are certain to produce second-tier regional powerhouses that will complement the already intense activities of the global giants. In view of the size of the market and its projected growth, it is not impossible that one or two Asian-based first-tier global giants may be spawned. 'Has it ever been written,' one Thai publisher asked, 'that an Asian cannot be a major player in regional or global media?'[258] Yet, as one 1996 report on Asian media for investors concluded, 'the Anglo-American (US, UK) dominance in media cannot be cracked in the near future.'[259]

The Middle East media have consolidated over the past decade, and are presently dominated by Saudi capital. Saudi investors are also bankrolling three major pan-Arab world satellite television ventures, all in collaboration with the media giants. A second-tier media group may emerge from these activities.[260] In India, the Modi group, one of that nation's five largest industrial concerns with annual sales of $2 billion, has targeted cable and satellite television as a primary focus of its opera-tions. On one hand, Modi is paving the 'road for U.S. fare in India' by working closely with the global giants. On the other hand, Modi has established ten entertainment companies, intends to begin production, and will establish its own cable channel. Its aim is to become a 'vertically integrated company.'[261] In East Asia several existing firms are position-ing themselves to get the inside track in cable and satellite broadcasting, alongside News Corporation and the global giants. These include the Hong Kong-based TVB International, which News Corporation attempted to buy in 1992 and which is challenging Star TV in India, Chinese Entertainment Television, and the Asia Broadcasting and Communications Network, a $500-million-dollar pan-Asian satellite broadcasting venture launched by the Thai M Group.[262] Filipino com-mercial broadcasting is dominated by ABS-CBN, valued at over $1 billion by *Forbes* magazine.[263] The Indian and Chinese state broadcast-ing companies, Doordarshan and Chinese Central Television (CCTV), have moved steadily into commercially oriented broadcasting. CCTV, in particular, is gearing up for commercial competition with a global enter-tainment satellite channel and an all-sports channel.[264]

Australian Kerry Packer's Publishing & Broadcasting (PBL) (1996 sales: $750 million) is an Australian conglomerate that provides News Corporation with competition. PBL owns the leading commercial tele-vision network, has magazine publishing interests, and a 17 percent stake in Fairfax, Australia's largest newspaper chain.[265] PBL was one of the first foreign firms to sign an agreement to cooperate on program-ming with China's CCTV, much to Murdoch's chagrin.[266] Packer also has a large stake in the New Regency film studio, which produces films that are distributed by Time Warner.[267]

Korea is slowly entering the global media system. The major industrial concerns are wakening to the importance of media; for example, each of Korea's four largest conglomerates (or chaebols) has applied to provide digital satellite broadcasting to that nation.[268] The Samsung Group has purchased a stake in New Regency Productions, which is affiliated with Time Warner. The Hyundai Group has a joint venture with Canal Plus for film production and Kolon Industries is negotiating with Disney on animation projects. The largest deal came in 1995 when Miky Lee, an heiress to the Samsung fortune, invested $300 million in DreamWorks, with the express interest of developing its Asian market.[269] Lee is also turning the food-processing company Cheil Jedang (1995 sales: $2.1 billion) into a pan-Asian media conglomerate with film production and distribution, multiplex theaters, and a music company. She is also considering the construction of an amusement park.[270]

Japan is notably absent as the home base for global media corporations. Of Japan's 227 firms that rank among the world's 1,000 largest firms (based upon market value) in 1996, only Sony is a serious media player – and the only Japanese firm with any global position – though several conglomerates have minor media interests.[271] This is a consequence of the low level of advertising in Japan, along with the laws and regulations imposed by U.S. authorities after World War II that limited conglomeration and multiple newspaper and broadcast station ownership.[272] (Regrettably, such anti-monopoly rules were not applied in the authorities' own country!) Japan's largest media organization is the public broadcaster, NHK (1995 revenues: $5.6 billion), which is technically advanced, vertically integrated, and strongly growth-oriented, but has minimal interests outside of Japan. Neither do Japan's smaller, private media powers, like the Toho Company (1996 sales: $1.6 billion), Asahi National Broadcasting Co. (1996 sales: $1.6 billion), Fuji Television Network (1996 sales: $2.6 billion), Tokyo Broadcasting System (1996 sales: $2.1 billion), and Nippon Television Network (NTV) (1996 sales: $2.2 billion), have any foreign presence.

The Japanese market is opening up to the global media giants, however, and the largest industrial conglomerates are making investments in media, especially satellite and cable television.[273] With regard to domestic and regional media investments, the largest Japanese concerns are entering the fray almost entirely through mergers and acquisitions or joint ventures with each other and with the existing first- and second-tier global media firms. Sumitomo and NTV are linked with TCI, Itochu and Toshiba with Time Warner, and Tokuma Shoten with

Disney.[274] Softbank, one of the fastest growing companies in Japan, whose annual sales increased from $800 million in 1995 to over $3 billion in 1996, is also the most aggressive Japanese media firm. It has a one-third stake in the digital satellite system Japan Sky Broadcasting, a joint venture with News Corporation and Sony to be launched in 1998. In 1996 Softbank purchased the U.S. Ziff-Davis publishing company for $2.1 billion. On a global level, while Japanese firms Sony and Matsushita did not reap rewards for their purchase of Hollywood studios in the late 1980s, Japanese investment banks are increasingly active in co-producing films with the media giants.[275] Japan is supplying capital and markets to the global media system, but little else.

CONCLUSION

The global media market is dominated by ten or so vertically integrated media conglomerates, most of which are based in the United States. Another thirty or forty significant supporting firms round out the meaningful positions in the system. These firms operate in oligopolistic markets with substantial barriers to entry. They compete vigorously on a non-price basis, but their competition is softened not only by common interests as oligopolists, but also by a vast array of joint ventures, strategic alliances, and cross-ownership among the leading firms. To no small extent, the hallmarks of the global media system are its financial underpinnings in advertising and its thoroughgoing commercialism. The global television system emphasizes a few areas of commercial promise: music videos, news, sports, children's fare, a few genres of filmed entertainment, and shopping. There is little that distinguishes the content provided by any of these firms from that of the balance of the commercial media.

The market is still in the process of rapid change, and more mergers, acquisitions, and joint ventures can be expected before the dust clears. One reason for the turmoil in the global communication market is the digital revolution which is eliminating the technological barriers that have divided media from telecommunications (telephony) and both of them from the computer and information industries. Some sense of these changes have emerged in this chapter as we discussed the involvement of telecommunications firms like AT&T with DirecTV, Concert (BT-MCI) with News Corporation, and U.S.West with Time Warner. We have also mentioned the alliance between NBC and Microsoft. These are all developments of the mid-1990s and they are only the tip of the iceberg. In this context the ultimate shape of the global media oligopoly will be indelibly associated with the fate of global telecommunication and computing. We devote Chapter 4 to the consideration of how the global media industry will address the 'communication revolution' and how the global media system can be reconciled with the 'information superhighway.'

How do we think culture happens? is produced?

4
GLOBAL MEDIA, THE INTERNET, AND THE DIGITAL REVOLUTION

During the 1990s, the shift to digital transmission of all forms of data has increased at an accelerated pace. This shift to computer language has already redefined the music industry and will eventually overtake film, radio, and television production and distribution.[1] In the future virtually all forms of data and information will be produced and stored in interchangeable digital bits. When combined with satellite communication and fiber optic-wired communication networks, digital communication becomes the 'information superhighway' or the 'Global Information Infrastructure' (GII), whereby individuals potentially can have instantaneous and global access to all forms of data, and can communicate with virtually anyone via a personal computer. The revolutionary implications of such a system are the stuff of much contemporary literature. At present the information superhighway largely remains to be constructed, but rudimentary digital communication networks – especially the Internet – are changing the media landscape. *rudimentary*

In this chapter we examine how the digital revolution and the Internet are developing and how they alter the vision of the global media presented in Chapters 2 and 3. To many of those closely connected to the digital revolution, the impending social changes will be revolutionary. 'Everything will be different,' U.S. Federal Communications Commission Chairman Reed Hundt states. 'The change is so extreme that many people have not grasped it.'[2] 'Our industry,' Microsoft Chairman Bill Gates notes, 'will be changing the way people do business, the way they learn and even the way they entertain themselves, far more than I think people outside our industry expect.'[3] With specific regard to media, some assert that computer communication will undermine the monopoly power of the media giants, opening a new era of more egalitarian and democratic communication. Nicholas Negroponte observes that 'the monolithic empires of mass media are dissolving into an array of cottage industries.'[4] 'The Internet represents the real information revolution,' Frank Beacham wrote early in 1995, 'the one that removes the governmental and corporate filters that have so long been in place with the traditional mass media.'[5] John Perry Barlow of the Electronic Frontier Foundation, in an extreme example, dismissed the importance of the global media mergers of the mid-1990s, stating that the media firms were merely rearranging 'deck chairs on the Titanic.' The iceberg, Barlow submits, will be the Internet with its 500 million channels.[6]

In our view, the evidence suggests that the Internet and the digital revolution do not pose an immediate or even foreseeable threat to the market power of the media giants. In the current political climate, moreover, it is likely that the global media firms will be able to incorporate the Internet and related computer networks into their empires, while the egalitarian potential of the technology is minimized. Yet we are at the beginning of the digital era, so prediction beyond broad brushstrokes is problematic. Hundt and Gates should be taken seriously. The nature of the communication system that the media giants do dominate is in the midst of sweeping change, introducing new players, new possibilities, stunning technological developments, and considerable instability.[7]

CONVERGENCE AND INSTABILITY

The shift to digital communication and other technological developments are breaking down barriers between traditional media industries and also between the broader media and communication sectors. The shift to digital formats and the ability to send all digital information over the same networks is removing the distinctions between them. 'Whereas it has always been a simple matter to distinguish between newspapers, broadcast television, cable television, computers, motion pictures, and the telephone companies,' one scholar notes, 'those distinctions are quickly eroding as a [sic] new, universal media looms on the horizon.'[8] In one of the better publicized developments, cable broadcasters and telephone companies are each capable of providing the other's services to their customers. This is broadly referred to as *convergence*, whereby the media, telecommunication (meaning primarily telephony), and computer industries find their activities are becoming increasingly the same. The traditional functions of telephones, television sets, and personal computers are merging. As they merge, manufacturers of one of them find they can/must now work in the other fields.[9] Computer software makers, who once serviced autonomous computers, now find they are crucially linked to both telecommunication and media firms. 'With the digitalization of all information then you have a common toolset to work with,' one computer executive states.[10]

When the global media system is thought of as part of a converging global communication system, it alters our perspective in two important ways. First, the 'info-communications' sector, as the International Telecommunication Union (ITU) terms it, is an enormous part of the global economy, with output valued at almost $1.5 trillion in 1994. This was divided between telecommunication (46 percent), computers (33 percent), and media (21 percent).[11] The info-communication sector has been growing at twice the rate of the balance of the global economy in the 1990s with no indication of a let-up.[12] Moreover, the fastest growing segment within the global communication industries is specifically international communication.[13] The importance of this sector for global capitalism can hardly be exaggerated. Sixteen of the sixty largest companies worldwide in terms of market capitalization fall into this sector.[14] In terms of annual revenues, eleven of the fifty largest firms in the world fall into the communication sector category.[15] If consumer electronic firms were included, as some argue they should be, along with all the firms that had partial interests in communication, the figures would be significantly higher.[16]

Second, global convergence has created greater uncertainty in what had been relatively stable global oligopolistic media, computer, and telecommunication markets. The situation is not unlike that discussed in Chapter 2 in regard to the global media market; the global media and communication firms in the larger 'info-communication' sector act as much out of fear of the unknown as from coherent visions of what a converging communication market might look like in ten or twenty years. All of these firms now need to be concerned not only about their immediate rivals but the prospect that firms from the other info-communication industries might move in on them. The response of these companies has been to engage in mergers and acquisitions (M&A) to build protective armor, as well as to establish joint ventures and strategic alliances with other firms to protect themselves from being blindsided while making forays into new terrain. In times of technological upheaval where nobody has a clear idea of exactly where things are heading, the smart course for a firm is to hedge its bets by getting involved in several options so it can be prepared to pounce on any one of them that shows commercial potential. 'It's not a question of if, but when,' AT&T's head of new media industries says, 'and there are real advantages in being first.'[17] In Europe alone, the value of M&A in the info-communications sector jumped 40 percent to $72 billion in 1996.[18] The merger specialists Broadview Associates anticipates that media/communication dealmaking will continue furiously for years or until the market stabilizes: 'The opportunity is just too big, and the risk/reward ratio too acute for even the most bullish to consider going alone.'[19] 'Today there's no company on earth that's strong enough to do everything,' MCI president Jerry Taylor states. 'The winners will be those who make partnerships work.'[20]

With the development of radically new digital technologies that are shaking the foundations of these industries, however, there are also much wider openings for start-up firms to enter the market than would ever be the case in more settled times. A few new giants will probably emerge, just as new industrial giants were formed with the emergence of film, broadcasting, cable, computers, and software. And the booming new markets, especially in East Asia, may provide the basis for a few new regional media and communication powerhouses. Most of the new great fortunes in digital communication, however, will be made by firms which get swallowed up by one of the existing giants after they have shown some new profitable application. There are tremendous advantages that accrue to the giants, not least of which are their immense cash resources and their ability to use their current markets to ease the transition into new ones.[21]

PRIVATIZATION AND DEREGULATION OF GLOBAL TELECOMMUNICATION

Everywhere, governments are preparing new laws and regulations for the digital era, but in virtually all of these debates the superiority of the market and the profit motive as the regulator of all branches of communication is taken as a given.[22] Nonmarket intervention is also dismissed as foolish, because regulation in times of technological upheaval might slow down the rate of change, and rapid change is presumed for the better. In these debates, the only justification for regulation is when the market does not provide enough competition.[23] There is little sense of markets having inherent flaws that must be addressed; as one observer puts it, governments have moved from being proactive policymakers to being the 'market policeman enforcing competition law.'[24] The liberal U.S. Aspen Institute, for example, argues that 'open-market, pro-competitive policies' for communication 'are unarguably sound, and ought to be adopted by all nations.' It dismisses the notion that governments might have to intervene to address flaws in the market as 'thinking the unthinkable.'[25] It is in the United States that the 'market policeman' notion of regulation has been in existence the longest, and based upon U.S. experience the record indicates that it has limited effect in enforcing competition, not to mention serving any broader public interest.

The single most important law affecting global telecommunications has been the U.S. Telecommunications Act of 1996, if only because it directly affects a majority of the giant communication firms in the world. The law removes barriers to entry and consolidation within the telecommunication industry and between it and closely related media and information industries. The core notion is to let the market determine the course of events. One business executive characterized the U.S. Telecommunications Act as a 'Magna Charta' for communication corporations. Similar laws have been or are being passed in the other developed countries.[26] The European Union, commissioned to establish a single European market, has been in the forefront of efforts to deregulate and privatize, or what is termed 'liberalize,' the telecommunication and information technology industries, and to make continental, rather than national, business empires the norm.[27] By 1998, all European telecom services will be at least partially privatized and the national markets deregulated. This process is not unopposed, however, as there are powerful national interests contesting deregulation as well as a general concern that immediate liberalization could lead to U.S. domination of European communication.[28] Nevertheless, although this liberalization process has had its fits and starts, the general trajectory is unmistakable.

It is in the realm of telecommunication that the move to privatization and deregulation is most significant, and the decline of public service standards has been precipitous. Prior to the mid-1980s, telecommunications was conducted almost entirely as national nonprofit – or, in the U.S., regulated – monopolies. These public telephone services often gave priority to subsidizing widespread public access that would have been shunned by purely profit-motivated institutions. The public telecommunication companies might have brought nonmarket public service standards to the Internet and the digital communications networks as they are developed. As late as 1978 a United Nations agency filed a report signed by seventy-eight nations stating that the emergence of private global communication networks 'could place national sovereignty in question.'[29] Those days are now a distant memory. The entire public sector of telecommunications is in the midst of an unprecedented privatization.[30] In every corner of the world, public systems are being sold off to private interests. One scholar says it is the most significant liquidation of public property since the Enclosure Acts in Britain.[31] Between 1984 and 1994, telecommunication privatizations were valued at $105 billion.[32] This was just the tip of the iceberg. The value of worldwide telecommunication equity offerings and mergers *doubled* from 1995 to 1996 to reach $135 billion.[33] Wall Street securities firms Merrill Lynch and Salomon forecast that worldwide telecom privatizations will provide 20 percent of investment banking income for the foreseeable future.[34]

What accounts for this burst of privatization and deregulation? There are several factors. First, the development of new digital and satellite technologies limited the ability of the traditional national telecommunication services to maintain monopoly control. Second, the traditional monopoly services were often bureaucratic and incompetent, thus breeding a public willingness to shake up the industry. Yet these two factors only explain why traditional monopolies were broken up, not why telecommunications had to be privatized and deregulated, subjecting the communication infrastructure of nations to the prerogatives of transnational communication firms and global capital markets. This liberalization was encouraged by slow economic growth and the general fiscal crises of nation states; the market offered the promise of huge capital investments and modernization leading to economic growth, all without cost to the taxpayer.

Moreover, communication was and is becoming central to the global market economy; business wanted and needed high-speed communication networks to manage global operations. In this context, the move toward privatized communication was the key to admission to the global economy, and there was simply no other alternative within the existing set of social relations. Accordingly, when Russia's plan to sell off its public telecommunications system to the Italian firm Stet collapsed in 1995, the business press reported that the episode had 'wide implications for the transition to capitalism.'[35] In many respects this need to have privatized communication to participate in global capitalism accounts for the lack of democratic participation in communication debates, and the narrow range of the debates that have ensued. The only issue to be debated was the speed of the liberalization program, not the merits of it.

The privatization and deregulation of communication has also been stimulated by the desire for profits by telecommunication firms and the investment bankers who coordinate these privatizations. Telecommunication tends to be the most lucrative activity traditionally under the control of the public sector. Moreover, these private interests work with the governments of the developed nations, and the institutions of global capitalism – the World Bank and the IMF[36] – to push these policies around the world.[37] To them it is simply axiomatic, as one European Bank for Reconstruction and Development official put it in 1995, that liberalized telecommunication is a 'vital element in moving to a free market economy and speeding growth.'[38] The United States has been the most aggressive government in demanding that nations liberalize their telecommunications, pushing for global, regional, and bilateral free trade agreements.[39] It argues that foreign competition must be permitted without any restriction because otherwise it would be impossible for competition to spring up against entrenched national monopolies.[40] It may be worth noting that the United States is the home of ten of the sixteen largest telecommunication firms in the world, and these are the firms that are the major beneficiaries of free trade.[41] Likewise, the United States aggressively pushes for global free trade in computers, another industry which its firms dominate.[42]

The drive for 'liberalization' culminated in the 'landmark' 1997 World Trade Organization telecommunications agreement. Signed by 68 countries representing 90 percent of the $600 billion per annum telecommunication services market, the agreement requires them to open their markets to foreign competition and to allow foreign companies to buy stakes in domestic operators. A crucial factor in getting the deal completed was having the largest telecom firms involved 'more directly in trade policymaking.'[43] AT&T hailed the WTO pact as 'an important step toward fully competitive markets.'[44] The U.S. trade representative and the EU trade commissioner both noted that the measure will spur development of the global information highway that 'increasingly provides the infrastructure for doing international business.'[45]

Despite the unilateral nature of the WTO agreement, the course of telecommunication liberalization has two very different faces. The major firms and developed nations all understand that a body like the WTO must serve as the 'global regulator' of the information highway if it is to reach its full commercial potential.[46] Yet in the negotiations between the United States, the European Union, and Japan, principle is jettisoned and the nations pursue protectionist courses if necessary to protect domestic firms.[47] Hence the United States forced the temporary postponement of the WTO's negotiations to liberalize telecommunication in 1996, in part to protect the powerful Motorola Corporation's digital satellite telephone system from European competition.[48]

The less powerful states of Eastern Europe and the Third World can likewise sometimes gain leverage and exact concessions in the privatization process by playing TNCs off against one another, and by allying with one or more of the major powers in their disputes. However, for these nations the general principles of privatization and liberalization are non-negotiable; the only issue is which foreign TNCs will get the best deals in combination with which local business interests. Telecommunications liberalization has improved services for business and the affluent in the developing world, but the principle of universal access has been compromised, if not abandoned. The 'reforms' have also led to numerous episodes of large-scale graft and corruption.[49] In Europe as well as the Third World, national labor movements, and the telecommunication workers in particular, have greeted privatization plans with waves of strike activity.[50]

This liberalization is leading to a sweeping reconstruction of global telecommunication. On the one hand, deregulation has led to a rash of mergers among the largest telecommunication firms, highlighted by the

1996 U.S. mergers of Nynex and Bell Atlantic, and Pacific Telesis and SBC Communications.[51] The mergers were carried out because the firms believed they needed to get larger to survive the shakeout in the global telecommunication industry.[52] On the other hand, the demise of public telecommunication monopolies has led to the disintegration of the international phone cartel, thereby opening up the highly profitable and rapidly growing sector of international telephony to private global networks.[53]

In the late 1990s, the world's largest telecommunication firms have raced to put together global alliances.[54] When British Telecommunication purchased MCI for some $20 billion in November 1996 to form Concert, it signaled that some of these alliances may turn into formal mergers. AT&T has allied with Singapore Telecom and four major European national firms to form World Partners, and Sprint, Deutsche Telekom, and France Telecom have formed Global One.[55] Deutsche Telekom and France Telecom own 20 percent of Sprint and are considering an outright purchase. Global One is also contemplating an alliance with Cable & Wireless.[56] The five remaining U.S. regional phone giants, GTE, and the other major national companies are all making their own efforts to form national and global alliances.[57] There is great pressure on telecom firms to link up with one of the few major alliances or find themselves cut out of the action. Concert (BT-MCI), for example, has 69 joint ventures and strategic alliances across the world.

The 1997 WTO telecommunications agreement should accelerate this process, igniting 'a wave of mergers and acquisitions,' *The Economist* noted, 'rather like the one inspired by America's telecom act last year.'[58] 'People aren't going to want to be left behind,' MCA president Gerald H. Taylor said. 'You're going to see a lot more movement into partnerships and joint ventures.'[59] There is every reason to anticipate many more mergers. The *Financial Times* states that the endpoint will possibly be 'a handful of giants, straddling the world market.'[60] MCI's Taylor concludes that 'There's probably going to be only four to six global gangs emerge over the next five years as all this sorts out.'[61] Nor will these 'global gangs' only concern themselves with international telephone and data transmission. Each of the giant telecom firms has moved aggressively into deregulated domestic telecommunications markets around the world, almost always in joint ventures with other global giants and local investors.[62] In these forays, the global firms and alliances have a decided advantage over the traditional national firms, due to the cost benefits they can offer business and the wealthy for global communication.[63]

As with the development of global media, global telecommunication firms are especially interested in the East Asian market. As the *Financial*

Times put it, the telecommunication firms and global alliances that are the 'winners in the east will inherit the earth.'[64] This gives the larger Asian governments far more negotiating power than the other Third World states. Sub-Saharan Africa, and much of the rest of the world, will receive minimal attention, except to service business and the upper classes.[65] Some experts argue that the telecommunications gap 'between the less developed and industrial countries is widening,' while even optimists see little hope of the Third World advancing relative to the developed world.[66] Industry analysts estimate that there is an annual shortfall of as much as $50 billion necessary for low-income nations to have modern telecommunication systems.[67] The ITU, which has seen its role of coordinating global telecommunication increasingly usurped by the World Bank, WTO, and IMF, has made what efforts it could to address the imbalance ignored and created by the market.[68] Yet the ITU has formally accepted liberalization as a beneficial process, and its most ambitious plan is to assist a for-profit telecommunication firm that plans to concentrate upon low-income nations.[69] One scholar concludes that it is unlikely that the ITU can have 'more than a marginal impact on the constraints faced by the developing nations.'[70]

THE NEW MEDIA PLAYERS

In the convergence of telecommunication, media, and computer industries, the telecommunication firms have mounted the first assault into new territory. They are entering traditional media, usually in joint ventures with other telecommunication firms and/or existing media giants. Telecommunication firms want to exploit their ability to provide television signals over their wires, and to protect themselves before cable broadcasting companies – like Time Warner and TCI – provide telephony over their cables. Several of these firms have explicit strategies to become active in media. Many of them are wealthy firms with strong cash flows, perfectly suited for acquisitions. Yet, we are still at the beginning of communication convergence in any meaningful sense; with few exceptions, none of the telecommunication–media ventures existed prior to the 1990s and most of them developed after 1994.

In terms of size, the world's largest telecommunication firms are Japan's NT&T (1995 sales: $82 billion), AT&T (1996 sales: $53 billion), Deutsche Telekom (1996 sales: $46 billion), Concert (BT-MCI) (1996 sales: $40 billion), France Telecom (1995 sales: $30 billion), the merged Bell Atlantic-Nynex (1995 sales: $27 billion) and Italy's Stet (1995 sales: $26 billion). Each is significantly larger than the largest global media giants, like Time Warner and Disney that enjoyed 1996 sales slightly

interactive TV

over $20 billion. The next tier of telecommunication firms, including GTE, the five other U.S. regional Bell companies, Spain's Telefonica, and the U.S. long-distance firm Sprint all have revenues in the $15 to $25 billion range. Most of these firms developed their strong positions through regional or national monopolies, but only one, NT&T, has failed to show global ambitions.

Among U.S. telecom firms, the regional Bell companies and GTE combined to launch two interactive television joint ventures – Tele-TV and Americast – in 1994–5. Disney is a partner in Americast. After much initial fanfare about how these services would directly challenge the dominance of cable companies over U.S. pay television, both have foundered and Tele-TV has effectively been disbanded. To some extent the telecom firms have decided that entering the long-distance telephony market or the Internet access market would be more profitable. Nevertheless, most of the large telecom firms still have investments in television, often 'wireless' cable, which offers digital pictures but none of the interactive potential of the original systems. GTE, SBC Communications, and BellSouth also have cable interests or plans for wired video networks in select markets around the nation.[71] But, on balance, the initial telecom forays into media have fallen short of even the most pessimistic estimates from 1994.

A few large U.S. telecom firms have maintained their commitment for media to become integrated into their core activities. Pacific Telesis, for example, the Baby Bell that merged with SBC Communications in 1996, began offering wireless cable to 5 million homes in Southern California in 1997.[72] Bell Atlantic-Nynex have soured on their Tele-TV interactive television plans, but they remain fairly significant media players. Bell Atlantic almost merged with TCI in 1994, and through its merger with Nynex it has come into several global media properties. Nynex has a significant stake in Nynex CableComms, one of Britain's largest cable operators, which in 1996 merged with units of Cable & Wireless and Bell Canada International to provide local and long-distance telephony, cable television, and Internet access all through one firm in the United Kingdom.[73] (Bell Canada, on its own, in 1997 launched ExpressVu, a Canadian satellite television service.[74]) Through its 50 percent stake in TelecomAsia Corporation, Nynex has cable and broadcast holdings in Thailand, India, and the Philippines. Nynex also has a $1.2 billion investment in Viacom.[75]

The telecom firm that has most aggressively recast itself as a media firm is the regional Bell company, U.S.West. In 1994 it purchased a 25 percent stake in Time Warner Entertainment (which includes Time Warner cable, HBO, and Warner Bros. film studios) for $2.5 billion. In 1996 U.S.West culminated several cable purchases by acquiring

Continental Cablevision, the third largest U.S. cable firm, for $10.8 billion. Through Continental, U.S.West now has a 10 percent stake in the PrimeStar satellite television service and a 50 percent stake in Video Cable Communication, one of Argentina's three main cable companies.[76] U.S.West became interested in media in Britain when it launched TeleWest in 1991 with TCI. It still has a 20 percent stake in the United Kingdom's largest cable provider.[77] Moreover, U.S.West has been active in other European media deals; in 1995 and 1996 it purchased stakes in cable companies in The Netherlands, Belgium, and the Czech Republic, where it has a 90 percent stake in the market-leading Kabel Plus.[78] At the same time U.S.West sold its interests in cable systems in Sweden, Norway, and Hungary because they were not well positioned to offer voice telephony.[79] Its cable wires now pass 16 million U.S. homes and 40 million worldwide. U.S.West is moving forward on cable telephony, interactive television, and Internet access along with its telephone business.[80]

Perhaps because they lack the monopolistic local markets of the regional Bells, the three largest U.S. long-distance carriers – AT&T, MCI, and Sprint – have been most aggressive in establishing global empires and adapting to digital and wireless technologies. AT&T split its disparate networks and manufacturing sectors into separate companies in the 1990s to eliminate the conflict of interest they had by working with each other's sector's competitors.[81] AT&T made its first breakthrough into media in 1996 when it purchased a 2.5 percent stake in DirecTV, with an option to increase its stake over five years to 30 percent.[82] Long-distance companies like AT&T (and BT-MCI with News Corporation) are seasoned marketers that can use their base of telephone customers as targets for selling their satellite television services. Sprint has dabbled in cable broadcasting but, like AT&T, its primary focus has been upon the Internet and wireless communication systems. Its global activities are primarily through the Global One alliance with Deutsche Telekom and France Telecom.[83] MCI, on the other hand, prior to its 1996 sale to BT which thereby inherits the media interests, made an emphatic commitment to media, not unlike that of U.S.West, reflected foremost in its $2 billion purchase of a 13.5 percent stake in News Corporation in 1995. MCI also has a 10 percent stake in the U.S. Sky Television, the digital satellite television service controlled by Echostar and News Corporation. MCI also has a 'sweeping' online alliance with Microsoft and a deal with Universal to sell music via the telephone and the Internet.[84]

Many of the other major European telecommunication firms have also moved into media ventures. Spain's Telefonica has interests in cable broadcasting ventures (and telecommunication firms) across Latin

America.[85] Telefonica also plans to become involved in satellite television joint ventures to the Spanish-speaking world.[86] As mentioned earlier, Cable & Wireless has merged its U.K. operations with Nynex Cablecomms to create a full service cable television–telephone–Internet access company. It also owns 58 percent of Hong Kong Telecom, which launched the most sophisticated version of 'video on demand' in the world in 1996. This is the technology that permits phone customers to use their telephone lines to order virtually any film over their television sets.[87] With Hong Kong's transfer to China in 1997, Hong Kong Telecom is in a position to capitalize upon the growth of Chinese commercial media, a prospect that has made Cable & Wireless the object of takeover rumors.[88] Deutsche Telekom and France Telecom are the telecommunication firms with the most media experience historically, having been leading cable broadcasting providers in their countries since well before convergence. Deutsche Telekom plans to digitize its German cable TV system, which serves half of Germany's 32 million TV households, thereby expanding the number of channels from thirty-one to over 150. In doing so, Deutsche Telekom will move to the front ranks of European media firms.[89]

THE INTERNET AS INFORMATION HIGHWAY

Much of the initial enthusiasm for interactive television dissipated with the emergence of the Internet as the global computer network by the mid-1990s. Likewise, the original efforts to establish proprietary computer networks – like America Online, Prodigy, and the Microsoft Network – were all revamped in 1995–6 to link them to the Internet. If consumers with computers and modems could have access to countless websites at no admission price, they were not going to be especially enthralled by interactive TV or expensive private computer services. The rise of the Internet was dramatic and caught almost everyone – including communication firms – by surprise. Developed with large subsidies by the U.S. Defense Department from the late1960s, the Internet links networks of computers that use the same protocols. By the early 1990s its use became common on U.S. campuses and it generated an alternative culture of cyberspace.[90] Commercialism was frowned upon and a 1995 advertising industry survey showed that two-thirds of U.S. adults opposed having advertising on the Internet.[91]

Two factors contributed to the burst in Internet activity. First, the establishment of the World Wide Web (WWW) as the easier-to-use multimedia portion of the Internet along with browser software by the mid-1990s were decisive in bringing the Internet closer to the mainstream. 'The WWW,' a 1995 report for investors stated, 'has almost single-handedly transformed the net from a members-only sandbox into a gigantic crossroads with strip malls, nouveau info-publishers, and EDI depots.'[92] The WWW offered access to seemingly limitless information and data and unprecedented possibilities for interactivity. 'For very little money, and with a modicum of computer skills, virtually anyone can create his or her own Web site,' the *New York Times* noted. 'Anyone with a modem is potentially a global pamphleteer.'[93]

Second, when the U.S. government turned its share of the Internet's computer 'backbone' over to seven firms including MCI and Sprint in 1995, 'an already compromised ban on commercial use of the Internet ended altogether.'[94] After the U.S. government withdrew its support, to the extent that any formal governance of the Internet existed, it was provided by the nonprofit 'Internet Society' of computer scientists who established protocols and standards for computers to employ if they wished to join the net.[95] With the passage of the 1996 Telecommunications Act, fundamental non-technical 'policy-making' for the Internet has been effectively turned over to the market, with whoever can generate the most profit in a position to set the terms for the development of cyberspace.

Although the Internet is inherently a global medium, its course is being determined primarily in the United States and a few other nations. Statistics vary widely, yet all studies show a 50 to 100 percent increase in Internet usage in the United States during 1996. One 1996 report concludes that 25 percent of U.S. households will have Internet access by the end of 1997 and that the figure will climb to around 45 percent by 2000.[96] Perhaps the extent of the boom is magnified in the culture since Internet access is so widespread among journalists, academics, executives, and others of the opinion-making classes.[97] Nonetheless, the pace of growth and change is numbing. 'We have a number of people who work [in the Internet] and I am always struck by the fact that they will say "what we thought 3 months ago has changed today",' a News Corporation executive stated in 1996.[98]

In popular parlance, the Internet has become the information highway. In 1995 the ITU gave the Internet 'a seven out of ten probability' that it would 'become a true GII.'[99] Nicholas Negroponte states that as entertainment fare moves to the Internet, 'the planet becomes a single media machine.'[100] Nonetheless, it will take a long time – perhaps decades – for the Internet to become the full-blown 'single media machine' in the United States, and longer than that everywhere else in the world. The Internet as 'media machine' would require dramatic (and by no means certain) improvements in both Internet software and technical hardware to accommodate such heavy usage. Most important, for digital communication networks to usurp traditional forms of communication would require an enormous increase in what is called bandwidth, meaning the speed at which digital data can flow between computers. Traditional telephone and cable wires can use digital compression techniques to provide considerable bandwidth, but to ensure that the Internet is the dominant medium will require massive investments in fiber optic wires. In a world lavishly and fully wired by fiber optic lines, data would move at the speed of light. The bandwidth problem becomes more acute as more people come online, because then there are more digital bits crowding the existing infrastructure, thereby slowing down the speed of transmission. It is one thing for a relatively small number of Internet users to use e-mail and download – often slowly – multimedia files; it is quite another thing for all of society to use the information highway for all forms of media, telephony, commerce, and the like. Bill Gates says low-cost interactive bandwidth 'is going to come very slowly,' with 'bandwidth bottlenecks' the 'biggest obstacle' that the Internet faces.[101] By some calculations, it would take investments in the hundreds of billions of dollars to provide 'broadband' capacity for the entire population of the United States, not to mention the world.

If media firms are not immediately affected by the rise of the Internet, such is not the case for computer manufacturers, consumer electronics firms, and computer software makers. Traditional personal computers were designed for stand-alone desktop usage, not networking. They tend to be expensive and difficult to use compared to other consumer appliances. The rise of the Internet has changed the way people use computers and computers are changing to accommodate the rise of networks. Stripped-down network computers or net PCs have been developed, as well as WebTV devices that permit browsing the Internet in a rudimentary fashion on one's television. In December 1996 the FCC approved technical standards for the development of digital television sets, making them compatible with personal computers and thereby opening the way for explicit battle between computer makers and television set manufacturers for control over the nature of the eventual home 'information/entertainment' appliance. This may be one of the main battlegrounds in the convergence of communication industries.[102]

The computer software industry, likewise, is in turmoil due to the Internet. Microsoft has dominated the PC software market, providing 80 percent of operating system software in the world.[103] As stand-alone computers are replaced by networked computers, Microsoft's traditional dominance is in jeopardy. Oracle, Sun Microsystems, and Netscape are attempting to keep the Internet free of Microsoft's dominance, thereby permitting themselves greater potential for profit. Microsoft has responded aggressively to the Internet challenge, seeking to convert the PC into the 'centre of home entertainment' run by Microsoft software.[104] Microsoft has worked assiduously to see that the technical specifications for the Internet are developed to suit Microsoft's domination of cyberspace.[105] 'I really shouldn't say this,' Bill Gates said about the importance of setting favorable industry standards, 'but in some ways it leads, in an individual product category, to a natural monopoly.'[106]

There are several distinct points at which software is necessary for the Internet to work, and Microsoft competes in all of them. (Indeed, Microsoft competes in Internet access and media content too, as we discuss below.) The most visible battle is for control of the potentially crucial 'browser' software, which is what people use to view and publish material on the WWW. Netscape seemingly had an insurmountable lead in 1995, but by 1997 Microsoft had used its immense resources and market power to catch up and arguably take the lead. The stakes are high, as the winner of this fight may have the power to establish standards for web usage and create the sort of monopoly Microsoft has had over stand-alone PC software. 'We are in the midst right now of the most titanic battle for market share we've ever seen on the planet,' said Internet venture capitalist John Doerr in 1996. 'Bigger than Coke and Pepsi.'[107]

The Internet is also forcing telecommunication firms to reevaluate their operations, especially with regard to the growing domain of providing Internet access. In the first half of the 1990s, providing Internet access was an industry of small independent firms which owned a computer and modems, and relied upon telephone lines.[108] With the WWW boom of 1995 and 1996, the telecommunication firms that controlled the infrastructure which handled the Internet traffic realized they were in the best position to dominate this market.[109] Moreover, this is a market where size is imperative, thus giving the global telecommunication alliances a distinct advantage over regional and national services. Even MFS, the most successful non-telecom access provider that provides high bandwidth access to business customers, merged with Worldcom, the fourth largest U.S. long-distance provider, in a $12.4 billion deal to remain competitive.[110] Telecommunication firms have extra incentive to move into the Internet access business because advances in software, computers, and bandwidth will make Internet telephony a more viable and far less expensive alternative to the traditional service.[111] Although it will be many years before the Internet could conceivably replace the telephone, one study estimates that the Internet will account for 16 percent of U.S. voice telephony by 2000.[112] Bill Gates, whose Microsoft company is responsible for the software that makes

Internet telephony viable, said in 1995, 'I don't know why you would want to be in the long distance business with that thing out there.'[113]

AT&T, Concert (BT-MCI), Sprint, Deutsche Telekom, and their global alliances all launched Internet access services in 1996 and have moved to the front of the industry.[114] The Baby Bells and other leading telecommunication firms are also offering Internet access.[115] 'This is the beginning of the end of the telephone as we know it,' an industry analyst commented in 1996. The telecommunication firms 'are committed to turning the phone line into an information utility conduit.'[116] MCI, for example, projected its Internet access revenues to increase from $100 million in 1996 to $2 billion by 2000.[117] Providing Internet service or access is becoming a major enterprise. In the United States it generated $1.4 billion in 1996 and this figure was expected to more than double or even triple in 1997; *The Economist* forecast that it could reach $30 billion by 2000.[118] Yet providing Internet service also remained an unprofitable business as the large players awaited a 'major shakeout' that would establish an oligopoly and yield profits.[119]

The telecom firms are not the only potential providers of Internet access. Indeed, this is where media firms begin to enter the picture as major actors. Cable broadcasting companies, in particular, are poised to use the cable modem to offer the finest bandwidth available, short of fiber optic wires. TCI, Comcast, and Cox Communications have invested several hundred million dollars in their @Home cable Internet access service.[120] Time Warner and TeleWest in the United Kingdom also launched Internet access service in 1996. The cable companies lack the telephone companies' links to the lucrative business market (as few offices are wired for cable television), but they are superbly positioned to develop and sell the Internet as an entertainment service to their existing cable customers.[121] John Doerr predicts that the cable modem 'will likely double the cash flow of the cable industry' in the United States by 2001.[122]

Internet access provision offers opportunities for media firms without cable properties as well. As current levels of competition have kept access rates depressed, access providers find that their profit comes from offering 'value-added' content to attract customers, and then to sell advertising to firms interested in reaching the access providers' clientele. The two largest non-telecom service providers, America Online and Microsoft, have in effect become Internet 'media' companies to distinguish their access service from the competition. And since they must rely upon telephone wires, unless they offer additional value it would be difficult to remain competitive access providers for very long. In this manner, traditional media firms find they have something of value for all Internet access providers, to the extent that they now need to provide

a distinct content package to attract customers. As one Viacom executive put it, media companies 'like us are in the ideal position to exploit
the Internet because you've got to find the hooks and reasons to bring
people in to a site and we are good at creating excitement and entertainment.'[123] Viacom has a joint venture with Sprint to provide its
media content exclusively to Sprint's Internet access service.[124] In
Britain, the BBC launched an Internet access service in 1997 in a joint
venture with a subsidiary of the Japanese Fujitsu Corporation. By purchasing access through the BBC, customers receive access to all of the
BBC's media fare in addition to Internet access.[125]

The other way media firms can capitalize on Internet access provision is through digital satellite broadcasting services. News Corporation
and DirecTV, for example, have already developed Internet access as a
service for business and consumers. News Corporation has a separate
company devoted to researching the interactive possibilities for its digital
satellite television ventures that will soon blanket the planet. Although
these satellite systems lack interactivity at present, News Corporation
and DirecTV anticipate that a rudimentary interactivity will be available within a few years. (Motorola and Teledesic, which is owned in part
by Bill Gates, are each launching low-orbiting non-broadcast satellite
systems that will offer wireless personal communication services and
Internet access to their customers by the early twenty-first century.
These services are intended to serve business customers in need of
mobile communication and are intended to complement, not replace,
wired broadband Internet access.) In the meantime, interactivity can be
provided through joint ventures with telephone companies, as News
Corporation has with MCI and BT and DirecTV has with AT&T. In
these arrangements, customers phone in their request for what they
want downloaded from the satellite to their computers or printers.[126] In
1997, News Corporation's British Sky Broadcasting will offer Internet
access to its customers, and the U.S. DirecTV launched its 'DirecPC'
Internet access service in 1996. At the very least, these digital services
will be able to hook up to computers and printers as well as TV sets, and
permit customers to browse the web and download data.[127] In 1997, for
example, an entire edition of *The Times* of London can be downloaded
via satellite to a computer in seven seconds.[128] News Corporation satellite ventures also plan to continually 'broadcast' the most popular 100
or 200 websites to its customers, as well as offering home banking and
home shopping. If these digital satellite systems prove attractive for
Internet access, it might provide their owners with the opportunity to
employ the profitable cross-selling and cross-promotional techniques
used across their other media properties.

THE INTERNET AS MASS MEDIUM

Although we can see the possible contours of a commercial Internet media system through the development of content-oriented Internet access services, the future of such enterprises is far from certain. One Internet commercial website producer calls the WWW 'ill-defined' as a medium. 'We are talking about a field where it's not even clear who should pay whom.'[129] Indeed, nobody is generating profit from Internet media content in 1997 and it is unclear if the medium will ever become especially lucrative for content providers. As long as that is the case, the Internet will hardly be in a position to overturn the dominance of television and traditional commercial media. One observer in 1996 compared the media firms to prospectors, noting that 'for media companies, the Internet today resembles a California gold-mining town in the 1840s, where the saloon and the general store prospered while the miners went broke.'[130] As one media executive put it, the Internet is 'not a business yet. . . . We lose money in significant amounts.'[131]

Yet all of the major media firms have significant stakes in Internet content, because none of them can afford to be outflanked by their competitors. Insofar as some evidence suggests that people watch 20 percent less television once they start using the Internet, media firms need to go online to maintain their audiences.[132] As Knight-Ridder's president of new media puts it 'We don't have a choice This is the future.'[133] 'Everyone is waiting for the killer application that will make this thing pay for itself,' one media executive said. 'We're in there getting the growth and the learning so that when the big revenue potential is there, we'll be ready.'[134] In 1996, however, two business analysts concluded that 'No "killer applications" have emerged for entertainment and social interaction via digital networks, apart possibly from the growth of e-mail and the equivalent of electronic chat lines over the Internet.'[135]

Most major U.S. newspapers and periodicals now produce online editions.[136] Likewise, all the major media firms have websites for their television, film, and music properties. By the end of 1996, over 400 television and 1,200 radio stations had established Internet websites.[137] The content is closely tied to their traditional fare, with some interactive applications.[138] Viacom's MTV, for example, has established a few online ventures to extend its dominance of music television to the Internet.[139]

But the media firms do not enjoy the same degree of leverage over Internet content as they have in their traditional oligopolistic media markets. The nature of the Internet is that anyone can produce a website – there is no physical scarcity as in broadcasting – and the costs are far lower than the costs of launching a traditional publication. For those who wish, websites can be produced at barely any expense. Yet regard-less of the technology, the highly open, egalitarian, and competitive nature of the Internet is being undermined by market forces even before it approaches being a mass medium. While anyone can start a website, it takes time and money to attract audiences and to compete with the expensive media firm websites that draw upon outside media resources.[140] Forrester Research estimated in 1996 that the average commercial website cost $2 million per year (and was losing $1 million annually).[141] Media firms can afford to be more patient than stand-alone commercial websites that have uncertain prospects. 'Brand build-ing is being done today,' one media executive said of his firm's Internet activities in 1996, 'for reward in 10 years' time.'[142] Media firm websites also enjoy ready-made audiences from traditional media that shift over to the WWW.[143] In addition, the media giants can promote their online activities incessantly to their traditional media audiences. 'The best thing to do,' the head of Warner Bros. Online stated in 1996, 'is to use your established media to build new media.'[144] Cox Interactive Media aggressively promotes the Cox websites through Cox's extensive news-paper, radio, and television properties. 'Without promotion, you're just a lemonade stand on the highway,' the head of Cox Interactive states. 'There is so much bad cholesterol clogging the arteries of the Internet now, it's very hard to establish a branded presence.'[145] Moreover, the largest media firms emerged by 1997 as the major source of capital for Internet content start-up ventures. These direct investments are meant to give the big media firms a better chance to anticipate and dominate any new developments in the rapidly changing realm of cyberspace.[146]

All of these factors combine to give the media websites and online activities tremendous leverage to negotiate deals with Internet access providers, digital satellite services, and Internet browser and crawler software services, assuring their websites and online activities of prom-inent attention when the Internet user turns on his or her computer. 'Internet technology,' the *New York Times* concluded in a piece on the corporate media dominance of cyberspace, 'has not rewritten the rules of competition for consumer media.' Size and market power still count. Indeed, the real question, the *Times* notes, is whether any commercial website can prosper unless it is part of or affiliated with a media giant.[147]

What seems probable, then, is a 'web within the web,' where the media firm websites and some other fortunate content producers are assured recognition and audiences, and less well-endowed websites drift off to the margins.[148] Already, most start-up commercial websites 'face a shake-out as deep-pocket rivals scoop up most of the limited pot of Web advertising dollars.'[149] The relevant media analogy for the Internet, then, is not that of broadcasting with its limited number of channels, but, rather, that of magazine or book publishing. Assuming no explicit state censorship, anyone can produce a publication, but the right to do so means little without distribution, resources, and publicity. At the same time, it is important to note that the Internet permits people who want it global access to the entirety of the 'marginal' online websites. This is a radical difference from the magazine or book publishing analogy, and one which suggests that the Internet should remain a vital tool for political organizing, even if its dominant trajectory is as a commercially driven entertainment vehicle.

The development of an elite commercial 'web within the web' may well be encouraged by the development of 'push' technology which permits some websites to be 'broadcast' constantly to personal computers, much as television signals are sent to home television sets.[150] By 1997 'push' technology galvanized hope for converting the Internet into a viable commercial mass medium. One U.S. investment research group forecast that 'push' technologies would account for $5.7 billion in Internet activity by 2000.[151] It may well reduce the importance of the browser software fight between Netscape and Microsoft, and shift the battle to the control and content of Internet 'webcasting.' *Business Week* concludes that 'push' technology provides 'a way out of the web maze.'[152]

The first-tier global media giants are using all of these methods to see themselves among those privileged Internet content providers who are being 'pushed' into people's attention and not getting left in obscurity. The giants are 'pushing' the types of sport and commercial news and entertainment that play well in broadcasting. CBS and Disney, for example, have developed major sports on-line services.[153] The General Electric–Microsoft joint venture MSNBC plans to join them. MSNBC is a key part of General Electric's strategy for global expansion.[154] 'MSNBC is not an appendage,' an NBC executive stated, 'This is the core business 10 years from now.'[155] Another NBC executive explains the rationale for the NBC–Microsoft joint venture. 'The whole idea was to establish a brand name early and be the leaders in a converged computer-television-video world.'[156] In 1997, MSNBC, CNN and News Corporation began 'pushing' 24-hour live video feeds over the Internet.[157] News Corporation also launched its *TV Guide Entertainment Network* website, to capitalize on the firm's widespread media properties. 'Existing trusted brands are the ones that are going to succeed,' stated the venture's director James Murdoch, Rupert's son and possible successor.[158] To complement its existing websites, in 1997 Time Warner established CityWeb, meant to replicate a TV network on the Internet with hundreds of local affiliates.[159] Disney launched an online kids' service in 1997 with basic and premium options and several different 'channels' targeting different youth demographic categories.[160] After failing in its effort to launch German digital television, Bertelsmann announced that it would concentrate on developing a widespread digital TV presence through the Internet.[161]

Most of the new major media players spawned by the Internet will come from the ranks of Internet access-providers, computer software-makers, or firms working closely with access-providers and software-makers. The leading software firms are growing at unrivaled double- and triple-digit annual rates, and they are uniquely positioned to coordinate content with distribution in the digital era. Oracle CEO Larry Ellison states that 'like petroleum a century ago, computer software has become the most important industry on earth . . . software is the fuel of the information age.'[162] Indeed, Oracle was the first software firm to move into interactive media, providing media server software for 'video-on-demand' and pay-per-view services in the early 1990s.[163] Netscape is not only owned in part by TCI and three other U.S. media firms (Hearst, Knight-Ridder, and Times Mirror); it also has working deals with most major media firms to help provide their content over the Internet.[164] 'Is there anybody Netscape Communications Corp. hasn't partnered with?', one trade publication asked after a flurry of media and communication firm alliances were announced in 1996.[165]

The striking new media firm wrought by the Internet is Microsoft. As an industry analyst puts it, 'They want to be a media company, an Internet access company, an Internet software company, and an Internet infrastructure company.'[166] Microsoft projects that the Internet will generate $13–15 billion in revenue by 2000, and its goal is to capture at least 10 percent of that market.[167] 'The Internet is like a gold rush,' Gates states, echoing many others. 'Fortunately, this is a gold rush where there really is gold.'[168] Microsoft has joint ventures with DreamWorks, DirecTV, AT&T, TCI, Nintendo, and MCI to mention but a few. 'Microsoft wants to get in bed with everybody,' a Wall Street analyst concludes.[169] Microsoft (1996 sales: $10.2 billion) brings unparalleled resources to its campaign to conquer the Internet. Not only has its annual growth of 30 percent made it one of the most profitable firms in the world by any measure, but it has an 'astounding' $7 billion in cash reserves, no debt, and less need for capital investment in plant and equipment to maintain its core business than most other firms.[170] According to the *Wall Street Journal*, Microsoft has funds 'about equal to the total of all the venture-capital pools available for technology investments.' Microsoft is deploying this money through industry-leading outlays in research and development ($2 billion in 1997) and, most striking, through an aggressive campaign of purchasing fledgling companies that have potentially viable commercial applications for software or for the

Internet. Between 1994 and 1996 Microsoft spent $1.5 billion to pur-chase or invest in forty-seven companies.[171] In April 1997 Microsoft paid $425 million for WebTV, the company that pioneered delivering Internet content over conventional television sets.

Developing Internet content is a central aspect of Microsoft's strategy for cyberspace, and its plans for the eventual converged world of PCs and televisions. In the long run, Microsoft believes, the ability to provide distinct and attractive content will be the factor that leads to success. This explains its MSNBC joint venture with NBC. In the late 1990s Microsoft is spending around $400 million on Internet content with little prospect for short-term return.[172]

But it is the Microsoft Network (MSN) that is at the center of Microsoft's strategy to become the 'premier force in online content.'[173] Microsoft provides customers with both Internet access and the MSN for the price other firms charge for Internet access alone; in this way the MSN can build up its customer base with relative ease.[174] MSN is a state-of-the-art website built on the advertising-supported model of commercial broadcasting, challenging traditional broadcasters for their viewers while preparing for the forthcoming market release of merged PC-TVs.[175] The Microsoft Network includes six television-style chan-nels designed to be of use to advertisers seeking specific target audiences. Microsoft has also developed premium web publications such as *Slate*, *Mungo Park*, and *Under Wire* in order to attract users and advertisers.[176] The MSN includes a series of localized Internet websites around the United States to provide local entertainment and sports news, and, of course, local advertising. Eventually the MSN may attempt to create electronic newspapers with classified advertisements and local news in major markets around the nation. 'It's not great news for newspapers,' a newspaper industry executive conceded.[177] 'The smart publishers are going to team up with Microsoft,' the president of the firm that owns the *Denver Post* and several other daily newspapers added.[178] Microsoft sees the MSN as generating a profit by 1999 and having annual revenues of between $1 and 2 billion by 2001.[179] As one industry analyst observes, 'This is another step along the way to having Bill Gates's face on the dollar bill.'[180]

The MSN's most direct competition comes from America Online (AOL) (1996 sales: $1.1 billion), which established itself as the dominant proprietary online service by 1994, and began to offer Internet access when the WWW wave became irresistible. With potentially less expens-ive Internet access alternatives, AOL is striving to become an online 'media powerhouse,' providing attractive entertainment content and interactive activities to lure customers.[181] As competition from the MSN and access providers drives down subscription prices, AOL is turning to advertising as the engine of revenue growth.[182] It has struck strategic alliances with numerous firms, including Microsoft, Netscape, TCI, and AT&T, parlaying its huge current base of subscribers for a niche in the evolving Internet content market.[183] AOL has established AOL Europe, a fifty-fifty joint venture with Bertelsmann, to duplicate its activities there.[184] It has a similar service in Japan in a joint venture with the mammoth Mitsui.[185]

The two primary means of generating revenue and profit for Internet content providers, as for commercial media, are through advertising and direct sales, or subscriptions. As the discussion of Microsoft and AOL indicated, it is advertising that is seen as the best hope for revenues in the short-term. Having Internet users pay content providers directly for access – or subscriptions – to websites has proven problematic; with all the free material, websites have discovered that 'users don't want to pay.'[186] Some publications like the *Wall Street Journal* and the *New York Times* are putting their websites on a subscription basis, but that option is generally available only to a select few media products which have built up brand names outside of the Internet.[187] One advertising industry executive stated that 'Most online ventures will not exist without advertising.'[188] As a Disney executive concluded in 1996, 'It's the direction the Web is going.'[189] The turn to advertising also enhances the power of the media giants to dominate the Internet; they can use their already existing ties to major advertisers to establish partnerships on the Web. In 1996, for example, Time Warner and Procter & Gamble established Parent Time in a fifty-fifty joint venture. This interactive website features material of interest to parents.[190] In 1996, a mere ten firms collected two-thirds of the $300 million spent to advertise on the Internet.[191]

Indeed, there is intense competition among Internet content providers and access services to attract advertising dollars. As a result, advertisers have the ability to play a large role in the development of editorial content, a situation often compared to the early days of U.S. commercial radio and television. Moreover, traditional distinct advertisements – as in broadcasting – are easily ignored in cyberspace, making them unattractive to marketers.[192] The Internet 'blurs the line' between advertisements and editorial content, *Advertising Age* observes.[193] 'The Web will be a lot more like a great retail experience,' the head of AT&T's Internet access service stated in 1995: 'If it's done well, you won't feel there's any tension between the consumerism and the entertainment.'[194] This blurred line has already caused concern about the integrity of Internet journalism and overall content, and it remains to be seen if this model will gain enough public acceptance to prove commercially viable.[195] The Internet presents other new problems for advertisers, not the least of which are how to determine the size of the audience and how to incorporate interactivity into the sales message.[196] It does not help advertisers that when websites request demographic data from their users to make it easier to sell advertising, it tends to sharply reduce the number of visitors to the site.[197] Advertisers hope that, as was the case with the commercialization of U.S. radio broadcasting, Internet users will gradually accept the commercialization of cyberspace and regard it as the natural state of affairs.

The turn to advertising gives web content providers great incentive to pattern their medium after commercial TV. 'Anything that can help the Web look, feel and act more like TV will provide a quantum leap for the advertising community in its acceptance of the Web,' one advertising executive observes, 'since TV video experience is the gold standard.'[198] Much of the ongoing technological innovation in the Internet has been directed to assist the Internet's development into a commercial medium like television, such as the 'push' technology mentioned above. 'It's the Internet for couch potatoes,' a Microsoft executive enthused.[199] The cable industry, in another example, opted for a modem that would make it far easier to receive content than to send messages.[200] By all accounts advertising will boom in the late 1990s, with industry forecasts ranging from $2.1 billion to as high as $5 billion by 2000.[201] But it will still be a minuscule portion of overall advertising spending, with negligible effect upon the advertising dollars flowing to traditional media for the foreseeable future.[202] And it remains to be seen if cyberspace will be as conducive to advertising as television has proved to be.

AOL CEO Steve Case states that active Internet usage will have to reach at least 30 percent of the population before subscription income becomes a prominent source of revenues.[203] It will be a gradual process; as *Business Week* observes, 'little by little, consumers are expected to become more accustomed to paying subscription fees – just as they moved from broadcast to cable TV.' One study estimates that 40 percent of Internet users will pay for services (beyond access fees) by 2000.[204] To promote the subscription principle, commercial websites are developing 'microtransactions,' meaning that access to the website will be free, but users will gain access to bonus material for a small price to be added to their monthly access charge. 'Bottom line on this is how do you get revenue for your content when most of the content is free?' asks the head of the Discovery Channel's website. 'I think the nickels and dimes will add up.'[205] One area where media firms are eager to employ the microtransactions concept is in selling music CDs, video CDs, and printed material directly to customers over the Internet in digital form for a small price. The customers would then print the digital data on their own disk in the case of music or film, and print it up on their printer for periodicals and books. Indeed, this is how many expect content producers to distribute their wares eventually, when the Internet's infrastructure is more developed.

An enormous barrier to the willingness of media firms to put content out over the Internet on a subscription or microtransaction basis is fear of what the media industry terms 'piracy.' The Internet is 'one gigantic copying machine,' a copyright lawyer states. 'All copyrighted works can now be digitised, and once on the Net, copying is effortless, costless, widespread, and immediate.'[206] The media and software industries are organizing nationally and globally to have digital copyright standards enacted to protect their control over digital content.[207] This is a complicated area, however, taking the law into uncharted territory. Many librarians, educators, and others oppose these media efforts, contending that the media giants want to extend copyright well beyond the traditional fair use standard, to the point of converting personal computers into 'vending machines.' The media giants' proposed copyright standards, one U.S. public interest group states, 'will make the World Wide Web look a lot less like a library and a lot more like a bookstore.'[208] In December 1996, the media giants won a major victory when 160 nations – urged on by the United States – agreed to extend copyright into cyberspace with the stated desire of encouraging the development of the Internet as a commercial medium.[209] This World Intellectual Property Organization agreement will require ratification by thirty nations to become a formal treaty, and the trade associations of the media industry have announced their plans to lobby aggressively in the United States and globally on behalf of the agreement.[210] Beyond copyright, the media giants are hard at work on encryption technology to make the copying of digital material more difficult, time-consuming, and expensive, if not impossible.

WHITHER THE INTERNET?

Although the future of the Internet as a mass medium remains unclear, two apparent sources of profitability – electronic commerce and providing private 'Intranets' to corporate clients – may go a long way toward determining the future use of cyberspace.[211] Through both of these mechanisms the Internet and digital communication networks are becoming even more tightly intertwined with the global market economy. A key barrier to electronic commerce – that is, the use of the web to buy and sell products and services – has been to 'bullet-proof the net' by creating a secure way to conduct credit card payments and other business. In view of the spectacular rewards, the software firms are racing to solve the problem.[212] By the late 1990s, a significant volume of banking, travel, even grocery shopping and much else will probably be conducted online.[213] Forecasts vary wildly, but one of the more conservative studies projects $6.6 billion in Internet commerce by 2000, with 20 percent of that for entertainment products.[214] The most explosive growth in Internet commerce should come from business-to-business sales, rather than business-to-consumer. Forrester Research projects this to be a $67 billion market by the year 2000, ten times the figure for consumer retailing through the Internet.[215] IBM's head of networking predicted in 1996 that once the security concerns eased, the value of transactions over the Internet would rise in just a few years to $1 trillion. By 2000, he stated, the Internet would be 'the world's largest, deepest, fastest, and most secure marketplace.'[216]

Intranets have been called the 'real' Internet phenomenon, providing an 'unstoppable market' for computer and software firms.[217] They are internal corporate networks linking employees worldwide and which follow Internet technology and permit users access to the Internet. But they are also fenced off from the Internet by 'firewalls,' which allow Intranet users to tap the WWW but prevent others from getting into the corporate network. This allows for considerably more security and speed. This is also, along with electronic commerce, where the profit lies for computer and software firms. From non-existence in 1994, 22 percent of the 1,000 largest U.S. firms had Intranets by the end of 1995, and 89 percent of the 500 largest U.S. firms were expected to install Intranets by 1998. Annual Intranet software sales are projected to increase from $400 million in 1996 to as much as $12 billion by 2000, dwarfing the sales projections for other types of Internet software by a factor of six.[218] 'That's where the money is,' Netscape's CEO states.[219] And through the development of Intranets, the market may have shown the way to a commercially viable Internet.

By the middle of 1996 the Internet teetered under the strain of its rapid growth; there was simply not enough bandwidth to accommodate the rapid increase in users. 'The World Wide Web,' the *Financial Times* reported, 'is turning into the World Wide Wait.'[220] A 1996 memo by U.S. government scientists warned that the Internet was in 'a disastrous state,' suffering from gridlock that might even lead to an outright blackout.[221] In October 1996 thirty-four U.S. universities announced plans for the formation of Internet II – in effect a massive Intranet – to reproduce the academic-centered activities and functions the Internet had been doing and planning to do prior to commercialization, and at ten times the speed of the existing Web.[222] The notion of 'moving the non-commercial traffic onto a separate network' was well received by some in the business community. Then 'the existing infrastructure could be turned over to purely commercial users and usage-based pricing plans introduced more easily.'[223]

Indeed, the 'anarchic' system of governance carried over from the Internet's early days appeared to be a hindrance to the commercial exploitation of the Internet. 'The framework that people cooperated in before is collapsing, and a new framework has yet to emerge,' one executive stated.[224] 'If this isn't addressed,' a Cisco Systems executive stated, 'the Internet is going to become the CB radio of the '90s.'[225] 'Is there a long-term future for the Internet unless it falls into the hands of a small group of firms?' one business analyst asked. His answer was 'Probably not.'[226] By the end of 1996, global telecommunication and software groups had coalesced to establish the Internet Law and Policy Forum (ILPF) to establish policies making the Web commercially viable.[227] Whether the ILPF succeeds or fails, the Internet has reached an impasse in its development. Acknowledging the problems, the Internet Society ceded some of its control in October 1996 to an international *ad hoc* committee representing telecommunication and media interests.[228]

Many industry figures believe that the Internet should be superseded by huge private 'Intranets' run by the global telecommunication alliances.[229] By the end of 1996 the rudiments of a purely commercial Internet infrastructure began to emerge. The telecommunication access providers like Concert and Sprint planned to offer high-speed 'limo service' for Internet users on their restricted networks.[230] These giant telecommunication firms and alliances are incorporating the Internet into their global full service communication networks that strive initially 'to provide multinational corporations with a single compatible worldwide system for voice and data.'[231] For non-business customers, these private Internet/Intranets would offer superior bandwidth as well as access to websites and services that would be unavailable to users of the broader Internet, or competitor private services.[232] Following this route, there will be a two-tiered or multi-tiered Internet industry with high-speed bandwidth options for those willing to pay, a low-speed clunker Internet for others, and nothing at all for the rest. The U.K. Cable & Wireless–Nynex 1996 merger suggests that cable broadcasting, and therefore media, may be incorporated into these global 'one-stop shopping' communication services, especially as they are directed at the consumer market.[233] 'The Internet will evolve along a similar path as broadcasting,' one of Wall Street's leading media analysts said in 1996. 'By the end of the decade four private data broadcasters will emerge that will bundle and package branded content on a global basis to a broad array of personal computers.'[234]

In keeping with the neoliberal political climate discussed at the beginning of this chapter and in Chapter 1, what little debate there is over the fate of the Internet tends to be predicated upon the premise of the superiority of the 'free market' as a regulatory mechanism. Any social problems not addressed by the 'magic of the market' will be resolved by the near-mystical powers of digital technology. The role of the political sphere, by this reasoning, is to assist the economy's need for 'efficiency' and 'competitiveness'; put more bluntly, the citizenry should sacrifice on behalf of those that own and control the economy, those who stand to profit from cyberspace.[235] It is ironic that the very existence of the Internet is due to massive government (taxpayer) subsidies long before it showed any commercial potential in the 'free market.' This is also the case to some extent with satellite communication and digital technology writ large. It is because of these state subsidies that U.S. firms have been in a position to dominate global markets. In contemporary U.S. discussions concerning the Internet, the role of the state in its development and the derivative right of the public to have a direct say in the Internet's future have dropped out of sight. In the new mythology the Internet is the result of daring entrepreneurs and eccentric tinkerers working in their garages. By this reasoning, the public has no rights in cyberspace except those that it can exercise as capitalists or as consumers. The Internet's future should be determined solely on the basis of what can generate the most profits.[236]

If the Internet develops along these lines, it will very likely enhance communication inequality between as well as within nations. In 1996, 64 percent of the Internet's host computers were in the United States and less than 6 percent were in Eastern Europe, Asia, Africa, the Middle East, and Latin America.[237] One 1996 study showed that 73.4 percent of Web users were in the United States and less than 4 percent were from the Third World.[238] 'The map of the world has been unsentimentally redrawn by computers,' the *Financial Times* observes. 'On that map, North America and Europe are hot zones with high per capita computer ownership, while the developing nations tend to be cold.'[239] The entire Internet system is predicated upon the use of English and, while that is changing, it is changing slowly.[240] And some expect that it will never change. Thanks to the fact that English is the global computer language, *The Economist* observes, 'The demand to learn English may be only in its infancy.'[241] In a geopolitical sense, two leading U.S. military and defense strategists assert that U.S. dominance of the Internet and all realms of global media and communication ensure that it is the twenty-first century, not the twentieth, that 'will turn out to be the period of America's greatest preeminence.' Among the attributes of this 'soft power,' they assert, is that it virtually requires nations to adopt the sort of 'free markets' that the U.S. firms tend to dominate.[242] Japan has been slow to adapt to the Internet, to some extent due to the prevalence of

English, but it is striving to establish itself as the center of Asia's emerging Internet system.[243]

The less-developed nations are gaining some ground relative to the United States – it would difficult to move in any other direction – but left to the market it is difficult to see Internet access becoming very widespread. In the less-developed countries, the strategy of Internet access providers 'is to go for business customers first and then, in theory, add consumers later.'[244] Latin America anticipates a boom in Internet use in the late 1990s, almost entirely among the upper and upper-middle classes; as one former AT&T Latin American executive notes, the commercially driven Internet 'wires marketers' to the 'Latin American elite.'[245] Indeed, when a Peruvian cooperative sought to bring inexpensive Internet access to the peasantry, the recently privatized national telephone company refused to provide the necessary equipment. The telephone company had plans to introduce its own commercial Internet access service.[246]

CONCLUSION: THE GLOBAL COMMUNICATION OLIGOPOLY

By the logic of the market and convergence, we should expect that the global media oligopoly will gradually evolve into a far broader global communication oligopoly over the next several decades. The media giants will link with the handful of telecommunication 'global gangs,' as the MCI president put it, and they will all strike deals with the leading computer firms. As one writer puts it, the goal of all the 'info-communication' firms is 'to ensure they are among what will end up being a handful of communication monoliths controlling both product and distribution networks in the future. . . . The basic aim of future M&A [mergers and acquisitions] is to control the transmission of three basic telecommunication products – voice, data and video.'[247] In short, the Internet and digital communication networks will not undermine the development of a global communication oligopoly; rather, they will be an integral aspect of it. As a market-driven system, it will be built to satisfy the needs of businesses and affluent consumers, as this is where the largest and easiest profits are to be found. The global computer industry, for example, made over 90 percent of its $225 billion in annual sales in 1995 to corporate customers.[248]

In the late 1990s it is evident how little the Internet influences the operations of the global media system. Rupert Murdoch, whose News Corporation has been perhaps the most aggressive of the media giants to explore the possibilities of cyberspace, states that establishing an information highway 'is going to take longer than people think.' He projects that it will take until at least 2010 or 2015 for a broadband network to reach fruition in the United States and Western Europe, and until the middle of the twenty-first century for it to begin to dominate elsewhere.[249] This is the clear consensus of opinion across the media and communications industries, and it explains the enormous investments in terrestrial broadcasting and digital satellite broadcasting that would be highly dubious if the broadband information highway was imminent. As Universal president Frank Biondi put it in 1996, media firms 'don't even think of the Internet as competition.'[250]

Perhaps the most striking change in the 1990s is how quickly the euphoria of those who saw the Internet as providing a qualitatively different and egalitarian type of journalism, politics, media, and culture has faded. The indications are that the substantive *content* of this commercial media in the Internet or any subsequent digital communication system will look much like what exists in the late 1990s. Frank Beacham, who enthused about the Internet as a public sphere outside of corporate or governmental control in early 1995, lamented one year later that the Internet was shifting 'from being a participatory medium that serves the interests of the public to being a broadcast medium where corporations deliver consumer-oriented information. Interactivity would be reduced to little more than sales transactions and email.'[251] Even *Fortune* magazine shows some regret about the Internet's present course. 'It's a far, far cry from the cherished vision of the Internet as a public network involving the free exchange of ideas.[252] Yet in this conclusion we must return to the chapter's point of departure: it is still unclear how the Internet will develop. More important, it is difficult to predict how people will respond to its continued commercial development. In this chapter we have assumed the rule of the market with a quiescent citizenry. Were control of cyberspace and communication to become the subject of political debate and struggle, all bets would be off concerning the Internet's future. In the end, this is a subject to be determined by politics, not technology.

5
MEDIA GLOBALIZATION (1): THE U.S. EXPERIENCE AND INFLUENCE

The consequences of the ongoing globalization of the media are difficult to disentangle from the effects of the parallel and closely related economic and technological changes in national and global economies. These are intertwined and reinforcing. What is more, their effects vary by place and over time, often taking many decades to fully work themselves out. Because the national and class stakes involved in these developments are high, this is an area of sharp controversy, with the generous use of emotion-laden words and phrases like freedom, free choice, diversity, democratization, and cultural imperialism.

Our view is that the most important effect of media globalization has been the spread and increasing and cumulating domination of a commercialized media, with consequences that flow from its nature and imperatives. With commercialization in place, closer integration into the global economy, and greater media, advertiser, and general corporate penetration readily follow. The short-term effects of media globalization and commercialization, however, have sometimes been benign or positive, and from some perspectives there have been and are likely to be future net benefits. In other cases, and as we see the broad sweep, the changes have been damaging and pose longer-term threats to democratic polities. The judgments here will rest in part on an appraisal of observable fact, in part on values, and in part on extrapolations of current trends into the future.

As noted in the Introduction, we give great weight to the effect of media developments on the quality of the public sphere, the places and forums where community issues are debated, and where facts and analyses pertinent to these issues are presented and discussed. Fundamental economic analysis of media processes suggests that commercialization of the media will be detrimental to the public sphere – public sphere programs do not sell well, and the positive benefits to society of a well-developed public sphere (an informed citizenry, a better working democratic order, possibly even greater social stability) are 'externalities' to private owners, who cannot capture revenue from these social benefits and therefore do not take them into account in programming.[1] This is a case of 'market failure,' with potentially seriously damaging social and political consequences. Similarly, if violence and sex sell well, they will be heavily employed in programming under competitive market conditions even if *their* consequences may be socially detrimental. Producing these negative externalities pays. Violence and sex also travel well, overcoming linguistic and cultural barriers by the power of their visuals in getting their basic messages across. They therefore tend to bulk large in international media transfers. As they enter this trade, the immediate impact of their messages and implicit values is far less important than their contribution to the process of consolidation of the commercial model.

In this chapter we examine, first, the long history and effects of having almost exclusively corporate-dominated, advertising-supported media in the United States. Second, we also examine some of the implications of the U.S. commercial model for the rest of the world as commercial media globalization increases in scope and power.

THE UNITED STATES AS EVOLUTIONARY MODEL

For many decades the United States has been the dominant world power and leading proponent and organizer of a neoliberal global order. Among the great powers, also, the United States is the country in which market domination of the media has been most extensive and complete. The new dynamics of the neoliberal world and globalizing media have been moving countries more or less rapidly into the commercial nexus. It is our belief that the United States therefore displays the model of a commercial media toward which other countries are moving and will continue to move. In countries that have a strong and respected public broadcasting tradition, powerful labor unions, and other democratic and grass roots forces, and resistant cultures, the pace may be slow and a complete transformation never realized. But virtually all countries are moving discernibly toward the U.S. model, and as we have noted the process is self-reinforcing: the global media, moving across borders, building alliances with local firms, constitute a formidable political force, and the growing commercial sectors cut into the market share of the public sectors, weakening their claims to public money, causing them to shrink or self-commercialize to maintain audiences, and they are under political and ideological attack in an increasingly market-dominated environment.

The background

The United States has a long commercial tradition in its print media, which have also gone through a prolonged and steady process of centralization. In the newspaper business, although there are thousands of papers, the combination of economies of scale and the dynamics of the advertising market have steadily reduced numbers in local markets,[2] so that by the 1990s there was only a single paper in 98 percent of the U.S. cities and towns that had any local newspaper at all.[3] Furthermore, large numbers of the local papers have become constituents of chain systems; the percentage of newspapers in chains increased from 20 to 80 percent between 1945 and 1989. Concentration has steadily increased in the print media across the board – in Bagdikian's measure, of the number of firms accounting for 50 percent or more of sectoral revenue, between 1983 and 1992 the number of magazine publishers accounting for a majority of revenue fell from twenty to two, the number of newspaper publishers went from twenty to eleven; and while there are more than 3,000 publishers of books, five of them account for half or more of industry revenue.[4]

There are three national newspapers in the United States – the *New York Times*, the *Wall Street Journal*, and *U.S.A Today* – and several others that aspire to that role – for example, the *Washington Post* and *Los Angeles Times* – which do compete with one another, and, along with the news agencies and government, set the agenda for the rest of the press and for broadcasters as well. This competition, and the professional standards that have evolved in the newspaper business over the years, has often yielded impressive news results; but these are elite institutions closely linked to the corporate community and government, and they tend to limit debate and investigative zeal within acceptable elite parameters.[5]

The U.S. commercial tradition was quickly extended to broadcasting in the 1920s and thereafter under a regime of weak regulation. Broadcasting arose first as a derivative of radio equipment manufacture, the producers needing regular broadcasts to stimulate radio sales. Initially, broadcasting was hailed for its potential contributions to education, religion, children's enlightenment, and high culture, and the idea that it would be a vehicle for advertising was considered outrageous. Then Secretary of Commerce (later President) Herbert Hoover stated in 1922 that 'It is inconceivable that we should allow so great a possibility for service to be drowned in advertising chatter.'[6] Even after commercial radio networks had achieved dominance, at the time of the passage of the Communications Act of 1934, it was accepted by the broadcasters themselves that their grant of rights to use public air channels was in exchange for their serving 'the public convenience, interest and necessity.' In the 1934 hearings, the National Association of Broadcasters acknowledged that it is the 'manifest duty' of the newly established regulator, the Federal Communications Commission (FCC), to assure an 'adequate public service,' which 'necessarily includes broadcasting of a considerable proportion of programs devoted to education, religion, labor, agricultural and similar activities concerned with human betterment.'[7]

In its 1946 report, *Public Service Responsibilities of Broadcast Licensees*, the FCC contended that 'sustaining programs' (i.e. those put on at the station's expense, unsupported by advertising) are the 'balance wheel' whereby 'the imbalance of a station's or network's program structure, which might otherwise result from commercial decisions concerning program structure, can be redressed.'[8] CBS's Frank Stanton is quoted to the same effect. The report referred to the sustaining programs as an 'irreplaceable' part of broadcasting, and public service performance in the interest of 'all substantial groups among the hearing public' as a fundamental standard and test in approving and renewing licenses.[9]

But as the commercial system matured, it became possible to sell time to advertisers for all hours of the day, and the price at which time could be sold depended on 'ratings,' which measure the audience size (and from 1970, its 'demographics,' which measure the income and spending potential of components of the audience). As time became salable and its price rose, the pressure for high ratings and good demographics increased; as the historian of U.S. television, Erik Barnouw, noted, 'The preemption of the schedule for commercial ends has put lethal pressure on other values and interests.'[10] A primary effect was the steady trend away from 'controversial' and modestly rated public service programs and toward entertainment. Richard Bunce found that by 1970, public affairs coverage had fallen to 2 percent of programming time, and the entire spectrum of public interest programming was far below that provided by public broadcasting systems in Canada, Great Britain, and elsewhere in the West.[11]

The decline in public service performance of the U.S. commercial broadcasters paralleled a steady increase in broadcasting station and network profitability. By 1970, the profits of major station owners was in the range of 30 to 50 percent of revenues, and much more on invested capital. Bunce estimated that for the period 1960–1972, the ratio of pretax income to depreciated tangible investments for the broadcast networks never fell below 50 percent a year.[12] These staggering profits did not alleviate broadcaster pressure for additional profits, because the workings of the market cause profits to be capitalized into higher stock values, which become the basis of calculation of rates of return for both old and new owners.

Growing advertiser hegemony

The force of competition and stress on the rate of return on capital, which comes to prevail in a free market, compels media firms to focus with increasing intensity on enlarging audience size and improving its 'quality,' as these will determine advertising rates. A recent audience decline for NBC's morning *Today Show*, moving it a full rating point behind ABC's *Good Morning America*, was the basis of a $280,000-a-day advertising income differential between the shows. Managements that fail to respond to market opportunities of this magnitude will be under pressure from owners and may be ousted by internal processes or takeovers. There is no room for soft-headed managers in a mature system, and in the United States the four top networks are now controlled by market-driven corporate owners. Independents, radio stations and networks, and cable systems are also commercial entities with the same priorities as the TV networks, and, with fewer resources and smaller market shares, they are at least as bottom-line-oriented as their larger rivals.

As competition has grown, with cable, VCRs, and direct satellite transmission encroaching on the traditional broadcasters, there has also been a steady increase in the influence of advertisers on TV programming (and on newspapers and magazines as well). Advertisers have been able to exact more and more 'editorial support' beyond the simple advertisement – major TV networks offer their 'stars' to sell commercials and appear at advertiser gatherings; they enter into joint promotional arrangements with advertisers, each pushing the other's offerings; they show 'infomercials' produced entirely by or for advertisers and displaying their products; and they co-produce programs with advertisers and gear others to advertiser requests and needs. 'Product placement,' in which branded products are displayed on the screen during regular shows, has become widespread in both TV and movies.[13]

As advertisers are the ultimate program funders, their demands for a suitable program environment for selling goods takes increasing effect under competitive conditions. A supportive environment does not challenge materialistic values and is not set in grim circumstances; it shows people who spend and gain status by acquisition and consumption, displayed in surroundings of wealth. In addition to favoring consumption as the solution to human happiness, advertisers do not want programs critical of or threatening to business or whose unconventional ideas disturb large constituencies.[14] Such requirements influence programming in broad structure and detail; plots regularly honor the family-oriented and denigrate the non- and anti-acquisitive looking to community solutions; programs are created that accommodate advertising easily (ABC's *Home Improvement* is beautifully suited to promoting home products); and stories are shaped in accordance with advertiser demands.[15] News programs have long been reoriented toward dramatic action, personalities, and other audience-attracting material.[16]

The orientation and shaping of both magazines and newspapers is increasingly dominated by the desire to capture advertising. Magazines are brought into existence on the basis of expected advertising revenue, and the planned format, tone, and targeted audience is often worked out in consultation with potential advertisers. For example, at the cost of $10 million, Time Warner 'is now showing advertisers a prototype for *Coastal Living*,' a magazine 'aimed at people who live on the coast as well as people who aspire to live there,' and 'with a median household income of $60,000.' Advertisers are offered a guaranteed rate base of 350,000, with a price of $16,000 for a full-page color advertisement.[17] Advertisers must be won and then kept, along with a suitable audience. The publisher of the magazine *Martha Stewart Living*, Shelley Waln, says that 'We package our assets for advertisers.'[18]

Major U.S. newspapers now all have lifestyle or fashion sections and frequent supplements on homes, technology, computers, men's clothes, and real estate, which blend together 'news' articles geared to the topic and advertisements for clothing, computers, and home furnishings. For example, the leading U.S. paper, the *New York Times*, ran a six-page article on March 28, 1993, on the big names (and advertisers) in fashion – Calvin Klein, Ralph Lauren, Donna Karan, Bill Blass, etc. – featured with photos and sample product lines, and badly eroding the distinction between editorial and advertisements.[19] In that same year, the *New York Times* sent out a solicitation letter to advertisers which read as follows:

> In an effort to educate the public and influence Washington decision-makers, The New York Times has planned a series of three special advertorials [ads with editorial content] presenting the positive economic and social benefits of NAFTA [North American Free Trade Agreement]. . . . I hope that some of your clients will actively participate in our rally for this important cause.

The compromising character of the solicitation is clear, but it is also evident that the ability to obtain such advertisements may well depend on (and influence) editorial positions taken.

Advertisements themselves are an increasingly important and even dominant cultural force in the United States. The money and creative talent expended on advertising is enormous. By 1972, members of the Screen Actors Guild 'were earning more from commercials than from theatrical films and television films *combined*.'[20] Commercials, says one advertising executive, are 'the focal point of creative effort.'[21] Expenditures on advertisements in the United States exceed $160 billion a year, with those on broadcasting alone exceeding $36 billion, and commercial messages extend their reach slowly but surely to every aspect of society, tying the sale of goods to every icon with whom a favorable association can be established. It is now an honor (as well as remunerative) to be shown peddling a commodity, and celebrities jump at the opportunity. Hard-pressed communities allow them on school buses, in school lavatories, and in advertisement-based news broadcasts in schoolrooms. The firm Cover Concepts Marketing Services has even introduced advertising into day-care centers and preschools; it 'has strung together a network of more than 22,000 day-care centers that pass along product samples, coupons and other promotions to toddlers and their parents.'[22] Olympic games and other sporting events are saturated with corporate logos and claims. 'Place-based' advertising now reaches from floor tiles to skywriting, from shopping bags to airsickness bags on planes.[23]

As Joseph Turow points out, the huge resources of advertisers and their dominance as funders 'gives them the power over the very structure of the media system' – they 'determine whether a public medium will survive' – and, in an advanced advertising environment like that of the United States, they are able 'to maximize the entire system's potential for selling.'[24] As values are built into media formats, advertisers' effective control of the formats that will prosper gives them command over the values that will be stressed.[25] Turow contends that this massive selling effort, and consequent dominance of advertiser interests under conditions of advanced technology, makes it possible for advertisers and the media to segregate people by income class, allowing concentrated service to the affluent and in the process creating 'the electronic equivalent of gated communities.'[26] Instead of unifying, the advertising regime divides.

In the United States, federal spending on the arts and humanities has been reduced to about $193 million a year, or under one-half of 1 percent of the sums spent on advertising in broadcasting. Public broadcasting is subsidized to the amount of $260 million per year. Despite their small size, public arts and broadcasting funding are both under constant conservative attack. In a market and entertainment culture, these outlays are often regarded as unnecessary or a threat, and tend to be marginalized. The values pushed by the enormous sums spent on advertising – the 'focal point of creative effort' and underwriter of TV programs – are the importance of material acquisition and consumption, not moral behavior, human solidarity, community, or aesthetic values. Indeed, much contemporary U.S. social analysis points to the striking and continuing long-term decline in civic involvement and social participation by large segments of the population. Although the commercial media hardly bear sole responsibility for this, they play a definite role.[27]

We mentioned in Chapter 2 that the huge global media conglomerates like Disney, Time Warner, and Viacom focus on cross-promotion and cross-selling as primary means of 'creating value.' This is closely linked to advertising at each level of the conglomerate operation. A book is published at one level; a movie based on the book is made at another level; toys and videos based on the movie are made at another level; and all of these commodities are promoted and sold at still other levels (magazines, video stores, theme parks). The flow of cultural artifacts from these pop cultural giants becomes of increasing importance in the general cultural environment.

The weakening public sphere

The maturing of commercial broadcasting not only substitutes entertainment for public service; the U.S. experience suggests that maturation brings with it a decline in variety of viewpoints and increased protection of establishment interests. A telling illustration is the handling of the Vietnam War, where, as Erik Barnouw notes:

> The Vietnam escalation of 1965–67 found commercial network television hewing fairly steadily to the administration line. Newscasts often seemed to be pipelines for government rationales and declarations. . . . Though a groundswell of opposition to the war was building at home and throughout much of the world, network television seemed at pains to insulate viewers from its impact. . . . Much sponsored entertainment was jingoistic.

The U.S. networks not only made none of the seriously critical documentaries on the war, during the early war years they barred access to outside documentaries. As Barnouw points out, 'this policy constituted *de facto* national censorship, though privately operated.'[28]

But while the mass protest against the war rarely found any outlets in commercial TV, it 'began to find occasional expression in NET [National Educational Television, a forerunner of PBS] programming in such series as *Black Journal, NET Journal, The Creative Person*, and – explosively – in the film *Inside North Vietnam*, a British documentarist's report on his 1967 visit to "the enemy".' This pattern helps to explain why Presidents Johnson and Nixon fought to rein in public broadcasting, with Nixon quite openly seeking to force it to deemphasize public affairs. The commercial systems did this naturally.

During the Gulf War of 1990–91, the U.S. commercial broadcasters, now more advertising-driven and centralized than ever before, were even more closely geared to government propaganda service. They protested only mildly at a system of gross censorship, gullibly accepted propaganda claims that were false, failed to explore serious issues essential to public understanding, and ultimately took on the role of propaganda chorus helping to sell the war. The commercial media were distressed by the fact that war scenes and reports were not providing a suitable advertising environment, and they tried to manufacture one with their enthusiasm and portrayal of the war as an exciting, aesthetically and technically attractive game.[29]

In-depth news presentations on U.S. TV reached their pinnacle with Edward R. Murrow's *See It Now* programs in the mid-1950s. There was a resurgence of news documentaries in the early 1960s in the wake of quiz show scandals in 1959, but subsequently the decline continued, despite occasional notable productions. Sponsors do not like controversy and depth – in either entertainment or non-fiction. Thus, in the years when environmental issues first became of national concern, NBC dropped the environmental series *In Which We Live* for want of sponsorship, although the major companies were all busily promoting commercials and other materials on the environment. Their materials, however, reassured, and did not explore the issue in depth or with any balance, as the NBC series did. A 1989 Audubon Society documentary on *Ancient Forests: Rage over Trees*, aired on Turner Broadcasting, had its advertisements withdrawn when logging interests protested. In that same year, an NBC docudrama on *Roe vs. Wade* ran without sponsors, and a program with Barbara Walters, also on the abortion issue, was unable to obtain sponsors, who openly rejected participation for fear of controversy.

Fear of 'fairness doctrine' requirements of balance also made serious programs that took a stand on an issue a threat to broadcasters; and watering them down to obviate challenges for lack of balance made them lifeless. Documentaries that appealed to sponsors were about travel, dining, dogs, flower shows, lifestyles of the rich, and celebrities past and present. In short, under the system of commercial sponsorship, the documentary was reduced to 'a small and largely neutralized fragment of network television, one that can scarcely rival the formative influence of "entertainment" and "commercials".' The form survived mainly in an aborted quasi-entertainment variant called 'pop doc,' specializing in brief vignettes, with a focus on individual villains, pursued by superstar entertainers, and settling 'for relatively superficial triumphs.'[30] 'Infotainment' has also come to the fore, with entertainers titillating audiences with 'information' about other entertainers.

Other public affairs programs with lower ratings, like discussion panels, were placed in weekend ghetto slots, and consisted mainly of unthreatening questions fed to guest officials. In the years before the

Reagan era *de facto* termination of 'public service' requirements, that obligation was met largely by public service announcements cleared through the Advertising Council, which provided a further means for the broadcasters to establish a record of public service without addressing any serious issue.

Children's programming and the centrality of violence

As with public affairs, the U.S. commercial system eventually ghettoized children's programming, with Saturday and Sunday morning fare that was largely cartoon entertainment with heavy doses of commercials. Between 1955 and 1970, weekday programming for children on network-affiliated TV stations in New York City fell from 33 to 5 hours. Only on Saturday did the children continue to get substantial time, but not with any new or non-entertainment programs.[31]

The failure of commercial TV in children's programming was so severe that a number of citizens' groups were formed during the 1960s to fight the commercial system. One, Action for Children's Television (ACT), formed in 1968, lodged a protest with the FCC in 1970 demanding reform. The FCC response in the 1970s was to introduce guidelines restricting children's advertising, plus encouragement of voluntary codes by the broadcasters. A major FCC study of children's TV published in 1979 concluded that children are 'drastically underserved.' And in that same year, a report on behalf of the advertising industry acknowledged that 'The Broadcasting Code and other efforts at industry standards are recognized as being ineffective.' Nevertheless, in 1983, the Reagan era FCC, in a further response to the ACT petition, declared that the broadcasters had *no* responsibility to children.

The situation deteriorated after 1983. According to Dale Kunkel, 'When "Captain Kangaroo" was removed from its Monday-through-Friday time slot in 1983 after 28 years on television, not a single regularly scheduled weekday children's program remained on any of the three commercial networks.'[32] Stephen Kline pointed out that 'Deregulation of television clearly resulted in a new promotional infrastructure more narrowly and purposively focused on promoting toys and other merchandise.' Toy manufacturers virtually took over children's TV on commercial stations, with a huge growth of 'program-length commercials' funded by toy manufacturers and prepared under their direction, with stories organized to feature the toys. The 'entertainment' was subordinated to merchandising; 'a story concept had to include a host of characters complete with various accoutrements and technologies, all of which would become saleable products.'[33]

A Children's Television Act of 1990 placed limits on advertising time and proclaimed that broadcasters had a duty to meet children's 'educational and informational needs,' but it failed to outlaw product-based programs, let alone straight advertising, and it left program standards vague. A regulatory requirement of a minimum of three hours per week of educational and informational programming for children was established, but definitions and meaningful time requirements were not specified. Toy-based programming, substantial advertising, and animated cartoons remain dominant; commercial imperatives continue to shape the secular trend of children's TV.

Children's programming of substance has long been left to public broadcasting, but there is no national policy or regular funding of children's programs even there. The development of cable specialty channels for children has altered the picture somewhat, but with minor exceptions their best offerings are reruns of older programs developed on public broadcasting; at worst, they provide standard commercial fare. And they are available only at a price, on cable. The poor performance of U.S. schoolchildren is often noted in the mass media, and is sometimes attributed in part to the underfunding of schools, but the foregone potential of TV broadcasting is never mentioned.

Although TV violence does build audiences, its huge presence is not based on its popularity at home, but rather on the fact that its dramatic ingredients are 'most suitable for aggressive international promotion.'[34] Under the pressure of commercial imperatives it therefore assumes a very important place on the TV screen. Professor George Gerbner and his associates have since 1967 compiled an annual television program Violence Profile and Violence Index. They have found that on average seven out of ten primetime programs use violence, and the rate of violent acts runs at between five and six per hour. Half of primetime dramatic characters engage in violence and about 10 percent kill, as they have done since 1967. Children's weekend programming 'remains saturated with violence,' with more than twenty-five acts of violence per hour, as it has done for many years.[35]

The degradation and plutocratization of politics

It is easy to exaggerate the quality of political life in the pre-TV era, but the maturing of commercial TV in the United States has had several significant negative effects on the political process. First, TV time in the United States must be purchased from the commercial broadcasters. This has made the quest for political office extremely expensive, as this powerful communications instrument has become a campaign imperative. Thomas Patterson notes that 'it is no coincidence that the 1964 presidential campaign was both the first to use advertisements heavily and the first in which overall campaign spending skyrocketed.'[36] This has reduced the democratic character of U.S. political life by further limiting the quest and attainment of office to the wealthy and those willing to serve the wealthy. Extending the franchise increased democratization in the United States; the escalating requirements of electoral finance in the regime of commercial broadcasting has reversed this trend, in the process reducing the diversity of debate and political options.

Second, the commercialization of broadcasting has further weakened democracy by delocalizing (nationalizing) politics, because, as Gerald Benjamin notes, 'appeals made in one place or to one group may be immediately communicated regionally or nationally. Thus the distributive politics of particular appeals to particular groups can no longer be made by candidates without their first calculating the possible effects on other groups in their electoral coalitions.'[37] The individual is more isolated, political participation tends to be reduced, and the idea of collective social action is weakened.

Third, the cost and importance of TV has put a premium on well-produced and carefully packaged 'spots' that provide effective imagery. Lasting 30 or 60 seconds, these spots are essentially advertisements that depend on images, formulas, and style. In this format, issues are downgraded. Just as programming and advertisements have tended to merge, with public affairs sharply downgraded, so are politics and advertisements merging, with issues carefully evaded and obfuscated. As Barnouw notes, the U.S. candidate for major political office 'no longer plans campaign speeches; he plans and produces "commercials".'[38]

TV news coverage of elections is also constricted in time and oriented to photo opportunities and entertainment values (personalities, drama, horse-racing). Frank Mankiewicz and Joel Swerdlow have pointed out that genuine intelligent discussion is avoided as 'bad television,' and with 1 minute and 15 seconds allotted to each candidate on the evening news (an extra 30 seconds on 'in-depth' presentations), issues are ruled out.[39] They are also ruled out by the networks' failure to investigate and report controversy that bites. George McGovern's charge in 1972 that the Nixon administration was seriously corrupt was true, but Nixon did not have to confront the charge on TV until well after the election.

Self-protective capabilities of a mature commercial system

The threat of a centralized, monolithic, state-controlled media system is well understood and feared in the West. What is little recognized or understood is the centralizing, ideologically monolithic, and self-protecting properties of an increasingly powerful commercial media system. U.S. experience suggests that once a commercial system is firmly in place it becomes difficult to challenge, and as its economic power increases so does its ability to keep threats at bay and gradually to remove all obstacles to commercial domination of the media.

In the realm of newspapers and magazines, citizens enjoy the right to launch new publications without state interference, but the market has rendered that right largely formal. Despite the exceptional profitability of the U.S. newspaper industry there has not been a single successful daily newspaper launched in an established market in the past 75 years. The market power of the newspaper chains helps make entry extraordinarily difficult. It is only slightly easier to launch a new magazine, and a large fraction of the successful new start-ups are launched by an existing media giant that can capitalize on its distribution, promotional and sales networks. In Hollywood, too, as we discussed in Chapters 2 and 3, no new studio has been successfully established in over 50 years. The market power of the established giants in these industries is formidable and is essentially uncontested.

In broadcasting, with its few channels on a publicly owned spectrum, there has been some political debate. But here also the commercial interests have been able to defeat and marginalize all efforts to establish a viable alternative to the commercial media system. Public broadcasting was marginalized in the early 1930s; the defeat of an amendment to the Communications Act of 1934 that would have reserved 25 percent of broadcasting space for educational and nonprofit operations confirmed the triumph of commercial broadcasting, and its power was steadily enlarged thereafter. A small segment was reserved for educational and other nonprofit broadcasting in the 1950s and after, but federal sponsorship and funding of public broadcasting did not come about until 1967, and one of the functions of public broadcasting was to relieve commercial broadcasters of a public service obligation that they did not want and were sloughing off. Even in the small niche reserved for it, public broadcasting has been a target of steady conservative attack for its excessive preoccupation with public affairs, and was subjected to a further financial crunch and politicization in the Reagan era.

Any organized opposition to commercial broadcasting collapsed following the 1934 Act, and from that time onward it has been subject to no serious threat of structural change or effective regulation. Regulation by the FCC, established in 1934, has been weak and rules limiting advertising and the transformation of programming away from public service steadily eroded in the face of broadcaster demands, until the final collapse of even nominal standards in the Reagan era.

As one illustration of the power of the industry to fend off virtually any threats, in the liberal environment of 1963 the FCC leadership decided to try to impose a formal restraint on commercial advertising, but only to the extent of making as the regulatory standard the limits suggested by the broadcasters' own trade association. This enraged the industry, which went to work on Congress, and the FCC quickly backed down.[40]

Another important illustration of the commercial broadcasting industry's self-protective power is found in the area of children's television. The country claims to revere children, and child abuse is given frequent and indignant attention. But although the erosion of children's programming, and the commercial exploitation of the residual ghettoized programs, occurred as the commercial networks were making record-breaking profits, and although substantial numbers of adults have been angered by this programming, it has taken place with only a muted outcry. The FCC has been pressed hard to do something about the situation by organized groups like ACT, but the mass media have not allowed this matter to become a serious issue. When, after a thirteen-year delay in dealing with an ACT petition to constrain abuses in children's television, the FCC decided in December 1983 that commercial broadcasters had no obligation to serve children, this decision was not even mentioned in the *New York Times*. In fact, during the years 1979–89, although many important petitions were submitted by ACT and decisions were made by the FCC that bore significantly on the commercial broadcasters' neglect and abuse of children, the *New York Times*, *Washington Post*, and *Los Angeles Times* had neither a front-page article nor an editorial on the subject. The dominant members of the press, most of whom had substantial broadcasting interests of their own, simply refused to make the huge failure of commercial broadcasters in children's programming a serious issue.

It is also enlightening to see how the principles of broadcasters' public service responsibility were gradually amended to accommodate broadcaster interests, without discussion or debate. As advertised programs displaced sustaining programs, and the 'balance wheel' disappeared, what gave way was any public interest standard. The industry defense was in terms of 'free speech' and the Alice-in-Wonderland principle that if the audience watches, the public interest is served. But the industry hardly needed a defense: raw power allowed the public interest standard to erode quietly, the issues undiscussed in any open debate, even as regards the enormous abuses and neglect in children's programming.

BEYOND THE UNITED STATES: INTRODUCTION

The globalization of the commercial model has come about partly by plan and partly by simple natural processes as profit-seeking companies seek out business opportunities across borders. The plan element encompasses the attempt by the U.S. government, and sometimes its allies, to encourage private enterprise, open economies, and market-based media systems throughout the world, to pry open markets, and to destabilize and overthrow non-market-friendly governments. Numerous official documents attest to a post-World War II design of U.S. leaders to use their dominant power to establish

> a strategic sphere of influence within the Western Hemisphere, domination of the Atlantic and Pacific oceans, an extensive system of outlying bases to enlarge the strategic frontier, and project American power. . . . [to facilitate] access to the resources and markets of most of Eurasia, [and to permit] denial of these resources to a prospective enemy, and the maintenance of nuclear superiority.'[41]

The most famous of these official documents – though hardly well-publicized – National Security Council Document 68, prepared in 1950, actually called for the destabilization and 'rollback' of the Soviet Union, a deliberately debilitating arms race, and a negotiated settlement only *after* the rollback, perhaps with a 'successor state.'[42]

During World War II, U.S. planners developed the concept of a 'Grand Area' that it was strategically necessary to bring under U.S. control, with a subordinate role fixed for Third World raw materials suppliers who would service the needs of the U.S. economy.[43] A 1954 National Security Council statement on U.S. policy toward Latin America is explicit that the United States supports governments that 'base their economies on a system of private enterprise and, as essential thereto . . . create a political and economic climate conducive to private investment.'[44] A large post-World War II U.S. program of military and police training of Third World personnel was explicitly designed to ensure their 'understanding of, and orientation toward, U.S. objectives.'[45] They were intensively educated on the threat of communist subversion, and did in fact serve U.S. ends in Latin America where, as political scientist Frederick Nunn pointed out, 'subject to U.S. military influence on anticommunism the professional army officer became hostile to any sort of populism.'[46]

U.S. goals and strategies were implemented by means of U.S. economic and military aid and political pressure, support given to indigenous forces serving U.S. aims, and sometimes more direct interventions, as in Guatemala in 1954 and Nicaragua in the 1980s. The United States was also able to mobilize help from the IMF, World Bank, and other institutions, and to use bilateral and multilateral agreements to serve these ends. There is a clear record of intentionality in their pursuit, which cannot be dismissed as a product of 'conspiracy theory.'

The most crucial requirement for the successful pursuit of the Grand Area plan was to get the proper institutional arrangements in place. Once that was accomplished, although constant surveillance and protection of those institutions was still necessary, and political obstructions to market transactions would have to be frequently fought, to a great extent the market system consolidates itself and spreads by itself. The internal political threats to market freedom may be reduced further by international accords – for example, the Canadian–U.S. Free Trade Agreement of 1988 and the North American Free Trade Agreeement (NAFTA) of 1993 pulled Canada and Mexico more closely into the global as well as regional system, reducing the freedom of the relevant populations to interfere with cross-border market decisions.

The post-World War II U.S. drive for open markets in communications was carried out in a campaign for what was called the 'free flow of information.' This meant the freedom of advertisers, sellers of communication hardware, publishers, motion picture producers, broadcasters, and telecommunications firms to do business abroad without constraint. This policy thrust reflected the economic strength and favorable competitive position of the U.S. communications industries. It was opposed by most other countries in varying degrees because of their relatively weak competitive position and desire to maintain economic, political, and communications independence and sovereignty.

The most conspicuous struggle over 'free flow,' which took place in the 1960s and 1970s, was between the United States and its major allies, on one side, and the majority of Third World countries (with Soviet bloc support), on the other. The Third World forces called for a New World Economic Order and New World Information Order, which would redistribute wealth and media resources from rich to poor countries and otherwise rectify existing imbalances. Not only was this rather hazy appeal denied, but the 1980s witnessed a widespread Third World economic and political collapse and return to dependency in the face of high interest rates, the debt crisis, and the aggressive deployment of economic and political muscle by the United States and other great powers. With a large fraction of its members necessitous borrowers from the IMF and World Bank, the Third World was quickly pressed into 'structural adjustments' that required not only budget and monetary cutbacks, but also privatization and a compulsory opening up of their economies to foreign private investment.

These developments, fortified by the GATT and NAFTA agreements, represented a triumph of U.S. postwar objectives, including the advancement of 'free flow' among other neoliberal principles, now widely accepted and institutionalized. This, in turn, paved the way for an accelerated globalization of the media, a process that now occurs mainly by market action and transactions among market participants as well as between them and local governments.

The neo-imperialism of constrained 'free choice'

Has this global tide of at least partially coerced commercialization been a manifestation of 'cultural imperialism' or 'cultural dependency'? These phrases are associated with analyses which claim that the economic and cultural power of the media and cultural artifacts of the United States and other dominant western powers have allowed them to dominate or unduly influence and put into a dependency relationship the media and cultures of less economically advanced countries. Many of these analyses have pointed to the imbalance in flow of cultural materials, with the United States a huge exporter (and small importer) of movies, popular music, TV programs, news, books, magazines, advertisements, and associated lifestyles and values.[47] Some of these analyses, however, have viewed the media and cultural output flows as merely one part of a larger structure of economic and political relationships.

Cultural imperialism and dependency models have been harshly criticized in recent years, reflecting in part the more conservative political climate, but grounded intellectually in the receding proportion of cross-border cultural flows coming from the United States, along with numerous micro-analyses showing that readers and viewers pick and choose what they want to hear and read and interpret imported materials from their own frames of reference. But these critics miss the point when they note the decline in the U.S. share of media exports and greater media exports from Brazil, Mexico, and Australia,[48] or when they cite varying interpretations of *Dallas* or other programs as manifesting effective resistance to foreign cultural incursions. The crucial incursion is the implantation of the model;[49] the secondary developments of importance are the growth, consolidation, and centralization of the commercial systems, their increasing integration into the global system, and the gradual effects of these processes on economies, political systems, and the cultural environment. The primary incursion defines the path that will be taken and brings the country in question into the orbit of interest of the dominant powers. This is the 'neo-imperialist' form that has replaced the older, cruder, and obsolete methods of colonialism.[50]

Furthermore, neo-imperial cultural power is not confined to the export of movies, magazines, and music. A great power like the United States has exercised influence in the process of doing general business, investing, building up sales branches and subsidiaries and networks of local agents; its lending agencies, private and governmental, have established important connections, alliances, and dependencies; its advertising agencies, following in the wake of home TNCs, control large advertising revenues, and they bring sophisticated techniques, advertising formulas and messages into the new terrain. The United States makes aid grants and influences international lending agencies, and often provides a flow of experts in a variety of fields. It has also made major investments in police and military support programs, deliberately designed to strengthen ties and firm up dependency relationships, and to exercise ideological influence.[51] Substantial numbers of elite members of Third World countries have sought education in the United States and other developed countries, which reinforces the ideological influence of the dominant powers, as does tourism and the communication between the home country and the frequently large number of immigrants to the United States and Western Europe.

The impact of globalization will understandably vary in intensity and speed of effects by the size and strength of the country in question, the strength and coherence of indigenous cultures, linguistic differences, and many other factors. A few countries, such as the United States, will be strong net exporters of 'effects,' while most will be net importers, although globalization means interpenetration and we would expect a degree of feedback in all or at least most cases. We would anticipate its having possible negative effects in four linked areas:

1. *Values.* Commercialization means the media's funding by selling advertising, and its global spread will therefore reinforce the stress on consumption as the primary end of life, and individualism and individual freedom to choose (especially among goods) as the fundamental desired social condition. This emphasis on individualism can be a progressive force in cases of government broadcasting monopolies and/or authoritarian systems, opening new vistas to deprived and oppressed peoples and threatening arbitrary rule and rulers. In other cases, and in the long run, however, this value intrusion strengthens materialistic values, weakens sympathetic feelings toward others, and tends to diminish the spirit of community and the strength of communal ties. This reduces the power of resistance to market forces at home and those encroaching from the outside. Arguably, in an interdependent world, and for a democratic order, individualism is not enough; carried to an extreme, it is dangerous.

2. *Displacement of the public sphere with entertainment.* As noted earlier, advertisers and the mainstream media seek large audiences with uncontroversial fare, so that hard news presented in depth, public affairs

analyses, debates, and documentaries, tend to disappear from prime listening hours in broadcasting. The modalities of entertainment also penetrate the residual elements of the public sphere with what in the United States is called 'happy news,' 'infotainment,' 'reality news,' and talk shows and 'news magazines' that stress personalities, conflict, and petty exposures of mainly minor crimes. Crime, sex, violence, spy stories, westerns, and dramas involving the climb to wealth and romance are favored and travel well. These have subtle political messages that comport with advertiser interests: individualism, the importance of consumption, hard work which (with luck) pays off in wealth, the threat of alien terrorists, and the need to confront them with force. Children's TV has gradually shriveled to proportions appropriate to the lesser command which children have over spending, and the programs that remain are, with modest exceptions, entertaining, not informative, and are closely tied to advertising and the sale of children's toys and other consumables.

3. Strengthening of conservative political forces. The centralizing and globalizing commercial media exercise a conservative political force. Closely linked to advertisers and the corporate community, of which they are members, the media support neoliberal economic policies that serve their own and the general TNC interest, but which undermine social democratic options. They are hostile to organized labor and complacent about increasing inequality of income and wealth, out of self-interest and linkage with advertisers and other members of a dominant elite. They press politicians to permit their own merger and other corporate strategies, to relieve themselves of regulatory obligations, and to help them weaken and dismantle public broadcasting systems.

Although the top media moguls tend to be extremely conservative and normally give especially warm support to conservative politicians, they find it expedient to do business with 'socialists' (Craxi–Berlusconi) and social democrats to assure acceptance and/or support of their own plans and needs. Their strong influence over all major parties makes it exceedingly difficult to contain the commercialization–globalization process. In many countries their conservative political influence has been manifested in the steady weakening of public broadcasting and shift to the right of editorial page commentaries and pundit opinion.

In dealing with Third World politics, the dominant media of the West have naturally aligned themselves with the interests and perspectives of the great powers and TNCs. These have been hostile to social democrats as well as radical nationalists, who fail to provide a 'favorable climate of investment,' and, in the words of one U.S. National Security Council document, pose a challenge by threatening to meet 'an increasingly popular demand for immediate improvement in the low living standards of the masses.'[52] In response to this threat, the United States sponsored the National Security State and military governments throughout its sphere of influence, and succeeded very well, as 'between 1960 and 1969, eighteen regimes in Latin America, of which eleven held office constitutionally, were overthrown by the military.'[53] The United States was an active or behind-the-scenes participant in many of these transfers of power. The new regimes invariably attacked and decimated trade unions and other social democratic forces, opened up the economies, and encouraged neoliberal transformations, and if they did not immediately commercialize the media at least created a political environment that helped expedite commercialization after the military regimes retreated to the barracks.[54] The dominant media of the West treated these lengthy interludes of state terror and class cleansing in a low-key manner and as regrettable features of Cold War policy.[55]

4. The erosion of local cultures. The impact of globalization on local cultures will vary enormously between the dominant and less dominant and subordinate, and the effects are hard to disentangle because of their symbiotic relationship to overall economic, political, and military penetration. Even the dominant cultures will be affected, not so much by feedback from others as by the reinforcement of the dominant culture by its success and power as an economic-political-cultural force. Not only will France, Japan, and Jamaica be Disneyfied; the United States itself is undergoing more rapid Disneyfication.

As for cultural effects on weaker countries, they are going to vary by indigenous forces of resistance, by class, by time span considered, and by the nature and scope of the intrusions from without. Strong cultures with linguistic barriers to Western intrusions, like Japan, withstand cultural penetration far better than do the Latin American cultures, where the elite at least have long been denationalized and subject to a strong pull and 'demonstration effect' from the West.[56] Cultural effects also depend on time horizons; a textual reading in Brazil today may be quite different from one taken twenty-five years later after a long period of saturation in advertising, stories, and news messages. We also think it very important to recognize that media effects are inseparable from broader economic, political, and cultural influences, such as external military occupation and rule, foreign indirect rule through sponsored authoritarian regimes (for example, Guatemala, Philippines under Marcos), military and police aid and training, economic and financial linkages, and tourism and educational exchanges, all of which are at least as unbalanced as media exports and imports.

6
MEDIA GLOBALIZATION (2): BEYOND THE UNITED STATES

The development of a global commercial media market and the related commercialization of national media systems has made the U.S. media experience described in Chapter 5 more salient to the rest of the world. In this chapter we provide seven brief national and regional case studies: of four developed nations – Canada, Great Britain, Italy, and New Zealand – and of three developing nations (and regions) – Brazil, the English-speaking Caribbean and India. With the partial exception of Italy, all of these case studies address areas with pronounced British or U.S. influence, past and present, which qualifies their general applicability. However, U.S. and British influence, and that of their globalizing transnational corporations (TNCs) and media firms, extends well beyond the countries examined here. Furthermore, in view of the on-going and increasing integration of nearly all nations into the global market economy, we believe that the patterns exhibited in these case studies are consistent with the contours described by the U.S. experience and are widely applicable.

CANADA: NEIGHBORLY INGESTION

Canada has had the fortune, good or bad, to abut the United States and to have a common language (except for the 20 percent minority French-speaking population). Of much greater size and dynamic, the United States long ago replaced Great Britain as Canada's main cultural and economic link, and in fact has gradually assumed a position of economic, political, and cultural preeminent influence, if not domination, over the smaller power. This rests to a considerable degree on economic integration, with extensive U.S. ownership and control of Canadian resources and manufacturing, and thus over ongoing investment activity. By 1963, 46 percent of Canadian manufacturing, 62 percent of petroleum and natural gas, and 52 percent of mining and smelting investment was controlled by U.S. interests.[1] As noted in Chapter 1, Canadian tariffs in the 1880s led to a burst of direct U.S. investment to

evade tariff barriers, and the flow of U.S. investment kept growing thereafter. It became commonplace among Canadian critics in the 1960s and
after to refer to their country as a 'branch-plant economy.' And the view
of such critics was that 'The final outcome of a branch-plant society is a
merging of value systems and a meshing of corporate and technocratic
elites which must ultimately call into question English Canada's willingness to pay the price of continued independence.'[2]

The integration of the corporate, technocratic, and financial elites
has continued apace. A large fraction of the Canadian business elite
works for or does extensive business with U.S. companies. The important financial sector of the Canadian economy is closely linked to that of
the United States by innumerable ties of ownership, corporate inter-
locks, joint ventures, and syndication and participation loans. A
significant minority of Canadian business leaders, however, are substantial transnational capitalists in their own right, and investment is not a
one-way street. The great entrepreneurial families of Canada have
invested heavily in the United States: the Reichmanns with large real
estate holdings in New York; the Bronfmans with major investments in
DuPont, Time Warner, and controlling MCA, and newspaper tycoon
Conrad Black owning almost 300 newspapers and shopping guides in
29 states in the United States (as well as the *Daily Telegraph* in London
and media interests in Israel and Australia).

The corporate and financial elite that dominates Canadian politics
through *de facto* control of both the Tory and Liberal parties is cos-
mopolitan in outlook – or, in more critical language, it is denationalized
– and has thrown its weight in favor of relatively unconstrained economic integration with the United States and a neoliberal world order.
Conrad Black, the newspaper tycoon, has repeatedly stated his preference for Canada's merging into the United States (with Quebec
preferably excluded!), and the *Wall Street Journal*, noting his refusal to
allow the *Daily Telegraph* to criticize a U.S. bombing attack on Libya in
1986, stated that Black is 'more pro-American than many Americans.'[3]
As the conservative philosopher George Grant put it in 1965, 'The
power of the American government to control Canada does not lie
primarily in its ability to exert direct pressure; the power lies in the fact
that the dominant classes in Canada see themselves at one with the continent in all essential matters.'[4]

In this process of slow fusion, Canada has become in many ways a
'miniature replica' of the dominant continental power. For instance,
Canada, although it has a multi-party system, like the United States has
two dominant parties that are not responsive to the demands of the mass
of ordinary citizens; its political leaders campaign on 'jobs first' and
then, upon attaining office, return to a priority attack on the budget

deficit; just as in the United States, they can quickly shift from the urgency of deficit reduction to expansion via tax cutting.[5] Canada has its Business Council on National Issues, a lobbying collective of business CEOs very reminiscent of (and with some overlapping membership in) the U.S. Business Roundtable. It has its rightwing thinktanks, Fraser, Howe, Mackenzie, and the Atlantic Institute for Market Studies, funded heavily by rightwing corporate foundations (Donner),[6] pressing the neoliberal agenda, closely paralleling the U.S. model of the American Enterprise Institute, Hoover, Heritage, and Manhattan Institute, funded by Olin, Bradley, etc. The ideological clichés and formulas pushed in Canada – 'family values'; the importance of containing 'big government,' the 'nanny state,' and 'deficits'; 'special interest groups,' used to refer to all social groups but those that are business-related; the need for 'downsizing' to make Canada 'competitive' – these are identical with those pushed by the dominant pundits and press in the United States.

The Canadian media, too, display many common features with those of the United States. The newspapers have become highly concentrated in Canada, even more so than in the United States, with control by very conservative businessmen who have learned how to make money by takeovers followed by ruthless downsizing and hollowing out of the captured and now minimalist entities.[7] Just as in the United States, aggressive rightwing pundits have taken hold in opinion columns and on talk shows, peddling the identical lines and using the same clichés employed by George Will, William Buckley, Rush Limbaugh, and Cathy Young. 'Family values' are extolled, North and South, while the economic policies supported by the pundits make family life insecure and difficult.

Despite this elite mimicking and frequent subservience, nationalism, pride, and the demands of cultural interests under assault have caused Canada to make continuous efforts over the years to protect its cultural industries from being overwhelmed by U.S. interests. It has used Canadian content rules in broadcasting, subsidies (broadcasting, motion pictures, books, theater, and other arts), limits on foreign ownership of Canadian media (broadcasting, cable, satellites, telephones, wireless communications), and tax discrimination in favor of domestic firms (magazines and newspapers). Some of these policies have been effective – the magazine industry market share of Canadian firms grew from 30 percent in 1970 to 68 percent in 1994, and Canadian newspapers are all home-owned, thanks to the disallowance of tax deductions for advertising in foreign-owned periodicals directed to Canadian audiences.[8] However, the U.S. presence remains massive – overwhelmingly so in motion pictures, dominant in videocassettes and music (although the TNCs that have increasingly dominated the recording industry do recognize differences in national tastes, and, in Canada, as elsewhere, they cultivate local artists for sale predominantly in Canada).

The most important effort at resistance to U.S. penetration and domination of the Canadian media began with legislation in 1932 and culminated in 1936 with the creation of the Canadian Broadcasting Corporation (CBC) as a Crown Corporation to control broadcasting. This followed the collapse of the Canadian motion picture industry in the face of Hollywood's advance, the rapid growth and domination of the magazine industry by U.S. companies, and the threat of domination of radio from across the border. Foreign control of radio would have made Canada a media satellite of the United States, and the nationalists prevailed in establishing CBC. However, the CBC was never well funded, and so private radio stations, and later commercial TV stations and networks, came into existence, some uncomfortably affiliated with CBC.

Although over the years commission after commission reiterated that CBC 'is not only the major instrument of Canadian culture, but also of culture in Canada' (the 1986 Task Force), CBC has never been given budget priority and has been increasingly vulnerable to the changing economic and broadcasting environment and neoliberal priorities. In exact parallel with the United States, the Canadian rightwing and neoliberals not liking CBC and its cultivation of a public sphere and some modest dissent and debate on community issues, CBC has been under attack and a budget crunch for many years.

Under Tory rule beginning in 1984, the CBC's budget was subject to heavy cuts, continued under the Liberals, aggregating 23 percent in real terms between 1983 and 1994; its total revenue continued to grow in real terms because its advertising income was enlarged. Its treatment by the government was far more ruthless than the military sector or overall federal spending. CBC's forced resort to advertising, along with slow budget growth, compromised its mission and programming, leading to criticism of the organization on *that* ground. A Mandate Review Committee report of January 1996, *Making Our Voices Heard* (popularly known as the Juneau Report, for its chairman, former regulatory chief Pierre Juneau), while lauding the CBC's work as essential to the preservation of cultural autonomy *and* broadcasting quality, nevertheless worked within the constraint of the dominant parties that insisted on further attrition of the CBC budget, and therefore tacitly accepted the shrinkage of this 'indispensable' institution. It criticizes CBC for having taken on advertising and compromised its capacity to program independently, but fails to note that this change of tack was imposed on the CBC by drastic budget cuts without reductions in CBC responsibilities. It proposes that the CBC abandon advertisements, letting the commercial broadcasters obtain that revenue, suggesting that this will allow the latter to do more Canadian programming – an implausible outcome. The Mandate Review Committee proposes that the CBC confine itself to Canadian programming, and be given new stable funding by means of a Communications Distribution Tax levied on cable, direct to home satellite companies, and non-residential phone service. This funding proposal has not been well received by the Canadian establishment.

The position of the CBC has also been profoundly affected (and its budget position weakened) by the growth of commercial television and the great proliferation of channels. Cable now reaches over 70 percent of Canadian households, and direct satellite reception through dishes reaches several hundred thousand households and is growing rapidly, although illegal. The new flood of channels produced 'an avalanche of American programming . . . now so great that Canadian children spend more time watching American television than they will spend in a Canadian school.'9 This merely accelerated a long trend, based, as in the motion picture industry, on the economics of commercial programming: U.S. programs are cheap compared to possible Canadian programs, and they are made to attract large audiences. Canadian content on the commercial networks is met by news, sports, and off-peak Canadian reruns, and it would shrivel further without content rules.

As in the United States, the growth of the commercial broadcasting media has tended to marginalize the public sphere and erode the quality of children's programming. In-depth treatments of public issues are sparse, and the news has been affected as well. David Taras claims that 'Canadian news executives made a conscious decision in the early 1980s to produce newscasts that were as fast-paced, abbreviated and action-filled as is American news.'10 Insofar as quality is offered in the commercial sector, it comes at a premium price and is not part of a universally available service.

Children's programming has been reduced in quantity and consists largely of U.S.-produced animation shows with minimal educational value and infused with toy and other advertisements as 'support.' André Caron and his colleagues have documented the great discrepancy in children's programming in Canada between public and private stations and anglophone and French Canadian markets: public ownership 'considerably widened the range of genres that are broadcast for children ...,' and in the anglophone commercial markets, U.S. productions were very prevalent and 'consisted almost exclusively of cartoon animation productions.'11 The situation is better in French Canada, where the language barrier and other factors have kept the children's TV environment at a higher level.

A large fraction, maybe over half, of Canadian households can directly tap U.S. networks from across the border. Canadians draw an impoverished children's fare from there; and Stephen Kline points out that as U.S. marketing practices on children's programs in the 1980s deteriorated (integrating toy-selling with programming policy), these could not only be seen directly in Canada, they were reproduced in Canadian syndicated programs on satellite and cable, although this was in violation of the Canadian regulatory code supposedly protecting children. Kline concludes:

> Mixed broadcasting systems and self-regulation provide minimal buffers to structural forces unleashed by globalized toy-marketing. The public broadcasters move out of children's production because they cannot draw the children's audiences, while self-regulation drifts closer to the business position to protect the domestic industry from unfairness created by restricted marketing. The changes continue to take place as long as there is no public protest or mobilization around children's issues.[12]

The impact of the United States on the Canadian media and society has been multileveled, cumulative, and of long duration. Integration of the two economies began in the nineteenth century and is now very great, and the flow of trade, music, books, motion pictures, travelers, immigration, and other cultural exchanges has been enormous. The business elites are closely linked and share a common ideology, and the similarities of the forms and expressions of neoliberal ideology, funded by parallel thinktanks and pundits, dominating commentary in similar media institutions – concentrated and advertisement-based newspapers, magazines, and commercial broadcasting entities – is impressive and certainly reflects in part the pressures and example of the dominant power. The erosion of the power and autonomy of CBC reflects the same forces that have exerted fiscal discipline on PBS and forced it into the commercial nexus.

On September 5, 1996, the Canadian Radio-Television and Communication Authority announced approval for twenty-three new Canadian private TV cable channels, although news reports say that 80 percent of Canadian viewers see no need for any new channels. Four days later, on September 9, CBC announced that a budget shortfall of $188 million would force a 1,400 staff reduction that is expected to have seriously damaging effects on local production, outreach, and quality.[13] Further planned reductions in 1998 will reduce CBC's full-time staff to half its 1984 level.[14] For the Liberals, as for the Conservatives, the market will suffice in broadcasting.

BRAZIL: MEDIA NEO- AND SUB-IMPERIALISM

Latin America is the U.S. 'backyard,' and the United States has long arrogated to itself the right to intervene there to serve its own perceived interests. U.S. Secretary of State Richard Olney stated back in 1895 that 'the United States is practically sovereign on this continent, and its fiat is law upon the subjects to which it confines its interposition.'[15] Because of this arrogance, along with the huge discrepancy in power between the United States and its southern neighbors, direct intervention has been frequent and the exercise of economic, political, and military pressure has been almost continuous.

As regards the media, throughout Latin America U.S. equipment manufacturers (radio, TV, and telecommunications), advertising agencies, press agencies, magazine publishers, and radio and TV broadcasters have pushed relentlessly for a commercial media. As Elizabeth Fox has noted:

> In many [Latin American] countries, the early public-service goals and government ownership, subsidy and regulation of broadcasting inevitably clashed with powerful national and international forces behind commercial broadcasting. Politically powerful national and foreign industries were interested in the media as advertising vehicles. . . . Commercial radio fulfilled industry's need for an advertising medium to reach the growing mass markets. . . . The government-subsidized educational, cultural and, at times, elitist radios were unable to compete with the unregulated expansion of commercial broadcasting and were soon driven out of business or sold to the private sector.[16]

Although Brazil is the largest and most powerful country in Latin America, its weak and financially strapped governments put up no resistance to the emergence of the commercial model of broadcasting in the 1920s and thereafter. As James Schwoch points out, 'Both promotion of American radio equipment and promotion of the American broadcasting style proved determinant in transplanting the American radio industry and American mass culture into Brazil.'[17] The Brazilian governments censored the media and tried to mobilize them for their propaganda goals, but made no effort to establish a public broadcasting system. As Fox notes,

> When television arrived in the mid-1950s, privately owned, commercially operated broadcasting was the norm in Latin America. A politically docile commercial system satisfied the demands of the governments and the ruling parties and enabled national and foreign industries to reach mass markets to advertise their products.[18]

Elizabeth Mahan points out that the processes of concentration and conglomeration which ensued 'are already fait accompli in Mexico and Brazil and underway in all commercial media systems in the region.'[19]

U.S. economic penetration of Brazil, already substantial, accelerated in the post-World War II era. By 1969, close to half of Brazilian industry was foreign-controlled, with U.S. firms owning a majority of assets in motor vehicles and pharmaceuticals and with a substantial presence elsewhere. A 1975 U.S. Senate report described this as 'denationalization' and 'decision dependence,' posing the threat of loss of sovereignty and vulnerability to private foreign economic power, a vulnerability 'likely to be much greater when utilized in tandem with U.S. foreign policy.'[20]

U.S. foreign policy toward Brazil was strongly intrusive in the 1950s and early 1960s. U.S. officials expected to be consulted over Brazilian actions and they did not hesitate to bully their Brazilian counterparts. They disliked the independence and social democratic tendencies of the governments of those years, which failed to quell peasant and other movements from below, and U.S. officials, in collusion with U.S. and Brazilian businessmen and military personnel, sought to undermine them. They did this by major covert subsidization of organizations designed to produce and disseminate propaganda, journalists, activist organizations of the Right, and Brazilian politicians. They encouraged and supported the military coup of 1964.[21] 'Within hours' of the coup, the U.S. Agency for International Development extended a large loan to the military junta, and the Inter-American Development Bank and World Bank lost no time in increasing their loans to Brazil 'dramatically.'[22]

In the years preceding the coup, the Brazilian media were penetrated and subverted by U.S. economic and political agents. U.S. advertising agencies, overwhelmingly dominant in Brazil and controlling the very large advertising budgets of U.S. transnationals, discriminated in favor of U.S. allied and other 'friendly' media, in the process driving out indigenous and unfriendly media.[23] *Reader's Digest* had a strong presence in Brazil, and was supplemented in the 1950s and 1960s with *Visao*, *Realidade*, and a number of other publications under unacknowledged U.S. control. The United States Information Service, U.S. Embassy, and Voice of America carried out a large news and book publishing and distribution operation, along with other propaganda activities.[24] The U.S. allied or controlled media included, most importantly, Robert Marinho's *O Globo* newspaper, which began to receive infusions of cash from Time-Life in 1962, contrary to Brazilian law, which prohibited all foreign investment in the media. The Time-Life connection may have been a cover for CIA control. In seeking a media vehicle in Brazil, Time-Life expressed an interest in helping to combat 'Castroism,' and a former Foreign Service officer in Brazil told the U.S. analyst of Brazil, Jan Black, that *O Globo* was CIA-owned or controlled.[25]

The large sums provided by Time-Life allowed Marinho to move rapidly into TV in 1965, and under the military regime of 1964–85 the Marinho–Globo empire grew to enormous dimensions. *O Globo* gave vigorous support to the pre-coup subversion process, and then to the coup itself; following the coup, the Marinho empire provided unstinting support to the military government up to its last year when, in the face of mass disapproval, it finally helped give the *coup de grâce* to direct military rule.[26]

The coup of 1964 had come just in the nick of time: the Brazilian legislature had embarked on an investigation of the foreign (U.S.) subsidization of literally hundreds of Brazilian politicians, as well as the possible illegality of the Time-Life investment in *O Globo*. The coup ended these inquiries, although public outcries led to a less-threatening investigation of Time-Life-Globo, whose recommendations were ignored by the military government.

Immediately after the 1964 coup, the Brazilian military government displayed exceptional, even groveling, subservience to the United States, which had underwritten the counter-revolution, and which was a model (economic and military, if not political) to the ruling generals, many of whom had trained in Panama.[27] For a period it was a crime to criticize the United States in Brazil. Eventually, however, the military regime became less subservient, deigning to defend powerful indigenous interests and occasionally taking political positions at odds with those of the United States. But this was an effective case of neo-imperialism in action. The United States had never 'controlled' Brazil, but its intervention – as in the case of Chile in 1973 – helped to crush the active movements from below and any possibility that Brazil would take an alternate development path. The generals led Brazil into the neoliberal world order, which was the prime U.S. objective.

As regards the Brazilian media as well, the coup assured a consolidation of the commercial system and an integration of the Brazilian media into the global media order. The huge inequalities built into the Brazilian economic order would be well protected by the rapidly concentrating and commercialized media, with Globo as its focal point. It would feature entertainment, in service to advertisers, and its politics would be mainly a depoliticizing blank, but under pressure would be suitably biased.[28] Venicio De Lima says that TV Globo in the 1970s, 'a perfect mirror of the regime, presented a Brazil without social conflict, repression, or poverty.'[29] A high official of Globo called it 'without any question, the best-finished product, the biggest success of the dictatorship. Globo made concrete an abstraction: Order and Progress.'[30]

The Globo system was rewarded by the generals with huge subsidies in the form of a taxpayer-financed telecommunications network and satellite system, a very large flow of government advertising, discrimination against rival networks, which helped sink several of them,[31] and a failure to enforce the constitutional rule that 'The means of social communication cannot, directly or indirectly, be an object of monopoly or oligopoly' (Article 220). The Globo system was permitted to expand both horizontally and vertically, the television system itself constituting what Roberto Amaral and Cesar Guimaraes describe as 'a private quasimonopoly of sound, image, and textual media.'[32] The Globo network absorbs some 80 percent of TV advertising revenue and 60 percent of all Brazilian advertising, and it also controls vast interests in other media sectors (including *O Globo*, the largest newspaper in Brazil, news and advertising agencies, record, printing and publishing companies, and all kinds of radio stations).

The ending of the military regime in 1985 did not curb the expansion of the Globo empire; the weak civil regimes that followed did not have the incentive or power to intrude, and in fact Marinho 'was assured by the incoming civilian administration of having a close friend, Antonio Carlos Maghalhaes, appointed to the powerful post of communications minister.'[33] Amaral and Guimaraes, writing in 1994, assert that Globo, by aggressively seeking control of the new technologies (subscription TV, CATV, cellular telephony, and new TV services) 'is moving toward a complete monopoly of all branches of the cultural industry.'

Like Televisa in Mexico, Globo's power has become so great that it attained some autonomy from its governmental sponsor and is by no means a puppet. But, like Televisa it is a part of an elite establishment and has a symbiotic and mutually supportive relationship with the government in power.[34] Just as Televisa has supported the PRI, so Globo supported the military government, then its neoliberal successors, and pushed hard for Collor in opposition to leftwing labor leader and candidate Lulu and the labor threat.

Both Globo and Televisa evolved from heavy dependence on U.S. capital and programming supply to a fair degree of independence. Their own home-produced materials now occupy a large fraction of programming space, and their own *telenova* productions are major exports. But their formats are derivative, and foreign supply is still far from negligible in programming, equipment, and source of advertisements. Globo is part of a global system in other ways as well: it owns an Italian TV station and has interests in a U.S. Latin-oriented network, and it has entered major joint venture arrangements with AT&T and Bradesco, a large private bank in Brazil, to bid for a privatizing Brazilian telephone system, and with News Corp, Televisa, and TCI, to provide a direct satellite broadcasting service to Latin America.

There is no doubt that the cultural effects of the spread of Globo programming and maturation and greater autonomy of the network are complex. Conrad Kottak stresses the liberalizing effects of the coming of TV in remote Brazilian villages, hungry for contacts with the outside world and influenced by more progressive (feminist, anti-authoritarian) perspectives coming from the urban centers.[35] At the same time, there is an isolating effect, a new individualist and consumerist ideology that begins to take hold. At the heart of the formats and programming adapted from the early dependency regime is the 'dominance of entertainment over educational or cultural programming' and the use of the soap opera, first 'sponsored by Colgate, a U.S. corporation wanting to sell soap in the region with the same advertising vehicle that had proved so successful in the United States.'[36] This form was capable of incorporating traditional oral folk cultures, but these were ultimately structured with the dominant themes being 'upward mobility and consumer consumption.'[37] As noted above, this system of positive messages, uplift, and evasion of political issues was just what the military dictatorship and advertising community wanted; it protected a system of immense inequality, helped to keep the public diverted, the public sphere shriveled and subtly biased, and inculcating values that keep people isolated and depoliticized.   use this

Kottak stresses the long time lags in effects on value systems, and envisages stages. In our view, the most important fact about Globo and the media system in place in Brazil is that it is advertisement-based and part of a global system that will press consumerist and neoliberal ideology, unremittingly and with vast resources. The Brazilian system is already running up against impressive local resistance (see Chapter 7), but that resistance faces a formidable and globally linked engine of propaganda that is still gathering strength and is likely to be hammering away decades from now.

GREAT BRITAIN: THE THATCHER–MURDOCH PUSH

Great Britain has had a long tradition of commercial print media, dominated for many decades by indigenous media moguls like Lord Beaverbrook, Lord Rothermere, and Lord Northcliffe. An unusual cultural conservatism, along with repulsion at the crass features of the emerging U.S. broadcasting system, led British conservatives to establish a non-commercial British Broadcasting Company (BBC) monopoly in the 1920s and 1930s, with a public service mandate and a certain degree of autonomy from the government, and funded by a license fee on receivers. Despite an elitist bent, the BBC attempted to offer a wide array of programs that would attract as well as 'improve' the British citizenry. It succeeded to an exceptional degree, and over the decades gave the BBC a world reputation for quality as well as a 'high degree of audience satisfaction' with its ongoing programs in Great Britain.[38]

When the BBC broadcasting monopoly was broken in 1955, with the establishment of Independent Television (ITV) as a second TV channel, the BBC public service tradition was so strong that the new commercial channel was not very commercial – it was obliged by contract to provide many specific public service programs, including substantial children's offerings, and, most importantly, advertising was disconnected from programming and thus had little programming influence. As the BBC depended on the license fee and ITV on advertising revenues, the duopoly 'produced programmes of high quality and prevented Gresham's Law, the bad driving out the good, from applying to British broadcasting. The new competition did the BBC Television Service a power of good.'[39]

Significant changes came to British broadcasting and print media in the Thatcher years, changes which in part reflected global forces. Thatcher brought to Great Britain a neoconservative ideology and faith in the market that had powerful domestic support but which was borrowed in good measure from a global network of intellectuals and thinktanks. The Thatcherite Tories shared the antipathy of neoconservatives in the United States toward the 'liberal media' and public service broadcasting, and Thatcher's ideology disdained the very idea of societal functions ('there is no such thing as society') or the possibility of systematic market failure. Thatcherite thought favored strong government and a subservient media, which added to its bias in favor of a commercial media and hostility to a subsidized public service and public sphere.

The result was a steady attack on the BBC, closely analogous to the Reagan era attack on PBS in the United States. In both cases, highly political appointments were made to supervisory and oversight positions, and political pressure and threats, along with funding cuts, were designed to damage and cow the public service.[40] In both cases a deliberate attempt was made to force the public broadcasters into the commercial nexus as an additional means of curbing dissent and shrinking the public sphere. Eventually, the Thatcher government succeeded in pushing through the Broadcasting Law of 1990, which provided for the auctioning off of the regional ITV companies and the creation of a new terrestrial channel, all to be funded by advertising. The earlier delinking of advertising and programming was ended, and the new companies, some with heavy debt burdens from the auction purchase, would be under pressure to 'lighten up' programming. The companies had committed themselves in the bidding to programming standards, but it did not take long for commercial difficulties to impel the companies to petition for relief, sometimes granted.[41] The crucial point, as we see it, is that the commercial model was elevated to dominance in broadcasting, with public service broadcasting relegated to 'junior partner,' as part of the Thatcher legacy.[42]

The introduction of commercial broadcasting in 1955 had been given impetus by U.S. advertising agencies in Great Britain,[43] and it was given a further strong push by Rupert Murdoch's successful introduction of satellite TV via British Sky Broadcasting (BSkyB), which began service in 1989. Murdoch was given an exemption from the European Union requirement of 50 percent European content, enabling him to concentrate on inexpensive foreign entertainment and sports. He was able to feed into homes not only through dishes (plus decoders), but also through cable systems.

Cable growth in Britain was stimulated by opening it to foreign entry and allowing the use of cable for telephone services. This encouraged large U.S. cable and phone companies to enter the business, and it took little time for British cable to fall under U.S. control. The largest cable operator in Great Britain is Telewest, a joint venture of TCI and U.S.West, a regional telephone company in the United States. A problem with this fusion of phone and cable service is that the primary interest of the entrants is phone service, not the provision of quality television; and even as regards phone service, the prized market is heavy business and affluent users. There is little likelihood that any kind of local content and public service broadcasting will come out of such a complex of interests.[44]

BSkyB and cable engage in 'cream skimming,' offering popular fare and audience-attracting special events, while neglecting anything profound, challenging, and merely contributing to the public sphere. Doing this at a price, they pull customers away from the BBC, forcing it to compete for audience share by moving away from public service broadcasting and weakening its support base and justification for privileged financing. As we noted in Chapter 2, the BBC has been encouraged and forced to seek alternative sources of funding; through BBC World Service Television it has offered a channel on Murdoch's Star system in Asia; it has a subscription channel on Murdoch's BSkyB; it entered into a partnership with Thames Television for co-production, and it joined with Pearson to launch extra satellite channels – BBC Prime, a general programming subscription service, and BBC World, an advertising-financed news service. These commercial efforts compromise BBC's commitment to universality of service and are likely to make its offerings across the board more attuned to the market. Furthermore, these efforts are not likely to come near solving the BBC's financial problems, while undermining the basis for continuation of the license fee.[45]

The British press underwent internationalization and centralization in the new milieu. The global media baron Rupert Murdoch was allowed to acquire four national newspapers, with an aggregate national audience share of 33 percent (in 1993). The Canadian media mogul Conrad Black acquired the *Daily Telegraph* in 1985; its 1993 market share was 7.4 percent. The foreign ownership share of the British national press thus aggregated a little over 40 percent. It was also more centralized, with four control groups commanding 82 percent of the national market.[46]

The British media were politicized and shifted to the right by the recent changes in structure and global links. Both Murdoch and Black are strongly political and aggressively conservative. Murdoch entered into a *de facto* alliance with Prime Minister Margaret Thatcher, getting the previously noted exemption from EU rules on European content for BSkyB, obtaining the political and legal support for his successful breaking of the printers' unions, and allowing him to acquire four national newspapers and 33 percent of the national market (along with other media interests) without interference from the Monopoly Commission. In return, Murdoch's newspapers gave hugely biased support to the Tories in the elections of 1987 and 1992, as did Black's *Daily Telegraph*. Former Conservative Party treasurer Lord McAlpine commented after the 1992 election that 'The real heroes of the campaign were the editors of the Tory press. . . . This was how the election was won.'[47]

Murdoch's power and bias is so great that Labour Party candidate Tony Blair traveled to a Murdoch meeting in Australia in 1995 to assure the mogul of his moderation and express hopes of friendlier electoral treatment. (Blair unilaterally abrogated a Labour Party platform demand for an investigation and program for dealing with media concentration.) It should be reiterated that while the forces of the right were being protected, the BBC was under steady attack and financial pressure in the years of Tory rule. This weakened a force that was not 'left' but provided some degree of openness to oppositional voices, and helped to shift the balance of media opinion further to the right.

Politicization also resulted from the fact that political decisions were continuously required in an environment of rapid technological change, new services, and cross-border moves following one another in rapid succession. And it was clear from the gifts Murdoch garnered from the Tories that suitable media bias would be rewarded. As noted, the Broadcasting Act of 1990 had ambiguities and loopholes leaving room for regulatory discretion, and a series of waiver requests and efforts to merge the regional companies followed. These made political leverage important. Greg Dyke, currently Chairman of Pearson's television interests, contends that political 'dependency' has been institutionalized 'with broadcasters constantly wanting favours and legislative action.'[48]

The effects of internationalization and the shift toward commercialization in Great Britain are hard to disentangle in the short period of the Thatcher–Major era and may be quite small. The institutional inertia of British broadcasting is strong and was capable of fending off the full force of the Thatcherite attack. But, as Colin Sparks states, 'Overall, there can be little doubt that the cumulative effects of the reregulation of British broadcasting is to shift it from a public service system towards a commercial system in which there remains a public service element.'[49]

ITALY: COMMERCIALISM'S RAPID ASCENT

For a long time, Italy had the commercial print media operating side by side with a publicly owned and controlled broadcasting system. In contrast with Anglo-U.S. practice, the Italian print media have been dominated to a considerable extent by industrial interests, each major business group wanted the prestige or power of controlling newspapers, news magazines, and other media entities. The Agnellis (Fiat) have controlled two national newspapers (*La Stampa* and *Corriere della Sera*), other local newspapers, major weeklies, the second largest book publisher, and a major advertising agency. Raul Gardini, another important industrialist (chemicals, cement, agricultural products), owned the leading Rome newspaper, *Il Messagero*, and *Italia Oggi*, and a Monte Carlo TV channel until his recent death. *Il Messagero* is now owned by real estate mogul Francesco Caltagirone; *Italia Oggi* by the Gruppo Class (Paolo Panerai), and TV MonteCarlo by the Cecchi Gori group, which owns over 50 percent of the movie theaters in Italy. Financier Carlo de Benedetti, through his increasingly tenuous control of Olivetti, has controlled the important newspaper, *La Repubblica*, a dozen provincial papers, the news magazine *L'Espresso*, one of the main radio networks, SPER, and a book publishing business, among other media interests.

De Benedetti has described the phenomenon of industrialist control of the major newspapers as one of the 'mafioso' sides of Italian life, but he indulges himself in it. The industrialists do not often directly intervene in their papers, 'but Italian journalists have a developed sense of their proprietors' interests which generally translates, at best, into an uncritical coverage of their business activities.'[50]

Until the late 1970s, Italian broadcasting was a state monopoly, with control of the three broadcasting channels of Radio Televisione Italia

(RAI) initially maintained by the Christian Democrats, but eventually divided between the three major political parties in a *lottizzazione* (division of patronage). The RAI channels were funded by a license fee, supplemented by advertising. They provided a system of public service broadcasting that was stodgy, with public sphere functions fatally compromised by political control.[51]

Italian broadcasting was radically transformed after a 1976 court decision which allowed virtually uncontrolled private broadcasting operations. This led to a huge expansion in station numbers (1,500 by 1982), followed by a shakeout and equally rapid concentration process. A builder and real estate mogul, Silvio Berlusconi, very conscious of the advertising possibilities of commercial TV (his honors dissertation in law from Milan university was entitled 'The newspaper advertising contract'), organized an advertising agency (Publitalia), and gradually expanded from a single TV network to control of three national networks, along with extensive other media and non-media interests. His holding company Finivest owns the largest cinema-producing, distribution, and theater operations in Italy, Mondadori, the largest book and magazine publisher, the advertising agency, the leading TV weekly, the newspaper *Il Giornale Nuovo*, whose legal ownership was transferred to his brother in 1993, along with a large department store chain, a major insurance and mutual fund company, and a leading soccer team. Berlusconi's 1993 share of the Italian broadcasting audience was 44.5 percent, RAI's was 46 percent; and Berlusconi controlled some 60 percent of TV advertising expenditure and 36 percent of all advertising in Italy. With three channels apiece, together commanding over 90 percent of the national audience, Berlusconi's and the RAI system have constituted a broadcasting duopoly.

In addition to assembling this immense concentration of economic and media power in Italy, Berlusconi globalized Italian broadcasting in several ways. First, his recognition of the enormous potential of TV as an advertising vehicle, and early establishment of his own complementary advertising agency, was based in part on observation of and contacts with U.S. and other foreign commercial TV operations which were notable 'money-creation machines.' He aggressively appropriated the foreign model and its tricks of the trade. (Product placement came early in Italy.) Second, he took advantage of the cheap foreign entertainment program supplies and models, mainly from the United States, and the movies, soaps, games, and talk shows became, along with sports programs, the program base for his media empire. Eventually, as he became better established, with large market share and resources, he reduced his dependence on foreign programming, but these, together with the adapted entertainment programming models, retained a very heavy weight.

What is more, his almost exclusive dependence on audience-building movies, soaps, game shows, and sports forced RAI to respond to defend its market share, which it did by expanding services and programming changes, many emulative of Berlusconi's. This helped push up the prices of foreign program imports, and also served to further transform the broadcast system from weak public service to advertisement-saturated light entertainment with a still flimsier public sphere.

Berlusconi also helped to integrate the Italian media into the global system by virtue of his aggressive pursuit of cross-border alliances and investments. Allied with the German media entrepreneur Leo Kirch, he shared investments in channels and stations in Germany, Italy, Spain, and France, and the two jointly financed a number of TV productions.

The rapid growth of the Berlusconi empire aroused widespread concern and opposition in Italy, based on the fear of concentrated economic and media power as well as distress at the swift commercialization of broadcasting. The Americanization and trivialization of programming and the aggressive intrusion of advertising, with intra-program interruptions as well as increasing advertising volume per hour, caused an outcry. Politicians and economic interests threatened by Berlusconi's power were also prominent in calls for reform. This opposition culminated in the passage of the weak and compromised Broadcasting Act of 1990, which failed to dislodge Berlusconi from his enormous power position, merely limiting him to his three national networks, and to a single radio or TV license (including cable stations or pay-TV services) in each area. It also put limits on cross-ownership between broadcasting and the daily press (a 20 percent ceiling on national newspaper circulation for a broadcaster), and overall media revenues to a single company (20 percent for a diversified owner, 25 percent for a media-only owner). The law also limited advertising time and breaks, and imposed European content requirements. Finally, it put in place a regulator (Guarantor) and a Viewer Consultative Group to police the Act and advise on policy, both relatively powerless.

The rise of the Berlusconi empire illustrates the intensifying politicization of the mass media under the globalization–commercialization process. Contrary to the idealized vision of commercialization, in which an impersonal market replaces a system under government rule or guidance, the process inevitably raises questions of excessive media power, and cross-border and cross-service alliances and encroachments arouse concern over both monopoly power and national sovereignty. Furthermore, the centralizing and globalizing firms need and seek political support for their advances, and their critics, rivals, and victims seek to contain them. In the Italian case, while there is no doubt that the media were already politicized before Berlusconi's entry, his appearance, growth, and widening activities intensifed the political stakes. His ability to grow reflected his friendship with and enthusiastic support by former Socialist Party head Bettino Craxi, under whose government (1983–7) the Berlusconi empire 'was rescued from various judicial enquiries and legal proceedings.'[52] Throughout the 1980s, and until Craxi fell under a corruption cloud, he and his party were able to nullify any threat to halt the rapid centralization process in broadcasting.[53]

Berlusconi's direct entrance into politics in 1993, and eventual victory, brief presidential tenure, and retreat, also highlights the exceptional politicization and power of the globalizing media. Berlusconi had always been interested in political power as well as making money. He had been a member of the secret, extreme rightwing P-2 organization, which was uncovered and outlawed in 1981. The collapse of the old political order created a new opportunity for him, and it was enormously advanced by his ownership of the dominant media empire. His commercial monopoly control, and the cultural as well as political effects of this control, had been widely criticized and challenged over the prior decade, and was the motivating force behind the 1990 Act. A referendum held in 1995 included, among other issues, a call for limiting ownership of broadcasting networks to one per group, which would have forced a divestment of two networks by Berlusconi (this referendum measure was defeated). In addition, the appropriateness of a dominant media owner running for high public office was of course a major campaign issue. He skillfully used his large media resources in a 'modern' campaign of intensive spot advertising of formulaic answers to issues that polls showed to be of public concern.

With Berlusconi's victory in the 1994 election, and his rapid dismissal of the board of directors of RAI, his principal rival broadcasting organization, questions about politicization and conflict of interest became more acute. The bias of his media empire with himself in office was notable: during Italy's largest postwar demonstration, with 1.5 million people in the streets protesting against the government budget, RAI broadcast three hours of live coverage; Berlusconi's anchorman on TG4 nightly news, Emilio Fede, had this to say: 'A protest parade was held today while other people in the country were trying to work.'[54]

Berlusconi was forced to step down as Prime Minister in 1994 under the pressure of investigations into his business empire and a collapse of his center–right coalition. He then lost a close election in 1996 to a center–left alliance headed by Romano Prodi, but his power is such that the Prodi government made no effort to dismantle the Berlusconi empire. He remains a brooding omnipresence in the Italian political economy.

BARBADOS, JAMAICA, AND THE CARIBBEAN ISLANDS:
DECOLONIZATION ABORTED

Like Canada, the Caribbean islands are close neighbors of the United States, but unlike Canada the islands are tiny, and most of them have only recently emerged from colonial status (Cuba, Haiti, and the Dominican Republic were freed in the nineteenth century; the recent wave of decolonization began in 1962 when Jamaica, the largest of thirteen British Caribbean colonies, became self-governing). As with many Third World former colonies, the economies of the newly freed Caribbean colonies were long geared to serving their colonial masters, mainly providing raw materials (bananas, coffee) and tourist facilities and services. They also had sharp class divisions closely paralleling ethnic and racial divisions, the small fraction of Caucasians/Europeans tending to be members of the affluent upper class, while the great mass of blacks, heirs of the plantation and slave populations, were the less affluent and poor.

The coming of independence to the islands was associated with a surge of nationalism and high hopes for improvement in the lives of ordinary people. This led to turmoil and intensified class and political struggle, most dramatically illustrated in the victory and rule of Michael Manley's People's National Party in Jamaica from 1972 to 1980, and the follow-up neoliberal regime of Edward Seaga. Economic conditions were not favorable for the tiny, divided, and fractured islands from 1962 to the present. Losing their privileged markets as colonial enclaves, and with price declines and instability in their export markets, they failed to attract foreign investment and were unable to mobilize it at home. Their economic difficulties pushed them into excessive borrowing and dependence on foreign banks and the IMF. The main exception as regards foreign investor interest was the tourist business. Stay-over tourist business increased sixfold between 1970 and 1994, and this was the only sector of the Caribbean economies that grew steadily in the 1980s. Many of the benefits of the tourism business go abroad (airlines, travel agencies; even local hotel rooms are 63 percent owned by foreigners), but tourism is now more important than sugar for Barbados and Jamaica, and the Barbados trade import deficit is covered by its tourism revenues (in 1993 the trade deficit was $330 million; tourist receipts were $502 million).[55]

Thus, the decolonized Caribbean countries have been economic failures since independence; the new globalizing economy has treated them harshly. They have not been able to generate the investment and jobs necessary to get the great mass of their citizenry out of poverty; their income distributions have worsened, and welfare states constructed in the early heady days of freedom have been eroded. A paradox noted by critics of the accommodation of island policy to the global economy has been the steady and large exodus of Caribbean peoples to the United States and Europe, forming sizable expatriate enclaves, simultaneously with the huge influx of tourists and growth of tourist facilities on islands unable to provide meaningful work for their own emigrating populations.

The decolonized islands have tended to evolve fairly quickly from colonial dependency on Great Britain to a neocolonial dependence on the United States. The United States was already an important trading partner of the islands, but its importance has greatly increased since 1962. This is also due to the growing debt dependency of the islands, and in the Cold War and especially in the Nixon and Reagan years by virtue of the aggressive politicization of U.S. policy, with aid and trade contingent on properly subservient foreign policy behavior and free market-oriented economic policy as well. The Manley government of Jamaica in the 1970s and into 1980 suffered aid cutoffs, embargo, harsh treatment by the IMF, and Chilean-type destabilization policies.[56] The successor and neoliberal Seaga government (1980–6) was treated with great generosity by the United States, although the extremely restrictive policies it was compelled to follow by the IMF eventually caused Seaga himself to refuse to comply with IMF demands.

One element of decolonization after 1962 was the retrieval by the larger islands (Barbados, Jamaica, and Trinidad) of government control over telecommunications, which had been monopolized in the colonial era by the British-based TNC, Cable & Wireless (C&W).[57] But under the global market and evolving technological conditions of telecommunications in the 1980s, C&W was able to gain majority control of the telephone systems in Jamaica and Barbados, and 49 percent ownership in Trinidad, while dominating in the other islands as well. This resulted from the rising costs of the new technologies (laying digital fiber systems, among others) and service extensions, the poor financial capabilities of the debt-burdened islands, and IMF pressures. The IMF served C&W well, urging privatization across the board, pressing Trinidad to sell to meet IMF obligations in 1989, and contributing to Jamaica's abandonment of majority control in 1987 (C&W's ownership rose from 9 to 79 percent). These actions, ironically carried out by Michael Manley's more 'understanding' and realistic government that had regained power, were severely criticized in Jamaica because it gave C&W a completely free hand as licensed monopolist of telecommunications, with a guaranteed 17.5 percent return on assets, but no service obligations or regulatory controls.[58]

An important aspect of the new dependency was the attractiveness of the Caribbean Islands to TNCs as a base for offshore information assembly and processing industries. The hard-pressed island governments eagerly sought this business, and to the low wages and proximity to the United States they added the advantages of tax holidays and high-tech teleports and digital microwave and telephone systems. Teleports and digital systems are, however, expensive, and were provided by foreign companies. Jamaica's teleport facilities, put in place by Digiport International – owned by AT&T (35 percent), C&W (35 percent) and Telecommunications Jamaica Ltd. (30 percent) – used hundreds of satellite circuits for high-speed transmission to the United States. Barbados External Communications Ltd., 55 percent owned by C&W, offered international direct dialing, international telex, facsimile, and international database access. These and other investments brought a modest number of jobs to the Islands, but ironies abound: despite the widespread technical advance to digitalization, only 12 percent of the households in the English-speaking Caribbean have telephones. Analyst John Lent says: 'Thus when the Caribbean was not used as a playground for U.S. tourists, it performed as a sweatshop for that nation's (and European) industrial leaders.'[59]

The Caribbean media at the time of decolonization were dominated by foreign companies and foreign (especially British) models. British newspaper moguls Roy Thomson and Cecil King owned major newspapers, although local capitalists and wealthy families were even more dominant. In broadcasting, the colonial governments had owned radio stations, although there was widespread radio station ownership by the British-based Diffusion International as well. Following independence, the foreign newspaper systems eventually exited, leaving local capital in charge of a concentrated, advertisement-based and conservative press.[60]

Following independence, governments continued to dominate broadcasting, considering radio (and then television) too important to be in the exclusive control of private parties, and helpful in protecting government interests and aiding development. On Barbados, a small island with only 250,000 citizens, TV is provided in the British tradition exclusively by the local government-owned and -sponsored Caribbean Broadcasting Company (CBC), which has a regular and pay-TV service. Radio is provided by CBC and two private radio stations. A Broadcasting Act of 1980 created a broadcasting regulatory authority and regularized the CBC system. CBC's program policy statement stresses national development objectives, to create a 'national awareness,' reliance on local materials, and participation by and feedback from the community.

These goals have never been even approximately met. As in the cases of the broadcasting authorities of Jamaica and Trinidad, a fatal weak-

ness of CBC has been its complete reliance on advertising revenue
(except for periodic government assistance to cover losses). There is no
license fee allocated to the public broadcaster, as with the BBC in Great
Britain. And Barbadian advertisers have been leery of controversy and
fearful of arousing politically the large majority of relatively poor blacks.
The showing of the U.S. TV hit *Roots* and the PBS series on the Civil
Rights Movement in the United States failed to obtain Barbadian sponsors because of advertisers' aversion to potentially critical political
messages. CBC staff claim that local products of a culturally oriented or
racially conscious nature are also rejected by advertisers 'as "too grass
roots" or "anti-white".'[61] A local producer claims that 'Anything that
will enlighten, especially programmes of an educational nature that will
uplift and cause Barbadians to question certain things, will never get
sponsorship.'[62]

Locally produced programs are enjoyed by Barbadian audiences, but
advertisers do not like them because of their dialects and frequently dis-
cordant images and themes; for these reasons the popular Jamaican
program *Oliver at Large* suffered from a paucity of sponsorship. Local
products are also more expensive than foreign materials, and the advertisers do not find the emphases on foreign lifestyles and the triviality of
the foreign imports problematic. Foreign imports account for some 90
percent of Barbadian TV programming. CBC offers local news, but it
depends heavily on CNN for its world news.[63]

Jamaica and Trinidad also have public broadcasting systems that are
entirely funded by advertising and whose dependence on foreign programming has, if anything, increased since independence. Jamaica has
been partially cabled and direct broadcasting satellite dishes have been
gaining steadily; programming received on the outlets is predominantly
of U.S. origin, but with significant contributions from Brazil, Mexico,
and Venezuela. Videocassettes are also important business in the
Islands, the goods again being mainly from the United States.

There are radio stations with a much larger fraction of indigenous
music and news, and these are much more heavily used by the less affluent Caribbean populations. Calypso competes well with U.S. rock on
local radio stations. Carnivals, reggae, and art festivals are powerful
forms of local self-expression, although somewhat corrupted by their
becoming major tourist attractions.

The impact of economic and media dependency on the Caribbean
cultures has been profound. The 'news' is to a large extent news about
non-Caribbeans; the lifestyle and value models offered in the mainstream media are largely U.S. and European; and although the
Caribbean islanders have their own (even exportable) musical, dance,
art, and literary forms, even these tend to be subordinated to those

imported by the marketing-savvy cultural TNCs from abroad. The latter take indigenous material from the Caribbean (and other areas as well) and adapt it to the demands of global sales, but in the process an indigenous form like *salsa* has been divested of many, if not all, of its oppositional elements.[64] The globally salable indigenous hybridized materials reenter the local culture, alongside the massive non-indigenous inflows in a system that Joseph Straubhaar has called 'asymmetrical interdependence.'[65] Much of the massive cultural inflow is based on sheer media source dependency; some is based on the importance of tourism, the affluent tourists' demands for news and culture, and the desire of the local cultural impresarios to serve (and avoid offending) them. The growth of satellite transmissions, arriving direct to home or through cable, and videocassettes, and the growing class divisions in the Caribbean, along with media domination by advertisers and governments unable to directly fund public broadcasting, has tended to strengthen the forces of commercialism and dependency – even further integrating Caribbean upper-class tastes into that of the dominant external cultures.

It has often been noted that Caribbean schoolchildren frequently know more about U.S. politics and history than they do about their own. They also learn and absorb the lessons of consumerism and gravitate to foreign models of speech, dress, and behavior.[66] Many adulate foreign icons and lifestyles and would like to emigrate to these superior cultures – attitudes arguably inculcated by what is shown in the media and displayed by the Caribbean elite. As John Lent points out, 'When local programming is attempted, very often it is a copy of something from the United States, the thinking being that the people will not accept anything else.'[67] It is certainly true that there is significant resistance, but the forces of commercialism and dependency have been exceptionally strong, and the tide continues to move in their direction. The statement of Barbados's first Prime Minister, on the eve of independence in 1966, that his country would 'not be found loitering on colonial premises after closing time,' has not yet been realized – Barbadians and their fellow islanders are still loitering.

NEW ZEALAND: OUTDOING THE HEARTLAND MODEL

New Zealand is a small but relatively affluent island state, formerly a part of the British Empire, and still closely tied to the West by tradition and economic and political ties. Like Great Britain, it is (or was) a modern welfare state, with a fairly strong trade union movement; its Labour Party has shared power with a conservative National Party and periodically controls the executive branch.

The New Zealand welfare state came under attack in the 1970s and 1980s, under the impact of oil price increases, global recession and high interest rates, growth slowdowns that created budget deficits and demands for austerity, and a new corporate aggressiveness. Neoliberal ideologues dominated the Labour Party, which took power in 1984, and they quickly put in place a structural adjustment program which was more drastic than that inaugurated by Margaret Thatcher in Great Britain. It featured tight money, radical cuts in social budgets and subsidies, devaluation, free exchange rates, tariff cuts, freedom of foreign investment, privatization, and attacks on the trade union movement and reduced labor protection. The macro-policy objective became inflation control, and unemployment soared and remained high for many years.

By the time the Labour government exited from power in 1990, the supposed benefits of the new regime had not materialized. New Zealand's external debt had quadrupled, productivity growth from 1984 through 1992 was only 0.9 percent, obtained mainly by labor cutbacks, and the country now suffered from much higher levels of poverty and chronic unemployment. The OECD, which enthusiastically approved such reforms, admitted that 'the economy was still suffering from sluggish growth, high and rising unemployment, and high real interest rates. This created a difficult investment environment.'[68] Despite the failed Labour Party policy, the National Party that succeeded it applied more of the same medicine, reinforcing the negative effects of its predecessor's policies. An important result of the Labour Party's radical move to the right and imposition of policies seriously damaging to their own mass constituency was that a majority of New Zealanders had no political representation. As in the United States and Canada, only neoliberal choices were on the restricted political menu.

The international financial community and mainstream media were nevertheless impressed and even enthralled by the 'brave recipe,' 'trail blazing economic reforms,' 'an international model for economic reform' (all from the London *Economist*, but duplicated in the *Financial Times*, *Wall Street Journal*, and Toronto *Globe and Mail*).[69] As Jane Kelsey points out, what the free market spokespersons

> were really applauding was the unimpeded imposition of a particular ideological model to which they adhered, notwithstanding its economic and social consequences. . . . The mission of New Zealand's change agents had been to initiate and entrench the 'right' policies, not to secure socially acceptable outcomes.[70]

In important respects the model imposed by the Labour Party was a foreign import, although it had strong support within the New Zealand business community, from its lobbying group the Business Council and its local thinktank, the Centre for Independent Studies. The main intellectual influence came from the Chicago School and its satellites. A number of New Zealand policy analysts and officials had studied in the United States, and during the reform process Treasury officials spent time in the United States in order to update their analyses; expert consultants were also brought in from there. There were also regular exchanges with IMF and World Bank personnel. As Kelsey notes, 'The US influence was so pervasive that these [Chicago School] theories were implemented in almost undiluted form,' with radical deregulation of the finance sector applied to New Zealand 'without its ever having been adopted as policy in the US.'[71]

The media and communications system were not exempt from the application of free market ideology. The public telephone company, Telecom, was sold off to U.S. giants Bell Atlantic and Ameritech in 1990, making New Zealand unique in allowing its basic communications infrastructure to be entirely foreign-owned. The Radiocommunications Act of 1989 introduced a pathbreakingly free-market broadcasting regime to New Zealand. Radio entry was opened up and new entrants flocked in. The two public TV channels were made wholly dependent on advertising, and were instructed by law to put profits (and provision of a dividend to the state) as first priority, public interest programming being a 'subsidiary' consideration. They were to compete with a third, private channel (TV3) established in 1987. Legislation of 1991 extended unrestricted media-ownership rights to foreign companies, allowing TV3 to come under the majority control of Canadian multinational CanWest. Auction of UHF spectrum resulted in the acquisition of frequencies covering 80 percent of New Zealand for the three-channel pay-TV operation of Sky Network Television, owned by a consortium led by Time Warner, Ameritech, and Bell Atlantic (the latter two being joint Telecom monopolists).

In the years before 1984, the New Zealand media had already been substantially commercialized. The print media were advertisement-based, and newspaper concentration was high – and became still higher in the 1980s as failures and mergers brought about a virtual duopoly in the 1990s, with the locally owned Wilson and Horton, and INL, 40 percent of which was owned by Rupert Murdoch, controlling 90 percent of metropolitan circulation and 65 percent of provincial sales.

New Zealand broadcasting had begun on a quasi-British BBC model, but that model had never been very closely realized; Labour and National governments had never relinquished the right to intervene in broadcasting policy ('broadcasting is too important to leave to the broadcasters alone,' said one Minister of Broadcasting). The license fee had never covered broadcasting expenses; its proportion of the state broadcasters' income fell from 43 percent in 1975 to only 16 percent in

1984, most of the balance being raised by advertising. The license fee reduction rested partly on political grounds; the conservative National Party, like Thatcher's Tories and U.S. conservatives, disliked an independent public broadcaster, and National Party leaders tried to defund it and force it into the commercial nexus. Conservative Prime Minister Muldoon regularly attacked public broadcasting, and tried to weaken it in the late 1970s both by open criticism and refusing to allow the license fee to rise as fast as the rate of inflation (which reached double figures in the late 1970s).[72]

The 1989 broadcasting legislation rested on the belief that competition, the profit motive, and open markets would yield optimum results in the field of broadcasting, as everywhere. It was assumed that the new technologies – cable, direct broadcast satellite, and digital compression – would proliferate channels and establish a new world of plenitude and widened choice. The radio spectrum was put up for auction, with rights sold (privately and without any public knowledge or feedback) for extended periods, without performance obligations.

The one exception to free market principles, put into the new legislation under pressure from opponents of the basic thrust of the act, and contrary to the desires of its sponsors, was the retention of a license fee to be handled by a newly created organization, New Zealand on the Air (NZOA). This fund was to help broadcasters finance worthy programs; over half of the $110 million available in the mid-1990s was being used to finance local production of programs reflecting New Zealand culture and meeting local needs ($6–7 million of this was funding children's program production).

The impact of the free market revolution on the New Zealand media has not been favorable to diversity, widening choice, the preservation of indigenous production of content, public service performance, or even competition. As noted above, the newspaper business has reached very high concentration levels through failure and merger. There was a great increase in commercial radio stations: from fifty-three in 1987 to 116 in 1993, concentrated heavily in the largest metropolitan markets, but with limited advertising many have been in financial straits. Some have gone over to 'multiplex radio' (numerous affiliates broadcasting out of the same studio); others are 'networking' (relying mainly on signals from one center). Many have scaled down their news coverage and concentrated on a very narrow range of popular genres; rather than filling niche spaces, they have focused on popular music from the 1960s to 1990s, which best meets the tastes of age groups with spending power. New Zealand studies show that it is the public stations which provide diversity – virtually all of the more numerous private stations compete for the same audience with similar fare.[73]

The impact of the new order on TV broadcasting has been dramatic. New Zealand TV has always relied heavily on foreign programs, given the small market and cost advantage of imports, but the new market regime intensified the pressure to rely on imports, so that apart from local news, sports, games, and talk shows there would be virtually no indigenous TV production without NZOA subsidies. The free marketers overestimated the prospective availability of new channels and the impact of new channels on diversity. Cable has not gotten off the ground in New Zealand, and the only substantial satellite-based competitor, Sky Network Television, with its pay-TV service of sports, movies, and news, has only 200,000 subscribers after five-and-a-half years. TVNZ's two channels still command 77 percent of the audience, TV3 19 percent, and Sky and the remainder 4 percent.

Program diversity fell markedly, contrary to predictions of proliferating choice. The oligopolistic rivals tend to offer the same type programs in primetime, a phenomenon observed frequently elsewhere.[74] By 1994, the program range had narrowed sharply: music, minority, religious, arts, and educational programming were gone from prime hours, reducing diversity and choice.[75]

The era after 1987 also witnessed a major increase in advertising time, with a primetime hourly average reaching 15 minutes by 1994, and station managers beginning to worry about audience anger and their possible approach to the 'switch-off point.' Programs were increasingly adapted to serve sponsor interests: editing cuts to allow advertising time, programs that would coordinate well with advertiser plans, and, increasingly, infomercials as a regular part of the schedule (one program is called *The Infomercial Hour*).

Under the commercial regime news was cut back; four regional news programs were eliminated in favor of a centrally produced current affairs show (*Holmes*), and a Maori news program *Te karere* was demoted in time slot. The news itself was gradually 'Americanized,' helped along by the importation of U.S. consultants who specialized in reshaping U.S. news formats to keep audiences watching.[76] Political scientist Joe Atkinson has shown how TV news on the major TVNZ *One Network News* has been made into shorter bites ('morselization') and 'has become a series of advertisements, teasers and "promos", interspersed with terse messages from authority or interviews with ordinary people, and dramatically embroidered with cinematic fictions of sex, violence, grief and natural disaster.'[77] Richard Prebble, the Minister of Information who helped to introduce the new order back in 1987, claimed in 1990 to be 'dismayed' by the changes: 'The 6 PM *Network News* should be renamed the Auckland crime show. The *Holmes* show should be described as entertainment and not current affairs and the *Frontline* programme should be called docudrama.'[78] These news formats involve a trivialization and depoliticization of news, exactly paralleling processes that have taken place in the United States.

Also paralleling the U.S. pattern has been the rapid erosion of children's TV. New Zealand has a vigorous children's TV lobby, which provides the only counterweight to the power of market forces. But as lobby leader Ruth Zanker stated at a World Summit on Television and Children in 1995, in New Zealand 'local child-centred television is battling for survival.'[79] Advertisements have penetrated even preschool children's programming, breaking a longstanding tacit rule. Entertainment has displaced the educational and informative, and there has been a narrowing of choice in types of programming. A study by Jeanette Forbes found a halving of program type offerings between 1982 and 1992; documentary, news, craft, science, natural history, music, and Maori children's programs had virtually disappeared by 1992; drama was reduced from 52 to two minutes a day; the one growth sector was animated cartoons, which increased fivefold. There was also a huge overall shrinkage of offerings for children.[80]

In sum, the realization in New Zealand of what one of its reforming leaders called 'the most open communications market in the world' was influenced in substantial measure by the international flow of ideology from the dominant centers to this small group of islands. It represents the consolidation of a commercial model already in place, but now more firmly entrenched, to the delight of the TNC community, IMF, and neoliberal governments abroad. Its effect on the public sphere has been strongly negative, as it has replicated and even pushed beyond the model laid out in the United States.

INDIA: PROGRESSIVE COMMERCIALIZATION

India inherited from the long British occupation a tradition of a private commercial press and a government-owned broadcasting system. That tradition prevailed for almost half a century after independence. The Indian press remained uncontrolled by government and free of official censorship (except for the eighteen-month 'emergency' under Prime Minister Indira Gandhi in the mid-1970s), even though the government retained firm control over broadcasting and censored it as a matter of course. The dominant press did, however, develop a close relationship with the government during the independence struggle, and it, and especially the English-language press, has only recently moved away from its 'cozy relationship with the political and bureaucratic establishment.'[81]

As with many countries emerging from colonial rule, the leaders of the Indian political establishment found it difficult to relinquish political control over broadcasting.[82] They preached freedom of the media, but could not bring themselves to practice it for such a convenient inherited instrument of control. Commission after commission urged that Doordarshan, the public broadcaster, be made more independent of government, but even leaders who had campaigned on tickets stressing broadcasting freedom (for example, V. P. Singh in the late 1980s) reneged on this promise after winning office. Government control was rationalized in terms of the need to use broadcasting for 'development' purposes, along with the destabilization threat of an uncontrolled broadcasting system in a society in which ethnic strife and huge inequalities were serious problems.

A major consequence of this politicized system was that the public broadcasting monopoly was over-bureaucratized and its performance was dull, corrupted by censorship and propaganda service, and unsuccessful in serving any development purpose.[83] It was held in contempt by the urban elite and middle class, who relied on the print media for news and news analysis. It is important to recognize that the alleged development purpose was inherently limited and at best mildly reformist. Indian independence was achieved without disturbance of the class divisions and vast inequalities of status and economic power that characterized the colonial system. Although the leaders of the independence movement were self-proclaimed 'socialists,' they did not socialize or redistribute landed property as did the leaders of South Korea, Taiwan, and China.

The media system of India was thus built on a system of great inequality, which it ultimately served to keep intact. In important respects there was a class division in media usage: the freer print media served the elite, whereas government-controlled Doordarshan was for the rural, poor, and mainly illiterate masses. This helped to pacify both the elite – permitted their own free press – and the vast majority, supplied paternalistically and inadequately by Doordarshan. For a long time this was done mainly by radio; only 28 percent of the population had theoretical access to TV signals before India's INSAT satellite of 1983, and the roughly $200 per capita income would not cover the cost of a TV set, and was also less than the average Indian telephone bill for the small telephone-using population.

Sevanti Ninan states that 'The first telecasts were for schools, and subsequently there came telecasts for farmers. Even today the poor and those dwelling in rural areas get their news from it, but do not necessarily buy the government propaganda that comes with it.' She goes on,

For close to eight years or more, prime-time television spots have preached the importance of family planning, immunization and giving equal status to female children. . . . In the same period, communal conflicts have also been addressed on television through fiction and public service spots, though no one knows for sure and how much effect.[84]

However, there was pressure on Doordarshan even in the early 1970s to service the New Delhi elite that owned TV receivers, and their presence contributed to an early shift to entertainment programming (approximately 62 percent by 1974).[85] Furthermore, although Doordarshan may have addressed communal conflict in 'fiction and public service spots,' it did not call attention to the huge inequalities and frequent outbreaks of protest and violence at mass deprivation; it taught self-help and the spiritual unity and greatness of India, and assured the people that their government cares.

Change came to Indian broadcasting, in part as a result of government self-interest. Mrs. Gandhi, Prime Minister from 1967 to 1978 and again from 1980 to 1984, put great stress on TV as a nation-builder, and especially in the early 1980s, with Independence Day and three televised international events in the offing for 1982–3, the government put high priority on the introduction of color TV, the launching of INSAT 1, and the great increase in number of transmitters (from fourteen in 1977 to 175 in 1985, with the TV signal reaching 392 million in the latter year). Manjunath Pendakur, noting the ironical fact that the vast majority of Indians could not afford to buy TV sets, contends that the TV-network building spree was intended in part 'simply to spread the magic and myth of the ruling family.'[86]

Competition was another force making for broadcasting change. As early as 1957, Doordarshan had been subjected to severe competition from a music station in Ceylon which had built up a large Indian audience; Doordarshan replied with its own similar station that recaptured some of the lost market.[87] It learned that market share requires films and film music, and these expanded as it began to take commercial spots in 1976. In 1980 it allowed advertising sponsors, and with the development of soap operas in the early 1980s it began to draw large audiences and to make a great deal of money. Its advertising revenues rose from $0.6 million in 1976 to as much as $300 million in 1990.[88] It became much more entertainment- and marketing-oriented; its soaps, begun as purportedly 'pro-development,' were quickly altered to meet the needs of advertisers (most importantly, six multinationals) – 'the family planning theme was diluted, family harmony was stressed instead, and the plot was speeded up' as primetime became entertainment-based.[89] India was increasingly regarded as an 'emerging market' by foreign TNCs in the

1980s, and Doordarshan was integrating into the global market system, serving advertisers who were anxious to reach the large Indian middle class of consumers.

Doordarshan's commercialization and self-financing was encouraged by the increasingly neoliberal governments of the 1980s and 1990s. The Indian budget was under frequent pressure in those years as a result of familiar factors: oil price increases, raw material price declines, high interest rates, recessions, and global competition. India had been forced to borrow from the IMF and World Bank beginning in 1980, and these institutions pressed India to open up the economy, privatize, and cut 'unnecessary' expenditures. From Mrs. Gandhi's years onward India steadily opened its doors to foreign investors, merchandisers, and advertising agencies.

In 1994, under pressure from Washington and the major U.S. motion picture studios, the Rao administration rescinded the ban on dubbing movies and allowed the direct import of foreign films. Warner Brothers and other Hollywood studios have since made important inroads, to the dismay of the Bombay movie industry.[90] The Rao administration put out feelers in 1994 looking toward opening up the Indian media to foreign investment, proposing allowing investments of up to 49 percent in Indian book, newspaper, and magazine companies. It also proposed that Doordarshan be allowed to enter into joint-venture production arrangements with foreign companies.[91] India's telecom business was also slowly opening up to foreign equipment and service operations under the influence of neoliberal ideology, IMF, World Bank, foreign government and supplier pressures, internal business demands, and the fact of massive and expensive unmet Indian telecom needs. Unfortunately, the priority needs that will be met by the new suppliers will be those of the business community and other payers, not those of the several hundred million still without a telephone service.[92]

Another potent force underlying Doordarshan's change in the 1980s and 1990s was the new threat of satellite transmission. CNN made its first big mark during the Gulf War in 1990–1. Interest was so intense that cable entrepreneurs quickly laid cables in several metropolitan areas, linked to their dishes, and CNN won a temporary elite audience. A more important development was the introduction of a five-channel satellite service in 1991 by Hong-Kong based Star TV, eventually controlled by Rupert Murdoch. This system was well received by the Indian elite, and the government was unwilling and/or unable to do anything about it. It was, of course, accessible only to the small minority who owned a TV set and could pay for a cable connection or dish and decoder. But that minority was influential, growing, and of particular interest to advertisers.

This was the beginning of a major influx; by early 1996 India had some forty cable and satellite channels operating, including BBC, MTV, CNN, Worldnet, Gulfnet, and Prime (a Dallas-based sports network). Perhaps the most important new channel was Zee TV, started in 1992, 49.9 percent owned by News Corp. (Murdoch), and offering popular programming to a broad middle class in Hindustani, Urdu, and English. By early 1996, Zee TV reportedly outdrew Doordarshan in primetime by 37 to 28 percent. Its popular quiz, game, talk, and phone-in shows offered flexible advertising breaks, put sponsors' names on programs, and 'offers greater selectivity of target audience than a mass channel like Doordarshan 1,' in the words of one advertising executive.[93]

Zee TV and the other new entrants provided less biased news and current affairs programming than Doordarshan, with more varied elite perspectives and with opposition politicians being given fuller coverage. Doordarshan was forced to respond, adding new channels and even allowing some uncensored news and news analysis. Zee TV and the other new media succeeded in arousing Doordarshan from its long bureaucratic lethargy and helped to break or weaken its – and therefore broadcasting's – political subservience. Under the threat of the new competition Doordarshan rapidly enlarged its TV reach throughout India and began to pay serious attention to audience responses.

In short, this is clearly a case where the influx of commercial enterprise improved the quality of the public sphere. But the public sphere in India still leaves a great deal to be desired. It remains a very much top-down system, now permitting a certain amount of debate and alternative views of the news from other elite interests, but with the mass of poor people still unrepresented. Both the new media, and increasingly Doordarshan, cater to advertisers and audiences of interest to advertisers. The new media are geared into pay systems, and have no intended universal reach, and Doordarshan's steady integration into the commercial nexus weighs ever more heavily on its programming. As Ninan points out,

> While programming for schools and farms persists to this day, these offerings are allocated shoestring budgets and are pushed off the air when sponsored presentations like cricket matches have to be accommodated. Meanwhile on prime time, soap operas, sitcoms and films reign. Doordarshan's latest stab at winning viewers away from competing channels has been a film channel. The fact that this can be a priority in a country where a third of the population (some 300 to 350 million people in a population of 950 million) still live at subsistence level is an indication of the waywardness of the television revolution.[94]

Doordarshan's failures in the past have put a blight on further possibilities of public broadcasting in India: the ideals of universal service and
viewing audiences as citizens, rather than satisfying paying consumers,
has been undermined by malperformance.

The shift of Doordarshan to a competitive and commercially oriented system has been progressive in the short run; the longer-term
consequences are less clear. The media are being integrated into a
global system that caters to those with effective demand and encourages
them to want and to spend more. They and the advertising community
are promoting 'an elitist consumerist culture within the larger society'[95]
of what is still a Third World country. Throughout the global system the
advertising–media–TNC–IMF collective has encouraged the implantation of neoliberal rules that rely on trickle-down from private investment
and cutbacks of the welfare state. This tendency has been evident in
India. Flaunting consumerism while shifting the balance of economic
and social policy toward investment incentives may be a dangerous
combination in a system of extreme inequality.

CONCLUSION

As can be seen from our cases studies, media globalization effects, while
still hard to sort out, are dominated by commercialization and its impact
on the public sphere. For smaller and less economically developed countries, there is a further force of economies of scale and technical and
promotional sophistication that greatly facilitates media and cultural
penetration by the great powers.

There is a strong tendency in the globalizing process for advertiser
preferences for light fare to prevail, giving zero weight to the positive
externalities of public service programming, and at the same time giving
full play to audience-attracting programs featuring sex and violence, all
in accord with market logic. Put otherwise, the globalizing media treat
audiences as consumers, not as citizens, and they are most attentive to
those with high incomes.

7

ALTERNATIVES TO THE STATUS QUO?

Our aim in the preceding chapters has been to establish the following four closely related points. First, a striking trend of the past decade has been the accelerated development of a global commercial media system which increasingly shapes the direction and content of national media in much of the world, although this process is meeting resistance and is far from complete. Second, this global commercial media system is dominated by some ten mostly U.S.-based transnational media conglomerates, with another thirty to forty very large, mostly North American and Western European firms occupying niche and regional markets. These firms not only operate in oligopolistic markets, but through numerous joint ventures and alliances have made the global media into a set of loosely knit cartels.[1] Third, the global media system is an indispensable component of the globalizing market economy as a whole. On the one hand, communication and information provide a large and growing area of investment. On the other hand, the global media provide a vital forum for advertisers and the promotion of demand and consumerist values that grease the wheels of the global market. Fourth, this global media system has fundamental structural flaws that limit its service to democracy and even stand as a barrier to the development of meaningful self-government. It tends to further centralize media control in a narrow business elite, whose offerings are shaped by advertiser interests; these in turn feature entertainment, the avoidance of controversy, minimal public participation, and the erosion of the public sphere.

In this concluding chapter we address two sets of issues. First, we examine the main arguments of those who consider the trends and effects of the globalization–commercialization process to be benign or positive. Second, we chronicle the widespread global efforts to establish and strengthen community and other noncommercial media, to publicize and organize around the flaws of the commercial media, and to push government communication and information policies away from service to advertisers and toward public service (i.e. nonmarket) principles. Although the short-term prospects for media (and social) reform appear poor, it is in these activities that we can see the embryonic forms of a genuine public sphere, where the audience is treated as citizens rather than as consumers.

THE DEFENSES OF GLOBALIZATION AND COMMERCIALIZATION

There are five main lines of defense of the media status quo and current globalization–commercialization trends.

The magic of the market

First and perhaps most important is the argument that, despite any limitations of the market, competition and the need to satisfy audiences ultimately compels the commercial media to 'give the people what they want.' The market, in this view, is a responsive mechanism, and in contrast with state bureaucracies, which can ignore audience reactions without peril, the market is driven to serve the consumer.

There is surely an important element of truth in this portrayal of the market. It must attract customers; consumers must receive value for their money, or they would not spend it, and listeners to and viewers of 'free' broadcasting must be induced to listen or watch and not switch stations. And the commercial media have proved to be very capable of providing a plethora of certain types of fare, such as action films and sporting events. Indeed, a great majority of people probably find satisfaction in some commercial programs and some, perhaps many, find satisfaction in a great deal of it.

There are, however, a number of core problems with using the market as the basis of a system of mass communication. First, the market treats its audiences as consumers, not citizens, so that serving a public sphere function is outside its purview. As we discussed earlier, its bottom-line objectives, along with the force of competition, cause it to marginalize the public sphere.[2] Second, although the market treats audiences as consumers rather than as citizens, it does not make consumers 'sovereign' in the sense of allowing them to choose what is offered. The right to choose programs rests with owners and managers, frequently in consultation with advertisers; the consumer audience has 'free choice' only among the offerings provided by the rulers of the market. If these rulers choose not to show a program on growing concentration in the media, the true sovereign has spoken, not the consumer. What Walter Hale Hamilton wrote in the 1930s holds true today: 'Business succeeds rather better than the state in imposing restraints upon individuals, because its imperatives are disguised as choices.'[3]

A third and related problem with the commercial media is that, being funded by advertisers, they service audiences on advertisers' terms. Advertisers want affluent audiences, and they want them to be provided with an atmosphere conducive to selling goods. This means a double-class (and antidemocratic) bias – programming formats are selected with an eye to advertiser interests; and, given the advertiser quest for affluent audiences, the audience 'vote' in the commercial system is weighted by spending capacity. We noted in Chapter 5 the FCC's acknowledgment back in 1946 that advertising and public service programming were incompatible – that advertisers want entertainment and light fare, and that public sphere programming would entail financial sacrifices on the part of broadcasters. As we also showed, with advertising eventually available in the United States for all time slots, public service program-ming was gradually sloughed off, a tendency that is observable globally.

A fourth problem with a market-based mass media is that its increas-ing centralization of ownership, links to advertisers, and dependence on politicians makes it conservative and hostile to dissent and debate on issues that challenge the status quo. It is for this reason that conservat-ives in Canada, Great Britain, and the United States have been hostile to public broadcasting (as well as the independent nonprofit sector) and have tried to defund it or push it into the commercial nexus. The com-mercial connection, instead of making for diversity of opinion, filters out dissent more consistently than public broadcasting, when the latter is given a modicum of autonomy.

A final problem with the market is that it is rarely fully competitive and may be subject to seriously monopolistic restraints. This is notably true in the media, where the sellers offer a differentiated product, where advertising, cross-selling, and economies of scale are important, and where entry is often difficult and concentration levels high. This non-competitive condition helps to explain the paradox that national audiences in many Third World countries are said to prefer local pro-gramming, whereas a great majority of programs actually shown are U.S.-made imports – small market diseconomies of scale allow the pur-chase of imports at 5 to 25 percent of the cost of equal quality local productions, and local advertisers often prefer the foreign-made pro-grams anyway for political reasons.[4] As another illustration, with its great monopoly power, the conservative-dominated U.S. cable system, TCI, was able to raise the price charged to a liberal channel, The 90s Channel, and drive it out of business, while favoring its own and allied rightwing channels.[5] Consumers are still 'free to choose' among the options decided upon by TCI, and if these consumers really want The 90s Channel they can always start their own cable system![6]

Professionalism and objectivity rules

A second major line of defense of the status quo and globalization–commercialization process rests on the rise of professionalism and rules of objectivity; these are alleged to be of increasing importance and to outweigh structural factors in affecting media performance. Media analyst Dan Hallin speaks of the maturing of professionalism as 'central to understanding how the media operate,' and its further improvement 'surely part of the answer' to protecting and rehabilitating the public sphere,[7] and he is not alone in this view. By the logic of this argument, flaws in journalism are a result of poorly constructed or insufficiently enforced professional standards, and can be largely remedied without major structural change.

As with the magic-of-the-market defense, there is a germ of truth in this perspective, as standards of professionalism do have effects and journalists' performance cannot be ascribed *in toto* to structural factors. But the heavy weight given to professionalism is not in any way justified; given its role, and the vagueness and flexibility of objectivity standards, professionalism has little impact on media agendas and can only rarely override the imperatives of ownership and advertiser interests and bottom-line pressures.

Professional journalism is a relatively recent phenomenon, even in the United States, where it was largely spawned. Throughout the nineteenth century, U.S. journalism was highly partisan, and newspapers and magazines were often closely tied to political parties. As the newspaper business became more concentrated by the beginning of the twentieth century, with advertising the main source of revenue, political partisanship became detrimental to business. It alienated customers who disagreed with the proprietor's biases. It made it difficult for news agencies and papers to sell their news product to other papers; a more factual and less opinionated product was more salable. And partisanship also made for more libel suits.[8] These factors contributed to the emergence of professional journalism, whose core idea was that the news should not be influenced by the political agendas of owners, advertisers, or the editors and reporters themselves. In one form this doctrine is characterized as 'objectivity,' according to which trained professionals apply 'neutral' news values so that accounts of public affairs tend toward sameness no matter who the reporter is or which medium carries the news.

Although the design of professionalism and objectivity rules was to show a journalism above the battle, they achieved this more in appearance than reality. Indeed, the interests of owners and advertisers were readily accommodated within the doctrine of professionalism and objectivity. What this doctrine established was a nominal rather than a substantive standard.[9] The objectivity rules called for citing credible sources, but economic considerations plus public acceptability and recognition value made for the media's heavy and uncritical reliance on officials. The rules called for 'balance' and the need to cite 'both sides,' but there may be more than two sides, and merely citing does not preclude serious favoritism. And objectivity rules say nothing about what slant to take, or what stories to select in the first place. With this flexibility in application of the rules, it is important that the hand of the owner always looms in the background with control over hiring, firing, and promotion. Those rewarded tend to be journalists who adhere closely to the 'policy' of the proprietor and do not stir up trouble.[10] Those penalized tend to be excessively preoccupied with the old dictum of 'comforting the afflicted and afflicting the comfortable.'

Nevertheless, the growth of journalist professionalism did bring a certain degree of autonomy to the newsroom and did permit journalists to pursue stories with more freedom from owner interference than had been the case in the nineteenth century. On some types of stories and in some contexts, reporters are able to do first-rate work, despite corporate control of the industry. But in many critical areas this kind of journalism is the exception and has been discouraged by bottom-line pressures, increasingly so in the last decade. In the world of the new media giants, each sector is expected to have a positive effect on the firm's earnings statement. Good journalism is expensive, and bottom-line results can be improved by staff cuts and filling the news gap with materials provided by the public relations industry, syndicated materials, and fillers. Furthermore, the media giants have major conflicts of interest in reporting on many crucial issues, such as taxation, trade, and labor policy, and there is little reason to believe that they will allow neutrality in the treatment of such matters. The past few years have witnessed several major editors and many journalists abandoning the profession in anger over these trends. James Squires, former editor of the *Chicago Tribune*, contends that the corporate takeover of the media has led to the 'death of journalism.'[11]

It should also be noted that the idea that 'professional' standards can protect creative media workers in entertainment, as opposed to journalism, from commercial imperatives, is not tenable. Commercial values are deeply embedded in commercial entertainment and, unlike journalism, there is little tradition of its being a public service area requiring protection from commercial influence. Creative workers in entertainment derive some protection from trade unions, along with the underwriters' interest in encouraging the creation of a salable entertainment product, which requires a certain degree of worker freedom. High-quality productions sometimes follow, but this is not a result of the protection of 'professional' standards, and the dampening effect of commercial pressures is all too common.

In sum, the professional status of journalism has afforded at best limited protection of journalists from bottom-line pressures. That protection has weakened under the force of increased concentration and commercialization. Any rejuvenation of the profession will require the alteration of the institutional conditions under which it operates.

The 'active audience'

A third major strand of argument in defense of the status quo and globalization–commercialization trend goes under the name of 'active audience' analysis. Active audience analysts contend that the power of media firms is exaggerated, as audiences routinely interpret corporate messages in ways that suit their own needs, not those of media proprietors or advertisers. In contrast with the professionalism argument, here the effective counter to structurally based forces is located in the audience itself. Active audience analysis also offers a variant of the argument that the 'market gives people what they want,' as the audience allegedly 'co-produces' the final outcome with the program organizer, reworking it in the listener-watcher's own frame of reference.[12]

This analysis has gained currency in global debates over cultural and media imperialism. The active audience analysts argue that the notion that media giants are brainwashing people into rejecting their own cultures and adapting U.S. or western culture is wrong. To the contrary, they argue, people around the world adapt global media fare to their own environment and use it creatively. This line of reasoning is appealing because it credits humanity with ingenuity and intelligence, and suggests that resistance to globalization and commercialization is more effective than it appears to be on the surface.

At their best, active audience analyses provide a useful corrective to the tendency to portray the media and their controllers as the exclusive determinants of political consciousness. The starting point for understanding the nature of global political culture is the global market economy, of which the media are only a part. That market economy is increasing global stratification, pressing home commercial values, and downgrading civic virtues. Its power has created a great paradox: an expansion of formal democracy, but a weakening of its substance and growing sense of political powerlessness.

But active audience analysis does not reach for a broader and more global frame of reference – that would involve 'meta-narratives,' which are rejected as unscientific, in favor of micro-analyses which focus on textual analysis and comparisons. This methodology imparts a strong apologetic thrust, as analyses of the readings of individual texts can only yield local conclusions and are almost certain to find variations among individuals and groups, hence reader 'freedom.' At its limit, this approach suggests that media control and consumer sovereignty are irrelevant – the consumer is always a 'co-producer' with those making media choices, and audience members will always be found with variant readings of media offerings. Implicitly, this could rationalize authoritarian control of the media, as audiences would inflect whatever was offered there as well. The approach misses the possibility of cumulative effects over time of ideological premises buried in images, lifestyles, and story frames, as well as the ability of those in control of the media to study and experiment with the means of overcoming audience resistance. It ignores the possibility of depoliticization resulting from massive programming of attractive entertainment and neglect of the public sphere.[13]

The global media system may not produce commercial robots, but it will provide billions of 'consumers' by means of a thoroughgoing and incessant indoctrination in commercial values, whether audiences like it or not. And it seems likely that over time this is going to have effects, probably large and almost certainly negative from the perspective of civic and communal values.

The new communications technologies

A fourth line of argument in defense of the ongoing globalization and commercialization trends claims that the new communications technologies have conquered the scarcity problem and provide new possibilities for competitive communication, thereby removing the monopoly power threat from the continuing expansion of the media giants. The argument is based on the capacity of digital TV systems to provide several hundred channels and, equally important, the emergence of the Internet to offer a forum to anyone at relatively modest expense. In Chapters 2 to 4, however, we showed how quickly the media and communications giants have taken charge of the new technologies and set them on an explicitly commercial course.

A proliferation of channels would seem to hold forth the potential for diversity and the intensive cultivation of niche markets serving neglected constituencies and the public sphere. But this is largely illusory if carried out within a commercial framework: the new channels tend to offer the same fare as the old, and instead of filling new niches they attempt to skim off some of the thinning cream in entertainment and sports. The grand irony is that the expansion of channels has increased, not reduced commercialism and advertiser power, as our discussions in Chapters 2,

4, and 5 indicated. To the extent that advertising is limited or unavailable, the alternative commercial course is to provide premium-priced
pay-TV channels. This is hardly a boon to the public sphere: not only
are these channels pitched to the affluent classes, but cable and satellite
television are monopolized gateways, whose owners have considerable
power to restrict channel access on commercial or political grounds.
Even a powerhouse can be excluded by a gateway-owner like Murdoch,
whose Asian satellites were made unavailable to CNN – 'Turner executives say News Corp. doesn't explicitly bar competitors; rather, it sets
economic terms that are so undesirable that a deal becomes unworkable.'[14] As noted earlier, this was the method employed by TCI to oust
and effectively destroy The 90s Channel.

The Internet in particular has inspired belief in a new age of democratic communication flowing from technological advance. Across the
globe, democratic forces and insurgent groups have been able to bypass
the global media system and communicate among themselves. There is
little doubt that the Internet is providing a superior mechanism for individuals and groups marginalized by the commercial media system to
communicate and share information quickly, in large quantity, and on a
global basis. For this reason alone, the Internet is a noteworthy historical development for democratic communication. Whether the Internet
can become a democratic mass medium, however, is another matter
altogether. Very large numbers cannot afford the technology accessing
the Internet, nor is there any reason to think they will be able to do so
for many years. Access may well be restricted as increasing numbers
eventually overwhelm its capacity. For the substantial numbers that do
obtain access, how do they know where to log in? The secret of mass
communication is making the information source widely known and
attractive. As the media and other business giants have invaded, colonized, and commercialized cyberspace (see Chapter 4), they have found
that it is through announcements and advertisements on their already
existing channels which reach millions that they can make substantial
numbers of people aware of and interested in their websites. Which is
another way of saying that existing command of audiences is the means
of getting cyberspace audiences – or that money and power outside of
the Internet is the basis for power within it.

No better alternatives

A final reason for support of the media status quo offered by its de-
fenders is that there are no viable alternatives to the developing
commercial system – non-market systems, it is argued, install a layer of
bureaucrats between media producers and consumers, and even the

best-intentioned bureaucrats over time grow arrogant in their largely unaccountable power. The failure of various communist regimes with their very unattractive media systems and appalling human rights records only reinforces the notion that there is no alternative to the market. Likewise, the mixed record of more benign government-run media and telecommunications systems supports the same conclusion.

There are very legitimate concerns over having state-run media and communication as an alternative to the market. However, government bureaucrats may be elected or appointed by democratically elected leaders, in which case they are not unaccountable. And commercial media decision-makers are accountable to owners and advertisers, not to a democratic constituency. Furthermore, we favor as a democratic alternative media that comprise a variety of autonomous and nonprofit entities. Such a so-called civic sector exists and is growing as grassroots movements respond to the centralization–commercialization process (see the next section). Finding and developing a democratic alternative to market-driven or exclusively governmentally dominated media systems may well be one of the central political tasks of our era.

THE GLOBAL STRUGGLE FOR DEMOCRATIC COMMUNICATIONS

Although the global media system seems every bit as entrenched as the global market economy, and has no shortage of advocates, it is generating opposition and resistance. Some of the loudest voices of dissent come from the anti-democratic, ultranationalist, fundamentalist right, that blames the media for middle-class economic distress, social turmoil, and moral decay, and would bring them under authoritarian discipline. But there is also a burgeoning global grassroots resistance, of individuals, groups, and organizations who perceive their (and society's) interests ignored, damaged, or threatened by the globalization and commercialization of the media and communication. Most of these groups are not opposed to global communication *per se*, but rather to global communications dominated by a handful of corporations driven by strictly commercial considerations. Although this activity is predominantly local or nationally based, global networks and alliances are also forming in response to corporate and media globalization.

This resistance faces a daunting task. Media corporations have always had the great advantage of controlling the flow of news that would inform people about any challenges to their power. The task of reforming the media becomes more difficult as they centralize and extend their reach across borders, and as pro-market policies become politically unchallengeable globally. In the 1970s and early 1980s, somewhat rosier times for visionaries of public service, the movement for a new world information and communication order was easily quashed by the United States, urged on by the dominant media firms. These firms and their vision of the world order are more dominant today.

The increasing hegemony of the market is especially important today because the digital revolution and convergence are forcing a rethinking of media and communications regulations and policies everywhere in the late 1990s. If the historical pattern for broadcasting holds true, decisions made in this and the following decade may establish the contours of the digital communication system for generations. It is in this context that public service is, regrettably, in retreat. Its interests have a potentially large support base in religious, educational, labor, and related non-profit organizations, but that base is fragmented and without large resources for organizing and lobbying. In the publicity vacuum that surrounds most communications policy-making, public interest groups are commonly left to hope that there will be splits among the powerful monied players that will leave an opening for extracting some public interest concessions. In the case of copyright and other intellectual property, for example, there are many nations and economic interests that are resisting the efforts of the media giants to establish stringent standards; these are the sorts of allies that might make a more public service-oriented copyright standard at least part of the policy debate. Without such allies, public interest lobbying has little leverage, and can only rarely exercise any influence over policy-making (an exception, even if a weak one, is the children's lobby, as is noted below).

For many decades, the most important communications policy struggles have been over the establishment and funding of public broadcasting, subsidies for the maintenance of independent film production and a diverse newspaper industry, laws limiting foreign ownership of domestic media, and local content rules. In the past decade, the debates over telecommunication deregulation and privatization have joined them in significance. Telecommunications is becoming an especially important media area as it is the logical domain for the establishment and supervision of digital computing networks, like the Internet. Moreover, the public policy questions surrounding broadcasting and telecommunications are very similar to those facing schools, universities, libraries, and museums, where commercial values are encroaching upon those traditionally public service sectors. In short, the current thrust is for the entire 'ideological' sphere of society to be brought into the market orbit. In the case of education, and to a lesser extent, telecommunication, workers' and citizens' groups provide a bulwark of resistance to rapid commercialization, but the present trend is very much toward market control. This is difficult to reconcile with a democratic communications system or polity.

Globalization and the growing power of the TNCs has made the containment of media concentration and centralization more difficult. The centralizing firms contend that they need greater size and vertical integration to compete in the global market, and their political power and the support of market forces (Wall Street loves these centralizing mergers) have essentially removed anti-trust barriers to media concentration. The political forces opposed to the recent U.S. mergers of Westinghouse and CBS, Disney and Capital Cities/ABC, and Time Warner and Turner were negligible. In short, the aim of media decentralization is politically utopian in the developed countries today; at this historical juncture it is extremely difficult to contain further centralization.

Instead of struggling to obstruct or turn back media centralization and commercialization, the forces of resistance have sought to educate and lobby for improved performance of the commercial media, they have tried to protect and strengthen public broadcasting, and, most important, they have struggled to create alternative media. In virtually every country there are groups – in some cases many groups – that engage in these activities, and their numbers grow. In the United States, for example, an organization called the Cultural Environment Movement (CEM) has been created, designed to combat the subordination of global culture to commercial principles by education and, hopefully, an eventual grassroots political movement. With a more constricted objective, the Center for Media Literacy holds regular classes on media literacy and supplies publications explaining how to understand and *use* the media. The media literacy movement is even stronger in Europe.

There are also many groups that monitor, criticize, and pressure the media, performing an educational and lobbying function at the same time.[15] In the United States, for example, the organization Fairness & Accuracy in Reporting (FAIR) publishes a bi-monthly critical journal *EXTRA!*, periodically publishes longer papers on particular issues (biased coverage of labor, conservative domination of public broadcasting talk shows), and has its own weekly radio program on media issues. It follows media performance and legislative issues and not only informs its readership but tries to mobilize them to act. A British organization pursuing a similar agenda is the Campaign for Press and Broadcasting Freedom (CPBF). Organizations have been formed in a number of countries to publicize media self-censorship – in the United States, Project Censored has done this since 1976, and a Project Censored Canada has been active since 1993.

Throughout the world, also, there are groups focused on studying, criticizing, and pressing for improvement in media programming for children. These *de facto* children's lobbies have arisen in response to the strongly negative effects of commercialization (and often less than superb performance of public broadcasters) on children's programming. They are loosely linked internationally, and in 1995 and 1996 had major international conferences in Australia and the Philippines. These lobbies have tried to exercise influence through persuasion of broadcasters – using evidence of malperformance, moral appeals, and threats – and efforts to get regulators and governments to compel broadcaster improvement. These lobbies have been relatively effective, because the number of aggrieved parents is large, posing a political threat, and the social desirability and morality of their positions are compelling. They can sometimes put the media establishment on the defensive, and they are fairly well organized and persistent. Unfortunately, however, the media are even better organized, and well positioned to control the debate, so that the victories of the children's lobbies have been modest and have not stemmed the secular drift to a deteriorated commercial media service for children.[16]

There have also been groups in each country seeking to protect the public broadcasting systems which have been under market and political siege. For example, in Great Britain there is a Voice of the Listener and Viewer (VLV), which holds conferences, publishes papers, and lobbies on behalf of public broadcasting.[17] In Canada, the Friends of Canadian Broadcasting, a 40,000-member group, fights for the protection of CBC; in France, the Media Télévisione Téléspectateur presses the public broadcasting case; and similar groups operate all over the globe. Furthermore, large numbers of individuals and lobbies such as the children's support groups recognize and appreciate the value of public broadcasting. Unfortunately, the committed support groups are small and weak and the larger forces of potential support are poorly organized and of uncertain loyalty. Public broadcasting has been weakened by the rise of specialty pay-TV cable channels, that have drained away support. Thus the savage cuts in public broadcasting funding in Canada, described in Chapter 6, have been carried through with minimal resistance.

The most vibrant and hopeful response to the trend toward globalization and commercialization has been the rise of community and public access radio and television stations and programs. These nonprofit and noncommercial media have been forming across the globe in literally scores of countries on every continent ranging from the United States and Germany to El Salvador, Haiti, and the Philippines. They have also been linking up in regional and global associations such as the World Association of Community Radio Broadcasters (AMARC) and the Global Alternative Media Association (GAMA). These global groups facilitate program exchanges and cooperation for political organizing. GAMA describes one of its core tasks as 'working to break the monopolies of the Western media giants.'[18] But while AMARC and GAMA are openly critical of global capitalism and the unfettered market, their primary lobbying effort has been to have spectrum space reserved nationally and globally for their activities.

Unlike traditional public broadcasters, community and public access broadcasters receive little or no public funding, and are usually directed by the staff or local community with minimal state interference. Many are one-person operations, offering radio programs to the local community by means of low-wattage transmitters, occasionally producing programs that are then sent around by satellite or by mailed videotape.[19] They involve public participation and genuine interaction, not vertical and one-way (top-down) communication and highly controlled interaction. They are democratic media in the true sense, and they regularly provide a community public sphere (which the mainstream media fail to do).

In a pioneering case in the United States, M'Banna Kantako, a 31-year-old black, blind, unemployed public-housing resident in Springfield, Illinois, organized Black Liberation Radio in 1986, out of frustration with the failure of the major media to provide news and entertainment to the black community. Operating illegally on a one-watt transmitter with a range of one mile, Kantako offered a genuine alternative to the black community. His example was widely emulated, and a 'free radio' movement emerged and numerous 'micro-radio' stations have gone on the air. Among such rebel stations in the Berkeley –San Francisco area, Stephen Dunifer's Free Radio Berkeley has been notable, for several reasons: it has used a mobile transmitter that allowed him to elude FCC attempts to close his operation; he has sold transmitting equipment to and helped organize dozens of similar stations; and he has successfully, if temporarily, resisted FCC closure efforts in court. It is enlightening to see the FCC struggling to close down such 'pirate' stations while quickly approving merger after merger of media giants with immense monopoly power.

There are several hundred legal community radio stations in the United States, although many have languished for want of continuity of programming and patchy quality. Pacifica Radio's five-station network has done yeoman work in providing alternative and high-quality radio programming and in developing a sizable and loyal audience. Radio has been even more important abroad, both in licensed and unlicensed operations. Radio Zinzine in Forcalquier, a small town in Upper Provence in France, provides an important model of constructive radio use. Organized by members of the progressive cooperative Longo Mai, Radio Zinzine, operating twenty-four hours a day, has given the local farmers and townspeople not only a more vigorous and action-oriented form of local news (as well as broader news coverage and entertainment), but also an avenue of communication among formerly isolated and consequently somewhat apathetic people. It has energized the local population, encouraged its participation in the station and politics, and made it a more genuine community.

Although community radio has often done wonders, and holds some promise for democratization of the media, its limits are evident. Quality journalism and entertainment require resources, technical facilities, experience, and institutional support; without these, media tend to stay small, local, and marginal, even if useful. Moreover, to the extent that community radio stations generate audiences, they are often subject to state harassment, sometimes at the urging of commercial interests. We noted the FCC's attempt to shut down Free Radio Berkeley, and Pacifica Radio in the United States and Radio Zinzine in France have also been subject to state attack. In Latin America, the persecution of community radio is commonplace. Brazil's commercial broadcasting firms, led by Globo, are pressing the state to limit the power and range of Brazil's 2,000 community stations.[20]

Television has been harder to democratize, because it is expensive to program and gaining access to distribution is difficult and costly. As we have described, commercial domination in the United States gradually marginalized public service. The proliferation of cable channels would seem to hold forth new democratic possibilities, and in the United States the rise of cable led to negotiated agreements between cable companies and communities requiring 'public access' channels and even demanding that the companies provide facilities, training, and sometimes money to help community groups. This led to a public access movement and the development of public access use at over 1,000 sites, and it also led to the development of program production for public access and satellite dish reception – most notably, Paper Tiger TV, and an affiliated Deep Dish Network, both assembling and producing quality programs, publicized in advance and transmitted through Manhattan Cable (Paper Tiger), and via satellite to alerted dish-owners and public access stations (Deep Dish).

In other countries also there has been a struggle to gain public access to cable channels, and as channel numbers multiply with digital compression some of these may become accessible. In many countries 'community cable,' TV cooperatives, and local TV stations have been organized to supply local needs on a noncommercial basis. In Saba, Colon, a farming community in Honduras, for example, a group of teachers organized a cooperative to install a cable system and transmit programs on community activities: sports, social, religious, and political events important to the local viewers are transmitted from 4 p.m. to 8 p.m. In Santa Rosa, Copan, in Honduras, similar technology was used, with programming of filmed local events, sports, news, and music, along with family advice. This was funded by members' fees and some local advertising.[21]

Closely related to the growth of community stations has been the development of video training and production. The fall in the price of video equipment has permitted a major expansion in the use of video productions by amateurs and semi-professionals, which are distributed through public access stations, other cable systems, and to organizations and groups for use in meetings, and public and private showings. There has been a rapid growth of film/video and public access training programs for community groups in practically every country in the world. In India, for example, where there are over 15,000 non-governmental organizations and thousands of schools and colleges looking for alternative video programs, an alternative video movement has sprung into existence to supply this demand for programs on ethnic strife and its roots and economic and environmental problems.[22]

In Latin America there were over 400 grassroots video projects in operation by 1989, and video activists have gone into the streets to create a mobile and truly local TV. Often linked to social movements, these projects have permitted close communication with, and within, local communities, and have been a prime educational and motivational tool of these movements. The Brazilian Association of Popular Video has embarked on an 'ABVP Goes to the Streets' project, which is attempting to establish a National Network of Street Television by installing TV screens on poles in open spaces in twenty-two cities, to exhibit videos produced by social movements, hopefully with audience interaction.[23]

A notable further example in Brazil has been TV Maxambomba, an experimental effort of the Popular Image Creation Center (CECIP), a nonprofit organization dedicated to producing alternative educational materials.[24] TV Maxambomba targeted Baixada, a large working-class district in Rio de Janiero, and the project has involved local video training, alternative filming of working-class materials, and screenings. Baixada's 300 residential associations were polled on member needs, and since 1989 the project's video production crews have gone into the neighborhoods on a nearly daily basis to make short videos of residents expressing their views on various topics (condom usage, clean water, sanitation); and, five nights a week, TV Maxambomba's crews set up moving exhibitions to show residents' comments along with other CECIP or local station video programs. A moderator tries to encourage people to discuss the issues. Maxambomba's videos often use the telenova format to attract audiences. Other similar efforts have fallen by the wayside for reasons of money shortages, technical weaknesses, and ennui at the video format, but TV Maxambomba has been a success, avoiding partisanship, and stimulating a real democratic dialogue.

Given its ease of use and low cost, activists have also seized upon the Internet as a venue to establish a nonprofit, noncommercial media sector. It has the further advantage of permitting nearly instantaneous global reach. And by linking the Internet to community broadcasting it may be possible to improve the quality of each of them. In countries like Mexico, China, and Saudi Arabia, the Internet has been a bulwark of democratic activism. However, it suffers in those countries, and elsewhere, from being limited to a small elite, with the bulk of the population excluded. The core problem for alternative media in its attempt to mobilize large numbers remains one of resources, or lack thereof; unless such resources can be found, or the public's interest is provoked by force of circumstance, it is hard to imagine community stations or the Internet providing a viable service for more than a small fraction of the population. This impoverished sector may remain harmlessly on the margins, along with the proponents of nonprofit media, with the ironic effect of 'proving' the freedom of the global media market while denying it in substance.

The central question is whether the various media activist groups can generate support from sympathetic larger aggregations such as religious bodies, labor, and educators, coalesce, and work to mobilize public opinion in favor of media reform. There is no shortage of ideas on how to create and support a viable nonprofit and noncommercial media, only a lack of finance and organized political muscle. The current wave of media activism is still in its nascent stage, so it is difficult to predict its future course. To succeed, the battle must be engaged locally, nationally, and globally. At the global level, media activists must not only join together but must also push for reinvigorating and reorienting public service groups like UNESCO and the ITU. The ultimate goal must be the establishment of a global, nonprofit public sphere to replace, or at least complement, the global commercial media market. Likewise, international groups like the WTO, IMF, and World Bank, which have been instrumental in pressing for the creation of a global commercial media and communication system, must be forced to cease their exclusive service to the TNC community, regardless of social and political costs. In this sense, again, the battle for democratic communication is part and parcel of the battle for a more just and democratic economy.

CONCLUSION

Few eras in history have approached this one for tumult and rapidity of change, and key hallmarks of the era have been the spread of an increasingly unfettered global capitalism, a global commercial media and communication system, and the development of revolutionary communication technologies.

For the short and medium term we expect both the global market and global commercial media to strengthen their positions worldwide, in the manner we have described earlier. But beyond that the future is very unclear and remains the subject of human political control. What is done now may significantly affect what is possible later. The system may be far more vulnerable and subject to change than appears to be the case at present. The global market system has not ushered in a liberal democratic utopia and history is not at an end; quite the reverse, as economic polarization, ethnic strife, and a market-based paralysis of democracy hold forth possibilities of rapid and substantial social, political, and economic upheaval. If it is to change, and in a positive way, it is important that people who are dissatisfied with the status quo should not be overcome and rendered truly powerless by a sense of hopelessness and cynicism. As Noam Chomsky said, 'if you act like there is no possibility for change, you guarantee that there will be no change.'

NOTES

NOTES TO INTRODUCTION

1. For example, in rural Tanzania, where conventional mass media are inadequate, oral communication plays a more important role in disseminating news, propaganda and tribal traditions. Ullamaija Kivikuru, *Tinned.Novelties or Creative Culture?* (University of Helsinki, Department of Communication, 1990), pp. 122–7.
2. 'Our analysis based on large national probability sample surveys indicates that long-term regular exposure to television tends to make an independent contribution to the feeling of living in a mean and gloomy world. The "lessons" range from aggression to desensitization and to a sense of vulnerability and dependence.' George Gerbner, 'Marketing global mayhem,' *the public*, 2 (1995), 73.
3. Jürgen Habermas, *The Structural Transformation of the Public Sphere* (Cambridge: Polity, 1984); James Curran, 'Mass media and democracy: a reappraisal,' in James Curran and Michael Gurevitch, *Mass Media and Society* (London: Edward Arnold, 1991).
4. Public service programs also encompass those serving small audiences – minorities, religious groups, and the like – some of which may involve the provision of niche entertainment.
5. Bob Franklin, *Packaging Politics* (London: Edward Arnold, 1994), pp. 79–81.
6. *Ibid.*, p. 61; Liz Curtis, *Ireland: The Propaganda War* (London: Pluto, 1984); David Miller, *Don't Mention the War: Northern Ireland, Propaganda, and the Media* (London: Pluto, 1994).
7. Michael Cockerell, Peter Hennessy, and David Walker, *Sources Close to the Prime Minister* (London: Macmillan, 1985). While attacking sources of potentially critical reports, in September 1989 the Thatcher government spent £76 million of taxpayers' money to propagandize for the privatization of electricity (Franklin, *Packaging Politics*, p. 7). Its outlays and propaganda effort during the miners' strike were far greater (Seumus Milne, *The Enemy Within: MI5, Maxwell and the Scargill Affair*, London: Verso, 1994).
8. An internal U.S. document speaks of people downwind from atomic test sites as a 'low use segment of the population,' a phrase never reproduced in the mainstream press. See Carole Gallagher, *American Ground Zero: The Secret Nuclear War* (Cambridge, MA: MIT Press, 1993). Also, Carole Gallagher, 'We are all downwinders,' interview in *Lies of Our Times*, April 1994, pp. 14–19.
9. See Noam Chomsky, *Necessary Illusions: Thought Control in Democratic Societies* (Boston: South End Press, 1989).

10. Taylor Branch, *Parting the Waters: America in the King Years 1954–63* (New York: Simon & Schuster, 1988); Nelson Blackstock, *The Cointelpro Papers: The FBI's Secret War on Political Freedom* (New York: Vintage, 1975).

11. Blackstock, *op. cit.*; Ross Gelbspan, *Break-ins, Death Threats and the FBI: The Covert War Against the Central American Movement* (Boston: South End Press, 1991).

12. See, especially, Tom Gervasi, *The Myth of Soviet Military Supremacy* (New York: Harper & Row, 1986).

13. See Philip Agee, *Inside the Company* (London: Stonehill, 1975); William Blum, *Killing Hope: U.S. and CIA Military Interventions since World War II* (Monroe, Maine: Common Courage Press, 1995), *passim*.

14. Edward Herman and Noam Chomsky, *Manufacturing Consent: The Political Economy of the Mass Media* (New York: Pantheon, 1988), pp. 98–9.

15. Alberto Manguel, 'Mexico: shooting the messenger,' *Globe and Mail* (Toronto), November 30, 1991. The article refers to fifty-five Mexican journalists having been killed or who had 'disappeared' since 1983.

16. Murray Fromson, 'Mexico's struggle for a free press,' in Richard Cole (ed.), *Communication in Latin America* (Wilmington, DE: Scholarly Resources, 1996), p. 117.

17. R. Karthigesu, 'Broadcasting deregulation in developing Asian nations: an examination of the nascent tendencies using Malaysia as a case study,' *Media, Culture & Society*, **16** (1994), 73–90.

18. Quoted in Brian Whitaker, *News Limited* (London: Minority Press Group, 1981), p. 20.

19. J. Blumler, M. Bynin, and T. Nossiter, 'Broadcasting finance and programme quality: an international review,' *European Journal of Communication*, **1** (1986), 343–64.

20. Stephen Kline, *Out of the Garden: Toys, TV, and Children's Culture in the Age of Marketing* (London: Verso, 1993), p. viii.

21. Ben Bagdikian, *The Media Monopoly*, 4th edn (Boston: Beacon, 1992), p. 157.

22. *Ibid.*, pp. 168–73.

23. Erik Barnouw pointed out the inappropriateness of a message selling painkillers to a program like *Roots*, describing the personal agonies of human slavery. *The Sponsor* (New York: Oxford University Press, 1978), p. 114.

24. *Ibid.*; Parts 1 and 2, especially pp. 101–22 on 'entertainment,' gives a great deal of evidence on the effects of sponsorship on the quality of entertainment, including values and political messages.

25. Edward Herman, 'The externalities effects of commercial and public broadcasting,' in Karle Nordenstreng and Herbert Schiller (eds), *Beyond National Sovereignty* (Norwood, NJ: Ablex, 1993).

NOTES TO CHAPTER 1

1. *The Wealth of Nations* (New York: Modern Library, 1937), pp. 528–9.

2. L. S. Stavrianos, *Global Rift: The Third World Comes of Age* (New York: William Morrow, 1981), pp. 52–61.

208   NOTES TO CHAPTER 1

3. See Oliver Boyd-Barrett, *The International News Agencies* (Beverly Hills: Sage, 1980).
4. Ian Jarvie, *Hollywood's Overseas Campaign: The North American Movie Trade, 1920–1950* (Cambridge and New York: Cambridge University Press, 1992), p. 330.
5. Tapio Varis, *The Impact of Transnational Corporations on Communications* (Tampere Peace Research Institute Reports, No. 10, 1975), p. 2.
6. Jarvie, p. 315.
7. These are the frequencies from around 550 to 1500 kilohertz, or what is regarded as the AM band today.
8. NBC was split in half in the early 1940s and the third U.S. network, the American Broadcasting Company (ABC) was formed.
9. Robert McChesney, *Telecommunications, Mass Media, and Democracy: The Battle for the Control of U.S. Broadcasting, 1925–1935* (New York: Oxford University Press, 1993).
10. Barnard Bumpus, *International Broadcasting* (UNESCO: International Commission for the Study of Communications Problems, Document 60, 1980), p. 1.
11. *Ibid.*, pp. 3–5.
12. Statement of Owen D. Young, Chairman of General Electric and founder of the Radio Corporation of America. Quoted in Emily S. Rosenberg, *Spreading the American Dream: American Economic and Cultural Expansion, 1890–1945* (New York: Hill & Wang, 1981), p. 95.
13. Jeremy Tunstall, *The Media Are American* (New York: Columbia University Press, 1977).
14. Varis, *Impact of Transnational Corporations*, p. 33.
15. Thomas Guback and Tapio Varis, *Transnational Communication and Cultural Industries* (Paris: UNESCO, 1982), p. 28.
16. Quoted in Thomas H. Guback, 'Film as international business,' *Journal of Communication*, **24** (1) (Winter 1974), 100.
17. Timothy Haight and Christopher Sterling, 'U.S. media industries abroad,' in *Mass Media: Aspen Institute Guide to Communication Industry Trends* (New York: Praeger, 1978), p. 396.
18. See Peter Golding, 'The international media and the political economy of publishing,' *Library Trends*, **26** (4) (Spring 1978), 453–67.
19. See Guback and Varis, pp. 18–19.
20. Robert S. Fortner, *International Communication: History, Conflict, and Control of the Global Metropolis* (Belmont, CA: Wadsworth, 1983), p. 180.
21. Cited in Guback and Varis, p. 9.
22. Fortner, p. 180.
23. Varis, p. 18.
24. See Chin-Chuan Lee, *Media Imperialism Reconsidered: The Homogenizing of Television Culture* (Beverly Hills, CA: Sage, 1979).
25. 'Business education,' *Journal of Peace Research*, **13** (1) (1976), 50–2.
26. Noreene Z. Janus, 'Advertising and the mass media in the era of the global corporation,' in Emile G. McAnany, Jorge Schnitman and Noreene Janus (eds), *Communication and Social Structure: Critical Studies in Mass Media Research*

(New York: Praeger, 1981), p. 294.

27. Karl Sauvant, 'Multinational enterprises and the transmission of culture: the international supply of advertising services and business education,' *Journal of Peace Research*, **13** (1) (1976), 52; Lee, *Media Imperialism Reconsidered*, p. 99.

28. Quoted in Sauvant, p. 50.

29. H. H. Wilson, *Pressure Group: The Campaign for Commercial Television* (London: Secker & Warburg, 1961).

30. Janus, p. 310; Sauvant, p. 51.

31. Mustapha Masmoudi, 'The new world information order,' *Journal of Communication*, **29** (2) (Spring 1979), 172–3.

32. Quoted in Frederick, p. 165.

33. UNESCO, *Many Voices, One World* (New York: UNESCO, 1980).

34. See Armand Mattelart, *Mapping World Communication: War, Progress, Culture* (Minneapolis: University of Minnesota Press, 1994), pp. 182–3.

35. William Preston, Edward Herman, and Herbert Schiller, *Hope and Folly: The United States and Unesco 1945–1985* (Minneapolis: University of Minnesota Press, 1989).

36. Herbert I. Schiller, *Mass Communications and American Empire* (2nd edn), (Boulder, CO: Westview Press, 1992), p. 24.

37. For an account of the scope of these changes and why they took place in this period, see Alfred Lewis and Gioia Pescetto, *EU and US Banking in the 1990s* (London: Academic Press Ltd., 1996), chapters 2 and 3.

38. 'The showdown in global banking,' *Business Week*, October 2, 1995, pp. 96–8.

39. UNCTAD, *World Investment Report 1994* (New York: UN, 1995), pp. 23–4, 131.

40. *Ibid.*, p. 143.

41. *Ibid.*, p. 141.

42. IFC, *Annual Report 1995*, p. 5.

43. Susan George and Fabrizio Sabelli, *Faith and Credit: The World Bank's Secular Empire* (Boulder, CO: Westview Press, 1994); Cheryl Payer, *The World Bank* (New York: Monthly Review Press, 1982).

44. George and Sabelli, *Faith and Credit*; Kevin Danaher (ed.), *Fifty Years Is Enough: The Case Against the World Bank and International Monetary Fund* (Boston: South End Press, 1994).

45. Alice Amsden, *Asia's Next Giant: South Korea and Late Industrialization* (New York: Oxford University Press, 1989); Robert Wade, *Governing the Market: Economic Theory and the Role of Government in East Asian Industrialization* (Princeton: Princeton University Press, 1990).

46. See the chapters by Leo Panitch and Manfred Bienefeld in Leo Panitch (ed.), *Between Globalism and Nationalism* (London: Merlin, 1994).

47. Wolfgang Streeck, 'Public power beyond the nation-state: the case of the European Community,' in Robert Boyer and Daniel Drache (eds), *States Against Markets* (Toronto: McGill-Queens University Press, 1994), p. 302. For further discussion of the Social Chapter's weakness, see Panitch, 'Globalisation and the state,' pp. 84–6.

48. The Maastricht Agreement was first rejected by the Danes. But it was put to a vote again after an intense 'educational' campaign, which was supportive of the agreement. They were not allowed a third try following some experience with the agreement.

49. See especially Paul Hirst and Grahame Thompson, *Globalization in Question: The International Economy and the Possibilities of Governance* (Cambridge, UK: Polity Press, 1996).

50. Peter Huber, 'Cyberpower,' *Forbes*, December 2, 1996, pp. 142–7.

51. On the active promotion of TNC investment abroad by the German government, see Folker Frobel, Jurgen Heinrichs, and Otto Kreye, *The New International Division of Labour* (New York: Cambridge University Press, 1980), p. 279.

52. The classic statement was that of Argentine Finance Minister Martinez de la Hoz during the rule of the generals: 'We enjoy the stability that the Armed Forces has guaranteed us. This plan can be fulfilled despite its lack of popular support. It has sufficient political support . . . that provided by the Armed Forces.' *Bulletin of the Argentine Information Service Center, Argentina Outreach*, March–April 1978, p. 3.

53. This is the most famous insight of Chicago School economist and Nobel Prize Laureate Ronald Coase's work, spelled out in his article 'The problem of social cost,' *Journal of Law and Economics*, October 1960.

54. See 'Over-regulating America: tomorrow's economic argument,' *The Economist*, July 27, 1996, pp. 19–21.

55. This was the economic policy objective put forward in June 1995 at a G-7 gathering; see in particular the remarks of Wim Duisenberg, president of the Bank for International Settlements, in the *Financial Times*, June 13, 1995, p. 1.

56. See Robert Eisner, *The Misunderstood Economy* (Boston: Harvard Business School, 1994), chapter 8; Edward Herman, 'The natural rate of unemployment,' *Z Magazine*, November 1994, pp. 62–5.

57. Edward Herman, 'Immiserating growth (2): The Third World,' *Z Magazine*, March 1995, pp. 22–7.

58. See Chapter 3, 'Privatization,' in Edward Herman, *Triumph of the Market* (Boston: South End Press, 1995), and citations given there.

59. See Alex Carey, *Taking the Risk Out of Democracy: Propaganda in the US and Australia* (Sydney, NSW: University of New South Wales Press, 1995); Edward Herman and Gerry O'Sullivan, *The 'Terrorism' Industry* (New York: Pantheon, 1990); John Saloma, *Ominous Politics: The New Conservative Labyrinth* (New York: Hill & Wang, 1984).

60. See Thomas Ferguson, *Golden Rule: The Investment Theory of Political Parties in a Money-Driven System* (Chicago: University of Chicago Press, 1995).

61. Cees J. Hamelink, *The Politics of World Communication: A Human Rights Perspective* (London: Sage, 1994), p. 33.

62. Jeremy Tunstall and Michael Palmer, *Media Moguls* (London: Routledge, 1991), p. 26.

63. National Technical Information Service, *Globalization of the Mass Media* (Washington, DC: Department of Commerce, 1993), pp. 20–1, 1–2.

64. Anthony Smith, *The Age of Behemoths: The Globalization of Mass Media Firms* (New York: Priority Press Publications, 1991), p. 23.
65. Fortner, p. 261.
66. Statistics and quotation in Tunstall and Palmer, p. 94.
67. Ben Bagdikian, *The Media Monopoly* (4th edn) (Boston: Beacon Press, 1992).
68. See Tunstall and Palmer, p. 221.
69. National Technical Information Service, p. 14.
70. Tunstall and Palmer, p. 209.
71. Schiller, pp. 14–15.
72. Schiller, p. 14.
73. Statement of Nick Nicolas. Quoted in U.S. House of Representatives, Committee of Energy and Commerce, 101st Congress, 1st Session, *Globalization of the Mass Media* (Washington, DC: U.S. Government Printing Office, 1990), p. 1.
74. Marc Doyle, *The Future of Television: A Global Overview of Programming, Advertising, Technology and Growth* (Lincolnwood, IL: NTC Business Books, 1993), p. 1.

NOTES TO CHAPTER 2

1. *Media and Entertainment*, Schroder Wertheim & Co. report, October 4, 1995, p. 3.
2. Jane L. Levere, 'Advertising,' *New York Times,* June 11, 1996, p. C6.
3. Ted Johnson, 'The upsizing of Hollywood,' *Variety*, March 18–24, 1996, p. 65.
4. 'A week in the life of German showbiz,' *Variety Global Media Report*, May 27 to June 2, 1996, pp. 16, 41.
5. Comment of Ed Wilson, president of Eyemark Entertainment. In Greg Spring, 'Cable, overseas deals beckon,' *Electronic Media*, May 20, 1996, p. 12.
6. 'Interview with Melissa T. Cook,' *Wall Street Transcript*, March 18, 1996, p. 2.
7. Ronald Grover, 'Lights, camera, less action,' *Business Week,* July 1, 1996, pp. 50, 52.
8. Gustavo Lombo, 'The land of opportunity,' *Forbes*, July 15, 1996, pp. 292–4.
9. 'European ratings snapshot,' *Variety*, October 14, 1996, p. 22.
10. *Our Creative Diversity: Report of the World Commission on Culture and Development* (Paris: World Commission on Culture and Development, 1995), p. 27.
11. Richard Tomkins, 'US tops poll on cultural exports,' *Financial Times*, December 4, 1996, p. 9.
12. 'Trade imbalance tops $6bn,' *Television Business International*, December 1996, p. 16.
13. David Rooney, 'Filmauro firing up exhib, distrib arms,' *Variety*, November 25 to December 1, 1996, p. 29.
14. Mark Landler, 'MTV finds increasing competition for foreign viewers,' *New York Times*, March 25, 1996, p. C7.

15. Andrew Geddes, 'TV finds no pan-Asian panacea,' *Advertising Age*, July 18, 1994.

16. Neel Chowdhury, 'STAR-TV shines in India,' *International Herald Tribune*, July 16, 1996, p. 15.

17. Comment of D. Bourse. Cited in Doug Wilson, *Strategies of the Media Giants* (London: Pearson Professional, 1996), p. 40.

18. John Tagliabue, 'Local flavor rules European TV,' *New York Times*, October 14, 1996, pp. C1, C3; Alice Rawsthorn, 'Hollywood goes global,' *Financial Times*, September 27, 1996, special section, p.x.

19. Alice Rawsthorn, 'World book market "faces further consolidation",' *Financial Times*, October 2, 1996, p. 16.

20. Alice Rawsthorn, 'Out of tune with the times,' *Financial Times*, June 25, 1996, p. 15.

21. Alice Rawsthorn, 'PolyGram is biggest music group,' *Financial Times*, May 9, 1996, p. 6; 'Musical chairs,' *The Economist*, December 23, 1995 – January 5, 1996, p. 78.

22. 'Music sales,' *Variety*, April 22–28, 1996, p. 7.

23. Alice Rawsthorn, 'Recorded music sales bound towards $40bn,' *Financial Times*, April 17, 1996, p. 5.

24. The trade publication is *Music Business International* magazine. Cited in Alice Rawsthorn, 'China to lead global music sales growth,' *Financial Times*, January 24, 1996, p. 7.

25. Harold L. Vogel, *Entertainment Industry Economics: A Guide for Financial Analysis*, 3rd edn (New York and Cambridge: Cambridge University Press, 1994), p. 40.

26. Comment of Ted Shugrue of Columbia TriStar Films (owned by Sony). Cited in Antonia Zerbisias, 'The world at their feet,' *The Toronto Star*, August 27, 1995, p. C1; see also Cäcilie Rohwedder, Lisa Bannon, and Eben Shapiro, 'Spending spree by German Kirch Group spells bonanza for Hollywood studios,' *Wall Street Journal*, August 1, 1996, p. B1.

27. Quotations of Greg Coote of Village Roadshow and David Davis of Houlihan, Lokey, Howard & Zukin. Cited in Leonard Klady, 'U.S. exhibs discover the joy of Plex O'Seas,' *Variety*, April 8–14, 1996, pp. 9, 14.

28. Andrew Tanzer and Robert La Franco, 'Luring Asians from their TV sets,' *Forbes*, June 3, 1996, p. 41.

29. 'Global fast forward,' *Variety*, April 22–28, 1996, p. 13.

30. Neil Weinberg, 'The fourth wave,' *Forbes*, November 20, 1996, p. 114; Peter M. Nichols, 'A new CD marvel awaits, but the horizon recedes,' *New York Times*, August 25, 1996, section 2, pp. 1, 20.

31. Cäcilie Rohwedder, Lisa Bannon, and Eben Shapiro, 'Spending spree by German Kirch Group spells bonanza for Hollywood studios,' *Wall Street Journal*, August 1, 1996, p. B1.

32. Bernard Weinraub, 'MCA in $2.5 billion sale of shows to German TV,' *New York Times*, July 31, 1996, p. C1.

33. Linda Lee, 'Film and TV output soars, spurring demand for studio space,' *New York Times*, January 20, 1997 pp. C1, C7.

34. Leonard Klady, 'Why mega-flicks click,' *Variety*, November 25 – December 1, 1996, p. 1.

35. John Lippman, "Hollywood reeled record $5.8 billion last year, boosted by blockbuster films,' *Wall Street Journal*, January 3, 1997, p. B2.

36. Bernard Weinraub, 'Media,' *New York Times*, January 6, 1997, p.C7.

37. Barbara Maltsby, 'The homogenization of Hollywood,' *Media Studies Journal*, **10** (2–3) (Spring/Summer 1996), 115.

38. Bill Carter, 'Pow! thwack! bam! no dubbing needed,' *New York Times*, Week in Review section, November 3, 1996, p. 6.

39. Neil Blackley, Pierre-Yves Gauthier, and Guy Lamming, *Pay TV in Europe* (London: Goldman Sachs, March 3, 1995), p. 1.

40. Comment of Jessica Reif. Cited in Lee Hall, 'Analysts offer cautious optimism for cable growth,' *Electronic Media*, April 1, 1996, p. 30.

41. Neil Blackley and Meg Geldens, 'The broadcast systems market,' *Europe Research*, June 14, 1996, p. 14.

42. Manjunath Pendakur and Jvotsna Kapur, 'Think globally, program locally: the privatization of Indian National Television,' paper presented to 'Democratizing communication: a comparative perspective on information and power,' January 23, 1995, p. 1.

43. Richard Parker, *The Future of Global Television News* (Joan Shorenstein Center on Press, Politics and Public Policy Research Paper R-13, Harvard University, September 1994), p. 5.

44. 'Switch it off,' *The Economist*, April 13, 1996, p. 15.

45. Heidi Dawley, 'The BBC as we know it is signing off,' *Business Week*, August 12, 1996, p. 50.

46. Sandy Tolan, 'Must NPR sell itself?' *New York Times*, July 16, 1996, p. A11.

47. See Helen Bunting and Paul Chapman, *The Future of the European Media Industry: Towards the 21st Century* (London: Pearson Professional, 1996), pp. 35–7.

48. Elizabeth Jensen, 'In funding squeeze, PBS cozies up to Madison Avenue "sponsors",' *Wall Street Journal*, July 3, 1996, p. B1.

49. Don Groves, 'Upping the ante: pubcaster confronts increased competition,' *Variety*, April 8–14, 1996, p. 45.

50. Raymond Snoddy, 'BBC seeks bigger international role,' *Financial Times*, January 11, 1996, p. 6.

51. Adam Dawtrey, 'BBC's private predicament,' *Variety*, September 2–8, 1996, p. 23.

52. Helen Bunting, *Global Media Companies, Volume 1* (London: Pearson Professional, 1995), p. 166; Meheroo Jussawalla, 'South East Asia,' in *Media Ownership and Control in the Age of Convergence* (London: International Institute of Communications, 1996), pp. 219–20.

53. Erich Broehm, 'Docu disagreement pushes BBC out of Arabian orbit,' *Variety*, April 15–21, 1996, p. 52.

54. Raymond Snoddy, 'BBC moves closer to US satellite deal,' *Financial Times*, September 28–29, 1996, p. 4; John Dempsey, 'Discovery goes global with Beeb,' *Variety*, September 30 – October 6, 1996, p. 62.

55. 'Number of TV channels "may top 4,000 in four years",' *Financial Times*, February 27, 1996, p. 8.

56. Elizabeth Lesly, Ronald Grover, and Neil Gross, 'Cable TV: a crisis looms,' *Business Week*, October 14, 1996, p. 103; Christopher Parkes, 'Arizona reaches for the sky with media deal,' *Financial Times*, July 1, 1996, p. 4.

57. Christopher Parkes, 'Television finds space to grow,' *Financial Times*, February 21, 1996, p. 13.

58. Raymond Snoddy, 'Broadcasters dish up a revolution,' *Financial Times*, October 6, 1995, p. 13.

59. Neil Weinberg and Robert La Franco, 'Yin, yang and you,' *Forbes*, March 10, 1997, p. 104.

60. Aaron Barnhart, 'Cable, cable everywhere but not a thing to watch,' *New York Times*, December 23, 1996, p. C7.

61. John Dempsey, 'Cable ops caught in the nets,' *Variety*, February 17–23, 1997, p. 1.

62. Raymond Snoddy, 'Information battle enters a new dimension,' *Financial Times*, June 10, 1996, p. 11; Raymond Snoddy, 'News Intl arm plans digital broadcast,' *Financial Times*, June 11, 1996, p. 22.

63. Jeff Cole, 'Mexico's plan to auction satellite system draws attention from U.S. operators,' *Wall Street Journal*, March 10, 1997, p. A3.

64. Bronwen Maddox and Raymond Snoddy, 'Media barons line up for digital star wars,' *Financial Times*, April 25, 1996, p. 8.

65. Mark Robichaux, 'As satellite TV soars, big firms crowd the skies,' *Wall Street Journal*, March 11, 1996, p. B1; Raymond Snoddy, 'Murdoch empire strikes back in US TV,' *Financial Times*, February 26, 1997, p. 19.

66. 'Radio Canada will end its international service,' *New York Times*, December 8, 1996, p. 12.

67. Raymond Snoddy, 'Former World Service chief scorns restructuring at BBC,' *Financial Times*, June 11, 1996, p. 8.

68. 'This is London, if we can afford it,' *The Economist*, January 6, 1996, p. 44.

69. John Ridding, 'Alcatel arm takes Euronews stake,' *Financial Times*, April 1–2, 1995, p. 5.

70. 'Euronews courts rival channels to take stakes,' *New Media Markets*, July 25, 1996, p. 7.

71. Marc Gunther, 'CNN envy,' *Fortune*, July 8, 1996, p. 124.

72. 'All news, all the time, any time soon?' *Business Week*, December 18, 1995, p. 42.

73. Chuck Ross, 'Ailes sets out to lead Fox into news business,' *Advertising Age*, July 1, 1996, p. 17.

74. Berlusconi's successful and explicit use of his media properties to promote his political agenda is perhaps most striking, though hardly exceptional. See Alexander Stille, 'The world's greatest salesman,' *New York Times Magazine*, March 17, 1996, p. 29.

75. Comment of unidentified executive. In Joe Mandese, 'Murdoch digs into more news,' *Advertising Age*, December 4, 1995, p. 33.

76. Ira Teinowicz, 'Court further bolsters commercial speech,' *Advertising Age*, May 27, 1996, p. 47.

77. Edward S. Herman, 'The media mega-mergers,' *Dollars and Sense*, No. 205, May–June 1996, pp. 8–13.

78. Mark Landler, 'In cable TV, more is less,' *New York Times*, Week in Review section, November 10, 1996, p. 4.

79. Andy Stern, 'Eurocrats set to clash on quota battleground,' *Variety*, February 12–18, 1996, p. 35.

80. Anthony DePalma, 'U.S. and Mexico reach accord over satellite TV transmission,' *New York Times*, November 9, 1996, p. 20.

81. Ira Teinowicz and Don Angus, 'U.S. joins the Canada ad fight,' *Advertising Age*, March 18, 1996, p. 44.

82. Anthony DePalma, 'World trade body opposes Canadian magazine tariffs,' *New York Times*, January 20, 1997, p. C8.

83. 'Digital dilemmas,' *The Economist*, March 23, 1996, p. 82; 'The revolution that could bring viewers 1,800 new channels,' *Financial Times*, April 25, 1996, p. 8.

84. Diane Summers, 'Norway may lose right to ban satellite advertising,' *Financial Times*, June 20, 1995, p. 1.

85. Neil Buckley, 'EU MPs to demand state TV protection,' *Financial Times*, September 18, 1996, p. 2.

86. Diane Summers and Andrew Jack, 'Brussels warning over French TV's health kick,' *Financial Times*, July 3, 1996, p. 3.

87. Julia Preston, 'With piracy booming in Mexico, U.S. industry's cries get louder,' *New York Times*, April 20, 1996, p. 20.

88. Andrew Hill, 'Piracy on the high Cs,' *Financial Times*, March 19, 1996, p. 6.

89. Joyce Barnathan, 'A pirate under every rock,' *Business Week*, June 17, 1996, p. 50.

90. Craig S. Smith, 'Counterfeit video compact disks in Asia may dwarf current copyright piracy,' *Wall Street Journal*, June 18, 1996, p. A12.

91. Seth Faison, 'U.S. and China agree on pact to fight piracy,' *New York Times*, June 18, 1996, pp. A1, A8; Marcus W. Brauchli, 'In a trade war, China takes the bigger hit,' *Wall Street Journal*, May 17, 1996, p. A10; Tony Walker, 'Beijing "steps up fight" against pirate CD makers,' *Financial Times*, April 22, 1996, p. 4.

92. Dennis Wharton, 'U.S., China avert war,' *Variety*, June 24–30, 1996, p. 135.

93. 'Piracy on the high Cs,' *The Economist*, February 17, 1996, p. 18.

94. 'Retribution for reproduction,' *The Economist*, May 18, 1996, p. 73.

95. Doug Wilson, *Strategies of the Media Giants* (London: Pearson Professional, 1996), p. 5.

96. Frank Biondi, 'A media tycoon's take on the 21st century,' *Business Week*, November 18, 1994, p. 190.

97. Helen Bunting, *U.S. Media Markets: Leading the World?* (London: Pearson Professional, 1995), p. 98.

98. Mark Landler, 'Think globally, program locally,' *Business Week*, November 18, 1994, pp. 186–9.

99. Helen Bunting, *U.S. Media Markets: Leading the World?* (London: Pearson Professional, 1995), pp. 99, 3.

100. 'Warner opens animation studio,' *Financial Times*, June 22–23, 1996, p. 4;

Julia Flynn and Katherine Ann Miller, 'Tinseltown on the Thames,' *Business Week*, August 5, 1996, pp. 47–8.

101. Diane Mermigas, "Still to come: smaller media alliances,' *Electronic Media*, February 5, 1996, p. 38.

102. Marlene Edmunds, 'Vertically integrated Schibsted rises to top,' *Variety*, October 14–20, 1996, p. 52.

103. Diane Mermigas, 'Media players mining for global gold,' *Electronic Media*, December 11, 1995, p. 18.

104. Comment of Porter Bibb, analyst for Ladenburg Thalmann & Co. Cited in Keith J. Kelly, 'Time Warner temblor topples structure,' *Advertising Age*, November 20, 1995, p. 6.

105. Comments of Michael J. Wolf, lead partner at Booz, Allen & Hamilton. Cited in Rita Koselka, 'Mergermania in Medialand,' *Forbes*, October 23, 1995, p. 254.

106. Koselka, *op. cit.*, p. 258.

107. Christopher Dixon, presentation to Association of Investment Management and Research, New York City, January 31, 1996, p. 4.

108. Marla Matzer, 'Contented kingdoms,' *Superbrands '97*, supplement to *Adweek*, October 7, 1996, pp. 30, 33.

109. Jeff Jensen, 'Viacom eyes venues for merchandising,' *Advertising Age*, April 6, 1996, p. 3.

110. Jeff Jensen, 'MCA/Universal grooms "Babe" for a new career as mass-market brand,' *Advertising Age*, April 29, 1996, p. 16.

111. Diane Mermigas, 'New day dawns for Universal Television,' *Electronic Media*, January 6, 1997, p. 24.

112. Jeff Jensen, 'Universal to present new image,' *Advertising Age*, July 1, 1996, p. 28.

113. Marla Matzer, 'Contented kingdoms,' *Brandweek*, special section of *Adweek*, October 7, 1996, p. 34.

114. Sally Goll Beatty, 'Turner lets some of its treasures moonlight for other marketers,' *Wall Street Journal*, May 22, 1996, p. B8; Chuck Ross, 'Heyer steering Turner into marketing alliances,' *Advertising Age*, April 22, 1996, p. 53.

115. Larry Dum, 'Pressure builds when a giant enters a niche,' *New York Times*, September 16, 1996, p. C4.

116. Joshua Levine, 'TV in the classroom,' *Forbes*, January 27, 1997, p. 98.

117. *Wall Street Journal*, January 29, 1997, p. B2.

118. 'Macworld,' *The Economist*, June 29, 1996, p. 62.

119. Alice Rawsthorn, 'PepsiCo. to feel force of Star Wars,' *Financial Times*, May 17, 1996, p. 21.

120. Diane Mermigas, 'Seagram eyes global arena for Universal,' *Electronic Media*, January 13, 1997, p. 94.

121. Laura Landro, 'Entertainment giants face pressure to cut costs, get into focus,' *Wall Street Journal*, February 11, 1997, pp. A1, A17.

122. Diane Mermigas, 'Liberty sees sports as key to global kingdom,' *Electronic Media*, May 13, 1996, p. 4.

123. Both the Viacom–Universal conflict over the US cable network and the

Time Warner–U.SWest conflict over Time Warner Entertainment are being negotiated and also considered by the court system as the book goes to press in March 1997. It is probable that both conflicts will be resolved by the end of the calendar year, with the joint ventures formally terminated.

124. Bernard Simon, 'Seagram to hold on to 15% stake in Time Warner,' *Financial Times*, June 1, 1995, p. 18.

125. Raymond Snoddy, 'Master of bits at home in the hub,' *Financial Times*, May 28, 1996, p. 17.

126. Catherine E. Celebrezze, 'The man who bought the media,' *EXTRA!*, **9** (2), March–April 1996, pp. 21–2.

127. Mark Robichaux, 'Tim Robertson turns TV's family channel into a major business,' *Wall Street Journal*, August 29, 1996, p. A6.

128. Linda Grant, 'Moneyman to the moguls,' *Fortune*, September 9, 1996, pp. 37–8.

129. Martin Peers, 'Wall Street looks overseas,' *Variety*, October 14–20, 1996, pp. 41–2.

130. Ronald Grover, 'Plenty of dreams, not enough work?' *Business Week*, July 22, 1996, p. 65.

131. Paula Dwyer, 'Can Rupert conquer Europe?' *Business Week*, March 25, 1996, p. 169.

132. Elizabeth Lesly, Gail DeGeorge and Ronald Grover, 'Sumner's last stand,' *Business Week*, March 3, 1997, p. 67.

133. Quoted in *Wisconsin State Journal*, February 9, 1996, p. A2.

134. Raymond Snoddy, 'Master of bits at home in the hub,' *Financial Times*, May 28, 1996, p. 17.

135. Elizabeth Jensen and Eben Shapiro, 'Time Warner's fight with News Corp. belies mutual dependence,' *Wall Street Journal*, October 28, 1996, p. A1.

136. Dixon, *op. cit.*, p. 2.

137. Laurel Wentz and Kevin Brown, 'Global marketers,' *Ad Age International*, November 1996, p. 115.

138. 'So what was the fuss about?' *The Economist*, June 22, 1996, p. 59.

139. Comments of Jack Trout. Cited in advertisement in *Advertising Age*, April 22, 1996, p. 7.

140. Chuck Ross, 'Global rules are proposed for measuring TV,' *Advertising Age*, August 12, 1996, p. 3.

141. *Advertising Expenditure Forecasts* (London: Zenith Media, December 1995), pp. 124–9.

142. Robert J. Coen, 'The advertising trends up to 2020,' paper presented to Marketing 2020 Conference, New York City, March 16, 1995.

143. Laura Petrecca, 'Coen sees hearty growth in ad spending for 1997,' *Advertising Age*, July 1, 1996, p. 10.

144. Calmetta Y. Coleman, 'U.S. agencies expand in Latin America,' *Wall Street Journal*, January 3, 1996, p. B2.

145. David Kilburn, 'Asia rising,' *Adweek*, August 19, 1996, p. 22.

146. Helen Bunting and Paul Chapman, *The Future of the European Media Industry:*

Towards the 21st Century (London: Pearson Professional, 1996), p. 13.

147. 'The Global 1000,' *Business Week*, July 8, 1996, pp. 46–89.

148. Mark Gleason, 'Big Bang of '86 is still shaping the ad world,' *Advertising Age*, April 22, 1996, p. 3.

149. R. Craig Endicott, 'Shops soar on growth of 9.2%, to $17 billion,' *Advertising Age*, April 15, 1996, p. s2.

150. Laurel Wentz and Sasha Emmons, ' "AAI" charts show yearly growth, consolidation,' *Ad Age International*, September 1996, p. 133.

151. Sally Goll Beatty, 'BDDP's management preparing a takeover bid for the agency,' *Wall Street Journal*, May 13, 1996, p. B4.

152. 'So what was all the fuss about?' *The Economist*, June 22, 1996, p. 59.

153. Anne-Michele Morice, 'Havas hopes new name and look turn heads around world,' *Wall Street Journal*, April 3, 1996, p. B10.

154. 'Publicis may spend up to $200 million to buy ad agencies,' *Wall Street Journal*, September 12, 1996, p. A5.

155. Sally Goll Beatty, 'Global needs challenge midsize agencies,' *Wall Street Journal*, December 14, 1995, p. B8.

156. Shiraz Sidva, 'An Indian campaign,' *Financial Times*, November 24, 1995, p. 14.

157. Noreen O'Leary, 'World tours single client,' *Adweek*, August 5, 1996, pp. 34–7.

158. 'A passion for variety,' *The Economist*, November 30, 1996, pp. 68, 71.

159. Greg Farrell, 'The world is their oyster,' *Adweek*, February 19, 1996; Stuart Elliott, 'Advertising,' *New York Times*, March 18, 1996, p. C9.

160. Sally Goll Beatty, 'Interpublic diversifies further with purchase of direct marketer,' *Wall Street Journal*, May 17, 1996, p. B8.

161. Jack O'Dwyer, *O'Dwyer's Directory of Public Relations Firms, 1996* (New York: J. R. O'Dwyer Co., Inc., 1996), p. A7.

162. 'Credits spiked to stop surfing,' *Variety*, December 23, 1996 – January 5, 1997, p. 32.

163. Mary Kuntz and Joseph Weber, 'The new hucksterism,' *Business Week*, July 1, 1996, pp. 77–84.

164. Chuck Ross, 'Fox-owned station in Chi. breaks program taboo,' *Advertising Age*, August 26, 1996, p. 2.

165. Nicholas Denton and Hugh Carnegy, 'Ad breaks may interrupt free Swedish phone calls,' *Financial Times*, January 20, 1997, p. 1.

166. Mary Kuntz and Joseph Weber, 'The new hucksterism,' *Business Week*, July 1, 1996, pp. 77–84.

167. Darren McDermott, 'All-American infomercials sizzle in Asia,' *Wall Street Journal*, June 25, 1996, p. B5.

168. P. J. Bednarski, 'A quantum leap in global infomercials,' *Electronic Media*, January 13, 1997, pp. EMI-2, EMI-10.

169. Sally Goll Beatty, ' "Sci-Fi Trader" on cable channel takes selling to new dimension,' *Wall Street Journal*, January 29, 1997, p. B2.

170. 'Sci-fi channel launches an entertainment program that sells,' *Adweek*, 1996: The Infomercial Special Sourcebook Issue, June 24, 1996, p. 34.

171. Michael Schneider, 'Brand name-dropping,' *Electronic Media*, August 26, 1996, pp. 1, 30.

172. David Leonhardt, 'Cue the soda can,' *Business Week*, June 24, 1996, pp. 64, 66.

173. Bradley Johnson and Kim Cleland, 'Apple, MCI tout "Independence",' *Advertising Age*, July 1, 1996, p. 3.

174. Stuart Elliott, 'The spot on the cutting-room floor,' *New York Times*, February 7, 1997, pp. C1–2.

175. Bruce Orwall, 'Disney chases live-action merchandising hits,' *Wall Street Journal*, November 27, 1996, pp. B1, B4.

176. Luisa Kroll, 'Entertainomercials,' *Forbes*, November 4, 1996, pp. 322, 324.

177. Sally Goll Beatty, 'CNBC will air a show owned, vetted by IBM,' *Wall Street Journal*, June 4, 1996, pp. B1, B8.

178. Jenny Holtz, 'NBC joins Paramount, P&G deal,' *Electronic Media*, November 20, 1995, p. 32.

179. 'Viacom's TV group forms 3-way venture for movie production,' *Wall Street Journal*, April 26, 1996, p. A5.

180. 'ESPN creates cross-company buy,' *Mediaweek*, September 2, 1996, p. 27.

181. Mark Gleason and Chuck Ross, 'Y&R, NBC mull massive linkup,' *Advertising Age*, September 16, 1996, pp. 1, 54.

182. Chris Petrikin, 'Is H'wood learning to go by the book?' *Variety*, December 16–22, 1996, pp. 1, 99. For an excellent analysis of this process, see Mark Crispin Miller, 'The crushing power of big publishing,' *The Nation*, March 17, 1997, pp. 11–18.

183. Andre Schiffrin, 'The corporatization of publishing,' *The Nation*, June 3, 1996, pp. 29–32.

184. Robin Pogrebin, 'At struggling Time Warner, Time Inc. is money,' *New York Times*, February 3, 1997, p. C1.

185. Bernard Weinraub, 'Hollywood success, with an aftertaste,' *New York Times*, January 7, 1997, p. B1.

186. See Robert W. McChesney, *Corporate Media and the Threat to Democracy* (New York: Seven Stories Press, 1997), pp. 17–29.

187. *Tyndall Report*, December 31, 1996.

188. 'Jordan brings the heart of the marketer to CBS-TV,' *Advertising Age*, February 3, 1997, p. 18.

189. Bill Carter and Richard Sandomir, 'The trophy in Eisner's deal,' *New York Times*, August 6, 1995, section 3, p. 11.

190. 'MTV: rocking all over the world,' *Financial Times*, July 4, 1995, p. 17.

191. World Commission on Culture and Development, *Our Creative Diversity* (Paris: UNESCO, 1995), p. 109.

192. Michela Wrong, 'Without a voice of its own,' *Financial Times*, February 19, 1997, p. 11.

193. Donald G. McNeil, Jr., 'A crank-up radio helps Africa tune in,' *New York Times*, February 16, 1996, p. A1.

194. Steven Erlanger, 'Russian press is free, free to go broke,' *New York Times*, July 6, 1995, p. A5.

195. Brian MacNair, 'Television in post-Soviet Russia: from monolith to mafia,' *Media, Culture & Society*, **18** (3) (July 1996), 489–99.

196. John Downing, *Internationalizing Media Theory* (Thousand Oaks, CA: Sage, 1996), pp. 132, 146.

197. 'Russia's judgment day,' *The Nation*, July 8, 1996.
198. Alan Riding, 'For a Czech film executive, it's all business,' *New York Times*, April 8, 1996, p. C9.
199. 'U.S. pic domination rankles Eastern Europe,' *Variety*, October 29–November 3, 1996, p. 32.
200. Cordelia Becker, 'Mittelstand makes an impression on the news stand,' *Financial Times*, March 5, 1996, p. 19; 'How an astrophysicist became a media mogul,' *The Economist*, August 3, 1996, p. 59.
201. Rick Richardson, 'Satellite, cable TV burgeoning in Poland,' *Variety*, April 15–21, 1996, p. M26; T. R. Smart, 'A handsome TV station – going once, going twice,' *Business Week*, May 27, 1996, p. 58.
202. Mark Landler, 'In Europe, an ex-ambassador's new empires,' *New York Times*, April 1, 1996, p. C3.
203. 'Eastern Europe's ailing press,' *New York Times*, August 6, 1996, p. A10.
204. 'Prepared Testimony of John Fox, Director, Open Society Institute, Before the House International Relations Committee Re: Foreign Aid Authorization,' Federal News Service, April 5, 1995; Steve Forbes, 'Airwaves for freedom,' *Forbes*, July 15, 1996, pp. 23–4.
205. John Thornhill, 'Russia's unfinished revolution,' *Financial Times*, May 30, 1996, p. 13.
206. Elizabeth Fox, 'Latin America,' in *Media Ownership and Control in the Age of Convergence* (London: International Institute of Communications, 1996), pp. 157–69.
207. Angus Foster, 'Contenders beam down,' *Financial Times*, September 12, 1995, p. 18; Jeffrey D. Zbar, 'Niche audiences are growing,' *Advertising Age International*, July 1996, pp. 118, 121.
208. 'Latin American snapshot: a look at key TV markets,' *Variety*, November 20, 1995, p. 19.
209. Andrew Paxman, 'Latin cable upsurge,' *Variety*, June 10–16, 1996, pp. 23, 28.
210. Jeffery D. Zbar, 'Conference extols Latin America,' *Advertising Age*, March 11, 1996.
211. Andrew Bailes and Neil Hollister, *Asian Cable and Satellite: Unrivalled Growth Opportunities* (London: Pearson Professional, 1996), pp. 44, 1.
212. Don Groves, 'Disney inks Indonesia vid deal,' *Variety*, June 3–9, 1996, p. 22.
213. Geoffrey Lee Martin, 'Rival media scions plot growth in Asia-Pacific,' *Advertising Age*, September 19, 1996, p. 46.
214. Louise Lucas, 'Asia TV race is a marathon, not a sprint,' *Financial Times*, July 27, 1995, p. 17.
215. Don Groves, 'Asia grows a money tree,' *Variety*, May 27–June 2, 1996, p. 13.
216. Janine Stein and Laurel Wentz, 'The new Asia,' *Ad Age International*, June 1996, p. 134.
217. Joseph M. Chan, 'Commercialization without independence: trends and tensions of media development in China,' in J. Cheng and M. Brosseau (eds), *China Review 1993* (Hong Kong: Chinese University Press, 1993), p. 25.2.

218. Orville Schell, 'Maoism *vs.* media in the marketplace,' *Media Studies Journal,* Summer 1995, pp. 33–42.
219. 'China's TV network to share programs with two concerns,' *Wall Street Journal,* February 7, 1996, p. B2; Tony Walker, 'China keeps tight grip on cable TV boom,' *Financial Times,* August 20, 1996, p. 5.
220. Craig Smith, 'China's huge consumer potential prompts industry survey boom,' *Wall Street Journal,* March 20, 1996, p. B5.
221. 'News corp. tries to forge link with Chinese,' *Wall Street Journal,* January 31, 1996, p. A6.
222. Mark Woods, 'Media giants court China TV market,' *Variety,* February 12–18, 1996, p. 37.
223. Comment by Christopher Dixon. Quoted in David Lieberman, 'Old guard tactic is old brand names,' *USA Today,* International edn, July 19, 1996, p. 8A.
224. Geraldine Fabrikant, 'Time Warner is licensing 12 films to its cable outlets,' *New York Times,* January 16, 1997, p. C10.

NOTES TO CHAPTER 3

1. Media sales figures will be provided for most of the firms under discussion in this chapter. These figures are taken from annual reports, publications, and stock brokerage reports. They are usually rounded off. Sometimes the figures given are estimates, especially if they are for 1996 or 1997.
2. 'Murdoch's empire,' *The Economist,* March 9, 1996, p. 68.
3. Geraldine Fabrikant, 'Murdoch bets heavily on a global vision,' *New York Times,* July 29, 1996, p. C1.
4. Cited in Ken Auletta, 'The pirate,' *New Yorker,* November 13, 1995, p. 80.
5. Mark Landler and Geraldine Fabrikant, 'Sumner and his discontents,' *New York Times,* January 19, 1996, p. C4.
6. Diane Mermigas, 'What's Murdoch want now? Programming,' *Electronic Media,* October 7, 1996, p. 8.
7. 'Ted Turner issues apology,' *Electronic Media,* October 7, 1996, p. 45. Turner apologized for his remark to the Anti-Defamation League, not to Murdoch.
8. Helen Bunting, *U.S. Media Markets: Leading the World* (London: Pearson Professional, 1995), p. 114.
9. Martin Peers, 'News Corp.,' *Variety,* August 26–September 1, 1996, p. 44.
10. Geraldine Fabrikant, 'Murdoch bets heavily on a global vision,' *New York Times,* July 29, 1996, p. C6.
11. Helen Bunting, *Global Media Companies: Volume 2, Rest of World* (London: Pearson Professional, 1995), p. 142.
12. 'Asian music unit for News Corp.,' *New York Times,* December 7, 1996, p. 20.
13. 'Murdoch's empire,' *The Economist,* March 9, 1996, p. 69.
14. Geraldine Fabrikant, 'Murdoch bets heavily on a global vision,' *New York Times,* July 29, 1996, p. C6.
15. Report on News Corporation, *Value Line,* March 1, 1996; Raymond Snoddy, 'Day of the dish for BSkyB,' *Financial Times,* August 22, 1996, p. 9.

16. 'News Corp.,' *Financial Times*, July 18, 1996, p. 12.

17. Quoted in Diane Mermigas, 'What's Murdoch want now? Programming,' *Electronic Media*, October 7, 1996, p. 8.

18. Hugo Dixon, 'BT and Murdoch plan UK digital TV venture,' *Financial Times*, May 18–19, 1996, p. 22.

19. Adam Dawtrey, 'U.K. digital hits ground running,' *Variety*, February 3–9, 1997, pp. 1, 62.

20. Michiyo Nakamoto, 'News Corp to set up Satellite TV service in Japan,' *Financial Times*, June 13, 1996, p. 13.

21. Andrew Paxman, 'Latin satcast deal "solid",' *Variety*, March 25–31, 1996, p. 87.

22. 'Murdoch plans ISkyB for April,' *Cable and Satellite Europe*, January 1997, p. 14.

23. Simon Holberton, 'News Corp raises stake in Star Television gamble,' *Financial Times*, October 11, 1995, p. 17.

24. David Kilburn, 'Asia rising,' *Adweek*, August 19, 1996, p. 26.

25. Andrew Bailes and Neil Hollister, *Asian Cable and Satellite: Unrivalled Growth Opportunities* (London: Pearson Professional, 1996), pp. 108, 131–3, 151–2.

26. 'Ship me somewhere east of Wapping,' *The Economist*, July 6, 1996, p. 58; Neel Chowdhury, 'STAR-TV shines in India,' *International Herald Tribune*, July 16, 1996, p. 15.

27. Tony Walker, 'China snubs Murdoch's TV "dreams",' *Financial Times*, August 15, 1996, p. 6.

28. Andrew Bailes and Neil Hollister, *Asian Cable and Satellite: Unrivalled Growth Opportunities* (London: Pearson Professional, 1996), pp. 98, 133.

29. Tony Walker, 'New move to catch the falling star,' *Financial Times*, March 26, 1996, p. 6.

30. Tony Walker, 'Murdoch opens China Web site,' *Financial Times*, January 16, 1997, p. 7.

31. Geraldine Fabrikant, 'Broadcasters bet on sports as first step in new markets,' *New York Times*, March 4, 1996, p. C4.

32. Diane Mermigas, 'Melding assets next step for team,' *Electronic Media*, October 9, 1995, p. 20.

33. Andrew Paxman, 'CBS says hola to news net,' *Variety*, July 1–14, 1996, p. 28.

34. Michael Mallory, 'Beavis & Butt-head take over the world,' *Variety*, June 24–30, 1996, pp. 106, 110.

35. Gary Levin, 'Pact between Dox, Marvel stamps FCN library card,' *Variety*, July 1–14, 1996, p. 25.

36. Tim Carvell and Joe McGowan, 'Showdown in Toontown,' *Fortune*, October 28, 1996, p. 102.

37. 'Warner opens animation studio,' *Financial Times*, June 22–23, 1996, p. 4.

38. Alice Rawsthorn, 'Disney faces rivals who are quick on the draw,' *Financial Times*, June 8–9, 1996, p. 9.

39. Jane L. Levere, 'Advertising,' *New York Times*, June 11, 1996, p. C6.

40. 'JSkyB,' *Financial Times*, June 13, 1996, p. 12.

41. Raymond Snoddy, 'Alliances for a digital future,' *Financial Times*, December 11, 1996, p. 1.

42. Diane Mermigas, 'Liberty sees sports as key to global kingdom,' *Electronic Media*, May 13, 1996, p. 31.
43. Raymond Snoddy and Simon Kuper, 'Money is the name of the game,' *Financial Times*, July 29–30, 1995, p. 10.
44. 'True fans,' *The Economist*, December 9, 1995, p. 13; 'Lording it,' *The Economist*, February 10, 1996, p. 57.
45. 'Swifter, higher, stronger, dearer,' *The Economist*, July 20, 1996, p. 18.
46. David Rowe, 'The global love-match: sport and television,' *Media, Culture & Society*, **18** (4) (October 1996), pp. 565–82.
47. David Greising, Linda Himelstein, Zachary Schiller, and Brian Bremner, 'Run, jump – and sell,' *Business Week*, July 29, 1996, p. 36.
48. Jane L. Levere, 'Advertising,' *New York Times*, June 11, 1996, p. C6.
49. Jeff Jensen, 'Reebok spots tip off new league,' *Advertising Age*, October 7, 1996, p. 18.
50. Michael Knisley, 'Rupeat,' *The Sporting News*, January 1, 1996, p. S1.
51. Michael Knisley, *ibid.*, pp. S1–S2.
52. Mark Robichaux and Elizabeth Jensen, 'News Corp. sets TCI programming deal, gears up to become global player,' *Wall Street Journal*, November 1, 1995, p. A4.
53. 'Fox sports for Brazil,' *Cable & Satellite Express*, February 6, 1997, p. 2.
54. Ray Richmond, 'Cable bases loading up with new sports webs,' *Variety*, October 14–20, 1996, p. 44.
55. Raymond Snoddy, 'Satellite rugby deal stirs debate over rights,' *Financial Times*, June 10, 1996, p. 6.
56. 'Swifter, higher, stronger, dearer,' *The Economist*, July 20, 1996, p. 18.
57. William Wchikson, Heidi Dawley, Monica Larner, and Andrew Robinson, 'Goodbye hoodlums, hello big money,' *Business Week*, September 23, 1996, p. 66.
58. *New Media Markets*, October 31, 1996, p. 20.
59. Jeff Jensen, 'Sports forum sizes up college ball,' *Advertising Age*, October 7, 1996, p. 52.
60. Joe Mandese, 'Murdoch adds football to list of global ambitions,' *Advertising Age*, June 13, 1994, p. 66.
61. Bethan Hutton and Patrick Harverson, 'Murdoch wins rugby super league court fight,' *Financial Times*, October 5–6, 1996, p. 3; *Forbes*, December 18, 1995, p. 222.
62. Diane Mermigas, 'Time Warner's Richard Parsons,' *Electronic Media*, January 22, 1996, p. 48; Helen Bunting, *Global Media Companies: Volume 2, Rest of World* (London: Pearson Professional, 1995), pp. 208–9.
63. Diane Mermigas, 'Levin looks to the future,' *Electronic Media*, October 9, 1995, pp. 20, 21.
64. Martin Dickson and Alice Rawsthorn, 'Bugs Bunny courts Yogi Bear,' *Financial Times*, August 31, 1995, p. 11; Michael Oneal, 'The unlikely mogul,' *Business Week*, December 11, 1995, p. 91.
65. Michiyo Nakamoto, 'Itochu, Toshiba in Time Warner plan,' *Financial Times*, August 30, 1995, p. 17.
66. Helen Bunting, *Global Media Companies: Volume 2, Rest of World* (London:

Pearson Professional, 1995), p. 215; Alice Rawsthorn, 'Time Warner to invest $220m in cinemas,' *Financial Times*, August 15, 1995, p. 7.

67. Elizabeth Guider, 'WB TV on BSkyB Euro beam,' *Variety*, June 24–30, 1996, p. 27.

68. Mark Woods, 'HBO Asia one in a million,' *Variety*, March 11–17, 1996, p. 41.

69. Andrew Bailes and Neil Hollister, *Asian Cable and Satellite: Unrivalled Growth Opportunities* (London: Pearson Professional, 1996), pp. 138–9.

70. Don Groves, 'HBO's expansion plan in Asia: platform, take it to Cinemax,' *Variety*, November 4–10, 1996, p. 37.

71. Eben Shapiro, 'New HBO honcho must hone pay network's creative edge,' *Wall Street Journal*, March 19, 1996, p. B1.

72. Marc Gunther, 'CNN envy,' *Fortune*, July 8, 1996, p. 124.

73. Shiraz Sidhva, 'CNN's India TV deal sparks opposition,' *Financial Times*, July 3, 1995, p. 4.

74. Richard Parker, *The Future of Global Television News* (Cambridge, MA.: The Joan Shorenstein Center for Press, Politics and Public Policy, 1994), p. 15.

75. Russell Shaw, 'CNN sets new service in Spanish,' *Electronic Media*, November 27, 1995, p. 52.

76. Geraldine Fabrikant, 'The looney tunes factor,' *New York Times*, September 12, 1995, pp. C1, C18.

77. Andrew Paxman, 'Latins gobble up animated product,' *Variety*, June 24–30, 1996, p. 104.

78. John Dempsey, 'Ted, time: new tower of cable,' *Variety*, July 22–28, 1996, pp. 1, 67.

79. Mark Woods, 'Warner signing on in Oz,' *Variety*, September 2–8, 1996, p. 32.

80. Elizabeth Guider, 'Kirch rules digital turf,' *Variety*, July 29–August 4, 1996, p. 30.

81. 'Murdoch's world from A to Z,' *New York Times*, July 29, 1996, p. C7.

82. Thomas R. King and Elizabeth Jensen, 'Disney brings personal touch to ABC's sagging line-up,' *Wall Street Journal*, May 17, 1996, p. B4.

83. Joe Mandese, 'Is it magic kingdom or an evil empire?' *Advertising Age*, August 7, 1995, p. 1.

84. Gary Levin, 'Disney, Mattel ink three-year deal,' *Variety*, April 8–14, 1996, p. 28.

85. Diane Mermigas, 'Disney's Eisner hints at plans for growth,' *Electronic Media*, February 19, 1996, p. 4.

86. Ken Auletta, 'Marriage, no honeymoon,' *New Yorker*, July 29, 1996, p. 29.

87. In January 1997 Disney announced plans to sell a portion of its newspaper and magazine interests.

88. Bruce Orwall, 'Pixar and Disney set exclusive deal for five new films,' *Wall Street Journal*, February 25, 1997, p. B7.

89. Bruce Orwall and Mark Robichaux, 'Disney plans cable network in a challenge to Viacom,' *Wall Street Journal*, December 20, 1996, p. B6.

90. Andrew Bailes and Neil Hollister, *Asian Cable and Satellite: Unrivalled Growth Opportunities* (London: Pearson Professional, 1996), p. 137.

91. 'Mickey Mao,' *The Economist*, August 3, 1996, p. 32.

92. 'Disney, its ABC unit combine divisions for international TV,' *Wall Street Journal*, June 20, 1996, p. B5; Raymond Snoddy, 'Cap Cities/ABC in inter-

national revamp,' *Financial Times*, June 26, 1996, p. 18.

93. Jon Lafayette, 'New Disney/ABC global unit looks ahead,' *Electronic Media*, July 1, 1996, p. 4.

94. 'Disney says it wants stakes in film channels,' *New Media Markets*, June 27, 1996, p. 14.

95. Jeff Jensen, 'Cable TV marketer of the year,' *Advertising Age*, December 9, 1996, p. s1.

96. Michael Oneal, 'Disney's kingdom,' *Business Week*, August 14, 1996, p. 33.

97. Joe Mandese, 'Is it magic kingdom or an evil empire?' *Advertising Age*, August 7, 1995, p. 4.

98. Andrew Bailes and Neil Hollister, *Asian Cable and Satellite: Unrivalled Growth Opportunities* (London: Pearson Professional, 1996), p. 144.

99. John Nelson, 'ESPN to add third channel,' *Wisconsin State Journal*, June 11, 1996, p. 2D.

100. Bill Carter and Richard Sandomir, 'The trophy in Eisner's big deal,' *New York Times*, August 6, 1995, section 3, p. 11.

101. *Advertising Age*, December 9, 1996, p. s2.

102. Wayne Walley, 'To the extreme,' *Electronic Media*, July 15, 1996, p. 3.

103. Scott Donaton and Chuck Ross, 'Petersen, ESPN plot weekly mag,' *Advertising Age*, October 21, 1996, p. 1.

104. 'Let the extreme games, like, man, begin,' *Adweek*, June 24, 1996, p. 22.

105. Kate Fitzgerald, 'Extreme-ly hot,' *Advertising Age*, June 24, 1996, p. 44.

106. Stuart Elliott, 'Advertising,' *New York Times*, June 21, 1996, p. C6.

107. Bruce Orwall, 'Field is crowded, but sports still score on TV,' *Wall Street Journal*, January 13, 1997, p. B8.

108. Kate Fitzgerald, 'Extreme-ly hot,' *Advertising Age*, June 24, 1996, p. 44.

109. Mark H. Gerstein, 'Report on Viacom, Inc.,' *Value Line*, March 22, 1996.

110. 'Murdoch's world from A to Z,' *New York Times*, July 29, 1996, p. C7.

111. Helen Bunting, *Global Media Companies: Volume 2, Rest of World* (London: Pearson Professional, 1995), p. 239.

112. Patrick M. Kelley, 'Viacom divisions collaborate on a line of children's books,' *Wall Street Journal*, March 4, 1996, p. B3.

113. 'Viacom's Paramount and Marvel to launch comic-book imprint,' *Wall Street Journal*, February 13, 1996, p. B7; Raymond Snoddy, 'Detour from the superhighway,' *Financial Times*, March 28, 1995, p. 15.

114. Diane Mermigas, 'Vexed Viacom vows upturn in soft stock via expansion,' *Electronic Media*, July 29, 1996, p. 23.

115. *Ibid.*

116. Comment by Dennis McAlpine, media analyst with Josephthal, Lyons & Ross. Cited in Michael Burgi, 'Summarily Sumner,' *Mediaweek*, January 22, 1996, p. 5.

117. Elizabeth Lesly, 'Chairman Fix-It at Viacom,' *Business Week*, April 15, 1996, pp. 42–3.

118. Raymond Snoddy, 'Viacom in Scandinavian deal,' *Financial Times*, September 17, 1996, p. 16; Elizabeth Guider and Michael Williams, 'Par-lay vous digital? TPS says oui to $500M,' *Variety*, September 30–October 6, 1996, p. 68.

119. Diane Mermigas, 'Vexed Viacom vows upturn in soft stock expansion,' *Electronic Media*, July 29, 1996, p. 23.

120. Wayne Walley, 'MTV plans custom-made services around the world,' *Electronic Media*, March 25, 1996, p. 27.

121. Geraldine Fabrikant, 'Blockbuster seeks to flex its muscles abroad,' *New York Times*, October 23, 1995, p. C7; Jeffrey D. Zbar, 'Blockbuster's new executives plot int'l growth,' *Advertising Age*, October 16, 1995, p. 38.

122. Anita M. Busch and Martin Peers, 'Suits strain MCA–Viacom ventures,' *Variety*, May 6–12, 1996, p. 23.

123. Peter Warg, 'Pay TV could be Mideast pipe dream,' *Variety*, June 3–9, 1996, p. 71.

124. Diane Mermigas, 'Vexed Viacom vows upturn in soft stock via expansion,' *Electronic Media*, July 29, 1996, p. 18.

125. 'USA Latino gets a new look,' *Variety*, August 19–25, 1996, p. 33.

126. *Wall Street Journal*, December 20, 1996, p. B6.

127. Debra Johnson, 'MTV to expand international reach,' *Broadcasting*, March 25, 1996, p. 64.

128. Michael Mallory, 'Beavis & Butt-head take over the world,' *Variety*, June 24–30, 1996, p. 106.

129. Wayne Walley, 'MTV plans custom-made services around the world,' *Electronic Media*, March 25, 1996, p. 27.

130. Jack Banks, *Monopoly Television! MTV's Quest to Control the Music* (Boulder, CO: Westview, 1996).

131. Alice Rawsthorn, 'MTV makes the big record groups dance to its tune,' *Financial Times*, July 4, 1995, p. 17.

132. J. Max Robins, 'Viacom faces the music, OKs MTV2,' *Variety*, March 4–10, 1996, p. 57.

133. Helen Bunting, *Global Media Companies: Volume 1, Europe* (London: Pearson Professional, 1995), pp. 25–6.

134. Judy Dempsey, 'Bertelsmann unit, Mitsui in licensing agreement,' *Financial Times*, January 11, 1996, p. 12; Judy Dempsey, 'Bertelsmann forecasts profits rise for full year,' *Financial Times*, March 29, 1996, p. 18.

135. 'Mitsui to take stake in Bertelsmann unit, forming partnership,' *Wall Street Journal*, November 18, 1996, p. B5.

136. Alice Rawsthorn, 'Thorn reveals music talks with Bertelsmann,' *Financial Times*, April 3, 1996, p. 22; Alice Rawsthorn, 'Bertelsmann forms music venture with Indian group,' *Financial Times*, June 28, 1995, p. 19.

137. Helen Bunting, *Global Media Markets: Volume 1, Europe* (London: Pearson Professional, 1995), p. 36.

138. Martin Du Bois, 'TV picture to change in Europe,' *Wall Street Journal*, April 3, 1996, p. A3.

139. Nathaniel C. Nash, 'New rules on ownership for German TV,' *New York Times*, October 30, 1995, p. C7.

140. Erik Kirschbaum, 'CLT's Delloye ankles on eve of Ufa merger,' *Variety*, June 24–30, 1996, p. 27.

141. Judy Dempsey, 'Bertelsmann faces need to rebuild bridges,' *Financial Times*, June 20, 1996, p. 17.

142. Erik Kirschbaum, 'German TV rivals sign a peace pact,' *Variety*, July 29 – August 4, 1996, pp. 1, 71.

143. Diane Mermigas, 'TCI covering all the bases,' *Electronic Media*, April 29, 1996, p. 21.

144. Lee Hall, 'TCI's gargantuan footprint grows,' *Electronic Media*, March 25, 1996, p. 20; Mark Robichaux, 'Knight-Ridder negotiating sale of cable stake to TCI,' *Wall Street Journal*, March 11, 1996, p. A3.

145. Diane Mermigas, 'Reborn TCI pins hopes on digital,' *Electronic Media*, November 4, 1996, pp. 1, 38.

146. Diane Mermigas, 'Obstacles slow TCI's multimedia journey,' *Electronic Media*, May 6, 1996, p. 19.

147. Geraldine Fabrikant, 'Tele-Communications to spin off satellite unit,' *New York Times*, June 20, 1996, p. C4; Mark Robichaux, 'TCI sets plan to spin off satellite unit,' *Wall Street Journal*, June 20, 1996, p. B8.

148. Mark Robichaux, 'TCI is cleared to spin off unit,' *Wall Street Journal*, November 18, 1996, p. B5.

149. Geraldine Fabrikant, 'A supporting actor takes center stage,' *New York Times*, May 15, 1996, pp. C1, C8.

150. 'Murdoch may make news net headlines with Malone,' *Variety*, May 27–June 2, 1996, p. 6.

151. Michael Schrage, 'Peter Barton,' *IQ*, February 26, 1996, p. 15.

152. Christopher Parkes, 'Malone longs for quiet life,' *Financial Times*, September 14, 1995, p. 20.

153. 'Channels for children set in U.S. and Latin America,' *Wall Street Journal*, August 29, 1996, p. B13.

154. Michelle Magee, 'Sumitomo making a discovery,' *Variety*, October 28–November 4, 1996, p. 48.

155. Diane Mermigas, 'Liberty sees sports as key to global kingdom,' *Electronic Media*, May 13, 1996, pp. 4, 31–3.

156. Diane Mermigas, 'Obstacles slow TCI's multimedia journey,' *Electronic Media*, May 6, 1996, p. 18.

157. 'Asia Business News in pact to create Japanese service,' *Wall Street Journal*, June 26, 1996, p. B5.

158. Raymond Snoddy, 'Flextech likely to secure BBC deal,' *Financial Times*, August 16, 1996, p. 16; 'Canal Plus planning ventures with TCI, Luxembourg firm,' *Wall Street Journal*, November 30, 1995, p. B10.

159. Andrew Bailes and Neil Hollister, *Asian Cable and Satellite: Unrivalled Growth Opportunities* (London: Pearson Professional, 1996), p. 140.

160. William Dawkins, 'Sumitomo to take on Star TV network,' *Financial Times*, July 9, 1996, p. 15.

161. Raymond Snoddy, 'TCI and Sega close to cable TV games deal,' *Financial Times*, January 23, 1996, p. 15.

162. Raymond Snoddy, 'Master of bits at home in the hub,' *Financial Times*, May 28, 1996, p. 17.

163. 'Malone's big retreat "doesn't extend" to UK,' *New Media Markets*, January 9, 1997, pp. 6–7.

164. Peter Bart, 'The gossip mill,' *Variety*, June 3–9, 1996, p. 6.

165. Report on Seagram Co., *Value Line*, May 17, 1996; Geraldine Fabrikant and Bernard Weinraub, 'Having gotten the part, Bronfman plays the mogul,' *New York Times*, February 4, 1996, section 3, pp. 1, 13.
166. Christopher Dixon, Paine Webber Note on Seagram, April 1, 1996.
167. Tony Jackson, 'Hangover risk in Hollywood,' *Financial Times*, April 11, 1995, p. 15.
168. Christopher Parkes, 'MCA to avoid Internet investment,' *Financial Times*, July 1, 1996, p. 17.
169. Thomas R. King, 'MCA's Osaka Park sounds start of global theme,' *Wall Street Journal*, February 6, 1996, p. A3.
170. Tony Walker, 'US group to invest in China entertainment,' *Financial Times*, November 11, 1996, p. 5.
171. Thomas R. King, 'Biondi's task: making peace with Redstone,' *Wall Street Journal*, April 24, 1996, p. B1; 'Pass the compost,' *The Economist*, March 23, 1996, p. 68.
172. Greg Spring, 'MCA-TV's R. Gregory Meidel,' *Electronic Media*, January 22, 1996, p. 84.
173. Eben Shapiro, 'Settlement talks between Seagram, Viacom fall apart,' *Wall Street Journal*, October 28, 1996, p. B2.
174. Judy Dempsey, 'German TV rivals buy rights from MCA,' *Financial Times*, July 31, 1996, p. 13.
175. Bernard Weinraub, 'MCA in $2.5 billion sale of shows to German TV,' *New York Times*, July 31, 1996, p. C1.
176. Diane Mermigas, 'New day dawns for Universal Television,' *Electronic Media*, January 6, 1997, p. 24.
177. Lisa Bannon, 'Seagram's MCA to sell programming to two rival German concerns,' *Wall Street Journal*, July 31, 1996, p. B2; Wayne Walley, '$2.5 billion MCA output deals latest in German spending spree,' *Electronic Media*, August 5, 1996, p. 29.
178. *Electronic Media*, January 6, 1997, p. 36.
179. 'PolyGram NV chooses Sanitsky, an agent, to head new TV unit,' *Wall Street Journal*, March 6, 1997, p. B6.
180. Report on PolyGram N.V., *Value Line*, May 17, 1996.
181. Martin Du Bois, 'PolyGram NV stock falls 9.2% after forecast,' *Wall Street Journal*, December 20, 1995, p. B5.
182. Alice Rawsthorn and William Dawkins, 'Schulhoh steals Sony's thunder,' *Financial Times*, December 7, 1995, p. 20.
183. Report on Sony Corp., *Value Line*, May 17, 1996; Jeffrey A. Trachtenberg and Eben Shapiro, 'Sony resignation brings speculation about possible suitors for movie unit,' *Wall Street Journal*, December 7, 1995, p. A3.
184. David P. Hamilton, 'Sony's Idei has no plans to sell any entertainment operations,' *Wall Street Journal*, January 15, 1996, p. A6.
185. Steven V. Brull, Neil Gross, and Robert D. Hof, 'Sony's new world,' *Business Week*, May 27, 1996, pp. 100–8.
186. 'Carving out a new future,' *The Economist*, June 1, 1996, p. 61.
187. Jim Carlton, 'Giants of video-game industry rallying for rebound,' *Wall Street Journal*, May 31, 1996, p. B3.

188. Joe Flint, 'Sony, CBS, 3 Arts pact,' *Variety*, July 15–21, 1996, p. 30.

189. 'The nightmare continues,' *The Economist*, September 21, 1996, p. 67; 'Why Sony loves TV,' *Fortune*, September 30, 1996, p. 134.

190. John Lippman, 'Can "the cable guy" repair Sony's fortunes?' *Wall Street Journal*, June 14, 1996, p. B5; Mir Maqbool Alam Khan, 'India's new Sony channel shakes the TV landscape,' *Ad Age International*, June 1996, p. i32.

191. Eben Shapiro and Cäcilie Rohwedder, 'Viacom close to sale to Kirch of rights to Paramount film and TV shows,' *Wall Street Journal*, April 3, 1996, p. B10.

192. Marc Gunther, 'How GE made NBC no. 1,' *Fortune*, February 3, 1997, pp. 92–100.

193. Raymond Snoddy, 'Tuned to a vision of the future,' *Financial Times*, March 11, 1996, p. 15.

194. Bill Carter, 'The peacock preens again,' *New York Times*, April 14, 1996, section 3, pp. 1, 10.

195. Michael Goldstein, 'How NBC won the triple crown,' *Business Week*, July 1, 1996, p. 33.

196. General Electric, *1995 Annual Report*, p. 13; Raymond Snoddy, 'NBC plans to aim TV channels at European PC users,' *Financial Times*, April 3, 1996, p. 16.

197. Laurel Wentz, 'NBC redirects its energy into making feeds global,' *Ad Age International*, February 1997, p. i2.

198. Michael Williams, 'Peacock wings into France on Canal +,' *Variety*, October 7–13, 1996, p. 37.

199. Greg Spring, 'Global cable tie binds NBC, National Geographic,' *Electronic Media*, December 9, 1996, p. 17.

200. Joe Mandese and Ira Teinowitz, 'A-B deals into NBC global buys,' *Advertising Age*, November 6, 1995, p. 28; Joseph Hanania, 'Media,' *New York Times*, December 18, 1995, p. C5.

201. Daniel Pearl, 'United News and MAI agree to merge, a sign of British media consolidation,' *Wall Street Journal*, February 9, 1996, p. B13.

202. Clyde H. Farnsworth, 'Media,' *New York Times*, June 24, 1996, p. C5.

203. Bernard Weinraub, 'Don't say no to Jeffrey,' *New York Times Sunday Magazine*, June 30, 1996, pp. 20–3.

204. Louise Kehoe, 'DreamWorks deal: say goodbye to Sillywood,' *Financial Times*, June 5, 1995, p. 11.

205. Diane Mermigas and Jenny Hontz, 'Four-way kid deal in works,' *Electronic Media*, November 20, 1995, p. 1.

206. Steven Lipin and Gabriella Stern, 'GM unveils sale of Hughes defense arm to Raytheon Co, in $9.5 billion accord,' *Wall Street Journal*, January 17, 1997, p. A3.

207. John J. Keller and Mark Robichaux, 'AT&T plans 50-state marketing blitz for DirecTV in latest assault on cable,' *Wall Street Journal*, June 24, 1996, pp. A3, A8.

208. Jeff Cole, 'Hughes Electronic revamps DirecTV to better expand its satellite services,' *Wall Street Journal*, November 12, 1996, p. B4.

209. Christopher Parkes, 'Hughes, PanAmSat in $32bn pact,' *Financial Times*, September 21–22, 1996, p. 5.

210. Eric Schine, 'Liftoff: Michael Armstrong has made Hughes an electronic and telecom contender,' *Business Week*, April 22, 1996, pp. 138–47.

211. Michiyo Nakamoto, 'Matsushita to buy stake in satellite broadcaster,' *Financial Times*, March 26, 1996, p. 18.

212. John Hopewell, 'New Sogecable digital bouquet smells like platform power play,' *Variety*, October 21–27, 1996, p. 210; Kerry A. Dolan, 'Crowded skies,' *Forbes*, July 29, 1996, p. 46.

213. 'Infinity buyout creates radio behemoth,' *Electronic Media*, June 24, 1996, p. 42.

214. Helen Bunting, *U.S. Media Markets: Leading the World?* (London: Pearson Professional, 1995), pp. 129–30; Report on Westinghouse, *Value Line*, March 22, 1996.

215. Timothy Aeppel, 'Westinghouse to spin off industrial operations,' *Wall Street Journal*, November 12, 1996, pp. A3, A20; Elizabeth Lesly, 'Good morning, CBS,' *Business Week*, June 3, 1996, p. 32; Kenneth N. Gilpin, 'Westinghouse considers split of business,' *New York Times*, June 11, 1996, pp. C1, C8; Claudia H. Deutsch, 'A move to prune at Westinghouse,' *New York Times*, August 28, 1996, pp. C1, C5.

216. Erle Norton and Elizabeth Jensen, 'Westinghouse's Infinity plan fails to excite investors,' *Wall Street Journal*, June 21, 1996, p. B4.

217. *Electronic Media*, January 6, 1997, p. 8.

218. Andrew Paxman, 'CBS says hola to News Net,' *Variety*, July 1–14, 1996, p. 28.

219. 'TeleNoticias Portuguese,' *Cable & Satellite Express*, January 9, 1997, p. 7.

220. Bill Carter, 'A late starter, CBS jumps in with its first cable channel,' *New York Times*, August 21, 1996, pp. C1, C5.

221. Geraldine Fabrikant, 'Westinghouse to buy country music units,' *New York Times*, February 11, 1997, p. C5.

222. The Lex Column, 'Westinghouse Electric,' *Financial Times*, June 21, 1996, 14.

223. John Hopewell, 'New Sogecable digital bouquet smells like platform power play,' *Variety*, October 21–27, 1996, p. 210; Michael Williams, 'Hungry for new markets, Canal+ swallows NetHold,' *Variety*, September 9–15, 1996, p. 6.

224. Judy Dempsey and Raymond Snoddy, 'European media alliance dies amid acrimony,' *Financial Times*, June 6, 1996, p. 14.

225. Raymond Snoddy, 'Canal Plus to end Bertelsmann pay-TV link,' *Financial Times*, June 21, 1996, p. 15.

226. Judy Dempsey, 'Kirch looks to build base for multimedia expansion,' *Financial Times*, July 21, 1995, p. 21.

227. 'Media players: who owns what,' *Variety*, May 27–June 2, 1996, p. 30; 'Lion in Winter,' *The Economist*, March 9, 1996, p. 67.

228. Cäcilie Rohwedder, Lisa Bannon, and Eben Shapiro, 'Spending sprees by German Kirch Group spells bonanza for Hollywood studios,' *Wall Street Journal*, August 1, 1996, pp. B1–B2.

229. Cecilia Zecchinelli, 'Telepiu takes off with digital,' *Variety*, August 5–11, 1996, p. 33.

230. Christopher Parkes, 'Kirch buys 7.5% stake in US film producer,' *Financial*

Times, October 5–6, 1996, p. 5.

231. Judy Dempsey, 'A jump up the television ratings,' *Financial Times*, July 19, 1996, p. 13.

232. Andrew Jack, 'Gaining critical mass at a stroke,' *Financial Times*, October 31, 1995, p. 18.

233. Mark M. Nelson, 'Alcatel to swap interests in magazines for 21% stake in France's Havas SA,' *Wall Street Journal*, October 26, 1995, p. B7.

234. Helen Bunting, *Global Media Companies: Volume 1, Europe* (London: Pearson Professional, 1995), pp. 145–56.

235. 'Berlusconi in the box,' *Financial Times*, May 24, 1996, p. 18.

236. Andrew Hill, 'Mediaset approves float price range,' *Financial Times*, May 31, 1996, p. 20.

237. Raymond Snoddy, 'Reed Elsevier has $5bn for acquisitions,' *Financial Times*, March 14, 1996, p. 22; Alice Rawsthorn, 'Reed turns over a new leaf,' *Financial Times*, July 19, 1995, p. 11.

238. Kenneth Zapp and Magda Palczny-Zapp, 'The wealth of nations,' *In These Times*, June 10, 1996, p. 19.

239. Paul Taylor, 'CME buys bank's stake in Czech TV group,' *Financial Times*, August 5, 1996, p. 17.

240. Diane Mermigas, 'Metromedia's new wave,' *Electronic Media*, February 12, 1996, pp. 1, 16.

241. Kevin Done, 'TV programme of expansion,' *Financial Times*, January 15, 1996, p. 8.

242. Cathy Meils, 'East Euro TV stations looking good for CEME,' *Variety*, March 4–10, 1996, p. 70; Cathy Meils, 'Nova profits explode in sophomore year report,' *Variety*, May 20–26, 1996, p. 24.

243. Lisa Gubernick, 'Chip off the old block,' *Forbes*, February 24, 1997, pp. 103–4.

244. Kevin Done, 'CME wins its first license to broadcast in Poland,' *Financial Times*, October 22, 1996, p. 16.

245. Andrew Paxman, 'Quiet Clarin making moves,' *Variety*, March 25–31, 1996, p. 60.

246. Thomas T. Vogel, Jr., 'Latin clan scours globe for media deals,' *Wall Street Journal*, September 18, 1996, p. A14.

247. Marcelo Cajueiro, 'Globo leads Brazilian charge,' *Variety*, June 3–9, 1996, p. 42.

248. Matt Moffett, 'Brazil's Globo evolves to maintain clout,' *Wall Street Journal*, December 4, 1996, p. A11.

249. Helen Bunting, *Global Media Companies: Volume 2, Rest of World* (London: Pearson Professional, 1995), pp. 55–60.

250. Andrew Paxman, 'Pay TV growth rate astounding,' *Variety*, November 4–10, 1996, p. 75.

251. Elisabeth Malkin, 'The Rupert Murdoch of Mexico?' *Business Week*, December 11, 1995, p. 61.

252. Craig Torres and Joel Millman, 'Televisa seeks to get big part in global play,' *Wall Street Journal*, May 30, 1996, p. A14.

253. Andrew Paxman, 'Trim Televisa looks abroad,' *Variety*, March 25–31,

1996, pp. 42, 60.

254. Andrew Paxman, 'Telenovela delirium,' *Variety*, October 7–13, 1996, p. 61.

255. Craig Torres and Joel Millman, 'Televisa seeks to get big part in global play,' *Wall Street Journal*, May 30, 1996, p. A14.

256. Brendan M. Case, 'Casting big nets for Latin American channel surfers,' *New York Times*, August 5, 1996, p. C7.

257. John Hopewell, 'Mexico's Televisa enters Spain fray,' *Variety*, December 2–8, 1996, p. 37.

258. Edward A. Gargan, 'Across Asia, an entrepreneur takes on the western press,' *New York Times*, December 11, 1995, p. C5.

259. Roger Wallis and Chong Ju Choi, *The Impact of Multimedia on the Entertainment Business* (London: Pearson Professional, 1996), p. 141.

260. Bassam Elbani, 'Saudis rule the high frontier,' *Financial Times*, August 26, 1996, p. 11.

261. Uma Da Cunha and Don Groves, 'Modi paves road for U.S. fare in India,' *Variety*, May 20–26, 1996, pp. 17–18; Janine Stein, 'India's Modi building an empire,' *Electronic Media*, December 4, 1995, pp. 52, 54.

262. Louise Lucas, 'Asia TV race is a marathon, not a sprint,' *Financial Times*, July 27, 1995, p. 17; Betsy Sharkey, 'As ever, East is East,' *Mediaweek*, May 13, 1996, pp. 17–18; Ted Bardacke, 'New satellite TV network set for Asia,' *Financial Times*, March 27, 1996, p. 14.

263. Danielle Nguyen, 'Value plays overseas,' *Forbes*, July 15, 1996, p. 312.

264. Janine Stein, 'China aims to conquer TV world,' *Electronic Media*, December 11, 1995, p. 22.

265. Nikki Tait, 'Packer empire rejuvenates its dynasty,' *Financial Times*, March 7, 1996, p. 19.

266. 'Packer signs China TV deal,' *Financial Times*, February 3–4, 1996, p. 4.

267. Martin Peers, 'Wannabes waffle as MGM deadline nears,' *Variety*, June 24–30, 1996, p. 137.

268. Yoo-Lim Lee, 'Giants vie for TV slots,' *Ad Age International*, June 1996, p. 12.

269. Andrew Pollack, 'Bringing Hollywood to Asia, with a "soft touch",' *New York Times*, July 5, 1996, pp. C1, C4.

270. 'DreamWorks East,' *Fortune*, October 28, 1996, p. 158.

271. 'The Business Week Global 1000,' *Business Week*, July 8, 1996, pp. 56–62.

272. D. Eleanor Westney, 'Mass media as business organizations: a U.S.–Japanese comparison,' in Susan Pharr and Ellis Krauss (eds), *Media and Politics in Japan* (Honolulu: University of Hawaii Press, 1996), pp. 54–6.

273. 'Reaching for the stars,' *The Economist*, October 5, 1996, pp. 63–4.

274. 'Disney, Toluma Shoten ink toon pact,' *Variety*, July 29–August 4, 1996, p. 12.

275. Andrew Hindes, 'Coin still goes H'wood,' *Variety*, September 16–22, 1996, pp. 49, 52.

NOTES TO CHAPTER 4

1. James Sterngold, 'Digital studios: it's the economy, stupid,' *New York Times*, December 25, 1995, p. 23.

2. Joel Brinkley, 'Defining TV's and computers for a future of high definition,' *New York Times*, December 2, 1996, p. C1.

3. Paul Taylor, 'Suppliers surf the Internet wave,' *Financial Times*, special section on Information Technology, December 4, 1996, p. 1.

4. Nicholas Negroponte, *Being Digital* (New York: Alfred A. Knopf, 1995), p. 57.

5. Frank Beacham, 'Questioning technology: tools for the revolution,' *Media Culture Review*, **4** (2) (1995), 18.

6. Quoted approvingly in Steven Levy, 'How the propeller heads stole the future,' *New York Times Magazine*, September 24, 1995, p. 59.

7. To predict the precise course of the Internet or the information highway would be nearly impossible. By 1997 even the best analysis of 1993 or 1994 looks woefully dated. In this chapter we endeavor to grasp the main dynamics at hand and what the probable course of the media/communication industries will be.

8. Jim Willis, *The Age of Multimedia and Turbonews* (Westport, CT: Praeger, 1994), p. ix.

9. Brian Gillooly with Jill Gambob, 'Sony plans to crack U.S. PC market,' *Information Week*, 4 December, 1995, p. 96; Alice Rawsthorn, 'Computer suppliers move into traditional electronics terrain,' *Financial Times*, July 19, 1996, special section, p. IV.

10. Cited in Doug Wilson, *Strategies of the Media Giants* (London: Pearson Professional, 1996), pp. 83, 77.

11. The media category in the ITU calculations only refers to film and broadcasting and does not include the print media of book publishing, magazines, and newspapers. Were they included, as seems appropriate for our purposes since the firms that dominate the media cross all these categories, the importance of media within the info-communications sector would rise, as would the importance of the sector in the overall global political economy.

12. International Telecommunication Union, *World Telecommunication Development Report* (Geneva: International Telecommunication Union, 1995), pp. 10, 1.

13. Harry M. Trebing and Maurice Estabrooks, 'The globalization of telecommunications: a study in the struggle to control markets and technology,' *Journal of Economic Issues*, **29** (2) (June 1995), 535.

14. 'FT 500,' *Financial Times*, FT 500 section, January 25, 1996, p. 2.

15. 'Fortune's Global 500,' *Fortune*, August 5, 1996, p. F1.

16. Roger Wallis and Chong Ju Choi, *The Impact of Multimedia on the Entertainment Industry* (London: Pearson Professional, 1996), p. 3.

17. 'The passion of the newly converted,' *The Economist*, June 8, 1996, p. 74.

18. *New Media Markets*, December 12, 1996, p. 16.

19. Paul Taylor, 'Media and electronic deals jump,' *Financial Times*, August 19, 1996, p. 17.

20. Tony Jackson, 'Plugged into partnerships,' *Financial Times*, November 2, 1995, p. 15.

21. Harry M. Trebing and Maurice Estabrooks, 'The globalization of telecommunications: a study in the struggle to control markets and technology,' *Journal of Economic Issues*. **29** (2) (June 1995). 537–8.

22. See, for example, 'Conferees agree to revise telecommunications law,' *New York Times*, December 21, 1995, p. C5.

23. See, for example, Richard Klingler, *The New Information Industry* (Washington, DC: Brookings Institution Press, 1996).

24. Alan Cane, 'Time for a lighter approach,' *Financial Times*, March 21, 1996, special section, p. II.

25. The Aspen Institute, *Building a Global Information Society* (Washington, DC: The Aspen Institute, 1996), pp. 55, 57.

26. Michael Lindemann, 'Expectations mixed on new telecoms law,' *Financial Times*, August 5, 1996, p. 2; Bernard Simon, 'Canada paves way for telecoms battle,' *Financial Times*, August 8, 1996, p. 3.

27. Emma Tucker, 'Brussels lifts bar on cable companies,' *Financial Times*, October 12, 1995, p. 2; Raymond Snoddy, 'Network for a future electronic superhighway,' *Financial Times*, October 3, 1995, p. 37; 'Communications, information technology firms ask EU to standardize regulations across Europe,' *Daily Report for Executives*, March 8, 1996, Section A, p. 46.

28. Guy de Jonquieres, 'EU split over liberalising telecoms,' *Financial Times*, March 13, 1996, p. 4.

29. Kevin Leppmann, 'Putting the public on hold,' *Dollars and Sense*, May/June 1996, p. 16.

30. 'Forthcoming worldwide telecom privatisations,' *Financial Times*, October 3, 1995, p. 23.

31. Kevin Leppmann, 'Putting the public on hold,' *Dollars and Sense*, May/June 1996, p. 17.

32. Conner Middelmann, 'Lines to investors buzz with avalanche of issues,' *Financial Times*, June 12, 1996, p. 19.

33. Nicholas Denton, 'Telecoms deals double in value to $135 bn,' *Financial Times*, January 6, 1997, p. 19.

34. Tony Jackson, 'Ringing rapid changes in telecoms,' *Financial Times*, February 12, 1996, p. 24.

35. Chrystia Freeland, 'Russia's privatisation: from bang to whimper,' *Financial Times*, December 29, 1995, p. 2.

36. Roberto Fonseca, 'Nicaragua: government gets only fair marks on annual IMF exam,' *Inter Press Service*, April 17, 1995; 'Treasury sets conditions for U.S. aid to Mexico,' *Reuters, Limited*, February 9, 1995; 'Mexico meets IMF requirements except reserves, official says,' *BNA International Business and Finance*, June 30, 1995; 'Venezuela may have to resort to the IMF; press claims government is considering petrol rise,' *America Regional Reports: Andean Group*, June 30, 1994; 'IMF approves loans for Bolivia,' *Deutsche Presse-Agentur*, December 19, 1994.

37. Gwen Urey, 'Infrastructure for global financial integration: the role of the World Bank,' in Bella Mody, Johannes M. Bauer, and Joseph D. Straubhaar (eds), *Telecommunication Politics: Ownership and Control of the Information Highway in Developing Countries* (Mahwah, NJ: Lawrence Erlbaum Associates, 1995), pp. 113–34.

38. Peter Marsh, 'Telecom rivalry "vital to growth",' *Financial Times*, April 10, 1995, p. 2.

39. 'Telecoms reform tops Asian agenda,' *Financial Times*, July 23, 1996, p. 3.
40. 'Teleconglomeration,' *The Economist*, April 6, 1996, pp. 16–18.
41. 'World's largest telecom companies,' *Electronic Media*, January 22, 1996, p. 166.
42. Bernard Wysocki, Jr., 'Computer industry pushes for free trade,' *Wall Street Journal*, March 18, 1996, p. A1; Guy de Jonquieres, 'Drive to dismantle electronics tariffs,' *Financial Times*, April 1, 1996, p. 4; Frances Williams, 'Washington attacks EU over computer tariffs,' *Financial Times*, May 23, 1996, p. 6.
43. Guy de Jonquieres, 'Template for trade talks,' *Financial Times*, February 18, 1997, p. 19.
44. Frances Williams and Alan Cane, 'Pact set to boost world telecoms,' *Financial Times*, February 17, 1997, p. 1.
45. Frances Williams, 'US, EU vie for credit on telecoms,' *Financial Times*, February 17, 1997, p. 3.
46. Alan Cane, 'Global regulator urged for information highway,' *Financial Times*, November 29, 1995, p. 18.
47. Jill Hills, 'US hegemony and GATT: the liberalisation of telecommunications,' *Media Development*, **40** (2) (1993), 8–12.
48. Paul Lewis, 'Telecom talks at trade body are postponed as U.S. balks,' *New York Times*, May 1, 1996, p. C1; 'U.S. trade policy,' *Financial Times*, April 29, 1996, p. 15.
49. Ted Bardacke, 'Thai telecom deal underlines shady business–politics links,' *Financial Times*, August 19, 1996, p. 3; Duncan Green, *Silent Revolution: The Rise of Market Economics in Latin America* (London: Cassell, 1995), p. 74; Dianne Solis, 'Mexican mogul "invested" millions with Salinas kin,' *Wall Street Journal*, January 30, 1996, p. A9; Conner Middelmann, 'Lustre slips from sell-offs,' *Financial Times*, September 19, 1995, p. 6; Christopher Bobinski, 'US group in row over Polish telecom deal,' *Financial Times*, December 19, 1995, p. 4.
50. Duncan Green, *Silent Revolution: The Rise of Market Economics in Latin America* (London: Cassell, 1995), p. 157; Roger Matthews, 'South African unions threaten strikes over sale of state assets,' *Financial Times*, December 9–10, 1995, p. 3; Mark Nicolson, 'Indian telecom workers strike nationwide,' *Financial Times*, June 20, 1995, p. 8; Sonali Verma, 'Indian telephone unions sign pact ending strike,' *The Reuters European Business Report*, June 23, 1995; Kerin Hope, 'Greek telecom sell-off prompts strike,' *Financial Times*, February 20, 1996, p. 2; David Buchan, 'Union threat to French telecom liberalisation,' *Financial Times*, March 7, 1996, p. 3.
51. Alan Cane, 'High-flyers seek second wind,' *Financial Times*, April 24, 1996, p. 13.
52. Kenneth Hart and Lane Cooper, 'Bell Atlantic set for global role?' *Communications Week International*, May 6, 1996, pp. 4, 8.
53. 'Telecom tangles,' *Financial Times*, April 9, 1996, p. 18; 'The lure of distance,' *The Economist*, April 6, 1996, p. 63.
54. Tony Jackson, 'MCI sees the future in "one-stop" services,' *Financial Times*, August 8, 1996, p. 15.

55. 'Global telecom alliances,' *Information Week*, November 13, 1995, p. 40; Michael Lindemann, 'Telecom operators launch global alliance,' *Financial Times*, February 1, 1996, p. 16.

56. Douglas Lavin, 'Cable & Wireless, Global One may ally, creating a rival to BT-MCI venture,' *Wall Street Journal*, November 11, 1996, p. B6.

57. 'And this is competition?' *The Economist*, April 27, 1996, pp. 67–70; Kenneth Hart and Malcolm Laws, 'GTE seeks to rival global carriers,' *Communications Week International*, June 24, 1996, pp. 1, 31.

58. 'Not quite magic,' *The Economist*, February 22, 1997, p. 73.

59. Mark Landler, 'Communication pact to favor growing giants,' *New York Times*, February 18, 1997, p. C1.

60. 'The world of giant telecoms,' *Financial Times*, April 2, 1996, p. 13.

61. John J. Keller and Gautam Nauk, 'PacTel–SBC merger is likely to ring in an era of alliances among Baby Bells,' *Wall Street Journal*, April 2, 1996, p. B1.

62. Erik Bohlen and Ove Granstrand (eds), *The Race to European Eminence: Who Are the Coming Tele-Service Operators?* (Amsterdam: Elsevier Science BV, 1994); Douglas Lavin, 'Italian telecommunications alliance is formed to challenge state monopoly,' *Wall Street Journal*, November 16, 1995, p. A12; 'Latin affairs,' *Communications Week International*, June 3, 1996, pp. 22–7; Alan Cane and Hugo Dixon, 'AT&T to launch nationwide telephone service in Britain,' *Financial Times*, September 23–24, 1995, p. 24; Shiraz Sidhva, 'Taking phones to rural India,' *Financial Times*, April 12, 1995, p. 7.

63. Alan Cane and Richard Waters, 'First of a new breed of telecoms operator,' *Financial Times*, August 28, 1996, p. 15.

64. Alan Cane, 'Winners in the east will inherit the earth,' *Financial Times*, April 9, 1996, special section on 'Asia-Pacific Telecommunications,' p. I.

65. Mark Landler, 'Have's and have-not's revisited,' *New York Times*, October 9, 1995, p. C4.

66. Paul Taylor, 'A two-tier infobahn,' *Financial Times*, May 13, 1996, p. 4; 'Forecast 2000,' *Forbes ASAP*, December 4, 1995, p. 78.

67. Alan Cane, 'Boost for third world telecoms projects expected,' *Financial Times*, June 7, 1996, p. 14.

68. Cees J. Hamelink, *The Politics of World Communication* (London: Sage, 1994).

69. Pekka Tarjanne, 'Telecom privatizations do work – if structured correctly,' *Communications Week International*, March 18, 1996, p. 9; Alan Cane, 'Boost for third world telecoms projects expected,' *Financial Times*, June 7, 1996, p. 14.

70. Jill Hills, 'The telecommunications rich and poor,' *Third World Quarterly*, **12** (2) (April 1990), 88.

71. 'Here's what other telco players are up to,' *Electronic Media*, December 16, 1996, p. 4.

72. Ronald Grover and Amy Barrett, 'Media/entertainment,' *Business Week*, January 13, 1997, p. 116.

73. Leslie Cauley and Sara Calian, 'Cable & Wireless, Bell Canada units to merge with Nynex's U.K. cable firm,' *Wall Street Journal*, October 23, 1996, p. A3.

74. John Urquhart, 'Canadian launch of satellite TV targets U.S. rivals,' *Wall Street Journal*, March 13, 1997, p. B15.

75. Andrew Bailes and Neil Hollister, *Asian Cable and Satellite* (London: Pearson Professional, 1996), pp. 140–1.

76. Michael Burgi, 'The Telco Express: US West pulls in,' *Cable*, April 29, 1996, pp. 16–19; Catherine Arnst and Peter Burrows, 'U.S.West's gauntlet won't just lie there,' *Business Week*, March 11, 1996, p. 32; Christopher Parkes, 'US West reinforces cable business with $11bn merger,' *Financial Times*, February 28, 1996, p. 1; Beatriz V. Goyoaga and Andrew Paxman, 'Latins cable-ready,' *Variety*, September 23–29, 1996, p. 57.

77. Randall L. Carlson, *The Information Superhighway* (New York: St. Martin's Press, 1996), p. 20.

78. *New Media Markets*, October 24, 1996, p. 23.

79. 'US West sells cable in European review,' *New Media Markets*, October 10, 1996, p. 11.

80. Ronald van de Krol, 'Philips and US West in Dutch cable TV deal,' *Financial Times*, May 13/14, 1995, p. 8; 'US West extends Dutch cable franchise,' *Broadcasting & Cable*, July 15, 1996, p. 46; Neil Buckley, 'US West joins BFr37bn Flemish telecoms tie-up,' *Financial Times*, May 30, 1996, p. 16; Vincent Boland, 'US West buys stake in Czech cable operator,' *Financial Times*, May 26, 1995, p. 16.

81. Louise Kehoe, 'AT&T's break-up is widely seen as a "divide and conquer" strategy,' *Financial Times*, October 3, 1995, p. 10.

82. Mark Landler, 'AT&T enters TV business via satellite broadcasting,' *New York Times*, January 23, 1996, pp. C1, C20; Jeff Cole, 'AT&T to buy 2.5 percent of GM's DirecTv Inc.,' *Wall Street Journal*, January 23, 1996, p. A2.

83. Diane Mermigas, 'Sprint stirs up interest with N.C. cable trial,' *Electronic Media*, January 29, 1996, p. 3; John J. Keller and Mark Robichaux, 'Sprint's Cable–TV alliance alters local-phone and wireless plans,' *Wall Street Journal*, February 22, 1996, p. A3.

84. 'MCI's future comes into focus,' *Business Week*, February 19, 1996, p. 69; Jeffrey A. Trachtenberg, 'MCI to offer 800 number that allows sampling and buying of music albums,' *Wall Street Journal*, October 27, 1995, p. B5; Kenneth Hart, 'Microsoft, MCI in partnership,' *Communications Week International*, February 5, 1996, p. 8.

85. Tom Burns, 'Telefonica strengthens position in Latin America,' *Financial Times*, October 23, 1995, p. 18; Tom Burns, 'Telefonica offshoot in agreement with Microsoft,' *Financial Times*, March 18, 1996, p. 19.

86. Kathy Morris, 'New conquistadors,' *Variety*, September 23–29, 1996, p. 90.

87. Louise Lucas, 'HK video on demand delayed,' *Financial Times*, February 29, 1996, p. 5.

88. John Ridding and Louise Lucas, 'Asian jewel in C&W's crown,' *Financial Times*, April 2, 1996, p. 25.

89. Frederick Studemann, 'Small screen, big ambitions,' *Financial Times*, September 23, 1996, p. 13.

90. Howard Rheingold, *The Virtual Community: Homesteading on the Virtual Frontier* (Reading, MA: Addison-Wesley, 1993); Douglas Rushkoff, *Cyberia: Life in the*

Trenches of Cyberspace (New York: HarperCollins, 1994).

91. Adrienne Ward Fawcett, 'Interactive awareness growing,' *Advertising Age*, October 16, 1995, p. 20.

92. From report of Forrester Research Group. Quoted in Paul Taylor, 'Revenues of $10bn forecast,' *Financial Times*, June 15, 1995, special section, p. IV.

93. John Markoff, 'If medium is the message, the message is the Web,' *New York Times*, November 20, 1995, p. C5.

94. Bart Ziegler, 'Slow crawl on the Internet,' *Wall Street Journal*, August 23, 1996, p. B1.

95. Michael Lipson, 'The organizational politics of a functioning anarchy: governance of the Internet,' paper presented to Midwest Political Science Association, Chicago, 1995.

96. *Television Business International*, December 1996, p. 62.

97. Mike Ivey, 'Expert rips "techno-classism",' *Capital Times*, April 10, 1996, p. 1C.

98. Comment of David Chance. Interviewed in Doug Wilson, *Strategies of the Media Giants* (London: Pearson Professional, 1996), p. 23.

99. International Telecommunication Union, *World Telecommunication Development Report* (Geneva: International Telecommunication Union, 1995), p. 19.

100. Negroponte, *Being Digital*, p. 178.

101. Brent Schlender, 'A conversation with the lords of Wintel,' *Fortune*, July 8, 1996, p. 46.

102. Joel Brinkley, 'F.C.C. clears new standard for digital TV,' *New York Times*, December 25, 1996, p. C1.

103. Amy Cortese, John Verity, Kathy Rebello, and Rob Hof, 'The software revolution,' *Business Week*, December 4, 1995, p. 78.

104. Louise Kehoe, 'Microsoft plans to make PCs centre of home entertainment,' *Financial Times*, April 1, 1996, p. 18.

105. John Markoff, 'Tomorrow, the World Wide Web?' *New York Times*, July 16, 1996, pp. C1, C5.

106. Peter Martin, 'Big guy embraces the Net,' *Financial Times*, June 13, 1996, p. 10.

107. Michael Schrage, 'John Doerr: Silicon Valley's most influential venture capitalist says Internet fever has only just begun,' *IQ*, July 8, 1996, p. 21.

108. Peter H. Lewis, 'The new Internet gatekeepers,' *New York Times*, November 13, 1995, pp. C1, C5.

109. Tim Jackson, 'Days numbered for independents,' *Financial Times*, August 28, 1995, p. 8.

110. John J. Keller and Gautam Naik, 'Merger poses a bold challenge to Bells,' *Wall Street Journal*, August 27, 1996, p. A3.

111. John W. Verity, 'Try beating these long-distance rates,' *Business Week*, April 22, 1996, pp. 131–2; Tim Jackson, 'Voices in the ether spook phone industry,' *Financial Times*, March 18, 1996, p. 9; John W. Verity, 'Calling all net surfers,' *Business Week*, August 5, 1996, p. 27.

112. Peter Coy, 'Can AT&T keep learning to love the Net?' *Business Week*, October 7. 1996. p. 130.

113. Ted Bunker, 'Calling for change; challenges facing communications industry; industry trend or event,' *LAN Magazine*, April 1996, p. 123.

114. Paul M. Eng, 'Surfing's big splash?' *Business Week*, March 11, 1996, p. 86; Catherine Arnst with Paul M. Eng, 'Info highway juggernaut,' *Business Week*, June 3, 1996, p. 44; BT–MCI announce global Internet backbone,' *Communications Week International*, June 24, 1996, p. 8; Alan Cane, 'BT, MCI Internet network set to go live,' *Financial Times*, June 10, 1996, p. 1; John Blau, 'Internet plays large role as Global One charts direction,' *Communications Week International*, February 19, 1996, p. 12.

115. Leslie Cauley, 'PacTel plans to offer access to Internet,' *Wall Street Journal*, May 28, 1996, p. A3; Leslie Cauley, 'A new calling: the Baby Bells hope to score big by offering easy Internet access,' *Wall Street Journal*, March 28, 1996, p. R18.

116. Peter H. Lewis, 'AT&T will offer no-fee Internet,' *New York Times*, February 28, 1996, p. A1.

117. Amy Barrett and Andrew Reinhardt, 'The "father of the net" has a problem child,' *Business Week*, September 30, 1996, p. 76.

118. 'Making a business of the bit buffet,' *The Economist*, March 8, 1997, pp. 75–6.

119. *Business Week*, January 13, 1997, p. 117; Bart Ziegler, 'Net is rarely pipeline to profit,' *Wall Street Journal*, August 23, 1996, p. B1.

120. Marc Gunther, 'The cable guys' big bet on the Net,' *Fortune*, November 25, 1996, pp. 102–8.

121. Mark Robichaux, 'Cable vendors plan big push on-line,' *Wall Street Journal*, November 29, 1995, p. A3; Ian Scales and Jeff Caruso, 'TeleWest aims to seize Internet initiative,' *Communications Week International*, May 20, 1996, p. 13; Edmond M. Rosenthal, '@Home takes on online world,' November 20, 1995, p. S-10.

122. Michael Schrage, 'John Doerr: Silicon Valley's most influential venture capitalist says Internet fever has only just begun,' *IQ*, July 8, 1996, p. 21.

123. Comment of Simon Guild. Quoted in Doug Wilson, *Strategies of the Media Giants* (London: Pearson Professional, 1996), p. 61.

124. 'Viacom, Sprint agree to develop and sell products over Internet,' *Wall Street Journal*, October 16, 1996, p. B5.

125. 'BBC will offer Internet access in spring of '97,' *Wall Street Journal*, September 23, 1996, p. A16.

126. Jeff Cole, 'Hughes's satellite-to-PC service now goes home,' *Wall Street Journal*, October 10, 1996, p. B10.

127. Raymond Snoddy, 'Information battle enters a new dimension,' *Financial Times*, June 10, 1996, p. 11; Raymond Snoddy, 'News Intl arm plans digital broadcast,' *Financial Times*, June 11, 1996, p. 22.

128. Raymond Snoddy, 'The "global village" begins to unfold,' *Financial Times*, special section on Global Business Outlook, January 7, 1997, p. 8.

129. Don Clark, 'Facing early losses, some Web publishers begin to pull the plug,' *Wall Street Journal*, January 14, 1997, p. A8.

130. Steve Lohr, 'The great mystery of Internet profits,' *New York Times*, June 17, 1996, p. C1.

131. Lee Hall, 'Internet's blooming, but little green to be seen,' *Electronic Media*, July 22, 1996, p. 12.

132. Raymond Snoddy, 'CNN digs its claws in,' *Financial Times*, December 9, 1996, p. 17.

133. Don Clarke, *Wall Street Journal*, January 14, 1997, p. A8.

134. Iver Peterson, 'Commitments and questions, on electronic newspapers,' *New York Times*, February 26, 1996, p. C5.

135. Roger Wallis and Chong Ju Choi, *The Impact of Multimedia on the Entertainment Business* (London: Pearson Professional, 1996), p. 1.

136. Iver Peterson, 'Commitments, and questions, on electronic newspapers,' *New York Times*, February 26, 1996, p. C5; Louise Kehoe, 'US newspapers link for the Internet,' *Financial Times*, April 20, 1995, p. 17.

137. Peggy Miles and Jeffrey Itell, 'Prime sites,' *Cable and Satellite Europe*, October 1996, p. 53.

138. Elizabeth Jensen, 'Off the dial,' *Wall Street Journal*, March 28, 1996, p. R18; Michael Burgi and Michael Krantz, 'Cable gets wired on Web,' *Mediaweek*, January 29, 1996, p. 6.

139. Kim Cleland, 'MTV, Yahoo! harmonize on music-oriented site!' *Advertising Age*, November 11, 1996, p. 44.

140. John Markoff, 'With a debut, a test of on-line publishing,' *New York Times*, November 13, 1995, p. C7.

141. Lee Hall, 'Internet's blooming, but little green to be seen,' *Electronic Media*, July 22, 1996, p. 12.

142. Lee Hall, 'Cox Interactive eyes synergy for projects,' *Advertising Age*, Interactive supplement, November 8, 1996, p. s8.

143. Geraldine Fabrikant, 'The young and the restless audience,' *New York Times*, April 8, 1996, pp. C1, C8.

144. Michael Schneider, 'When two worlds collide,' *Electronic Media*, June 17, 1996, p. 34.

145. Lee Hall, 'Internet's blooming, but little green to be seen,' *Electronic Media*, July 22, 1996, p. 12.

146. Stephanie N. Mehta, 'On-line upstarts tap big media companies for funds,' *Wall Street Journal*, January 28, 1997, p. B2.

147. Steve Lohr, 'Digital commerce: the old media dinosaurs seem to be having a rebirth. Don't blame cloning,' *New York Times*, March 10, 1997, p. C5.

148. 'Webs within the Web,' *Financial Times*, June 24, 1996, p. 16.

149. *Wall Street Journal*, January 14, 1997, p. A1.

150. Tim Jackson, 'Push power,' *Financial Times*, January 6, 1997, p. 13.

151. Geoffrey Nairn, 'Turning the net on its head,' *Financial Times*, March 5, 1997, information technology section, p. 12.

152. Amy Cortese, 'A way out of the web maze,' *Business Week*, February 24, 1997, pp. 94–104.

153. Steve Lohr, 'CBS to buy one-third stake in Sportsline,' *New York Times*, March 4, 1997, p. C11.

154. Diane Mermigas, 'Microsoft, NBC deal fits GE's plans,' *Electronic Media*, December 18–25, 1995, pp. 1, 75; Tony Jackson and Andrew Gowers, 'Big enough to make mistakes,' *Financial Times*, December 21, 1995, p. 11.

155. Elizabeth Lesly and Kathy Rebello, 'Network meets Net,' *Business Week*, July 15, 1996, p. 68.

156. Frank Rose, 'The end of TV as we know it,' *Fortune*, December 23, 1996, p. 2.

157. Don Clark and Kyle Pope, 'NBC to provide live video feeds over the Internet,' *Wall Street Journal*, March 7, 1997, p. B6; Seth Schiesel, 'CNN is planning to provide live video feed as part of its web service,' *New York Times*, March 10, 1997, p. C10.

158. Laurence Zukerman, 'Murdoch again tries his luck on line,' *New York Times*, January 13, 1997, p. C8.

159. Chuck Ross, 'Warner sets Net venture for local TV' *Advertising Age*, January 6, 1997, p. 1.

160. Chuck Ross, 'Disney eyes two-tier kids site, says source,' *Advertising Age*, January 6, 1997, p. 125.

161. *Digital Broadcasting Europe*, October 16, 1996, p. 2.

162. Cited in Doug Wilson, *Strategies of the Media Giants* (London: Pearson Professional, 1996), pp. 83, 77.

163. Tim Clark, 'Oracle's Hollywood splash,' *Advertising Age*, February 14, 1994, p. 14.

164. Louise Kehoe, 'Media companies take up Netscape stakes,' *Financial Times*, April 8–9, 1996, p. 8; Kenneth Hart, 'Netscape moves to entrench real-time multimedia on Net,' *Communications Week International*, February 19, 1996, p. 17; Joan Indiana Rigdon, 'Netscape teams with Web publishers; technology surpasses Microsoft deals,' *Wall Street Journal*, August 19, 1996, p. B6.

165. Stephanie Stahl, 'Netscape, HP team,' *Information Week*, May 20, 1996, p. 35.

166. Peter H. Lewis, 'Microsoft is set to detail plan for foray into the Internet,' *New York Times*, October 10, 1996, p. C1.

167. Geoffrey Wheelwright and Louise Kehoe, 'Gates cast his lines for a Net profit,' *Financial Times*, October 21, 1996, p. 9.

168. *Financial Times*, Information Technology section, December 4, 1996, p. 1.

169. Christopher Dixon, presentation to Association of Investment Management and Research, New York City, January 31, 1996.

170. 'Citizen Gates,' *The Economist*, November 23, 1996, p. 69.

171. David Bank, 'Microsoft's problem is what many firms just wish they had,' *Wall Street Journal*, January 17, 1997, p. A9.

172. Don Clark, 'Microsoft's on-line service goes to a TV format,' *Wall Street Journal*, December 9, 1996, p. B8.

173. Cathy Taylor, 'Doing the "media thing",' *Mediaweek*, October 21, 1996, p. 40.

174. Cathy Taylor, 'Gates' $100mil gamble,' *Mediaweek*, October 14, 1996, p. 5.

175. Chuck Ross and Bradley Johnson, 'Microsoft links sites as network buy,' *Advertising Age*, August 12, 1996, p. 16; Bradley Johnson, 'MSN spells out Web ad strategy,' *Advertising Age*, May 13, 1996, p. 38.

176. Cathy Taylor, ' "Slate" aims high on ads,' *Mediaweek*, June 10, 1996, p. 8; Keith J. Kelly and Bradley Johnson, 'Microsoft on big trek with Webzine,' *Advertising Age*, May 27, 1996, pp. 1, 43.

177. 'Don Clark, 'Microsoft taps into local media's turf,' *Wall Street Journal*, April 22, 1996, p. B5.

178. G. Bruce Knecht, 'Microsoft puts newspapers in highanxiety.com,' *Wall Street Journal*, July 15, 1996, pp. B1, B3.

179. Kathy Rebello, 'Honey, what's on Microsoft?,' *Business Week*, October 21, 1996, p. 134.

180. Peter H. Lewis, 'Microsoft offering news without charge on Internet,' *New York Times*, April 30, 1996, p. C4.

181. Amy Barrett, 'We have to be prime time,' *Business Week*, April 15, 1996, p. 87.

182. Amy Barrett and Paul M. Eng, 'AOL downloads a new growth plan,' *Business Week*, October 14, 1996, pp. 85–6.

183. Mark Gimein, 'AOL seeks online hegemony,' *Mediaweek*, March 18, 1996, p. 4; Chuck Ross, 'AOL, TCI are talking team-up,' *Advertising Age*, March 4, 1996, p. 6; Cathy Taylor, 'The Net takes the local,' *Mediaweek*, July 22, 1996, p. 14.

184. Doug Wilson, *Strategies of the Media Giants* (London: Pearson Professional, 1996), p. 9.

185. 'Mitsui to take stake in Bertelsmann unit, forming partnership,' *Wall Street Journal*, November 16, 1996, p. B5.

186. Mike Allen, 'Web magazine at a halt and seeking readers' aid,' *New York Times*, May 28, 1996, p. C2.

187. Patrick M. Reilly, 'Slim ad sales force publishers to put a price on Web services,' *Wall Street Journal*, May 8, 1996, p. B8; Anya Sacharow, 'New Web site spun by "journal",' *Mediaweek*, April 29, 1996, pp. 4–5.

188. Jeff Jensen, 'Agencies envision Web of networks,' *Advertising Age*, August 23, 1995, p. 8.

189. Laura Rich, 'Disney's new attraction: banners,' *Adweek*, September 30, 1996, p. 38.

190. Chuck Ross, 'Time Warner, P&G join forces on Internet,' *Advertising Age*, October 28, 1996, pp. 1, 52.

191. *Wall Street Journal*, January 14, 1997, p. A1.

192. Scott Donaton and Chuck Ross, 'P&G, Conde casting Web deal,' *Advertising Age*, July 1, 1996, pp. 1, 27; Debra Aho Williamson and Jane Hodges, 'Editorial lines blur as advertisers create sites,' *Advertising Age*, February 26, 1996, p. s9.

193. Kim Cleland, 'Web narrows gap between ads, editorial,' *Advertising Age*, Interactive section, November 4, 1996, p. s3.

194. Michael Krantz, 'The Webmeister of AT&T,' *Mediaweek*, November 20, 1995, p. 17.

195. Wendy S. Williams, 'The online threat to independent journalism,' *EXTRA!*, November/December 1996, pp. 22–3.

196. Laurie Freeman, 'Internet visitors' traffic jam makes buyers Web wary,' *Advertising Age*, July 22, 1996, p. s14.

197. 'Slate, an on-line magazine, to stay-free,' *New York Times*, January 13, 1997, p. C10.

198. Eric Garland, 'I want my Web TV,' *Mediaweek*, November 16, 1996, p. 46.

199. David Bank, 'How Net is becoming more like television to draw advert-

isers,' *Wall Street Journal*, December 13, 1996, p. A1.

200. Louise Daly, 'US cable operators agree modem specification,' *New Media Markets*, December 19, 1996, p. 8.

201. Keith J. Kelly and Chuck Ross, 'Bright prospects seen for cable TV, new media,' *Advertising Age*, August 19, 1996, p. 8; Lee Hall, 'Internet's blooming, but little green to be seen,' *Electronic Media*, July 22, 1996, p. 12; Clinton Wilder, 'The Web "ads" up,' *Information Week*, August 5, 1996, p. 41.

202. Winston Fletcher, 'Net facts burst ads bubble,' *Financial Times*, October 7, 1996, p. 13.

203. Roger Wallis and Chong Ju Choi, *The Impact of Multimedia on the Entertainment Business* (London: Pearson Professional, 1996), p. 79.

204. Kathy Rebello, Larry Armstrong, and Amy Cortese, 'Making money on the Net,' *Business Week*, September 23, 1996, p. 118.

205. Charles Waltner, 'Turning pocket change to big dough on the Net,' *Advertising Age*, April 22, 1996, p. 22.

206. 'The property of the mind,' *The Economist*, July 27, 1996, p. 57.

207. Alice Rawsthorn, 'Copyright dilemmas in digital arena,' *Financial Times*, July 10, 1995, p. 9; Alice Rawsthorn, 'Music industry seeks digital copyright,' *Financial Times*, September 26, 1995, p. 4; Emma Tucker, 'Music industry seeks rights on superhighway,' *Financial Times*, October 31, 1995; Denise Caruso, 'Should an extension of current copyright law, tweaked a bit, govern the Internet?' *New York Times*, July 15, 1996, p. C5.

208. 'Let the browser beware: copyright comes to cyberspace,' *infoActive*, 2 (3) (1996), pp. 1, 2.

209. Seth Schiesel, 'Global agreement reached to widen law on copyright,' *New York Times*, December 21, 1996, pp. 1, 22.

210. 'RIAA pushes Congress to OK copyright pact,' *Variety*, January 27–February 2, 1997, p. 24.

211. Louise Kehoe and Paul Taylor, 'Sign on for the Internet gold rush,' in *A–Z of the Internet* (London: Financial Times, 1996), p. 4.

212. John W. Verity and Rob Hof, 'Bullet-proofing the net,' *Business Week*, November 13, 1995, p. 98.

213. George Graham, 'Rise of Internet threatens traditional banks' market,' *Financial Times*, August 12, 1996, p. 1; 'Tripping out on the Web,' *The Economist*, August 3, 1996, pp. 54–5; Clinton Wilder, 'E-commerce emerges,' *Information Week*, June 17, 1996, pp. 14–15; Louise Kehoe, 'Oracle and Verifone in Internet commerce venture,' *Financial Times*, February 22, 1996, p. 16; 'Selling in cyberspace,' *Wall Street Journal Reports*, June 17, 1996; Chuck Ross, 'TCI and P&G in cyber-huddle,' *Advertising Age*, April 1, 1996, pp. 1, 60.

214. 'Wired for action,' *Wall Street Journal*, special section on the Internet, December 9, 1996, p. R18.

215. 'Suited, surfing and shopping,' *The Economist*, January 25, 1997, p. 59.

216. Paul Taylor, 'Internet users "likely to reach 500m by 2000",' *Financial Times*, May 13, 1996, p. 4.

217. Paul Taylor, 'First the Internet: now the Intranet phenomenon,' *Financial*

Times, April 3, 1996, special section on 'Information Technology,' p. I.

218. Steve Lohr, 'For the Internet, I.B.M. to stick to what it knows,' *New York Times*, September 2, 1996, p. 22.

219. Robert D. Hof, Kathy Rebello, and Amy Cortese, 'Cyberspace showdown,' *Business Week*, October 7, 1996, p. 35.

220. Louise Kehoe, 'Trapped in the Web traffic jam,' *Financial Times*, October 16, 1996, p. 10.

221. Bart Ziegler, 'Slow crawl on the Internet,' *Wall Street Journal*, August 23, 1996, p. B1.

222. 'An Ivy League of an I-way?' *Business Week*, October 21, 1996, p. 46.

223. Geoffrey Nairn, 'A crucial year ahead for the "Net",' *Financial Times*, January 8, 1997, special section on 'Information Technology', p. 6.

224. Peter Coy, Robert D. Hof, and Paul C. Judge, 'Has the Net finally reached the wall?' *Business Week*, August 26, 1996, pp. 62–6.

225. Bart Ziegler, 'Slow crawl on the Internet,' *Wall Street Journal*, August 23, 1996, p. B1.

226. John Kay, 'Threats to Bill Gates and the Internet,' *Financial Times*, December 15, 1996, p. 10.

227. Kenneth Hart, 'Power struggle over Net's fate,' *Communications Week International*, September 23, 1996, p. 4.

228. Kenneth Hart, 'New setup takes hold of Net,' *Communications Week International*, October 21, 1996, p. 8.

229. George Gilder, 'Telecosm: feasting on the giant peach,' *Forbes ASAP*, August 26, 1996, pp. 85–6; Interview with Mark Wood, Reuters executive, cited in Doug Wilson, *Strategies of the Media Giants* (London: Pearson Professional, 1996), p. 107.

230. Peter Coy, 'Limo service for cruising the Net,' *Business Week*, June 24, 1996, p. 46; Alan Cane, 'The backbone of MCI's Net battle,' *Financial Times*, June 11, 1996, p. 17.

231. Tony Jackson, 'Big carriers a-wooing go,' *Financial Times*, October 3, 1995, special section, page 8.

232 See, for example, Thomas E. Weber, 'MTV says, "I want my Web-site fee," seeking to make the Internet pay off,' *Wall Street Journal*, November 29, 1996, p. B2.

233. 'MCI offers Internet, phone, paging package to business customers,' *Wall Street Journal*, September 13, 1996, p. B5.

234. Christopher Dixon, presentation to Association for Investment Management and Research, New York City, January 31, 1996.

235. Heather Menzies, *Whose Brave New World? The Information Highway and the New Economy* (Toronto: Between the Lines, 1996).

236. Adam D. Thierer, 'End free ride on the Internet,' *Wall Street Journal*, March 7, 1997, p. A14.

237. 'Where Internet host computers are located,' *Business Week*, April 1, 1996, p. 36.

238. Robin Frost, 'Web's heavy U.S. accent grates on overseas ears,' *Wall Street Journal*, September 26, 1996, p. B4.

239. Martin Mulligan, 'A rickshaw on the infobahn,' *Financial Times*, March 4, 1996, p. 13.

240. Candee Wilde, 'Industry moving to multilingual Internet,' *Communications Week International*, March 4, 1996, p. 22.

241. 'The coming global tongue,' *The Economist*, December 21, 1996, p. 78.

242. Joseph S. Nye, Jr. and William A. Owens, 'America's information edge,' *Foreign Affairs*, March–April, 1996, pp. 20–36.

243. Richard Vadon, 'Drowning, not surfing,' *Financial Times*, January 22, 1996, p. 7; Nick Ingelbrecht, 'Japanese corporates build Asian backbone,' *Communications Week International*, May 6, 1996, p. 14.

244. 'Developing the highway,' *Communications Week International*, June 24, 1996, p. 9; Howard W. French, 'On the Internet, Africa is far behind,' *New York Times*, November 17, 1995, p. A8.

245. Fernando J. Espuelas, 'Internet wires marketers to Latin American elite,' *Ad Age International*, November 1996, p. 112.

246. Calvin Sims, 'A Web entree for Peruvians without PC's,' *New York Times*, May 27, 1996, p. 25.

247. Danielle Robinson, 'Opening up the markets in US telecoms,' *Independent*, February 13, 1996, p. 24.

248. Lee Gomes, 'H-P aims at high end of business computing market,' *Wall Street Journal*, May 29, 1996, p. B4.

249. Raymond Snoddy and Alan Cane, 'Full multimedia impact years away, says Murdoch,' *Financial Times*, May 12, 1995, p. 1.

250. David Lieberman, 'Old guard tactic is old brand names,' *USA Today*, Int, edn, July 19, 1996, p. 8A.

251. Frank Beacham, 'Net loss,' *EXTRA!*, May–June 1996, p. 16.

252. J. William Gurley and Michael H. Martin, 'The price isn't right on the Internet,' *Fortune*, January 13, 1997, p. 154.

NOTES TO CHAPTER 5

1. Edward Herman, 'The externalities effects of commercial and public broadcasting,' in Karle Nordenstreng and Herbert Schiller (eds), *Beyond National Sovereignty* (Norwood, NJ: Ablex, 1993), Chapter 5.

2. For an analysis of the dynamics of the advertising market, see C. Edwin Baker, *Advertising and a Democratic Press* (Princeton: Princeton University Press, 1994), Chapter 1.

3. Ben Bagdikian, *The Media Monopoly* (Boston: Beacon, 1992), p. 119.

4. *Ibid.*, pp. ix–x.

5. See Edward S. Herman and Noam Chomsky, *Manufacturing Consent: The Political Economy of the Mass Media* (New York: Pantheon, 1988); Martin Lee and Norman Solomon, *Unreliable Sources* (New York: Lyle Stuart, 1990); Lawrence C. Soley, *The News Shapers* (New York: Praeger, 1992).

6. Quoted in Federal Trade Commission, *Public Service Responsibilities of Broadcast Licensees* (Washington, DC: FCC, 1946), p. 41.

7. *Ibid.*, p. 10.

8. *Ibid.*, p. 12.

9. *Ibid.*

10. Erik Barnouw, *The Sponsor* (New York: Oxford University Press, 1978), p. 95.

11. Richard Bunce, *Television in the Corporate Interest* (New York: Praeger, 1976), pp. 27–31; J. Blumler, M. Bynin, and T. Nossiter, 'Broadcasting finance and Programme quality: an international review,' *European Journal of Communication*, 1 (1986), 348–50.

12. Bunce, *op. cit.*, p. 97.

13. For extensive details, see Robin Andersen, *Consumer Culture and TV programming* (Boulder, CO: Westview, 1995), pp. 5–6, 45–6, and Matthew P. McAllister, *The Commercialization of American Culture* (Thousand Oaks, CA: Sage, 1996), *passim.*

14. In its classic report of 1946, the FCC noted that Procter & Gamble has been described as having 'a policy never to offend a single listener' (*Public Responsibilities*, p. 17). See the quotation from Procter & Gamble's more recent rules for acceptable programs in the Introduction; and see further, Bagdikian, *Media Monopoly*, Chapter 9; Andersen, *Consumer Culture*, Chapters 1–5.

15. See Andersen, *op. cit.*, Chapter 5.

16. Jerry Jacobs, *Changing Channels: Issues and Realities in Television News* (Mountain View, CA: Mayfield, 1990); Dan Hallin, 'Network news,' in Todd Gitlin (ed.), *Watching Television* (New York: Pantheon, 1986); James Fallows, *Breaking the News: How the Media Undermine Democracy* (New York: Pantheon, 1996), Chapter 2.

17. Keith Kelley, '"Coastal living" enjoys $10 mil Time Inc. kickoff,' *Advertising Age*, October 28, 1996, p. 12.

18. 'Magazine of the Year,' *Advertising Age*, March 11, 1996, p. s11.

19. For other illustrations just from the *New York Times*, see Andersen, *op. cit.*, pp. 48–50.

20. Barnouw, *op. cit.*, p. 81.

21. *Ibid.*

22. Paulette Thomas, 'Show and tell: advertisers take pitches to preschools,' *Wall Street Journal*, October 28, 1996, p. B1.

23. McAllister, *Commercialization of American Culture*, Chapter 3.

24. *Breaking Up America* (Chicago: University of Chicago Press, 1997), pp. 2, 11, 200.

25. *Ibid.*, p. 5.

26. *Ibid.*, p. 2.

27. TV is the main culprit in Robert Putnam's 'The strange disappearance of Civic America,' *The American Prospect*, Winter 1996, 34–48.

28. Barnouw, *The Sponsor*, p. 138.

29. See, especially, Douglas Kellner, *The Persian Gulf TV War* (Boulder, CO: Westview, 1992); Hamid Mowlana, George Gerbner, and Herbert Schiller (eds), *Triumph of the Image* (Boulder, CO: Westview, 1992); Andersen, *Consumer Culture*, Chapter 8.

30. Barnouw, *The Sponsor*, p. 138.

31. Edward Palmer, *Television and America's Children: A Crisis of Neglect* (New York: Oxford, 1988).

32. 'From a raised eyebrow to a turned back: the FCC and children's product-related programming,' *Journal of Communication*, 38 (4) (1988), 97.

33. *Out of the Garden*, pp. 197, 317, and Chapters 5–7.
34. George Gerbner, 'Marketing global mayhem,' *the public*, **2** (2) (1995), 74. See also Paul Farhi, 'TV violence adds punch to the overseas market,' *Washington Post National Weekly Edition*, February 13–19, 1995, p. 21.
35. George Gerbner and Nancy Signorielli, 'Violence profile 1967 through 1988–89: enduring patterns,' mimeo, January 1990.
36. 'Television and election strategy,' in G. Benjamin (ed.), *The Communications Revolution in Politics* (New York: Academy of Political Science, 1982), pp. 33–4.
37. *Ibid.*, p. 5.
38. Barnouw, *The Sponsor*, p. 76.
39. Frank Mankiewicz and Joel Swerdlow, *Remote Control* (New York: Ballantine, 1979), p. 101.
40. E. Krasnow, E. Longley, and H. Terry, *The Politics of Broadcast Regulation* (New York: St. Martin's Press, 1982), pp. 194–6.
41. This is diplomatic historian Melvyn Leffler's summary, in 'The American conception of national security and the beginning of the Cold War, 1945–8,' *American Historical Review*, April 1984, 379.
42. For a discussion of this document, see Noam Chomsky, *Deterring Democracy* (London: Verso, 1991), pp. 10–19.
43. For a discussion of this concept, and citations to document sources, *ibid.*, pp. 45–8.
44. National Security Council, 'United States objectives and courses of action with respect to Latin America,' *Foreign Relations of the United States, 1952–1954*, Vol. 4 (1955), p. 81.
45. *Ibid.*, p. 86.
46. Quoted in Jan Black, *United States Penetration of Brazil* (Philadelphia: University of Pennsylvania Press, 1978), p. 194. On U.S. training programs, see also Miles Wolpin, *Military Aid and Counterrevolution in the Third World* (Lexington, MA: Lexington, 1972).
47. In one estimate, the U.S. controls 85 percent of the world's trade in audio-visual products; in the United States itself, all foreign programs, including English language films and TV programs, take less than 2 percent of U.S. gross box office receipts and occupy less than 2 percent of TV airtime. See Patricia Edgar, 'Breaking new ground for global partnerships for children's rights and the media,' paper given at the first Asian Summit on Children's Rights and the Media, Manila, July 2–5, 1996, pp. 1–2.
48. John Sinclair, Elizabeth Jacka, and Stuart Cunningham (eds), *New Patterns in Global Television* (New York: Oxford University Press, 1996).
49. 'As Emile McAnany has observed, the question of foreign versus domestic ownership and control of the "cultural industries" has turned out to be much less formative of patterns of international media development than the implantation of the model in terms of which cultural industrialization has proceeded: that is, the question of "public" or "private". . .' (John Sinclair, 'Neither West nor Third World: the Mexican television industry within the NWICO debate,' *Media, Culture & Society*, **12** (1990), 348).

50. See John Gallagher and Ronald Robinson, 'The imperialism of free trade,' *Economic History Review*, **6** (1) (1953), 1–15.

51. For details on the ideological impact of U.S. training programs, see Wolpin, *Military Aid and Counterrevolution in the Third World*.

52. 'United States objectives and courses of action with respect to Latin America,' *Foreign Relations of the United States 1952–1954*, Vol. 4 (1955), p. 81.

53. Black, *United States Penetration of Brazil*, p. 161.

54. In Chile, for example, the *El Mercurio* newspaper, which had been funded and used by the CIA in the overthrow of the elected Allende government in 1973, prospered under the Pinochet dictatorship, and now dominates the print media. The neoliberal regime which followed the dictatorship, and operates under constraints inherited from that seventeen-year regime, has allowed a steady commercialization and concentration process throughout the media. See John Vanden Heuvel and Everette Dennis, *Changing Patterns: Latin America's Vital Media* (New York: Freedom Forum Center, 1995), pp. 119–26.

55. See Edward Herman, *The Real Terror Network* (Boston: South End Press, 1982), Chapter 4.

56. For a comparison of Latin and Japanese elites on this pull, see David Felix, 'Interrelations between consumption, economic growth and income distribution in Latin America since 1899: a comparative perspective,' Working Paper No. 4, Department of Economics, Washington University, St. Louis, especially pp. 33–40.

NOTES TO CHAPTER 6

1. Kari Levitt, *Silent Surrender: The American Economic Empire in Canada* (New York: Liveright, 1970), pp. 60–1.

2. *Ibid.*, p. 142.

3. Lawrence Ingrassia and Suzanne McGee, 'Canadian press baron who baits journalists raises sights in U.S.,' *Wall Street Journal*, November 8, 1994, p. A10.

4. George Grant, *Lament for a Nation* (Toronto: McClelland and Stewart, 1965), p. 41.

5. Duncan Cameron, 'Tax cuts,' *Canadian Forum*, October 1996, p. 3.

6. See Krishna Rau, 'A million for your thoughts,' *Canadian Forum*, July/August 1996, pp. 11–17.

7. For details, see James Winter, *Democracy's Oxygen* (Montreal: Black Rose, 1996).

8. Lon Dubinsky, 'Periodical publishing,' in Michael Dorland (ed.), *The Cultural Industries in Canada* (Toronto: Lorimer, 1996), pp. 43–4.

9. David Taras, 'The new undefended border: American television, Canadian audiences and the Canadian Broadcasting System,' in Rob Kroes (ed.), *Within the US Orbit: Small National Cultures Vis-à-vis the United States* (Amsterdam: VU University Press, 1991), p. 192.

10. *Ibid.*, p. 199.

11. 'An analysis of Canadian children's programming and preferences

1992–1993,' Centre for Youth and Media Studies, University of Montreal, pp. 129–33.

12. Stephen Kline, *Out of the Garden* (London: Verso, 1993), pp. 272–3.

13. Antonia Zerbisias, 'Broadcast bonanza,' *The Toronto Star*, September 5, 1996, p. C1; Christopher Harris, 'Up to 1,400 CBC staff face cut,' *The Globe and Mail*, September 9, 1996, p. 1.

14. Daryl Duke, 'The final cut?' *Canadian Forum*, November 1996, pp. 14–17.

15. Quoted in Walter LaFeber, *The New Empire: An Interpretation of American Expansion 1860–1898* (Ithaca, NY: Cornell University Press, 1963), p. 262.

16. Elizabeth Fox, *Media and Politics in Latin America* (Beverly Hills, CA: Sage, 1988), p. 13.

17. James Schwoch, *The American Radio Industry and Its Latin American Activities, 1900–1939* (Urbana, IL: University of Illinois Press, 1990), p. 106.

18. Elizabeth Fox, *op. cit.*, p. 15.

19. Elizabeth Mahan, 'Media politics and society in Latin America,' *LARR*, **31** (2) (1996), 148.

20. Richard Newfarmer and Willard Mueller, *Multinational Corporations in Brazil and Mexico: Structural Sources of Economic and Noneconomic Power*, Report to the Subcommittee on Multinational Corporations of the Senate Foreign Relations Committee. Washington, DC: Government Printing Office, 1975, p. 152.

21. Jan Black, *United States Penetration of Brazil* (Philadelphia: University of Pennsylvania Press, 1978), *passim*.

22. *Ibid.*, p. 49.

23. *Ibid.*, pp. 105–7.

24. *Ibid.*, pp. 96–102.

25. *Ibid.*, p. 102, n. 22.

26. Venicio A. De Lima, 'The state, television, and political power in Brazil,' *Critical Studies in Mass Communication*, 5 (1988), 108–28.

27. Black, *op. cit.*, pp. 50–1.

28. De Lima gives some telling illustrations (*op. cit.*, pp. 108–28).

29. *Ibid.*, p. 120.

30. Quoted in *ibid.*

31. Roberto Amaral and Cesar Guimaraes, 'Media monopoly in Brazil,' *Journal of Communication*, Autumn 1994, p. 33.

32. *Ibid.*, p. 26.

33. Matt Moffett, 'Brazil's Marinhos evolve to keep clout,' *Wall Street Journal*, December 4, 1995, p. A9.

34. These points are stressed by both De Lima, *op. cit.*, and Amaral and Guimaraes, *op. cit.*

35. Conrad Kottak, *Prime-Time Society: An Anthropological Analysis of Television and Culture* (Belmont, CA: Wadsworth, 1991).

36. Joseph D. Straubhaar, 'The electronic media in Brazil,' in Richard R. Cole (ed.), *Communication in Latin America* (Wilmington, DE: Scholarly Resources Inc., 1996), p. 225.

37. *Ibid.*, p. 229.

38. Stephen Hearst, 'Broadcasting regulation in Britain,' in Jay Blumler (ed.),

Television and the Public Interest (London: Sage, 1992), p. 75.

39. *Ibid.*, p. 67.

40. Colin Sparks, 'The future of public service broadcasting in Britain,' *Critical Studies in Mass Communication*, **12** (1995), 328–9.

41. For details, see Sparks, *ibid.*, pp. 331–3.

42. This is Colin Sparks's conclusion; *ibid.*, p. 340.

43. See H. H. Wilson, *Pressure Group: The Campaign for Commercial Television in England* (New Brunswick: Rutgers University Press, 1961), pp. 133–40.

44. For a good discussion of this set of issues, see Graham Murdock, 'Money talks: broadcasting finance and public culture,' in Stuart Hood (ed.), *Behind the Screens: The Structure of British Broadcasting in the 1990s* (London: Lawrence & Wishart, 1996), pp. 160–7.

45. For a good discussion, see *ibid.*, pp. 167–181.

46. For a full account, see Colin Sparks, 'Concentration and market entry in the UK national daily press,' *European Journal of Communication*, **10** (2) (1995).

47. Quoted by Lord Hollick in Brian Groombridge and Jocelyn Hay, *The Price of Choice* (London: John Libbey, 1994), p. 9.

48. Raymond Snoddy, 'Broadcasters' political "dependency" attacked,' *Financial Times*, August 27–28, 1994, p. 7.

49. Sparks, 'Future of public service broadcasting', *op. cit.*, p. 340.

50. John Wyles, 'A man of his word, and that of La Republica,' *Financial Times*, April 12, 1989, p. 25.

51. On the history of government control of RAI, see John F. Kramer, 'Italian entrepreneurial initiatives: public service broadcasting in transition,' in Robert Avery (ed.), *Public Service Broadcasting in a Multichannel Environment* (New York: Longman, 1993), pp. 112–19.

52. Jeremy Tunstall and Michael Palmer, *Media Moguls* (London: Routledge, 1991), p. 173.

53. See Alexander Stille, 'The world's greatest salesman,' *New York Times Magazine*, March 17, 1996, p. 28.

54. Lisa Bannon, 'As faithful as Fido, Italian anchorman sticks by Berlusconi,' *Wall Street Journal*, December 19, 1994, p. A10.

55. Polly Patillo, *Last Resorts: The Cost of Tourism in the Caribbean* (London: Cassell, 1996), Chapter 1.

56. Anthony Payne, *Politics in Jamaica* (New York: St. Martin's Press, 1988), Chapter 5.

57. This paragraph is based on Hopeton S. Dunn, 'A one-way street just off the global digital superhighway,' in Hopeton S. Dunn (ed.), *Globalization, Communications and Caribbean Identity* (New York: St. Martin's Press, 1994), Chapter 8.

58. *Ibid.*

59. 'The North American wave: communication technology in the Caribbean,' in Gerald Sussman and John Lent (eds), *Transnational Communications: Wiring the Third World* (Newbury Park, CA: Sage, 1991), p. 68.

60. See John Lent, *Mass Communication in the Caribbean* (Ames: Iowa State University Press, 1990), Chapters 3–4.

61. Cheryl Renee Gooch, '"Loitering on colonial premises after closing time": an analysis of television programming policy in Barbados,' in Dunn (ed.), *op. cit.*, p. 107.

62. *Ibid.*, pp. 107–8.

63. Mark D. Alleyne, 'Barbados,' in Stuart Surlin and Walter Soderlund (eds), *Mass Media and the Caribbean* (New York: Gordon & Breach, 1990), p. 59.

64. Elizabeth Mahan, 'Cultural industries and cultural identity: will NAFTA make a difference?,' *SLAPC*, **14** (1995), 21.

65. Joseph D. Straubhaar, 'Cultural imperialism: a media effects approach,' *Critical Studies in Mass Communication*, **8** (1991), 39–59.

66. For evidence on these effects, see Hilary Brown, 'American media impact on Jamaican youth: the cultural dependency hypothesis,' in Dunn, *op. cit.*, Chapter 4; Lynette Lashley, 'Television and the Americanization of Trinbagonian youth: a study of six secondary schools,' in *ibid.*, Chapter 5.

67. 'Communication technology in the Caribbean,' p. 84.

68. OECD, *New Zealand Country Report 1993* (Paris: OECD, 1993), p. 13. Quoted in Jane Kelsey, *Economic Fundamentalism* (London: Pluto Press, 1995), p. 6.

69. *Ibid.*, p. 8.

70. *Ibid.*, p. 11.

71. *Ibid.*, pp. 54–5.

72. Alan Cocker, 'Broadcasting myths and political realities: New Zealand's experience in comparative perspective,' *Political Science*, **46** (2) (December 1994), 250–2.

73. 'Diversity, in the form of a classical music station and a national information service is provided by the non-commercial and publicly funded National Radio and Concert FM' (Alan Cocker, *'A Toaster with Pictures': The Deregulation of Broadcasting in New Zealand*, Ph.D. Thesis, University of Auckland, 1996, p. 260). The present case study depends heavily on this excellent dissertation.

74. See above, pp. 143–6.

75. Cocker, *op. cit.*, pp. 246–8.

76. Joe Atkinson, 'The "Americanisation" of One Network News,' *The Australasian Journal of American Studies*, July 1994, 1–26.

77. Joe Atkinson, 'The state, the media and thin democracy,' in Andrew Sharp (ed.), *Leap into the Dark: The Changing Role of the State in New Zealand since 1984* (Auckland: Auckland University Press, 1994), pp. 152–62.

78. Quoted from a New Zealand newspaper in Cocker, *op. cit.*, p. 230.

79. Ruth Zanker, 'Lobbying in New Zealand,' March 16, 1995.

80. Forbes's unpublished paper is summarized in Cocker, *op. cit.*, pp. 282–3 and Appendix 3.

81. Hamish McDonald, 'Paper tigers,' *Far Eastern Economic Review*, October 5, 1995, p. 24.

82. R. Karthigesu, 'Broadcasting deregulation in developing Asian nations,' *Media, Culture & Society*, **16** (1994).

83. See Mehra Masani, *Broadcasting and the People* (New Delhi: National Book Trust, 1976); Arvind Rajagopal, 'The rise of national programming: the

case of Indian television,' *Media, Culture & Society*, **15** (1993), 94–6.

84. Sevanti Ninan, 'Transforming television in India,' *Media Studies Journal*, Summer 1995, 47–8.

85. Masani, *op. cit.*, p. 85.

86. 'Political economy of television in India,' in Lent and Sussman, *Transnational Communications*, p. 248.

87. Arvind Rajagopal, 'The rise of national programming: the case of Indian television,' *Media, Culture & Society*, **15** (1993), 92–3.

88. Arvind Singhal and Everett M. Rogers, *India's Information Revolution* (New Delhi: Sage, 1989), p. 79.

89. Rajagopal, *op. cit.*, pp. 103–4.

90. Jonathan Karp, 'Bollywood blues,' *Far Eastern Economic Review*, December 22, 1994, p. 50.

91. Suman Dubey, 'India's plan to draw foreign media investment sparks outcry from local outlets, rival parties,' *Asian Wall Street Journal*, September 5, 1994.

92. Bella Mody, 'State consolidation through liberalization of telecommunications services in India,' *Journal of Communication*, **45** (4) (1995).

93. Mir Maqbool Alam Khan, 'Preparing for war, Zee revises selling tactics,' *Advertising Age*, January 15, 1996, p. 14.

94. Ninan, *op. cit.*, p. 50.

95. Michael Griffin, K. Viswanath, and Dona Schwartz, 'Gender advertising in the US and India: exporting cultural stereotypes,' *Media, Culture & Society*, **16** (1994), 503. This article discusses the extent to which women's advertisements in major Indian media are almost exact replicas of those in the United States in cultural stereotyping of women's roles.

NOTES TO CHAPTER 7

1. For an account of the interrelations between two giants, see Elizabeth Jensen and Eben Shapiro, 'Time Warner's fight with News Corp. belies mutual dependence,' *Wall Street Journal*, October 28, 1996, p. 1.

2. See Introduction and Chapter 5 above.

3. Quoted in James Rorty, *Order on the Air* (New York: John Day, 1934), p. 10.

4. See the application of these points to Barbados in Chapter 6 above.

5. *EXTRA!* Update, December 1995, p. 1. This means of exclusion is common, and can even be used to block the entry of powerful content providers. Turner insiders told *Wall Street Journal* reporters that this was the means by which Murdoch excluded Turner's CNN and Cartoon Network from showing on his Asian satellites – 'Turner executives say News Corp. doesn't explicitly bar competitors; rather it sets economic terms that are so undesirable that a deal becomes unworkable' (Jensen and Shapiro, 'Time Warner's fight with News Corp. belies mutual dependence,' p. A6).

6. A famous line by the U.S. wit and media analyst A. J. Liebling was that the country has a free press in the sense that anybody 'in the ten-million-dollar category is free to buy or found a paper in a great city like New York or Chicago, and anybody with around a million (plus a lot of sporting blood)

is free to try it in a place of mediocre size like Worcester, Mass. As to us, we are free to buy a paper or not, as we wish' (*The Press*, New York: Ballantine, 1961, p. 15).

7. Dan Hallin, *We Keep America on Top of the World* (London: Routledge, 1994), p. 13.

8. See Gaye Tuchman, 'Objectivity as strategic ritual,' *American Journal of Sociology*, **77** (4) (1972).

9. See Tuchman, 'Objectivity as strategic ritual'; Dan Schiller, *Objectivity and the News* (Philadelphia: University of Pennsylvania Press, 1981); Bagdikian, *Media Monopoly*, 4th edn (Boston: Beacon Press, 1992), pp. 179–81; Lance Bennett, *The Politics of Illusion* (New York: Longman, 1988), Chapter 4.

10. On the concept of policy and its enforcement, see Warren Breed, 'Social control in the newsroom,' *Social Forces*, (1955), 326–36.

11. James Squires, *Read All About It: The Corporate Takeover of America's Newspapers* (New York: Times Books, 1993).

12. See in particular, John Fiske, *Television Culture* (London: Methuen, 1987), p. 317.

13. See Herbert Schiller, *Culture Inc.: The Corporate Takeover of Public Expression* (New York: Oxford University Press, 1989), Chapter 7; William Seaman, 'Active audience theory: pointless populism,' *Media, Culture & Society* (1992), 301–11.

14. Elizabeth Jensen and Eben Shapiro, 'Time Warner's fight with News Corp. belies mutual dependence,' *Wall Street Journal*, October 28, 1996, p. A6.

15. For a discussion of consumer groups interested in the media in Europe, see Jeremy Mitchell and Jay Blumler (eds), *Television and the Viewer Interest* (London: John Libbey, 1994).

16. See the discussions in Chapters 5 and 6 of the problems faced by the children's lobby in the United States and New Zealand.

17. VLV has a wider range of operations than serving public broadcasting, but this is one of its roles. See Brian Groombridge and Jocelyn Hay, *The Price of Choice: Public Service Broadcasting in a Competitive European Market Place* (London: John Libbey, 1995).

18. Global Alternative Media Association, Internet Post, 1996, FIC@oln.cpomlink.org.

19. Since 1986, David Barsamian in the United States has operated an Alternative Radio program that produces and distributes an hour-long public affairs show once a week, consisting mainly of interviews with distinguished dissidents on issues of the day. The program is distributed to hundreds of radio stations by satellite, and is sent overseas on videotapes.

20. 'Community radios: a controversial topic,' *Barricada International*, September 1996, 28.

21. Vidéaszimut, 'Breaking barriers,' *Clips* (September 1994), p. 3.

22. K. P. Sasi, 'New communication technologies, environment and social action,' Paper delivered at International Communication Association meeting in Dublin in 1990.

23. This paragraph draws on Vicki Mayer, 'For the people and by the people:

TV Maxambomba's regeneration of popular cinema,' paper presented at Latin American Popular Culture Conference, New Orleans, 1996.

24. Vidéaszimut, 'Television in the streets,' *Clips* (December 1994), p. 3.

INDEX